International Litigation and the Quest for Reasonableness

International Litigation and the Quest for Reasonableness

Essays in Private International Law

ANDREAS F. LOWENFELD
Herbert and Rose Rubin Professor of International Law
New York University School of Law

CLARENDON PRESS · OXFORD
1996

Oxford University Press, Walton Street, Oxford OX2 6DP
Oxford New York
Athens Auckland Bangkok Bombay
Calcutta Cape Town Dar es Salaam Delhi
Florence Hong Kong Istanbul Karachi
Kuala Lumpur Madras Madrid Melbourne
Mexico City Nairobi Paris Singapore
Taipei Tokyo Toronto
and associated companies in
Berlin Ibadan

Published in the United States
by Oxford University Press Inc., New York

British Library Cataloguing in Publication Data
Data available

Library of Congress Cataloging in Publication Data
Lowenfeld, Andreas F., 1930–
International litigation and the quest for reasonableness: essays in private international law / Andreas F. Lowenfeld.
p. cm.
Includes bibliographical references.
1. Civil procedure (international law) 2. Jurisdiction (International law) 3. Conflict of laws. I. Title.
K7615.6.L69 1996
340.9—dc20 95–47048
ISBN 0–19–826059–8

1 3 5 7 9 10 8 6 4 2

Typeset by Vera A. Keep & Theresa M. Murphy, Cheltenham
Printed in Great Britain
on acid-free paper by
Bookcraft Ltd., Midsomer Norton, Avon

PREFACE

This volume is not a Treatise on Private International Law, but a set of essays, derived from lectures prepared for delivery in the General Course on Private International Law at the Hague Academy of International Law in the summer of 1994.

A number of subjects usually addressed in texts on private international law are not addressed at all or are addressed only by way of comparison with the principal topics. I have sought to focus here on areas that are of great concern both to lawyers advising participants in international transactions and to governments, but that have usually not been treated either in books on private international law or in books on public international law. The inevitable cost of this different focus has been to sacrifice some subjects commonly covered under the heading of Private International Law, in particular choice of law in wholly private transactions such as contracts and torts, and family law. On the other hand, I believe these essays, taken together, may bridge a gap that has long been too wide between 'public' and 'private' international lawyers and their disciplines.

It seemed natural to me—though it surprised some of the participants—that a course devoted to problems of litigation should be presented in large measure through cases rather than solely through doctrine. Thus each of the chapters except the brief summary at the end contains a detailed discussion of at least one judicial decision, most more than one. The decisions selected for discussion are not necessarily authoritative, and all are subjected to critique; what the decisions have in common—regardless of level of decision or country of origin—is that they are illustrative of the topics addressed, and that they seem likely to stimulate the reader to think about the chosen topics in specific contexts. 'Further reading' inspired by any of the essays should generally start with the decisions reported on in the text.

I believe these essays contain a good deal of information not generally available; they also contain a good many opinions, some firm, some tentative. I trust the reader will be able to see distinctly where fact ends and opinion begins. The data are solid, and the footnotes are thorough, even where the conclusions may fail to convince.

Finally, a few words about the relation of these essays to the American Law Institute's *Restatement of Foreign Relations Law* (1987), a project with which I had the privilege to be associated for close to a decade. On the one hand my work on the *Restatement* formed and informed much of my thinking on the topics addressed in these essays; on the other hand I thought it would be interesting to an audience largely unfamiliar with Restatements in general and with the *Restatement of Foreign Relations Law* in particular to see how that collective work has approached some of the topics addressed in these essays, and how American courts, in turn, have responded to the approach of the *Restatement*. In a number of instances I have sought in this volume to build on and go beyond the consensus reflected in the *Restatement*. In doing so, I express only my own views and do not purport to speak for my fellow Reporters or the American Law Institute.

Andreas F. Lowenfeld

SUMMARY CONTENTS

CONTENTS

TABLE OF CASES*

* Principal cases discussed in the text are shown in bold type.

TABLE OF STATUTES AND RULES

TABLE OF TREATIES

MULTILATERAL TREATIES

BILATERAL TREATIES AND AGREEMENTS

1

Private International Law Redefined

A. INTRODUCTION

Fifteen years ago, I gave a short course at the Hague Academy of International Law entitled 'Public Law in the International Arena'.[1] My purpose then was to break down the to me unconvincing separation between public and private international law, by focusing on those areas in which private and public interests, and often the interests of two or more states, collided. The lectures were well received—in the sense that they stirred a good deal of comment and reaction, and no little controversy. The lectures also contributed to the agenda, and the approach, of Part IV of the American Law Institute's *Restatement (Third) of the Foreign Relations Law* (1987), with which I was associated for close to a decade, and that work in turn stimulated my case- and textbook on *International Litigation and Arbitration* (1993). The essays collected in this volume continue my pursuit of that area of the law, addressed both to private parties and to states and their agencies, and relying on all the resources known to lawyers—judicial decisions, national and international treaties and conventions, custom and practice, and, yes, common sense or what the *Restatement* calls reasonableness.

Some readers may be disappointed that I propose to omit, except as incidental subjects, many of the topics traditionally included in the course on Private International Law. It is not that I am uninterested in contracts and torts, in decedent succession, in marriage and divorce.[2] But these traditional subjects have been well mined by others, and some choices have been necessary to the effort to make of these essays a volume to be read, rather than a reference book. Whether the topics I have chosen justify a full-blown treatise, I do not know; no one, so far as I am aware, has undertaken such a project. I do believe it is possible to articulate and illustrate some principles that will raise the level of discussion, possibly develop some consensus, and sharpen the debate where consensus remains elusive.

[1] Andreas F. Lowenfeld, 'Public Law in the International Arena: Conflict of Laws, International Law, and Some Suggestions for their Interaction' (1979) 163 *Recueil des Cours* 311.

[2] Indeed, I teach all of these subjects in my course on Conflict of Laws, and have a book to prove it: Andreas F. Lowenfeld, *Conflict of Laws, Federal, State, and International Perspectives* (Matthew Bender, 1986 plus 1990 Supplement).

I considered setting out the principles at the beginning. I prefer however, to leave that task to the end, even at the risk of some puzzlement at the outset. If it turns out that the several topics do not lend themselves to a common approach, that, too, will have taught us a lesson. In any event, no lawyer since Moses has written in stone, and it may well be that the illustrations and inquiries are more important to lawyers, officials, legislators, judges—even to the professors—than principles too abstract or too dogmatic to be truly useful.

My perspective is that of an American, which is an advantage in the sense that in respect to our focus here, the United States has more of everything than any other country—more lawyers, more litigation, more efforts to exercise extraterritorial jurisdiction, more judgments that shock some non-Americans. But I am an internationalist, and a scholar, and far from a spokesman for all the views and practices of the United States government or United States courts. If I do sound from time to time like an advocate, it is for a method or approach, not for any country, industry, or cause.

B. PRIVATE INTERNATIONAL LAW REDEFINED

The term 'Private International Law', when one thinks about it, is a rather odd phrase. As best one can tell,[3] the term was first used by Joseph Story, that remarkable figure of the early nineteenth century who was not only a Justice of the United States Supreme Court for more than thirty years, but also the first American legal scholar to be taken seriously outside the United States. Story had no doubt that conflict of laws was a branch of *public* law—'a most interesting and important branch of public law';[4] he wanted to establish that conflict of laws was a branch of the law of nations:

> This branch of public law may be fitly denominated private international law, since it is chiefly seen and felt in its application to the common business of private persons, and rarely rises to the dignity of national negotiations, or national controversies.[5]

My focus here partly follows Story's definition, in that all of the problems we deal with here concern the 'common business of private persons'. Many of our topics, however, do 'rise to the dignity', as he put it, of national negotiations or national controversies—or, as we would put it today, *inter*national negotiations and *inter*national controversies.

[3] See Friedrich K. Juenger, *Choice of Law and Multistate Justice* (1993) 4.

[4] Joseph Story, *Commentaries on the Conflict of Laws, Foreign and Domestic* (1st edn. 1834), § 9. In all, eight editions of Story's Commentaries on the Conflict of Laws were published, the last one in 1883. The second edition was edited by his son, and later editions were prepared by other editors. Only the first edition was Story's alone, and it is the one to which references are made herein.

[5] *Ibid.*

In the closing paragraph of his treatise, Story looked towards the establishment of a 'general system of international jurisprudence, which shall elevate the policy, subserve the interests, and promote the common convenience of all nations'.[6] 'We may thus indulge in the hope', Story continued, 'that, at no distant period, the comity of nations will be but another name for the justice of nations.'

I venture no similar grandiose hope here. I do believe, however, that Story was right to think of conflict of laws as part of the law of nations, and that the term that he introduced and that has gained currency in Great Britain and throughout Europe is misunderstood by those who regard private international law as sharply distinct from public law or public international law. Thus my definition and approach are very different from those of Batiffol and Lagarde, who define private international law as the collection of rules applicable solely to private persons in their international relations.[7] Moreover, I believe that, while the discussion in this volume does not address the cosmic issues of war and peace, of nuclear weapons and terrorist assaults, it does deal with legitimate and serious concerns of private persons and of states, and surely of lawyers, embraced within what Story calls the comity of nations.

C. PRIVATE INTERNATIONAL LAW WITHOUT CHOICE OF LAW

I want to make only one more general observation, before undertaking a narrative that will illustrate many of the issues that will recur throughout the volume. In a traditional 'private' law suit involving, say, a dispute about a contract concluded in Patria and to be performed (or partly performed) in Xandia, an important issue may well be whether the law of Patria or the law of Xandia will be applied. On some issues, such as formation of the contract and breach, the law of the two states is likely to be the same or close to the same; when one comes to excuse for non-performance, scope and measure of damages, possibly even capacity to contract, the choice between applying Patrian or Xandian law may well be critical to the outcome of the case. I do not want here to discuss when application of one law or the other would be more appropriate; my point is that this question will be addressed whether suit is brought in Xandia or in Patria. The choice of forum, whether made in advance by contract or made by the plaintiff in initiating the suit, will not necessarily decide the choice of law question, let alone the outcome of the action. The Xandian court may well apply the law

[6] Story, *Conflict of Laws*, § 645.

[7] 'l'ensemble des règles applicable aux seules personnes privées dans les relations de la société internationale': H. Batiffol and P. Lagarde, *Droit Internationale Privé* (7th edn., 1981), 2–3. The same definition appears in previous editions of Batiffol's treatise.

of Patria (place of conclusion of the contract), the Patrian court may well apply the law of Xandia (place of performance), and if the contract was formed by telephone or fax, one or both courts may well want to make a preliminary finding about where the contract was concluded.[8]

Suppose, in contrast, that the issue in controversy is not about whether a contract was formed or how to measure damages for its breach. Suppose, instead, that the plaintiff asserts that he purchased securities from the defendant on the basis of representations that give rise to liability under the securities laws of Patria. The defendant asserts that it did not act in Patria and that the laws of Patria do not apply to the transaction.[9] If suit is brought in Xandia, say because it is the defendant's principal domicile, it turns out that the courts of that state will almost certainly not apply the securities law of Patria. If the statement of claim does not allege a cause of action under the laws of Xandia, the Xandian court will simply dismiss the action. Correspondingly, if the suit is brought in Patria, defendant will assert (if it has any basis for doing so) that the Patrian court has no jurisdiction over it, and that in any event the laws of Patria do not apply to it as to the transaction in question. If the courts of Patria conclude that they have judicial jurisdiction over the defendant, they will decide whether the laws of Patria are applicable, possibly by reference to criteria that are to be explored in Chapter 3. If the answer is affirmative, the defendant's liability will be judged by the law of Patria; if not, the case will be dismissed, again without any examination of whether liability might be shown under the law of Xandia.

Why should this be so? Why should the courts of Xandia not be prepared

[8] Compare *Entores Ltd* v. *Miles Far East Corporation* [1955] 2 QB 327 (UK Ct. App.). Held: contract formed at place where telex evidencing meeting of minds was received, in contrast to a contract concluded by mail, which would be deemed to have been formed where the acceptance was dispatched. Accord: *Brinkibon Ltd* v. *Stahag Stahl und Stahlwarenhandelsgesellschaft mbH* [1983] 2 A. C. 34 (HL (E)).

[9] For an interesting recent case of this kind involving a claim under the famous rule 10b–5 of the US securities laws, see, e.g., *Alfadda* v. *Fenn*, 935 F. 2d 475 (2d. Cir. 1991), cert. denied, 501 U.S. 1005 (1991). The plaintiffs were residents and nationals of Saudi Arabia and Bahrain, who had purchased shares in a Netherlands Antilles Company on the basis of a prospectus issued outside the United States and stating that the shares were not to be sold in the United States. The plaintiffs alleged that the promoters included two American citizens, that the prospectus and the transaction itself had been prepared in the United States, and that the proceeds of the stock offering were to be used in investments in the US energy industry. Further, the plaintiffs alleged that, contrary to representations in the prospectus, the promoters had doubled the number of shares sold, thus diluting the plaintiffs' holdings, and that some of the shares had been sold to subsidiaries of US firms. The district court dismissed the action on the basis that the alleged fraud was perpetrated outside the United States: *Alfadda* v. *Fenn*, 751 F. Supp. 1114 (S.D. N.Y. 1990). The Court of Appeals reinstated the action, on the ground that conduct both before and after the sale of shares to plaintiff was part of a single scheme and that thus the transaction as described in the complaint met the test of conduct in the United States sufficient to support application of US securities law. For a still more recent securities case blending the conduct and the effects test, see *Itoba Ltd* v. *LEP Group Plc.*, 54 F.3d 118 (2d Cir. 1995).

to adjudicate a claim under the securities laws of Patria, just as they would be prepared to adjudicate a claim that depended on the definition of a bona fide purchaser under the law of Patria.[10] Why should the courts of Patria focus only on whether Patrian law applies, without considering either claims or defences under the law of Patria, as they would, for instance in a defamation case.[11]

The answer to both questions, of course, is 'Well, securities law is public law, and public law is different. States don't apply the public law of other states.' I want to develop, and to challenge this proposition throughout the volume. At this first stage, I want to point out only that if the choice of law is not, as one might expect, between the law of Patria and the law of Xandia, but between the law of Patria and dismissal or between the law of Xandia and dismissal, then the issues of judicial jurisdiction, and related topics such as *forum non conveniens*, anti-suit injunctions, *lis pendens*, and the like become critically important—much more so than we are accustomed to. In ordinary actions involving parties or activities in more than one state, I think that choice of law plays a kind of mediating role among the laws of the states touched in some way by the transaction or controversy. When the opportunity to engage in choice of law is absent, the mediating rôle is absent as well. What is left is a struggle over jurisdiction—to prescribe and to adjudicate—that may reflect the genuine interest of states or may just reflect the interests of the combatants, each contending that international law is on its side. It is this branch of international law that will form one of the principal themes of these essays—not wholly private (if indeed law can ever be) nor wholly public, but an interlacing of several strands that we will try, throughout this volume, to disentangle.

D. A FIRST ILLUSTRATIVE CASE: THE LAKER LITIGATION

I want to start, by way of illustration, with the story of Freddie Laker, a young English businessman who sought in the 1970s to take on the

[10] For a dramatic case of the latter, see *Macmillan* v. *Bishopsgate PLC et al.* ([1995] 3 All ER 747 High Ct. Chancery 1993), att'd Ct. App. 1995 involving the fall of the House of Maxwell, and in particular involving the question whether unauthorized pledges of securities of an American corporation given in England were to be judged under the English law of restitution or under the American (New York) law applicable to *bona fide* purchasers (or holders in due course) of investment securities. After a trial lasting many months and involving numerous experts, the court decided that New York law governed, and interpreted provisions of the New York Uniform Commercial Code that had not previously been construed or applied by any court in New York or indeed the United States.

[11] Article 137 of the new Swiss Private International Law seems to provide for the possibility that Swiss courts might apply the competition law of another country, if the alleged restraint of competition directly affected the injured party in that country's market. So far as I know no case has expressly involved this provision, and no other country's laws contain a similar provision. For the suggestion that arbitrators in Switzerland should be guided by Article 137, see Ch. 9, sect. D.

international airline establishment and to provide low-cost, 'no frills' service between Britain and the United States. The story illustrates many of the topics to be explored in more depth hereafter, and takes place in several of the fora relevant to our inquiry. First some background.

International civil aviation since the close of World War II has been governed by a dual regime: (1) the right to operate commercial airline services between different states over specified routes has been subject to bilateral air service agreements, pursuant to which each state's authorities designate one or more of its flag carriers to operate the services agreed upon; (2) fares have been set not by governments, but by periodic multilateral conferences conducted by the International Air Transport Association (IATA). Typically, fares were set for six-month periods—roughly the summer season and the winter season—and the fare agreements covered not only the basic fare, but permitted discounts and surcharges, the width of seats, the charge for inflight movies and drinks, and so on. The underlying premise was that fares needed to be uniform from point to point, and to bear a fixed relation to each other, so that, for instance, the fare for New York–Amsterdam and New York–Paris would be the same, *x* per cent higher than New York–London and *y* per cent lower than Chicago–Paris or New York–Rome. On a given route, the same fare would apply regardless of the carrier providing the service. In theory, fares set through the IATA procedures were subject to approval by governments; in fact, only the United States, among major aviation states, ever disapproved IATA fares, and this happened only rarely.[12]

Of course, concerted rate-making under the auspices of IATA was in United States eyes a restraint of trade, but in the age of regulation (as contrasted with deregulation) a trade-off was authorized by the U.S. Congress whereby agreements among airlines were to be submitted to the Civil Aeronautics Board for approval. Approval of an agreement carried with it exemption from the antitrust laws to the extent necessary to carry out the approved agreement; disapproval would bring exposure to suit under the antitrust laws, not only by the U.S. government, but also by private parties seeking treble damages.[13]

In 1946 the United States Civil Aeronautics Board (CAB) decided to approve the IATA conference rate-making procedures, subject to submission to the CAB of individual fare-setting agreements.[14] Generally the CAB went through the motions of investigating IATA fare resolutions (i.e., in form exercising jurisdiction), but then approved the resolutions

[12] Much (though not all) of this has changed in the last few years, but it is substantially accurate as of the time relevant to our story here.

[13] See Federal Aviation Act §§ 412, 414, 49 U.S.C. §§ 1382, 1384 (1938–78). In 1978 the Act was modified so that antitrust immunity was no longer automatic; for present purposes, however, the descriptions in the text are sufficient.

[14] *ATA Traffic Conference Resolution*, 6 C.A.B. 639 (1946).

and avoided conflict. In the beginning of 1963 the CAB disapproved an IATA fare resolution—known as the Chandler fares[15]—that would have raised international air fares by about five per cent, at a time when the majority of the CAB thought fares should be coming down. Not only IATA and the international airline establishment but most governments united in resisting and protesting the American government's action, going so far as to threaten to seize aircraft and to terminate the landing rights of United States flag carriers. In part the opposition to the action of the CAB was due to a difference in judgment about the proper direction of air fares just as jet planes were replacing propeller aircraft on all major long-haul routes. More important, however, was the reaction, led by Great Britain but joined in by most of the world's industrial countries, that the United States had attempted to exercise unilateral jurisdiction over a matter that was properly committed to multilateral negotiation and decision. Eventually the United States government backed down, and the Chandler fares were permitted to go into effect at least until the next IATA fare conference, which was promptly convened.[16]

No doubt the United States had jurisdiction—to prescribe and to enforce—in respect of air travel between the United States and foreign countries; the CAB was not undertaking to pass on fares charged by foreign airlines between Calcutta and Kuala Lumpur. But the Chandler fare controversy of 1963 was an early case—not the first and certainly not the last case but a highly publicized one—in which the attempt by the United States government to exercise jurisdiction over an activity that touched upon many states was regarded as overreaching—unreasonable and ultimately unlawful.

I was a young lawyer in the United States State Department at the time, and I had a good deal of sympathy with the initial decision of the CAB disapproving the increased fares, particularly since it was clear that no other government had looked seriously into how the airlines that had agreed not to compete on price were setting their fares, and considering further that a preponderance of the affected customers—some two-thirds of passengers across the North Atlantic—were American. On the other hand, it was striking that the United States stood all alone, and that the other countries, all of which also had jurisdiction to prescribe, took a different position from that of the United States—on supervision over IATA, or on the level of air fares, or both. It was then that I first began to think about whether it might be possible to develop some criteria for the allocation of regulatory jurisdiction over activities touching upon more than one state. I also began to wonder whether for purposes of such

[15] The name came from the town of Chandler, Arizona, where the conference that agreed on the fares in question had held its session.

[16] For detailed exploration of the Chandler fare controversy including more technical issues of international and aviation law, see A. Chayes, T. Ehrlich, A. Lowenfeld, International Legal Process (1968) ch. VIII; A. Lowenfeld, Aviation Law (2d edn., 1981), ch. 2, §§ 7–9.5.

allocation one could properly distinguish between a decision to regulate (as the United States had made in the Chandler fare episode) and a decision not to regulate (as the British and others had made in Chandler).[17]

As background to the Laker litigation, the discussion of IATA may seem to have been an excessive digression; as background to our overall theme, however, I think it is not irrelevant.[18] Coming back to Freddie Laker, for seven years he alternately battled British and American authorities for permission for his 'Skytrain Service' across the Atlantic, at fares substantially below IATA fares. Finally, after litigation on both sides of the Atlantic, Laker Airways received permission from both countries and in September 1977 Skytrain began operations.[19]

For several years Laker Airways was very successful, operating as many as forty scheduled flights per week across the Atlantic, in addition to numerous charter flights, and carrying one passenger in seven between Britain and the United States. The IATA carriers fought back, with a variety of stand-by and advance-purchase flights, but Laker kept expanding its services, to new cities and with more flights. Prime Minister Thatcher, who had come into office in 1979 preaching return to old-fashioned entrepreneurial spirit, bestowed a knighthood on Mr Laker, who was thereafter known as Sir Freddie.

In the early 1980s, Laker's fortunes began to turn. In part, it seems that the airline had expanded too fast. As interest rates and fuel prices rose sharply while travel was reduced, Laker Airways began to feel a credit

[17] As a government official some years before I became an academic, I could not express my thoughts and doubts fully; my first published writing on this question, which has occupied me for more than three decades, was a book review of Lawrence Ebb, *International Business: Regulation and Protection* (1964); 78 Harv. L. Rev. 1699 (1965). I wrote there:

> I do not think there is a universal principle that economic regulation must stop at the national frontier, and I would not advise creating one. It seems to me that the fact that commerce is conducted on an international scale—that it has significant contacts with more than one state—should not immunize it from regulation. In a situation involving more than one country, if country *A* wishes to regulate and country *B* does not, it seems to me equally fair to criticize *B* for attempting to impose its will beyond its borders as it is to criticize *A* for attempting to exercise its jurisdiction extraterritorially.

78 Harv. L. Rev. at 1703–4. For a somewhat different and more searching discussion of the issue of regulation *v.* non-regulation, see Ch. 2 at 26–7 *infra*.

[18] A second, similar episode of the U.S. against the world occurred in 1978, when the CAB issued a 'show cause order' why IATA fares should not be disapproved, thus denying antitrust immunity to the airlines participating in IATA fare conferences, nearly all of which operated to and from the United States. The order provoked a major controversy, with virtually every country alleging that the United States had exceeded its jurisdiction to prescribe. Eventually the CAB retreated by restoring antitrust immunity to the IATA agreements, but it withheld permission to the U.S.-flag carriers to participate in IATA conference ratemaking. See A. Lowenfeld, *Aviation Law*, n. 16 *supra*, ch. V §§ 4.4–4.5.

[19] When Freddie Laker stepped off the first flight of his Skytrain to New York from London on September 26, 1977, he told the crowd at JFK Airport:

> My friends . . . Tonight I am a fugitive. We are all part of the biggest jailbreak on Earth. For tonight, we have all escaped from the IATA prison.

Quoted in *Aviation Week and Space Technology*, October 3, 1977, 28.

squeeze. Moreover, Laker's debts were largely in dollars while much of its revenue was in sterling, which in the relevant period was falling sharply in relation to the dollar. Laker, however, alleged that the downturn was due to a double conspiracy. First, the major IATA carriers, he claimed, had engaged in predatory price-cutting designed to drive Laker Airways out of business; secondly, the major carriers, led by British Airways but including also Pan American, TWA, KLM, Sabena, and other airlines, had conspired to pressure Laker's creditors—banks and equipment manufacturers—to deny Laker further extensions of credit. On February 5, 1982, Laker Airways ceased operating, and shortly thereafter went into liquidation.

In November 1982, Laker Airways Ltd, represented by its liquidator (a partner in the London office of a Big Eight accounting firm) brought an action against British Airways and the other major IATA airlines plus McDonnell Douglas, the aircraft manufacturer, based on the allegations described and demanding treble damages coming to more than one billion dollars ($350 million × three). Where were these claims filed? In a United States court, of course—in particular the U.S. District Court for the District of Columbia. There was no doubt that the court had judicial jurisdiction over all the defendant carriers; they all operated to the United States and had at least ticket offices in Washington, D.C. But should United States antitrust law be applied to conduct—competitive or anti-competitive—involving international air transport? In prior cases—notably in the Chandler controversy and again in 1978[20]—the United States Government had said yes, but had backed down in the face of massive opposition. This time, however, the matter was before a U.S. court, and the initiative came from a private party—indeed a foreign party.

British Airways did not wait for decision by the U.S. District Court. Instead, on January 21, 1983, BA filed an action against Laker in the High Court of Justice in London, seeking a declaration of non-liability to Laker and a permanent injunction to prevent Laker from continuing to pursue its action in the United States. British Caledonian (B-Cal), Lufthansa, and Swissair joined in the action shortly thereafter. On January 24, Laker applied to the district court in Washington for a preliminary injunction to restrain Pan American, TWA, McDonnell Douglas, KLM, and Sabena from joining the action in London. Judge Greene in the District of Columbia granted a Temporary Restraining Order and set the matter down for a hearing.

Thus by the end of January 1983, an initial action was pending in Washington, a suit to enjoin that action was pending in London, and an anti-anti-suit injunction was pending in Washington.

How should we look at this situation? One view that appeals to me is

[20] See n. 18 *supra*.

that all anti-suit injunctions are wrong, especially injunctions issued in one state designed to restrain proceedings in another state. Even if the courts of State *A* are not prepared to recognize judgments rendered by the courts of *B*, they ought not to interfere with litigation in progress in *B*. On that view, the anti-suit injunction pending in London ought to be refused, and the anti-anti-suit injunction pending in Washington ought also to be refused. But what if the London court does not share this view? Should the court in Washington nevertheless refuse the counter injunction, on the ground that two wrongs don't make a right?

Another way to look at the situation would be to ask where the underlying action should be heard. On one level the controversy is between one English party, Laker, and another English party, British Airways, as principal defendant. But the action is not one for personal injuries suffered aboard a ship which can be heard in one country as well as in another.[21] As we have already seen, an English court might apply American or Portuguese tort law, but it would not apply American antitrust law. Thus if the English court restrains the English plaintiff from proceeding in an American court, it will in effect deny it all recovery, without ever having heard the merits of the case. Does it follow that, even if it does not share our distaste for anti-suit injunctions,[22] the English court should not enjoin Laker's action in the United States? I think so. Does this conclusion lead to the further conclusion that the American judge should not hesitate to grant the anti-anti-suit injunction, in order to keep as many parties as possible in the litigation brought before the only court that has a chance to reach the merits? I think so as well, but I am not sure. And I would not go so far as to suggest that the American judge should permit Laker Airways to continue the action in Washington as long as an injunction against it was outstanding.[23]

[21] See, e.g., *Castanho* v. *Brown & Root (U.K.) Ltd* [1981] AC 460 (HL (E)), affirming reversal of an antisuit injunction issued by the High Court against a Portuguese sailor who had first brought his claim for injuries in England where the injury occurred, but had been persuaded to drop that action in favor of an action in Texas, where his damages were likely to be substantially higher and his legal fees could be taken care of on a contingency basis. For the American phase of this case see *Castanho* v. *Jackson Marine, Inc.*, 484 F. Supp. 201 (E.D. Tex. 1980), appeal dismissed, 650 F.2d 546 (5th Cir. 1980), sustaining jurisdiction of the federal court in Texas against the parent corporation of the chain of enterprises in charge of the ship on which the accident occurred, and refusing to dismiss on grounds of *forum non conveniens*.

For more on the issue of the liability of parent corporations for obligations of their subsidiaries, see Ch. 5.

[22] See *Société Nationale Industrielle Aèrospatiale* v. *Lee Kui Jak* [1987] AC 871 (PC), reversing refusal by a court in Brunei to issue an injunction against suit in Texas by the widow of a passenger killed in a plane crash against the manufacturer, because the other defendant (the airline) could not be sued there.

[23] In fact, after the temporary injunction issued by the English court had been in effect for ten months, Judge Greene appointed a private Washington lawyer as *amicus curiae*, to advise him on the available options. *Laker Airways Ltd* v. *Pan American World Airways*, 577 F. Supp. 348 (D.D.C. Nov. 17, 1983). The *amicus* laid out several options, including the appointment of

The story, at all events, continued as follows:

March 2, 1983, Mr Justice Parker, in London, sets the application for an injunction down for hearing on March 21, but grants a temporary injunction against any further steps by Laker against BA in the American action.

March 9, 1983, after hearing, Judge Greene in the District of Columbia, issues an injunction restraining Pan American, TWA, KLM, Sabena, and McDonnell Douglas from joining the anti-suit action in London, holding that the 'public interest clearly favors a full airing of Laker's claims envisioned by the Sherman Act'.[24]

May 20, 1983, Mr Justice Parker in London, after a hearing, holds that the injunctive relief requested by British Airways is not justified.[25] True, antitrust actions are penal in nature, as confirmed by Parliament in adopting the Protection of Trading Interests Act;[26] but this principle 'cannot be regarded as a sound foundation' for enjoining the bringing of an antitrust action by a British company against other British companies arising out of business carried on by all parties in both countries and subject to both countries' laws.[27] However, Mr Justice Parker continues the March 2 temporary injunction pending appeal.

June 27, 1983, the United Kingdom Minister for Trade and Industry issues an order under authority of the Protection of Trading Interests Act prohibiting British Airways and B-Cal from complying with United States antitrust measures or furnishing any documents in the United Kingdom to any U.S. court, or to a U.S. grand jury that had begun to look into Laker's allegations.[28]

July 26, 1983, the Court of Appeal in London reverses the decision of Mr Justice Parker and issues a permanent injunction restraining Laker from taking any steps in the American action against British Airways and B-Cal.[29] Sir John Donaldson, Master of the Rolls, it seems, is somewhat embarrassed:

a guardian *ad litem*, as for a child or for an incompetent person, but not including an instruction to Laker to carry on the litigation itself.

[24] *Laker Airways Ltd* v. *Pan American World Airways*, 559 F. Supp. 1124 (D.D.C. March 9, 1983). The judge wrote:

> The Court exceedingly regrets that it must issue an injunction in this case. However, it is worth emphasizing that this Court had no part in precipitating the current dispute. The lawsuit pending before it was proceeding in its normal course, when the British court, without appropriate regard for the principles of comity, proceeded to interfere with that action.

Id. at 1138. Two months later, Judge Greene granted partial summary judgment to Laker rejecting dismissal of the action on grounds of *forum non conveniens*: *Laker Airways Ltd* v. *Pan American World Airways*, 568 F. Supp. 84 (D.D.C. May 3, 1983).

[25] *British Airways Board* v. *Laker Airways Ltd* [1983] 3 WLR 544, 549, [1984] QB 142, 147.

[26] The Act is discussed in Ch. 7, Sect. D.

[27] [1983] 3 WLR at 564, [1984] QB at 163.

[28] Protection of Trading Interests (U.S. Antitrust Measures) Order 1983, S.I. 1983 900, and General Directions thereunder, quoted in the decision of the Court of Appeal.

[29] *British Airways Board* v. *Laker Airways Ltd* [1983] 3 WLR 544, 569 (C.A.), [1984] QB 142, 169.

First let it be said, and said loud and clear, that no one has ever suggested that the United States District Court is without jurisdiction to try Laker's complaint against the Appellants both under the Sherman and Clayton Acts and in respect of the commission of an intentional tort. Both Appellants carry on business in the United States of America sufficiently to make them amenable to the jurisdiction of its courts. If any such submission had been made, it would have been rejected out of hand.

Second, let it be said at no less volume and with no less clarity that no submission has been made to this Court that the civil procedures of the United States courts and, in particular, the system of pre-trial discovery by the taking of depositions, the administration of interrogatories and the disclosure of documents, the limited circumstances in which a successful defendant would be awarded costs and the conduct of litigation upon the basis of contingency fees are in any way to be criticized. They are different from English civil procedures, but the days are long past when the English courts and judges thought that there was only one way of administering justice and that was the English way. Each nation must decide for itself which way is appropriate to its need and there is nothing strange in two nations which enjoy a common legal heritage and could be described as 'cousins-in-law' rightly deciding that different procedures suited them best.

Third, let it be said no less loudly and clearly that neither the English courts nor the English judges entertain any feelings of hostility towards the American anti-trust laws or would ever wish to denigrate that or any other American law. Judicial comity is shorthand for good neighbourliness, common courtesy and mutual respect between those who labour in adjoining judicial vineyards. In the context of the United Kingdom and the United States, this comes naturally and, so far as we are concerned, effortlessly.[30]

Nevertheless, the effect of the order under the Protection of Trading Interests Act rendered the U.S. action 'wholly untriable'. 'To allow Laker to proceed with its claim in these circumstances', the Court of Appeal concluded, 'would amount to a total denial of justice to [British Airways and B-Cal].'[31] There was something strange about action by the British government disabling British Airways from obtaining justice in an American court by prohibiting it from responding to discovery requests issued in the American action, as was pointed out later in the House of Lords.[32] But as an assertion of British national interest in a British court, the action by the British Minister, supported in court by Her Majesty's Attorney General, though unusual, was quite clear. Before the controversy could be taken further in the British courts, however, the scene shifted back to Washington.

March 6, 1984, after the House of Lords has granted leave to appeal but before the appeal is heard, the U.S. Court of Appeals for the District of

[30] [1983] 3 WLR at 575, [1984] QB at 185–6.

[31] [1983] 3 WLR at 591, [1984] QB at 202.

[32] See *British Airways Board* v. *Laker Airways Ltd* [1983] AC 58 at 94, [1984] 3 WLR 413 at 433–4, discussed below.

Columbia Circuit issues a decision in the appeal by the foreign carriers from the order of Judge Greene enjoining them (as well as Pan American and TWA) from joining British Airways' suit in London. By a two to one vote, the U.S. Court of Appeals affirms Judge Greene's order.[33] Judge Wilkey, for the majority, writes:

> The conflict in jurisdiction we confront today has been precipitated by the attempts of another country to insulate its own business entities from the necessity of complying with legislation of our country designed to protect this country's domestic policies. At the root of the conflict are the fundamentally opposed policies of the United States and Great Britain regarding the desirability, scope and implementation of legislation controlling anticompetitive and restrictive business practices.[34]

The court concludes that it has 'neither the authority nor the institutional resources' to resolve the underlying conflict, or the competing claims of jurisdiction, which it suggests should be submitted to diplomatic and executive channels. Meanwhile, it acts to preserve the district court's jurisdiction, and upholds that court's anti-anti-suit injunction. Judge Starr, in dissent, says no evidence has been presented of the sovereign interest of the United States in the action, whereas the fact that the British government has an interest has been plainly demonstrated. He would therefore have pulled back from 'what will be viewed by many of our friends and allies as a rather parochial American outlook'.[35] We come back to Judge Wilkey's claim of inability to weigh competing interests in Chapter 3. Meanwhile back to London.

July 19, 1984, the House of Lords is ready with its decision, and it reverses.[36] It was clear that all the airlines involved were subject to U.S. legislative jurisdiction, including the U.S. anti-trust laws. Since no cause of action under these laws is justifiable in an English court, only one forum is competent to hear the claim, i.e., the U.S. court. As Lord Diplock says in the principal speech:

> For an English court to enjoin the claimant from having access to that foreign court is, in effect, to take upon itself a one-sided jurisdiction to determine the claim upon the merits *against* the claimant but also to prevent its being decided upon the merits *in his favour*.[37]

[33] *Laker Airways Ltd* v. *Sabena, Belgian World Airlines*, 731 F.2d 909 (D.C. Cir. 1984).

[34] *Id.* at 955–6.

[35] 731 F.2d at 956–7 (Starr, J. dissenting).

[36] *British Airways Board* v. *Laker Airways Ltd* [1984] 3 WLR 413, [1983] AC 58 (HL(E)).

[37] [1984] 3 WLR at 420, [1985] AC at 80, emphasis in the original. In a subsequent decision, an anti-suit injunction was issued barring Laker from proceeding in a U.S. court against a British bank, which, as the Court of Appeal held, had no relevant presence in, and (unlike the airlines) had not submitted itself to the jurisdiction of the United States: *Midland Bank Plc* v. *Laker Airways Ltd* [1986] 2 WLR 707, [1986] QB 689 (CA). The further application by the bank for a declaration of non-liability was denied.

Thus the Laker action was not the kind of case in which it might be open to the English court to hold that one forum was clearly more suitable than another. It was a single-forum case, and the English courts should not deny the plaintiff (Laker) the opportunity to present its claim in that forum. Concerning the expression of governmental interest by the Attorney General and the Secretary of State under the Protection of Trading Interest Act, Lord Diplock wrote:

> For my part, I regard this as a dubious advantage, for the litigation between Laker, B.A. and B.C. both in the United States and in England falls within the field of private law, where the sources of the public policy to which courts of justice give effect in litigation between subject and subject are to be found in judicial decisions and in legislation and not in the views of the executive government except in the relatively narrow field of international relations between sovereign states which is still reserved to the prerogative.[38]

The story does not quite end there, and we will return to the underlying subject of weighing conflicting interests in Chapter 3. For the time being, however, I think we have opened up quite enough issues, I hope in a way that enables the recorder to think about them with an actual controversy, not just abstract formulae, in mind. We have brought up:

—national jurisdiction to prescribe with respect to activity carried out in more than one nation;
—the question of a convenient or inconvenient forum;
—the availability and desirability of anti-suit injunctions;
—the role of governmental interests in private litigation;
—the distinctions between civil and 'penal' actions; and between compensatory and 'punitive damages'.

In the background, and in the minds of the judges whom we have quoted, other problems loom:

—transnational discovery;
—blocking statutes;
—enforcement of foreign judgments;
—the relation of national law to international agreements; and
—the extent to which courts may inquire into the motives of governments.

I make no commitment that by the end of the volume the reader will come away with what Americans call 'Black Letter' solutions to all—or even to any—of these issues. I do undertake that, if the reader pursues the discussion to the end, he or she will feel more comfortable—I hesitate to say enlightened—in approaching these problems, whether from the point of view of a practising lawyer, a public official, a judge, or a scholar.

[38] [1984] 3 WLR at 425, [1985] AC at 85.

2

The Limits of Jurisdiction to Prescribe

Having opened up so many subjects in the first chapter, I hope to explore them one by one in the succeeding chapters. I want to start with a search for the limits, if any, of national jurisdiction over transnational activity.

A. LOOKING FOR A NEUTRAL TERM

Everyone understands that a state has jurisdiction over activities carried out wholly within that state, i.e., where both conduct and effect are confined to the state that exercises jurisdiction to apply its law. All other exercise of jurisdiction seems to be referred to as extraterritorial jurisdiction, with more than a hint that 'extraterritorial' means 'exorbitant', if not 'illegal'. I think it is unfortunate that the term 'extraterritorial jurisdiction' has acquired this pejorative cast.

A great many activities involve conduct in more than one state; others involve conduct in one state and effect in another. To suggest that such activity may or should be carried out without reference to the law of any state is to suggest a kind of Antarctica,[1] a no man's land greater than any of us would tolerate for a world inhabited by people, not penguins. Whether one thinks of export/import transactions, of shipping or aviation or telecommunications, of investment across frontiers, or of myriad other activities, it is inconceivable that law is simply excluded. Of course there will be overlap, inconsistent values, even direct conflict. It is our task to sort these out, to devise some rules, or at least guidelines, that can help in distinguishing between genuine and spurious interests, promote accommodation between public and private interests, and between interests of different states.

I believe the search for appropriate limits on the exercise of jurisdiction

[1] See Antarctica Treaty signed at Washington, Dec. 1, 1959, 12. U.S.T. 794, T.I.A.S. 4780, 402 UNTS 71. For a recent decision of the U.S. Supreme Court, holding that the widow of a member of an American scientific expedition could not recover under the U.S. Federal Tort Claims Act for a fatal injury sustained by her husband in Antarctica on account of the U.S. government's alleged negligence, see *Smith* v. *United States*, 507 U.S. 197 (1993). The statute excluded claims 'arising in a foreign country', 28 U.S.C. § 2680(k), but though Antarctica is not a country, the Court held that the Tort Claims Act made the United States liable 'under circumstances where the United States, if a private person, would be liable to the claimant *in accordance with the law of the place where the act or omission occurred*', 28 U.S.C. § 1346(b), and there is no such law.

is a worthwhile pursuit. The search for a satisfactory definition of extraterritorial jurisdiction, on the other hand, is doomed to failure: 'extraterritorial jurisdiction', like 'bureaucratic', is a term that could never be rescued from its unattractive reputation. When we wish to praise the achievement of a government employee, we call him or her a creative official, perhaps a devoted civil servant, never a bureaucrat. Similarly, when we appreciate the accomplishment of a state—for combatting securities fraud, or catching drug traffickers, for instance—we call it national vigilance, not sound exercise of extraterritorial jurisdiction.

Throughout these essays, I will refer to jurisdiction to prescribe, or regulatory jurisdiction, perhaps jurisdiction to enforce—all, I submit, neutral terms. But I want to begin with a warning: when you read a book or article, or attend a symposium with 'extraterritorial jurisdiction' in the title, be advised that the authors or editors or sponsors are attempting to communicate an attitude before the audience has read or heard a single phrase.

B. JURISDICTION TO PRESCRIBE AND CHOICE OF LAW

Having, for present purposes at least, banished the word 'extraterritorial' from the discussion, I am left nevertheless with the word 'jurisdiction'. I think that word is perfectly appropriate, in that it neither attracts nor repels, apart from the context in which it is employed. But here, too, we must be careful. To students of conflict of laws, jurisdiction sometimes is deemed related to power, and especially when focused on courts, to an inquiry that yields a yes/no answer, like a light switch that is either on or off, in contrast to choice of the proper or applicable law, which is understood to involve selection among two or more potentially applicable solutions, each of which falls within the power of the decision-maker. I prefer to think of jurisdiction to prescribe as a question of authority, not power. To pursue the analogy of the light switch, it is helpful to think of a traffic light, sometimes red, sometimes green, but—as in the interesting cases of purely private controversies touching upon more than one system of laws—often yellow. Yellow indicates caution, the need to evaluate and, I would argue, to balance the respective interests, public and private.

There is one difference between the typical private choice of law case and most cases involving jurisdiction to prescribe. In a purely private law case, the court in the forum state *A* will decide whether to apply the law of *A*—say the seller's principal place of business, or the law of state *B*, the buyer's principal place of business or the place of performance of the obligation in question. We saw in connection with the *Laker* litigation dicussed in Chapter 1 that there is virtually no chance that the courts of *A* will apply the public law of *B*, or that the courts of *B* will apply the public law of *A*. But this does not necessarily mean that the courts of *A* will apply the law of *A* to every international controversy coming before them in which one party seeks to invoke the law of *A*. What it does mean is that the choice for the courts of *A*—the choice of law—is between applying the law of *A* and dismissing the action. I do not suggest that this difference is insignificant.

I do suggest, however, that the techniques of choice of law analysis—of private international law more narrowly defined than I have proposed here—are relevant and helpful. My submission is that the issues of jurisdiction to prescribe can and should be addressed by reference to contacts, interests, and expectations—that is to say meaningful contacts, genuine interests, and justified expectations—rather than by reference to the traditional vocabulary of public international law, focused on the over-used concept of sovereignty.

C. THE APPROACH OF THE RESTATEMENT

Having called for attention to meaningful contacts, genuine interests, and justified expectations, it is incumbent on me to put some content into these phrases. Fortunately I do not have to start with Adam and Eve. I have the advantage of having worked for close to a decade to formulate, explain, and illustrate a set of criteria addressed to the problem we are discussing, as one of the Reporters of the American Law Institute's *Restatement of Foreign Relations Law* published in 1987.[2] I propose to use the approach of the *Restatement* as the theme for the remainder of this Chapter.

A *Restatement of the Law*, as it has existed in the United States since the 1920s, is a collective work, involving drafting by a small team of reporters, review and critique by specialist advisers, and further review and approval by the Council of the Institute, made up of leaders of the profession who are generally not specialists in the field to which the particular *Restatement* is addressed. Once the Council has given its approval of some or all of a *Restatement*, the draft is submitted for discussion and ultimately adoption by vote of the membership of the Institute, which consists of several thousand lawyers, judges, and law professors independent of the government and of any particular cause.[3] Typically *Restatements* look something like

[2] American Law Institute, *Restatement (Third) of the Foreign Relations Law of the United States* (1987). The subject here discussed is reflected in Part IV of that work, particularly §§ 401–416.

[3] Of course not all members of the American Law Institute attend the Annual Meeting, or take part in any given vote. Typically, however, by the time a Restatement is submitted for final approval, drafts have been circulated for several years, and all who are interested have had an opportunity to be heard. Portions of the *Restatement (Third) of Foreign Relations Law* were brought before eight Annual Meetings (1980–7).

European codes, in that they contain numbered Rules (printed in black letters), followed by Comments and Reporters' Notes, in descending order of authority. *Restatements* generally have more prestige and influence than works by individual scholars, but they have no official status.

The *Restatement of Foreign Relations Law* is directed to the law of the United States concerned with international relations: the sections that I want to quote and elaborate on are asserted to state international law. Consistently with my approach here and elsewhere,[4] they do not distinguish sharply between public and private international law.

Leaving aside certain special or universal bases for jurisdiction to prescribe, the *Restatement* sets forth the principal bases of jurisdiction to prescribe—territoriality and nationality (§ 402). It invites some controversy by including effect as well as conduct within the territory of the state seeking to exercise jurisdiction under the rubric of territoriality (§ 402(1)(c)[5]). But while territoriality or nationality are *necessary* conditions for the lawful exercise of jurisdiction to prescribe, according to the *Restatement* they are *not sufficient*. Section 403(1) states:

> Even when one of the bases for jurisdiction under § 402 is present, a state may not exercise jurisdiction to prescribe law with respect to a person or activity having connections with another state when the exercise of jurisdiction is unreasonable.

We will explore hereafter the guidance offered by the *Restatement* in interpreting the standard of reasonableness. Even if the factors listed do not completely satisfy, I want to stress the importance of this first point. By providing that existence of one of the accepted links between an activity and a state is a necessary condition to application of its law but not a sufficient condition, the *Restatement* holds up a yellow light in all situations touching on more than one state. The *Restatement* says—to courts and to governments—that they are facing a yellow signal: stop, think, evaluate.

It is time to turn to the list of factors—the guidance for the required evaluation. Section 403(2) reads:

> Whether exercise of jurisdiction over a person or activity is unreasonable is determined by evaluating all relevant factors, including, where appropriate:
> (a) the link of the activity to the territory of the regulating state, i.e., the extent to which the activity takes place within the territory, or has substantial, direct, and foreseeable effect upon or in the territory;
> (b) the connections, such as nationality, residence, or economic activity, between the regulating state and the person principally responsible for the

[4] See my 1979 Hague Lectures, Ch. 1, n. 1 *supra*, 321–2.

[5] To be precise, s. 402(1)(c) speaks of

> conduct outside [the state's] territory that *has or is intended to have substantial effect* within its territory.

More on effects jurisdiction in Ch. 3.

activity to be regulated, or between that state and those whom the regulation is designed to protect;

(c) the character of the activity to be regulated, the importance of regulation to the regulating state, the extent to which other states regulate such activities, and the degree to which the desirability of such regulation is generally accepted;

(d) the existence of justified expectations that might be protected or hurt by the regulation;

(e) the importance of the regulation to the international political, legal, or economic system;

(f) the extent to which the regulation is consistent with the traditions of the international system;

(g) the extent to which another state may have an interest in regulating the activity; and

(h) the likelihood of conflict with regulation by another state.[6]

No one, as far as I know, has said that these factors are wrong—in the sense that one or another of them is irrelevant or misleading. Quite a few people—lawyers, judges, and academics—have said that the factors are unhelpful because they are too general, or because they call on judges (and others) to perform a task of evaluation or balancing that they cannot perform. My friend Professor Juenger, for example, writes that the concept of jurisdiction to prescribe is a poor problem solver which needs a *deus ex machina*, and that the *Restatement* finds that *deus ex machina* in what is loosely called 'comity'.[7] He goes on to quote a judge from the state of Louisiana in the 1820s to the effect that 'comity is, and ever must be, uncertain'.[8]

In fact the *Restatement* avoids the use of the word 'comity', not so much because it is uncertain but because it, too, comes with a tradition that it makes it something less than law, whereas the *Restatement* asserts that the principles of reasonableness are law.[9] Juenger asserts that the list of factors in the *Restatement* demonstrates that comity is as nebulous as the public policy exception involved in private choice of law controversies though

[6] Note that this list is similar to the list I proposed in my 1979 Hague Lectures, Ch. 1, n. 1 *supra*, at 328–9, but not quite the same. The 1979 list, in turn, drew on the general guidelines for exercising the choice of law function in the *Restatement (Second) of Conflict of Laws*, § 6 (1971), as well as on the pioneering work of Kingman Brewster, Jr., *Antitrust and American Business Abroad* (1958), 446–8.

[7] Friedrich K. Juenger, 'Constitutional Control of Extraterritoriality?: A Comment on Professor Brilmayer's Appraisal', 50 *Law & Contemp. Prob.* No. 3, 39 at 45 (1987).

[8] *Saul* v. *His Creditors*, 5 Mar. (n.s.) 569, at 596 (La. 1827).

[9] See *Restatement (Third) of Foreign Relations Law* § 403, Comment *a*. Also, comity often carries with it a presumption of reciprocity. The *Restatement* rejects reciprocity in this context, because if it is unreasonable and therefore unlawful for state *A* to exercise jurisdiction over an activity centered in state *B*, it cannot, other things being equal, be reasonable to exercise jurisdiction over the same activity when centered in state *C*, just because *C*'s position is different from *B*'s or is unascertainable.

their purposes are diametrically opposed. 'While public policy invokes the *lex fori* to ward off undesirable foreign law', he writes, 'comity is used to curtail unreasonable impositions of forum law.'[10] I think the contrast pointed out by Juenger between 'public policy' and what he calls 'comity' is instructive, but I would resist his characterization of the two techniques as 'equally unhelpful'. They are unhelpful only if one believes that the search for the applicable law—public or private—can yield precise formulations, like the laws of gravity or the laws relating the boiling point of water to the altitude above sealevel. Further, I think that the distrust that students of choice of law have of public policy—a distrust that I share—comes from the frequent use of that term as a substitute for thought and as a bridge to 'hometown justice'; the recognition that a foreign state *B* has an interest in regulation of a given activity which weighs against the exercise of jurisdiction to prescribe by State *A*, it seems to me, need not be a substitute for thought. On the contrary, it should be an invitation for thought, and the *Restatement* list of factors offers suggestions for what to think about in the course of reaching a decision.

Rather than exploring each of the factors listed, I want to illustrate the process of thinking about the exercise of jurisdiction called for by the *Restatement* by presenting in some detail a case that recently came before the United States Supreme Court. It is important to bear in mind that the object of the inquiry is not to see how a particular set of facts or allegations fits within the list of factors set out in § 403(2); the object is to ascertain whether application of the law of a given state is reasonable by standards that can be shared by the international community.

D. TESTING THE RESTATEMENT APPROACH: THE INSURANCE ANTI-TRUST CASE[11]

In 1986, nineteen states of the United States, along with a number of local governments and private parties, brought a massive antitrust action in the federal district court for the Northern District of California alleging a conspiracy among members of the insurance industry in the United States and abroad (i) to sell only 'claims made' liability insurance policies and to stop selling occurrence-based or so-called 'long-tail' liability insurance

[10] Juenger, n. 7 *supra*, 45.

[11] In the Supreme Court, the case is reported as *Hartford Fire Insurance Co.* v. *California*, 113 S.Ct. 2891 (1993); the District Court opinion, entitled *Insurance Antitrust Litigation*, is reported in 723 F. Supp. 464 (N.D. Cal. 1989); the opinion of the Court of Appeals is reported under the same title in 938 F.2d. 919 (9th Cir. 1991). The author was of counsel to the English defendants in the U.S. Supreme Court. However, the effort here is to present the case as objectively as possible, and nothing here stated is attributable to the defendants or to the law firm that represented them.

policies;[12] and (ii) to exclude coverage for sudden accidental pollution from general liability policies. The defendants were four major domestic insurance companies, a number of domestic reinsurers, brokers, and insurance associations, plus several foreign insurers—in particular a number of underwriting agencies at Lloyd's of London and two English individuals associated with the reinsurance market at Lloyd's.

All defendants moved to dismiss the action. The domestic insurers' and reinsurers' principal defense, which need not concern us much here, was the so-called McCarran-Ferguson Act, which largely exempts insurance companies organized in the United States from the antitrust laws, provided they are regulated by individual states.[13] The foreign defendants, who were not shielded by the McCarran Act, did not deny that when they declined to offer reinsurance to American insurance companies except under conditions satisfactory to them, their action had effects in the United States. Indeed it was their heavy losses in the United States in the preceding years, particularly in suits arising from claims of asbestos-related injuries, that had led to what they regarded as sound business decisions. Nor did they contest the assertion of judicial jurisdiction over them on the basis of agreement to supply services in California. They argued, however, that they had acted in England in full compliance with English law and policy, and that under applicable principles of international law and comity, the London insurance market was not subject to American antitrust law. To put it in our terms, the London defendants argued that it would be unreasonable, and therefore unlawful, to apply U.S. law to their activities carried out on the London insurance market in full compliance with English law.

The District Court agreed with the defendants, holding 'that the *conflict* with English law and policy which would result from the extra-territorial application of the [U.S.] antitrust laws in this case is not outweighed by other factors'.[14] The Court of Appeals reversed, on the basis that the alleged *effect* in the United States from defendants' conduct did outweigh the significant conflict with English law and policy.[15] Thus by the time the case reached the Supreme Court one opinion had stressed the place of conduct—England, the other the place of the effect—the United States. Though the two decisions in the lower courts and much of the argument

[12] An occurrence-based insurance policy has the effect that the insurer cannot close its books on policies issued for a given period until many years after the end of the term of the policy. Particularly with respect to claims arising out of buildings constructed with asbestos, or claims involving underground pollution, the insurance industry in the 1980s found itself in severe difficulties from these 'long-tail' claims. On the other hand, a 'claims made' policy might leave insureds unprotected at the time when injuries were first detected and claims were initiated.

[13] 15 U.S.C. § 1012 *et seq.* § 1012(b) provides in pertinent part that 'No Act of Congress shall be construed to invalidate, impair, or supersede any law enacted by any State for the purpose of regulating the business of insurance.' The exemption does not apply to any agreement 'to boycott, coerce, or intimidate.'

[14] 723 F.Supp. at 490.

[15] 938 F.2d at 934.

before the Supreme Court turned on the well-known *Timberlane* case,[16] both the majority and the dissent sought guidance primarily from the *Restatement.*

How then would evaluation according to the *Restatement* criteria resolve the *Insurance Antitrust* case? One way to look at the case would be simply to ask whether it was reasonable for the U.S. District Court in San Francisco to supervise the understandings and arrangements of English insurance underwriters practising their profession in London. Doubtless that was how the defendants thought about the suit when they first heard about it. It would not have occurred to them to invite an American lawyer to the meetings at which they discussed 'claims made' versus 'occurrence-based' reinsurance. But the defendants understood that they were reinsuring risks originally covered by policies issued in the United States to American insureds, and they could not deny that their proposed arrangements, if successful, would have effect in the United States. In the best case, they would keep all their American customers, and their exposure to losses would be significantly reduced. Seen from the United States, one could not conclude *a priori* that it would be unreasonable to exercise jurisdiction to apply United States law to activity intended to have substantial effect in the United States. Thus the search for the 'reasonable' or, as the *Restatement* prefers, 'not unreasonable' approach to the problem needs to go further. The question is whether section 403(2) of the *Restatement* illuminates that search.

Factor (*a*) on the *Restatement's* list—the link of the activity to the territory of the regulating state—would point to England, i.e., away from exercise of jurisdiction by the United States.

Factor (*b*)—the link of nationality or residence between the regulating state and the defendants—points away from exercising jurisdiction, but the link between the regulating state and those whom the regulation is designed to protect points to exercise of jurisdiction by the United States.

Factor (*c*)—the character of the regulation, and the importance of the regulation to the regulatory state, calls for some reflection. If we were concerned with application by the United States of its laws against narcotics, we would say the case for exercise of jurisdiction was strong, and the opposition weak or non-existent.[17] Regulation of securities fraud is not practised with the same vigor in other countries as in the United States, but no country affirmatively supports such activity. At one time the United States was almost alone in enforcing antitrust or competition law; at

[16] *Timberlane Lumber Co.* v. *Bank of America, N.T. & S.A.*, 549 F.2d 597 (9th Cir. 1976), discussed in my earlier Hague Lectures, 169 *Rec. des Cours* at 407–8, and in the *Restatement (Third) of Foreign Relations Law* at § 415, Reporters' Note 4.

[17] See, e.g., *United States* v. *King*, 552 F.2d 833, 850–1 (9th Cir. 1976), certiorari denied, 430 U.S. 966 (1977), sustaining a conviction in the United States for unlawful distribution in Japan of heroin intended for importation into the United States.

present it can no longer be said that the desirability of such regulation in general is questioned, but of course the reach of such regulation remains in question, as in the present case. I would add that the fact that the United States government was not itself involved as a plaintiff, and that Congress had largely yielded antitrust jurisdiction over the insurance industry to the states, diminishes the 'importance of regulation to the regulating state'; not everyone would agree, however, because of the importance assigned in United States law to private antitrust actions and because of the status of the principal plaintiffs as state public officials.

Factor (*d*)—justified expectations—is also difficult. If instead of reinsuring American insurance policies, defendants were selling, say, children's clothing to the United States, they would expect that their merchandise was required to comply with American law, for instance the Flammable Fabrics Act.[18] They would not be justified in expecting that if their fabrics complied with British fabric standards, they would be free from regulation, or from liability in case of injury, in respect of clothes shipped to the United States. The direction of flow of reinsurance, however, is not self-evident. I think it is justifiable to look at this activity as involving American insurers bringing their product—primary insurance—to the reinsurance market in London, in other words inward trade from the point of view of Great Britain. If that view is accepted, the justified expectation of the participants in the London reinsurance market would be that only English and not American regulation applies to their conduct. The London reinsurers, on this view, are not like British Airways, with three hundred flights a week between Britain and the United States and a market without doubt subject to the laws of both the United States and the United Kingdom.[19] It must be conceded that this view of the conduct of reinsurance across national frontiers is not the only possible one; but consider whether (prior to this case) it would have been reasonable to expect London underwriters to invite an American lawyer to a meeting to discuss reinsuring long-tail policies.

Factor (*e*)—the importance of the regulation to the international system might be significant in the context of applying national law to enforce internationally agreed sanctions, as in the case of Rhodesia (1965–1979) or Iraq (1990–present). No case could be made that this factor supported application of U.S. law to the London reinsurance market; a case could be made that maintenance of the global insurance market at Lloyd's of London free from national controls was important to the world's economy as a whole.

Factor (*f*)—consistency of the regulation with the traditions of the international system—was included in the set of factors primarily with reference

[18] 15 U.S.C. §§ 1191–1240. [19] See Ch. 1, sect. D.

to maritime law, which by centuries-old custom limits the jurisdiction to prescribe of port states and commits most jurisdiction, including wages and working conditions of the crew, compensation for injuries, and safety requirements, either to the flag state or to international treaty.[20] In the *Insurance Antitrust* case this factor would seem to play no part.

Factors (*g*) and (*h*) were critical to the *Insurance Antitrust* case. Clearly the United Kingdom had a strong interest in regulating the activity in question. Indeed there had been several Lloyd's Acts since the nineteenth century, the most recent one in 1982, and several Royal Commissions since then had been directed to look into the problems of the insurance market at Lloyd's. Both lower courts had concluded that there was likelihood of conflict between British law and policy and application of U.S. antitrust law. But neither judgment had defined conflict, and the argument was made to the Supreme Court that there was no conflict at all, because no order of the British government had *required* the conduct here challenged.

The understanding of 'conflict', as we shall see, divided the members of the U.S. Supreme Court. We will come back to that question and to the opinions of the Supreme Court justices shortly. Meanwhile, it is not inappropriate to ask whether looking at the case in light of the factors set out in the Restatement has illuminated the issues. I believe that it has done so. That the process has not yielded a single unequivocal answer should not surprise those of us accustomed to search for the law of the state which has 'the most significant relationship' to the transaction in question,[21] or with which the contract is most closely connected.[22] We have learned, I submit, to be skeptical of formulas for choice of law that yield quick solutions free from all doubt.

What the effort to apply the criteria of the *Restatement* to a particular controversy has shown is that the *Insurance Antitrust* case is a borderline case, which suggests on the one hand that the issue of jurisdiction to prescribe is worth litigating, and on the other hand that neither side should be outraged if it fails to prevail. That is already a substantial advance, when compared with such controversies as the *Nylon Patent* litigation in the 1950s[23] or the various controversies concerning shipping, aviation and

[20] For affirmation of this statement by the U.S. Supreme Court in the context of efforts to apply United States law, see, e.g., *Lauritzen* v. *Larsen*, 345 U.S. 571 (1953) and *Romero* v. *International Terminal Operating Co.*, 358 U.S. 354 (1959) both involving efforts by crew members of foreign flag ships to take advantage of American law concerning personal injury; and *McCulloch* v. *Sociedad Nacional de Marineros de Honduras*, 372 U.S. 10 (1963), rejecting efforts by U.S.-based unions to organize workers aboard a foreign-flag ship on the basis that the ships were owned by a U.S. Company and were engaged in commerce of the United States.

[21] Compare American Law Institute, *Restatement (Second) of Conflict of Laws*, § 145 (torts), § 188 (contracts) (1971).

[22] Compare the EEC Convention on the Law Applicable to Contractual Obligations 1980 (the Rome Convention), Art. 4.

[23] See *United States* v. *Imperial Chemical Industries*, 105 F. Supp. 215 (S.D.N.Y. 1952) in which a U.S. Court ordered the British company ICI not to assert its British patent to prevent

the uranium trade of the 1960s and 1970s,[24] not to speak of such episodes as the Siberian Pipeline case of 1981–2, which started as a response by the United States to the proclamation of martial law in Poland and ended up as a major confrontation between the United States and the European Community and its member states.[25] But of course the *Restatement* seeks to achieve more than just cooling down tempers. It seeks to give guidance to deciding close cases, guidance useful to courts, counsel, and governments. With that in mind, we return to the *Insurance Antitrust* case in the United States Supreme Court.

Five justices, in an opinion by Justice Souter, upheld application of U.S. antitrust law to the English defendants. Four justices, with Justice Scalia writing, dissented. For the majority, Justice Souter wrote:

> whether a court with Sherman Act jurisdiction should ever decline to exercise such jurisdiction on grounds of international comity . . . we need not decide . . ., for . . . international comity would not counsel against exercising jurisdiction in the circumstances alleged here.
>
> The only substantial question in this case is whether 'there is in fact a true conflict between domestic and foreign law.' . . . The London reinsurers contend that applying the [Sherman] Act to their conduct would conflict significantly with British law, and the British government, appearing before us as *amicus curiae*, concurs . . . They assert that Parliament has established a comprehensive regulatory scheme over the London reinsurance market and that the conduct alleged here was perfectly consistent with British law and policy. But this is not to state a conflict.[26]

Thus the majority was able to avoid deciding between the approach of the District Court which considered the *conflict* between United States and

importation of nylon into Great Britain; *British Nylon Spinners Ltd.* v. *Imperial Chemical Industries I* [1953] Ch. 19 (U.K. CA, 1952), temporarily restraining ICI from obeying the order of the U.S. court; and *British Nylon Spinners Ltd.* v. *Imperial Chemical Industries, Ltd. II* [1955] Ch. 37, ordering ICI to carry out its contract granting an exclusive license to BNS notwithstanding the order of the U.S. court. See also, e.g., Otto Kahn-Freund, 'English Contracts and American Anti-Trust Law—The Nylon Patent Case' (1955), 18 *Mod. L. Rev.* 65, expressing the view that the U.S. Court's assertion of jurisdiction constituted a violation of public international law.

[24] See, e.g., the controversy over the so-called § 21 orders of the U.S. Federal Maritime Commission (Board), described in A. Chayes, T. Erlich, and A. Lowenfeld, *International Legal Process* ch. VI, 'National Sovereignty and Private Regulation: Ocean Cargo Rates' (1968); the controversy about the U.S. Civil Aeronautics Board's 'Order to Show Cause' why IATA's conference rate-making should not be disapproved, described in A. Lowenfeld, *Aviation Law*, ch. 5, §§ 4.4–4.5 (2nd edn., 1981); and the controversy concerning the uranium cartel, described in Ch. 7, sect. E. For brief citations to the principal sources, see *Restatement (Third) of Foreign Relations Law*, § 403, Reporters' Notes 1, 6, and 8; § 415, Reporters' Notes 4, 5, and 9; § 442, Reporters' Notes 1, 3, 4, and 8.

[25] This episode has been covered extensively in a variety of books and articles. My own account appears in A. Lowenfeld, *Trade Controls for Political Ends* (2nd edn., 1983), ch. II, pp. 267–306.

[26] 113 S.Ct. at 2910.

British law as decisive, and the view of the Court of Appeals, which viewed the *effect* of the challenged activity in the United States as controlling, in spite of the conflict with British law and policy. But *was* there not a conflict relevant to determining the reasonableness of a proposed exercise of jurisdiction, as the four dissenters believed?

It seems clear that if the British government had *ordered* the London underwriters to stop selling long-tail policies, Justice Souter would have viewed the case as presenting a 'true conflict'; though one cannot be sure, there is good reason to believe that he, or at least some of his colleagues in the narrow majority, would have come round to the position of the dissenters that exercise of jurisdiction to apply U.S. law to the challenged activity would be unreasonable.[27] But making a true conflict depend on the foreign government's command, I submit, is to confuse the foreign compulsion defense with the question of conflict of jurisdiction. Surely no state that takes its obligations under international law seriously would require a person to do an act in another state that is prohibited by the law of that state, or punish a person for doing an act in another state that was required by the law of that state.[28]

Suppose that British law had provided that any agreements among underwriters concerning the terms and conditions of reinsurance policies must be submitted to the Minister of Trade for approval, and that the agreements here challenged had been submitted and approved. That would not rise to the level of compulsion, but it would be unequivocal evidence of the British government's exercise of jurisdiction to prescribe. Would it meet Justice Souter's threshold of conflict? Would it make more convincing Justice Scalia's conclusion that Great Britain had established 'a comprehensive regulatory scheme governing the London reinsurance markets'[29] which conflicted with the application of U.S. antitrust law? What about a statutory scheme according to which agreements among underwriters had to be submitted to the Minister and would go into effect thirty days after submission unless *dis*approved. We need not answer this ques-

[27] Indeed, Justice Scalia expressed the dissenting view much more vigorously. After going one-by-one through the factors listed in § 403(2) of the *Restatement*, he concluded:

> Rarely would these factors point more clearly against application of United States law . . . Considering these factors, I think it unimaginable that an assertion of legislative jurisdiction by the United States would be considered reasonable, and therefore it is inappropriate to assume, in the absence of statutory indication to the contrary, that Congress has made such an assertion.

113 S.Ct. at 2921 (dissenting opinion).

[28] This formulation, spelled out in somewhat greater detail, appears in § 441 of the *Restatement*. It goes without saying that the reference is to lawful orders of the foreign state, and could not be used to excuse torture, genocide, or similar crimes.

For more on the foreign compulsion defense, see Ch. 7, sect. D.

[29] 113 S.Ct. at 2921.

tion, or other possible variations.[30] My point is that there is a significant space between such indifference on the part of state *B* as to make the exercise of jurisdiction by state *A* not unreasonable, and such compulsion by state *B* as would be required, in Justice Souter's view, to create a 'true conflict'.

I must concede that, while this point is clear enough to me, it seems not to have been successfully presented in the *Restatement*. The majority opinion in the Supreme Court points to a comment to § 403 that says no conflict exists where a person subject to regulation by two states can comply with the laws of both.[31] The predicate to that statement, however, is a situation in which it is not unreasonable for both states to exercise jurisdiction consistently with the criteria of § 403(2). Where we left the inquiry, and where the majority and the dissent split in the *Insurance Antitrust* case, was in exploring whether exercise of jurisdiction by state *A* (here the United States) would be reasonable in the first place. That inquiry, in the scheme of the *Restatement*, involves an assessment of all of the relevant factors, including, but not limited to, the interests of the two states and the potential for conflict if *A* exercises jurisdiction to apply its own law.

* * *

Is the approach of the *Restatement*, then, a failure? I do not think so. Only four of the Justices undertook to apply the methodology of the *Restatement*, and I believe they came out correctly, though I might not have gone quite as far as Justice Scalia did in writing that 'rarely would these factors point more clearly against application of United States law'.[32]

As for the majority, though it quotes several times from the *Restatement*, it really takes a quite different approach. (1) The Court starts by saying that the United States has jurisdiction, because minimum contacts with the United States are present, whereas the *Restatement* says that minimum contacts are only a necessary and not a sufficient condition for exercise of jurisdiction to prescribe. (2) The Court says that only comity might counsel against exercising jurisdiction, whereas the *Restatement* purports to set out a rule of law.[33] (3) The clearest divergence between the majority in

[30] e.g., another variation might involve approval (or non-disapproval) by an industry committee serving under delegation from the government.

[31] *Restatement*, § 403, Comment e. The illustration given in the comment, not quoted by Justice Souter, is of a multinational enterprise required by State *A* to keep its books on a cash basis, and by state *B* to keep its books on an accrual basis. Keeping its records in two ways is merely a nuisance for the enterprise, and neither state is required to defer to the other.

[32] 113 S.Ct. at 2921, quoted more fully at n. 27 *supra*. As suggested above, I believe that if the evidence of affirmative action by the British government in approving or directing the challenged conduct had been stronger, the factor of potential conflict would have weighed more heavily, and the balance would have tipped more clearly in favor of non-application of U. S. law.

[33] See text at n. 9 *supra*.

Insurance Antitrust and the *Restatement* comes not in the definition of 'conflict', though, as we have seen, that determines the outcome in the case before it. The real divergence comes in the final sentence of the Court's discussion. 'We have no need in this case', the Court writes, 'to address other considerations that might inform a decision to refrain from the exercise of jurisdiction on grounds of international comity.'[34] The *Restatement* approach requires that the 'other considerations' be addressed in all cases.

However one feels about the outcome of the *Insurance Antitrust* case, this is where, in my view, the majority opinion of the United States Supreme Court is most disappointing, and where I hope it will not be followed in other decisions, in the United States and elsewhere.

Reasonableness, the interests of states, and the possibility of balancing these interests are explored further in the next chapter.

[34] 113 S.Ct. at 2911.

3

More on Jurisdiction to Prescribe: Of Effects and Balancing

The discussion in Chapter 2 of the *Insurance Antitrust* case before the U.S. Supreme Court may have left the reader in a somewhat dissatisfied state. It is not just that the approach of the *Restatement* that I have been espousing fell one vote short. More important for our inquiry, the majority accepted effects jurisdiction without any discussion, and by defining 'conflict' in terms of black and white, the majority avoided having to say anything about balancing of competing interests, which is most needed—as well as sharply debated—with respect to the gray areas.

A. EFFECTS JURISDICTION AND ITS DISCONTENTS

Simply defined, effects jurisdiction is an assertion by a state that its law applies (or may apply) to regulate conduct that has or is intended to have effect within its territory, even when the conduct itself takes place outside its territory. The assertion may be made in court, or by governmental order, and it may be made on private as well as public initiative. Since by definition the challenged conduct takes place in some other state, effects jurisdiction may well involve competing interests, and jurisdiction should not be exercised without some thought. But I have never understood why effects jurisdiction has become as controversial as it has become, why the European Court of Justice, for example, though it seems to accept the effects principle, carefully avoids saying so.

Actually effects jurisdiction is not controversial in the context, for instance, of shots fired from state *B* into state *A*.[1] Nor, I think, would there

[1] The paradigm case, easily talked about, is actually hard to find in the law reports. One example is *Simpson* v. *The State*, 92 Ga. 41 (1893), sustaining conviction under the law of Georgia of a man who, while standing on the bank of the Savannah River which formed the boundary between South Carolina and Georgia, fired two shots at a man in a boat on the Georgia side of the river's main channel. In fact the shots did not hit the man in the boat, but, as the court said, 'the balls did strike the water in close proximity to him within this State, and therefore it is certain that they took effect in Georgia': *id.* at 42.

As early as 1826, the British Parliament adopted the following statute: 'Where any Felony or Misdemeanour . . . shall be begun in one county and completed in another, such Felony or Misdemeanour may be dealt with, inquired of, tried, determined and punished in any of the said Counties, in the same Manner as if it had been actually and wholly committed therein': 7 Geo. IV, c. 64, s. XII, quoted also in Jennings, n. 6 *infra*, at 157.

be much controversy over assertion by state *A* of jurisdiction to punish (and if necessary demand the extradition of) a person who mailed a letter from state *B* to a person in state *A* containing threats and demanding money.[2] Many readers will be familiar with the famous *Reinwater* case,[3] involving discharge of 10,000 tons of chlorides per day by a French company into the Rhine in the Alsace. The European Court of Justice, interpreting the Brussels Convention,[4] upheld the assertion of judicial jurisdiction by the Dutch court based on an allegation that nursery gardens in Holland were damaged by the discharge some 500 kilometers upstream. That is certainly effects jurisdiction, or as Americans call it, 'long-arm jurisdiction'. More significant for the present discussion, following the decision of the European Court of Justice, the Netherlands courts applied Dutch law concerning environmental damage to the merits of the dispute, rejecting the defense that the defendant's conduct was lawful where it took place.[5] That clearly is effects jurisdiction as we have defined it, that is application of the law of the state where the harm occurred by a court of that state, notwithstanding different rules applicable at the place where the conduct occurred. Yet so far as I know exercise of prescriptive jurisdiction in these circumstances has not been regarded as excessive or exorbitant.

Why, then, does a red flag go up when effects jurisdiction is applied to antitrust or competition law? Professor Jennings (as he then was) wrestled with that question nearly forty years ago,[6] in the context of the first post-war wave of American cartel cases, notably *Alcoa*,[7] and *ICI*.[8] Jennings' basic proposition was quite close to that of the *Restatement*:

> It is reasonable to say . . . that international law will permit a State to exercise extraterritorial jurisdiction provided that State's legitimate interests (legitimate that is to say by tests accepted in the common practice of States) are involved; but against this must be set also the legitimate and reasonable interests of the State whose territory is primarily concerned, for the extraterritorial exercise of jurisdiction must not be permitted to extend to the point where the local law is

[2] The example is suggested by *Treacy* v. *Director of Public Prosecutions* [1971] AC 537 (HL(E)), though in that case the issue was assertion of jurisdiction by the state *from* which the blackmailing letter was sent, i.e., state *B* in our example.

[3] *Bier* v. *Mines de Potasse d'Alsace, SA* [1976] ECR 1735, [1977] 1 CMLR284 (ECJ, Nov. 30 [1976].

[4] EEC Convention on Jurisdiction and the Enforcement of Judgments of Sept. 27, 1968, Art. 5(3).

[5] *Mines de Potasse d'Alsace SA* v. *Bier*, Hooge Raad (Sup. Ct.) Sept. 23, 1988 [1989] Nederlandse Jurisprudentie 743.

[6] R. Y. Jennings, 'Extraterritorial Jurisdiction and the United States Antitrust Laws' (1957) 22 Brit. Yb. Int'l Law 146.

[7] *United States* v. *Aluminum Co. of America*, 148 F.2d 416 (2d Cir. 1945).

[8] *United States* v. *Imperial Chemical Industries Ltd.*, 100 F.Supp. 504 (S.D.N.Y. 1951), 105 F.Supp. 215 (S.D.N.Y. 1952). Jennings also discusses *United States* v. *National Lead Co.*, 63 F.Supp. 513 (S.D.N.Y. 1943), aff'd. 332 U.S. 319 (1947); *United States* v. *Timken Roller Bearing Co.*, 83 F.Supp. 284 (N.D. Ill. 1949), aff'd. 341 U.S. 593 (1951); and *United States* v. *General Electric Co.*, 82 F.Supp. 753 (D.N.J. 1949), 115 F.Supp. 835 (D.N.J. 1953).

supplanted; where in fact it becomes an interference by one State in the affairs of another.[9]

Jennings thought the doctrine of abuse of rights might help: '[a] State has a right to extraterritorial jurisdiction where its legitimate interests are concerned, but the right may be abused and it is abused when it becomes essentially an interference with the exercise of the local territorial jurisdiction'.[10] That statement, especially if one asks (i) what is meant by *legitimate* interests of state *A*, and (ii) what is meant by *essentially* an interference with the state of conduct, sounds like an invitation to balance competing interests, and on the whole like an acceptance of jurisdiction on the basis of effects in the territory of the acting state.

> In relation to elementary cases of direct physical injury, such as homicide, this is unexceptionable, for here the 'effect' which is meant is an essential ingredient of the crime. Once we move out of the sphere of direct physical consequences, however, to employ the formula of 'effects' is to enter upon a very slippery slope . . . If . . . it were permissible to found objective territorial jurisdiction upon the territoriality of more or less remote repercussions of an act wholly performed in another country, then there were virtually no limit to a State's territorial jurisdiction.[11]

Putting the case in terms of 'remote repercussions' is of course easy. Judge Learned Hand himself, in *Alcoa*, was careful to stress that he did not conceive the effects principle as reaching remote repercussions.[12] He would not, for instance, apply American labor law to a labor dispute in Italy, though the output of the firm in question was destined for export to the United States and thus the progress of the labor dispute might affect supply and price of the product in question in the United States.[13] Judge Hand dealt with the danger that 'mere repercussions' might be used to support application of United States law where it should not be applied by requiring both *intent* to affect the American market and actual *effect* in that market. True, Hand left himself open to criticism that was not slow in coming by holding that, once intent was established, *effect* in the United States would be inferred unless the defendant carried the burden of proof

[9] Jennings, n. 6 *supra*, at 153.

[10] *Ibid.*

[11] *Id.* at 159.

[12] *Judge Hand wrote:*

> Almost any limitation of the supply of goods in Europe, for example, or in South America, may have repercussions in the United States if there is trade between the two. Yet when one considers the international complications likely to arise from an effort in this country to treat such agreements as unlawful, it is safe to assume that Congress certainly did not intend the [Sherman] Act to cover them.

148 F.2d at 443.

[13] The same point is made more explicitly in my earlier Hague Lectures, Ch. 1, n. 1 *supra*, 163 *Recueil des Cours* at 381 and n. 137.

that there had been no effect upon the market that U.S. antitrust law was created to protect.[14]

Later formulations, therefore, have generally spoken of 'direct and substantial' effect on the commerce of the United States, sometimes also adding 'foreseeable'.[15] I would have thought that, when producers who sold regularly to the United States agreed to limit production, as in *Alcoa*, or when producers of the same product agreed to divide markets and not to challenge each other's patents, as in the *Nylon* and *Light Bulb* cartels, such facts would meet a 'direct and substantial' effects test against a contention that 'mere repercussions' were involved. But the critics, particularly in England, disagreed. Even as measured and moderate analysis as that offered by Jennings in 1957 places *Alcoa* and the cases building upon it in the category of *some effects* and *mere repercussions*.[16] Thus Jennings was able to retain the concept of 'objective jurisdiction' for homicide and, one suspects, for product liability as well, but nevertheless to conclude that assertion of jurisdiction to apply the American antitrust laws is too far down on the slippery slope.

But at the end of the day—or for present purposes at the end of Jennings' article—the underlying conflict emerges:

> even allowing a most liberal view of the limits of *extra*territorial jurisdiction, these cases still offend against the ultimate limit because they are an attempt to export into other countries and to make operate there what are after all peculiarly American political notions.[17]

In other words, the real problem is not with the effects principle, but with American antitrust law. When American concepts of competition law spread to Europe—notably to Germany and to the European Community, so does the effects principle. But while Professor Jennings' statement about 'after all peculiarly American political notions' no longer stands, the resistance to the effects principle as applied to competition law survives, even when it does not prevail.

[14] See, e.g., Jennings, n. 6 *supra*, 160, n. 1, expressing at least gentle doubt about Judge Hand's inferences of both intent and effect.

[15] See, e.g., *United States* v. *General Electric Co.*, 82 F.Supp. 753 at 891 (D.N.J. 1949); *United States* v. *Watchmakers of Switzerland Information Center Inc.*, 1963 CCH Trade Cas. ¶ 70,600 (S.D.N.Y. 1962), modified 1965 CCH Trade Cas. ¶ 71,352 (S.D.N.Y. 1969); *Timberlane Lumber Co.* v. *Bank of America N.T. & S.A.*, 549 F.2d 597 at 610–2 (9th Cir. 1976). The *Restatement* speaks in § 402(1)(c), the general section, and § 415, the section on application of antitrust law, of 'substantial effect' without the additional word 'direct' but always subject to the requirement of reasonableness. As quoted in Chapter 2, the guidelines for determining reasonableness in § 403(2) speak in paragraph (a) of 'the extent to which the activity . . . has substantial, direct, and foreseeable effect upon or in the territory'.

[16] Jennings, n. 6 *supra*, at 175.

[17] *Ibid.*

B. EFFECTS JURISDICTION IN THE EUROPEAN COMMUNITY

1. The *Dyestuffs* Case (1972)

The famous *Dyestuffs* case[18] was the second instance in which Imperial Chemical Industries took its place in the select group of cases familiar to all international lawyers. The charge was simple. Three uniform price increases in most aniline dyes took place in countries in the Community—15 per cent in January 1964 in Italy, the Netherlands, Belgium, and Luxembourg; 15 per cent in January 1965 on the products in Germany, and 10 per cent in all five countries on dyes that had not been covered in the first price increase; then 8 per cent more on all dyes on October 16, 1967 in Germany, the Netherlands, Belgium, and Luxembourg, and 12 per cent in France. The European Commission suspected concerted pricing in violation of Article 85(1) of the Treaty of Rome, and initiated an investigation pursuant to Article 3 of Regulation 17. The Commission sent a letter and a notice of the proceeding to some sixty producers of dyestuffs established both inside and outside the Community. Among the recipients of the letter, for example, were Ciba, Sandoz, and Geigy in Switzerland, Du Pont in the United States—and ICI, with headquarters in London. In July 1969, the Commission adopted a decision holding that the price increases were not mere parallelism but had resulted from prohibited agreements. Ten companies were ordered to pay fines of 50,000 European Units of Account each, including ICI.[19] The Commission held that its decision was equally applicable to enterprises established inside or, like ICI, outside the Common Market, since Article 85 prohibits as incompatible with the Common Market all agreements and concerted practices 'which may affect trade between Member States and which have as their object or effect the prevention, restriction or distortion of competition within the Common Market'. Thus the Commission held that the effects principle was stated right in the Treaty of Rome itself, requiring not intent plus effect, as in *Alcoa*, but intent ('object') *or* effect. 'It does not matter, therefore', the Commission concluded, 'whether the enterprises that cause such restraints on competition have their seat within or outside of the Community.'[20]

ICI applied to the European Court of Justice for annulment of the decision, on the ground that the decision represented an exercise of

[18] *Imperial Chemical Industries Ltd* v. *Commission*, Case 48/69, [1972] ECR 619, [1972] CMLR 557 (ECJ, July 14, 1972).

[19] Commission Decision of 24 July 1969, [1969] JO L195/11. One company's fine was only 40,000 EUA, because it had not participated in the third price rise.

[20] *Ibid.* at 16. It is interesting that the decision states that, with respect to the four firms that do not have their seat within the Community, service may be made on their wholly controlled subsidiaries.

extraterritorial jurisdiction contrary to international law.[21] ICI accompanied its application by an opinion of Professor Jennings, and it was Jennings' opinion that became the principal focus of the Court's opinion. Jennings drew the same distinction that he had drawn in the article a decade earlier from which I have quoted, except that while he had no trouble describing the U.S. antitrust law as penal law—a subject to which we will return in Chapter 6 on foreign judgments—he could not quite put the competition articles of the Treaty of Rome in that category. As the Court summarized:

> Professor Jennings observes that in respect of penal offences which amount to common crimes generally recognized as such, States have somewhat relaxed the principle of the territoriality of the penal law. On the other hand, restraint of trade laws belong not to that category where State practice permits a wide discretion but rather to the category of *public law* peculiar to a State *or group of States*, which should therefore be territorially confined unless there is a specific permissive rule.[22]

Citing European consultants to the *Second* (i.e., previous) *Restatement of Foreign Relations Law*, Jennings referred to the view that the exercise of jurisdiction based on territory is not justified as regards conduct occurring abroad and producing effects within the territory 'unless the contested conduct and its effects are generally recognized as constituent elements of a crime or tort under the laws of States that have reasonably developed legal systems'.[23]

It was harder in 1969 than in 1957 to suggest that only the United States disapproved of trusts, cartels, and other restrictive trade practices.[24] The

[21] ICI's other challenges to the Commission's decision are not relevant to the present discussion. The Swiss companies also challenged the jurisdiction of the Commission, but *ICI* was treated as the principal case.

[22] [1972] ECR at 624. The italics are mine.

[23] [1972] ECR at 625. In fact the quoted words appear almost verbatim in § 18(a) of *Restatement (Second) of Foreign Relations Law of the United States* (1965). Professor Stanley Metzger, in a review of the *Restatement*, sharply criticized this passage, pointing out that it was not contained in prior drafts and suggesting that the late addition was the result of lobbying by lawyers for international oil companies: Metzger, 'The Restatement of the Foreign Relations Law of the United States: Bases and Conflicts of Jurisdiction', 41 N.Y.U.L.Rev. 7, 13–17 (1966). It seems likely that Jennings' consultants and Metzger's special interest pleaders were the same people, viewed from opposite vantage points.

[24] 20 years later, in the Ninth Edition of *Oppenheim's International Law* (1992), edited by Sir Robert Jennings (by now President of the International Court of Justice) and Sir Arthur Watts the same point reappears, but further toned down (i, 474–6):

> The justification for such assertions of jurisdiction on the basis of an alleged 'effects' principle of jurisdiction has not been generally accepted, and the matter is still one of controversy. The exercise of jurisdiction because of the effects of an act within the state may amount to no more than an 'objective' application of the territorial principle of jurisdiction, but where the effects relied on are not a constituent part of the offence in question but are mere consequences or repercussions of the act done, the legitimate bounds of the territorial principle of jurisdiction are overstepped, particularly if the effects are only incidental and insubstantial: in this lies the danger of impropriety in resort to the

United Kingdom, however, was still outside the Community, and indeed its *Aide-Mémoire*, not referred to by the Court but widely available, was much more blunt than the opinion of Professor Jennings submitted by ICI:

> [T]he United Kingdom Government have . . . consistently objected to the assumption of extra-territorial jurisdiction in anti-trust matters by the courts or authorities of a foreign state when that jurisdiction is based upon what is termed the 'effects doctrine'—that is to say, the doctrine that territorial jurisdiction over conduct which has occurred wholly outside the territory of the State claiming jurisdiction may be justified because of the economic 'effects' of such conduct within the territory of that State.
>
> . . .
>
> So far as substantive jurisdiction is concerned, the United Kingdom Government are of the view that the decision of the Commission incorporates an interpretation of the relevant provisions of the E.E.C. Treaty which is not justified by the accepted principles of international law . . .
>
> The territorial principle justifies proceedings against foreigners and foreign companies only in respect of conduct which consists in whole or in part of some activity by them in the territory of the State claiming jurisdiction. A State should not exercise jurisdiction against a foreigner who, or a foreign company which has committed no act within its territory.[25]

The Commission had two answers to the contentions of ICI and the United Kingdom government. First, ICI had several subsidiaries operating within the Community, and when it gave instructions to these subsidiaries to raise prices, this constituted conduct—forbidden conduct—within the Common Market.

Second, relying on the *Lotus* case,[26] jurisdiction on the basis of effects is consistent with the objective theory of jurisdiction, and is not limited to penal laws of the traditional kind. While *Alcoa* may have been interpreted too broadly, going so far as to support injunctions directed to firms established abroad ordering amendments to contracts made between foreigners

> 'effects' principle as a basis for jurisdiction and the doubtful consistency of that principle with international law. Concern expressed by many other states has led certain United States courts to have some regard to the legitimate interests of other states, by requiring not only that the foreign conduct of aliens must have actual or intended effects within the United States, causing sufficient injury there, but also that 'the interests of, and links to, the US—including the magnitude of the effects on American foreign commerce—are sufficiently strong, *vis-à-vis* those of other nations, to justify the assertion of extra-territorial authority'. By balancing the competing interests of the states concerned in this way some of the more serious excesses of an effects doctrine may in practice be avoided in particular cases, although objections of principle are still likely to remain.

[25] UK: *Aide-Mémoire* to the Commission of the European Communities, Oct. 20 1969 in the *Dyestuffs* case, repr. in International Law Assoc., Report of the 54th Conference, 185–8 (The Hague 1970); A. V. Lowe, *Extraterritorial Jurisdiction: An Annotated Collection of Legal Materials* (1983), 144–7.

[26] *The S.S. Lotus (France* v. *Turkey)* [1927] P.C.I.J. Ser. A, No. 10.

abroad—evidently a reference to the first *ICI* case[27]—here the Community was seeking only to apply its law within its own territory.[28]

The Advocate General, M. Henri Mayras, clearly preferred the second argument. On imputing conduct of a subsidiary to a parent corporation, the Advocate General thought the position of the Commission is 'somewhat uncertain', and, besides, adopting it would seem to indicate 'hesitation, if not a certain unwillingness' to adopt the effects doctrine, a hesitation that M. Mayras did not share.[29] He concluded that the effect of the practices by ICI *et al.* 'was not merely direct; it was obviously foreseeable, . . . [and] the effect was substantial'.[30] It is interesting that the Advocate General took up the reference to the *Restatement* and the use made of it by Jennings:

> [A]lthough the Restatement of Foreign Relations Law renders the application of the 'effects' doctrine subject to the condition that the conduct from which those effects flow must be generally recognized to be reprehensible under the law of States which 'have reasonably developed legal systems,' I do not think that this condition is unfulfilled as regards conduct interfering with competition. For in most developed and industrialized countries substantive law forbids and suppresses, either by penal or by administrative means, agreements which adversely affect competition. This is indeed the case . . . in the United Kingdom and in Switzerland, and who would have the temerity to suggest that they do not have 'reasonably developed' legal systems?[31]

And yet? The Court of Justice upheld the Commission, but it could not quite bring itself to rely on the effects principle:

> Since a concerted practice is involved, it is first necessary to ascertain whether the conduct of the applicant has had effects within the Common Market.
>
> It appears from what has already been said that the increases at issue were put into effect within the Common Market and concerned competition between producers operating within it.
>
> Therefore the actions for which the fine at issue has been imposed constitute practices carried on directly within the Common Market.
>
> It follows from what has been said in considering the submission relating to the existence of concerted practices, that the applicant company decided on increases in the selling prices of its products to users in the Common Market, and that these increases were of a uniform nature in line with increases decided upon by the other producers involved.[32]

[27] *United States* v. *Imperial Chemical Industries, Ltd.*, 105 F.Supp. 215 (S.D.N.Y. 1952).

[28] *Dyestuffs* case, n. 18 *supra*, at 627–9 (ECR).

[29] [1972] ECR, at 693. The French original reads, at 699, 'la position de la Commission n'est pas, sur ce terrain, des plus solides'.

[30] Opinion of Advocate-General Mayras delivered on May 2, 1972, *Dyestuffs* case [1972] ECR, 665 at 693, 694.

[31] *Id.* 694.

[32] *Id.* 662.

One would expect the next sentence to read something like, 'Since the effect within the territory of the Community has been established, the applicant ICI is liable for the fine assessed by the Commission.' The Court, however, took a quite different direction:

> By making use of its power to control its subsidiaries established in the Community, the applicant was able to ensure that its decision was implemented on that market.
>
> . . .
>
> The fact that a subsidiary has separate legal personality is not sufficient to exclude the possibility of imputing its conduct to the parent company.
>
> . . .
>
> In effect the Telex messages relating to the 1964 increase, which the applicant sent to its subsidiaries in the Common Market, gave the addressees orders as to the prices which they were to charge and the other conditions of sale which they were to apply in dealing with their customers.
>
> In the absence of evidence to the contrary, it must be assumed that on the occasion of the increases of 1965 and 1967 the applicant acted in a similar fashion in its relations with its subsidiaries established in the Common Market.
>
> In the circumstances the formal separation between these companies, resulting from their separate legal personality, cannot outweigh the unity of their conduct on the market for the purposes of applying the rules on competition.
>
> It was in fact the applicant undertaking which brought the concerted practice into being within the Common Market.
>
> The submission as to lack of jurisdiction raised by the applicant must therefore be declared to be unfounded.[33]

Of course, by imputing the conduct of subsidiaries to a parent corporation, the Court of Justice was not immunizing itself from criticism[34]—criticism to which we will return in Chapter 5. And the Court did not reject jurisdiction on the basis of the effects principle. But without undermining enforcement of the Community's competition law, the Court succeeded in avoiding the 'E' word—an achievement that the Court appears to have considered important and worthwhile.

2. The *Wood Pulp* Case (1988)

Time passed. In the United States, jurisdiction on the basis of effects was subjected to more sophisticated analysis, notably in the *Timberlane* case decided in 1976,[35] to which we shall return shortly, as well as in *Restatement*

[33] *Id.* 662–3.

[34] See, e.g., F. A. Mann, 'The Dyestuffs Case in the Court of Justice of the European Communities' (1973) 22 Int'l & Comp. L.Q. 35 at 49–50.

[35] *Timberlane Lumber Co.* v. *Bank of America N.T. & SA*, 549 F.2d 595 (9th Cir. 1976), discussed at 42–3 *infra*.

(Third).[36] In the Federal Republic of Germany, which had codified the effects principle in its competition law,[37] two important decisions of the Supreme Court defined the parameters of application of that law to conduct outside the territory of the Federal Republic.[38]

The issue did not come up again directly before the European Court of Justice until 1988—once more, as one might expect, in a cartel case, this time concerning wood pulp.[39] The Commission had found that some thirty-four firms producing bleached sulphate pulp in Sweden, Finland, Canada, and the United States for sale in the Community had engaged in concerted pricing over a six-year period, affecting some 60 per cent of consumption within the Common Market. Moreover, nine American companies had participated in a so-called Webb-Pomerene association, which acted as a co-ordinating agency for export prices, as permitted under a special exemption to the U.S. antitrust laws;[40] the association, KEA, did not itself make or sell wood pulp, but it was named a respondent by the Commission and a fine was assessed against it.[41]

Again, all of the firms applied to the Court of Justice to annul the decision. They pointed out that in *Dyestuffs* the Advocate General had urged support of jurisdiction on the basis of the effects doctrine, but that the Court had upheld the Commission's decision only on the basis of activities of the defendants' branches or subsidiaries established within the territory of the Common Market. The United Kingdom, by now a member of the European Community, intervened in the case, for the most part to support the decision of the Commission, but also, it seems, to preserve as much as it could of its position in the long-running quarrel with the United States. The British position now conceded that a firm established outside the Common Market could be subject to Community law on the basis of activity within the Common Market carried out not only through branches or subsidiaries but also through agents. 'That', said the British memorial,

[36] See § 402 comment *d* and Reporters' Note 2; § 403 and Reporters' Note 3; § 415 and comment *d*, Reporters' Notes 3, 4, and 9.

[37] Gesetz gegen Wettbewerbsbeschränkungen (GWB), § 98(2):

> This law is applicable to all restraints on competition that have effect within the territory where this law is in force, even if they are caused outside of said territory.

[38] Compare the *Oil Pipelines case*, Decision of July 12, 1973, 25 BGHSt 208, with the *Organic Pigments* case, Decision of May 29, 1979, 74 BGHZ 322. See, e.g., Gerhard Kegel, *Internationales Privatrecht* (7th edn., 1995), 890–3; David J. Gerber, 'The Extraterritorial Application of the German Antitrust Laws', 77 Am. J. Int'l L. 756, esp. 764–9 (1983).

[39] *Re Wood Pulp Cartel: Ahlström* Oy v. *Commission*, Case 89/85, [1988] ECR 5193, [1988] 4 CMLR 901 (ECJ, Sept. 27, 1988).

[40] Under the Webb-Pomerene Act of 1918, 40 Stat. 517, 15 U.S.C. § 62, firms may enter into associations to co-ordinate their export activities, provided they file certain information with the Federal Trade Commission and that they do not act in restraint of trade within the United States. See, generally, Wilbur Fugate, *Foreign Commerce and the Antitrust Laws* (4th edn., 1991), ch. 7.

[41] Commission Decision of Dec. 19, 1984, [1990] OJ L85/1. The Commission's discussion of the international law points appear in paras. 77–9, L85/14–15.

'is merely an illustration of the application of the principle of territoriality.'[42] But if a firm or association had neither subsidiaries or branches nor agents within the Community, and was not selling directly into the Community, as was true of KEA, exercise of jurisdiction by the Community would not be justified.

The Commission replied that while the price recommendations of KEA had been made outside the Community, the 'substantial, foreseeable and direct effect of that conduct' had been a restriction of competition within the Common Market, 'that is to say an effect which clearly took place within the Community':[43]

> There is nothing in international law which obliges the Commission to interpret away the word 'effect' in Article 85 of the Treaty [of Rome] as soon as that effect is produced across international boundaries. Although the effects doctrine is still contested under international law, the Commission considers that the objections come primarily from the United Kingdom and not from the OECD or other countries. The Commission maintains that in that respect, the Community should not be subject to a more restrictive jurisdictional criterion than that accepted for States.[44]

Once again the Advocate General (not the same person, but also a French jurist, M. Marco Darmon) supported the Commission and jurisdiction on the basis of effects. After a long and wide-ranging review of the literature as well as American case law from *American Banana*[45] (1909) through *Alcoa*[46] (1945) to *Timberlane*[47] (1976), *Mannington Mills*[48] (1979), and *Laker*[49] (1984), as well as the two *Restatements* (1965 and 1987), the Advocate General concluded: 'there is no rule of international law which is capable of being relied upon against the criterion of the direct, substantial and foreseeable effect. Nor does the concept of international comity, in view of its uncertain scope, militate against that criterion either.'[50]

Still, the Court of Justice was not prepared to accept the effects principle directly. It took the small additional step suggested by the United Kingdom, to attribute to the foreign firms not only activity conducted through branches or subsidiaries, but also activity conducted through independently owned agents within the Community:

> [A]n infringement of Article 85, such as the conclusion of an agreement which has had the effect of restricting competition within the common market, consists of conduct made up of two elements, the formation of the agreement, decision or concerted practice and the implementation thereof. If the applicability of prohibi-

[42] [1988] ECR at 5206. [43] *Id.* at 5212. [44] *Id.* at 5213.
[45] *American Banana Co.* v. *United Fruit Co.*, 213 U.S. 347 (1909).
[46] n. 7 *supra*.
[47] *Timberlane Lumber Co.* v. *Bank of America N.T. & S.A.*, 549 F.2d. 597 (9th Cir. 1976).
[48] *Mannington Mills Inc.* v. *Congoleum Corp.*, 595 F.2d 1287 (3d Cir. 1979).
[49] See Ch. 1, sect. D. [50] [1988] ECR at 5227.

tions laid down under competition law were made to depend on the place where the agreement, decision or concerted practice was formed, the result would obviously be to give undertakings an easy means of evading those prohibitions. The decisive factor is therefore the place where [the agreement] is implemented.

The producers in this case implemented their pricing agreement within the common market. It is immaterial in that respect whether or not they had recourse to subsidiaries, agents, sub-agents, or branches within the Community in order to make their contacts with purchasers within the Community.[51]

But as to KEA, which had neither subsidiaries nor agents within the Community and did not 'implement' the agreements, the decision of the Commission must be declared void.[52]

Again, as in *Dyestuffs*, the Court did not expressly reject the effects principle, or hold it contrary to international law. But it did not accept the submissions of the Commission and the Advocate General, and it must be conceded, I think, that the British intervention carried the day.

I find the Court's decision with respect to KEA difficult to accept, and the stress on *implementing* the challenged agreement within the territory of the European Community unpersuasive. One wonders, for example, how, *mutatis mutandis*, the Court of Justice (not the United Kingdom) would view the *Insurance Antitrust* case. With minor exceptions, the American insurance companies were neither parents nor subsidiaries of the English reinsurers, and it would do violence to the law of insurance to regard the primary insurers as agents of the reinsurers. But would the close questions raised in that case[53] be resolved simply by saying that the collective decisions not to reinsure long-tail policies or to require pollution exclusion clauses were implemented in London?

What about a conspiracy that was halted before it could be implemented? Would the Court of Justice take the same attitude that it took in *Wood Pulp* to exercise of jurisdiction not linked to competition law? How, for instance, would the Court of Justice treat a case such as has come before U.S. courts more than once, of a conspiracy to ship heroin to the United States, stopped before it could be implemented?[54]

Or what about the situation presented in *Alcoa* itself, where the claim was that defendants had withheld supplies from the market pursuant to an agreement designed to raise prices. It seems clear that such an agreement, if directed to the European Common Market, would come within the text of Article 85, in that it had as its 'object or effect the prevention, restriction

[51] [1988] ECR at 5243.

[52] *Id.* at 5245. For the substantive phase of the case, substantially cutting down the Commission's decision, see *A. Ahlström Oy* v. *Commission*, 1993 1 CEC 466, [1993] 4 CMLR, 407 (ECJ (5th Chamber), Mar. 31, 1993).

[53] See Ch. 2, 20–2 *supra*.

[54] See, e.g., *United States* v. *King*, 552 F.2d 833, 850–2 (9th Cir. 1976), cert. denied, 430 U.S. 966 (1977).

or distortion of competition within the common market'. Yet if, as in *Alcoa*, the agreement was made in Switzerland by firms not established in the Community, it might not pass the test crafted by the Court of Justice in *Wood Pulp*.

In an interesting article making some of the same points that I have made but expressing more satisfaction with the decision than I do, Lange and Sandage conclude that the Court 'managed to steer a middle course between the broad view of *Alcoa* and the restrictive view put forward by the British Government'.[55] I am not sure that the Court's judgment is really a middle course, though clearly the position of the United Kingdom has moved toward the center since the *ICI* cases of two earlier generations. Lange and Sandage write: 'What remains unclear is the extent to which this policy reflects a legal limitation on the Commission's power, or instead is simply an exercise of discretion.'[56] If the Court is really exercising its discretion to curb the discretion of the Commission, then it must be engaging in a kind of balancing of interests without saying so. It might, for example, come out differently in the heroin case, or, say, in the case of a bomb planted in the Middle East on an airliner bound for Paris or London but disarmed before it exploded—i.e., before the conspiracy was *implemented*. If that is so, then, as the Court of Justice sees it, there is a different standard for competition law—or perhaps for all economic regulation—than for criminal law or for narcotics or for terrorism. But if that is the solution, it can only be, as it seems to me, because the interest of the state (or group of states) seeking to exercise jurisdiction is stronger, and the countervailing interest of the other possibly concerned state is non-existent, weaker, or not entitled to equal respect. That conclusion, I submit, brings us back to balancing, to which I now turn.

C. THE QUESTION OF BALANCING

1. Balancing and the Effects Doctrine

I accept the term 'balancing' because it has come to be understood as engaging in a process which I believe is necessary, possible and required, i.e., a process of evaluation to determine whether a proposed exercise of

[55] Dieter G. F. Lange and John Byron Sandage, 'The Wood Pulp Decision and Its Implications for the Scope of EC Competition Law', (1989) 26 *Common Mkt. L. Rev.* 139, 164. Dr. Mann, on the other hand, who had criticized the *Dyestuffs* case, n. 34 *supra*, liked *Wood Pulp* even less. 'Its only satisfactory aspect', he wrote, 'is that the United States is being repaid in its own coin, as it had frequently been warned might happen': F. A. Mann, 'The Public International Law of Restrictive Practices in the European Court of Justice', (1989) 38 *Int'l & Comp. LQ*, 375, 377.

[56] Lange and Sandage, n. 55 *supra*, 165.

jurisdiction supported by minimum contacts would or would not be unreasonable.[57]

I prefer the word 'evaluation', because I worry about the figure of a scale with only two weights—'them' and 'us'—and I believe that some of the criticism of balancing is attributable to that misleading metaphor. I continue to be disappointed and surprised when I see otherwise temperate persons becoming furious with the idea that courts—or indeed legislators and officials—can and should engage in balancing. Dr. F. A. Mann, for example, wrote:

> [W]hether one speaks of analysis or of balancing, interests are in law a bad and misleading guide. It is contact that matters . . . The so-called balancing of interests is nothing but a political consideration; it is not the subjective or political interest, but the objective test of the closeness of connection, of a sufficiently weighty point of contact between the facts and their legal assessment that is relevant.[58]

With all respect to a most learned man with whom I shared many interests over many years and a warm friendship for the last seven years of his life, I disagree.

Of course, for Dr. Mann, and for the British government (at least in its earlier pronouncements[59]) there is no need to balance in the context that we have been discussing. Their answer to assertion of jurisdiction on the basis of effects is 'Just say "no"'. Correspondingly, for the majority of the Supreme Court in the *Insurance Antitrust* case, there is no need (absent foreign compulsion) to balance. Once effects in the state exercising jurisdiction have been shown, 'Just say "yes"'. For my part, I continue to prefer the approach of Judge Choy, first set out in the *Timberlane* case in the context of assertion of jurisdiction to apply U.S. antitrust law to alleged anticompetitive activity by defendants in Honduras, directed to monopolizing the exportation of lumber from Honduras to the United States.[60] The complaint did allege intent to cause effect in the United States. But

[57] See *Restatement*, §§ 402 and 403, discussed in Ch. 2, sect. B, *supra*.

[58] F. A. Mann, 'The Doctrine of International Jurisdiction Revisited after Twenty Years' (1984—III) 186 *Recueil des Cours* 9, 30–1. Dr. Mann was particularly irate at the 'calamitous influence', as he put it, of the approach of 'interest analysis' of Professor Brainerd Currie in American conflict of laws. I share some of Mann's skepticism of Currie, because often in the context of married women's contracts or automobile guest statutes and similar controversies the purported 'state interests' are spurious or invented for the occasion. In the cases we are discussing here, the interests of states—at least some of the asserted interests—are genuine. Moreover, Currie nearly always resolved these conflicts in favor of the law of the forum. See, e.g., B. Currie, 'Notes on Methods and Objectives in the Conflict of Laws', 1959 *Duke LJ* 171, 178 (repr. in B. Currie, *Selected Essays on the Conflict of Laws* (1963), 177, 183–4).

[59] See, e.g., its 1969 *Aide-Mémoire* to the European Commission quoted at n. 25 *supra*.

[60] *Timberlane Lumber Co.* v. *Bank of America N.T. & S.A.*, 549 F.2d 597 (9th Cir. 1976). See also the majority opinion by Judge Weis in *Mannington Mills, Inc.* v. *Congoleum Corp.*, 595 F.2d 1287 (3d Cir. 1979).

'[t]he effects test by itself is incomplete because it fails to consider other nations' interests. Nor does it expressly take into account the full nature of the relationship between the actors and this country.'[61]

Judge Choy pointed out that addition of the word 'substantial' to the effects principle may silently incorporate the habit of balancing, with 'substantial' as a flexible standard that varies with other factors, including the requirement of *intent*, suggested by *Alcoa*, and the distinction between American and foreign citizens. 'The failure to articulate these other elements in addition to the standard effects analysis', Judge Choy went on, 'is costly, however, for it is more likely that they will be overlooked or slighted in interpreting past decisions and reaching new ones.'[62] In particular, Judge Choy directed the district court to address:

> the additional question which is unique to the international setting of whether the interests of, and links to, the United States—including the magnitude of the effect on American foreign commerce—are sufficiently strong, vis-à-vis those of other nations, to justify an assertion of extraterritorial authority.

The *Restatement*, as we saw, follows Judge Choy's approach, generalized in three ways: § 403 is not limited to antitrust, it is not limited to the United States, and it is stated as a proposition of law—international law—not just discretion or good sense. And lest the Reporters be accused of pretentiousness—or, worse, poor scholarship—in asserting that their views rise to the dignity of law, I would refer the reader to Sir Gerald Fitzmaurice, not only an eminent member of the World Court for many years, but in general a stout defender of the British view of international law. 'It is true', Judge Fitzmaurice wrote in his separate opinion in the *Barcelona Traction* case,[63]

> that under present conditions, international law does not impose hard and fast rules on States delimiting spheres of national jurisdiction . . . It does however . . . involve for every State an obligation to exercise moderation and restraint as to the extent of the jurisdiction assumed by its courts in cases having a foreign element, and to avoid undue encroachment on a jurisdiction more properly appertaining to, or more appropriately exercisable by another state.[64]

Fitzmaurice speaks of *moderation* and *restraint*, of *undue encroachment* and of *appropriate* exercise of jurisdiction—all words that can be summed up in the term *reasonableness*. Most important, Fitzmaurice speaks of an *obligation*, as does the *Restatement*.[65]

[61] 549 F.2d at 611–12.

[62] *Id.* 612.

[63] *Barcelona Traction, Light & Power Company* case (*Belgium* v. *Spain*) [1970] ICJ Rep. 3.

[64] *Id.* 105 (separate opinion).

[65] And as did the previous *Restatement*. However, § 40 of *Restatement (Second)* (1965) set out the obligation, and the factors to be considered in the context of enforcement jurisdiction; *Restatement (Third)* focuses the obligation at the stage of jurisdiction to prescribe.

2. Balancing and Reasonableness

Are reasonableness and balancing inevitably linked? I think so. One can be reasonable in judging without explicitly engaging in balancing, though as Judge Choy pointed out in *Timberlane* and as the *Wood Pulp* case illustrates, there are dangers in not setting the process out explicitly. And since balancing is not an exact science, it does not guarantee a result that all will find reasonable. But I disagree strongly with those who, like Judge Prentice Marshall in the American phase of the *Uranium* litigation, wrote that balancing of interests of the United States and foreign states is 'simply impossible'.[66] In my view thoughtful judges faced with close questions of law instinctively search for reasonableness and balance competing interests, even when, like Molière's hero, they do not know, or may even deny, that they are doing so.[67]

I promised in the first chapter to come back to the *Laker* case in the context of balancing. In the English phase of the case, it is clear that the House of Lords weighed the conflicting interests and discounted the interest of the United Kingdom, although that interest had been expressly asserted to the Court of Appeal by the Attorney General. Since the American interest was evidently an important one, it made sense to lift the injunction and to permit the exercise of jurisdiction in the United States to proceed. In the American *Laker* case,[68] decided by the U.S. Court of Appeals after the decision of the Court of Appeal in England but before the decision of the House of Lords, Judge Starr, in dissent, had wondered out loud what sovereign interest of the United States had been shown comparable to the clearly demonstrated interest of the British government.[69] That remark, it seems, provoked Judge Wilkey for the majority into a lengthy attack on interest balancing and in particular on the approach of the *Restatement* and of Judges Choy and Weis:[70]

> Most proposals for interest balancing consist of a long list of national contacts to be evaluated and weighed against those of the foreign country. These interests may be relevant to the desirability of allocating jurisdiction to a particular national forum. However, their usefulness breaks down when a court is faced with the task of selecting one forum's prescriptive jurisdiction over that of another.
>
> Many of the contacts to be balanced are already evaluated when assessing the

[66] In re *Uranium Antitrust Litigation: Westinghouse Electric Corp.* v. *Rio Algom Limited*, 480 F.Supp. 1138 at 1148 (N.D. Ill. 1979), discussed in Ch. 7, sect. E(4).

[67] See Molière, *Le Bourgeois Gentilhomme*, Act II, sc. 4:

M. Jourdain:	Par ma foi! quand je dis: 'Nicole, apportez-moi mes pantoufles, et me donnez mon bonnet de nuit', c'est de la prose?
Maître de Philosophie:	Oui Monsieur.
M. Jourdain:	Par ma foi! il y a plus de quarante ans que je dis de la prose sans que j'en susse rien.

[68] *Laker Airways Ltd* v. *Sabena Belgian World Airlines*, 731 F.2d 909 (D.C. Cir. 1984).

[69] *Id.* 956–7 (Starr, J. dissenting).

[70] *Id.* 948–53.

existence of a sufficient basis for exercising prescriptive jurisdiction. Other factors, such as 'the extent to which another state may have an interest in regulating the activity,' and 'the likelihood of conflict with regulation by other states' are essentially neutral in deciding between competing assertions of jurisdiction. Pursuing these inquiries only leads to the obvious conclusion that jurisdiction could be exercised or that there is a conflict, but does not suggest the best avenue of conflict resolution. These types of factors are not useful in resolving the controversy.

And so on.[71]

In fairness, it must be recalled that Judge Wilkey was addressing the situation—the very rare situation—where the court of a foreign nation had enjoined a party from pursuing its action before his court. The situation before Judge Wilkey had thus gone well beyond the question faced in *Insurance Antitrust* or *Wood Pulp*, where the courts had to decide only whether exercise of jurisdiction to apply the law of the forum was proper. Judge Wilkey, in short, faced a situation that even Justice Souter in *Insurance Antitrust* would have regarded as a 'true conflict', though we cannot be sure how he would have gone about resolving it.

Judge Wilkey did concede that 'international law prohibits the assertion of prescriptive jurisdiction unsupported by reasonable links between the forum and the controversy',[72] which is the basic position of the *Restatement*, if by 'forum' one understands not a court but the source of the law in question. Thus I believe Judge Wilkey does not reject reasonableness in assessing jurisdiction to prescribe. But he answers 'no' to the question to which I earlier answered 'yes'—whether reasonableness and balancing are inevitably linked. Of course, as Wilkey continued, there is no 'line of reasonableness which separates jurisdiction to prescribe into neatly adjoining compartments of national jurisdiction'.[73] That does not make me give up on balancing, or on reasonableness, though perhaps it is clearer now than it was at page 42 why I prefer the term evaluation to the term balancing.

I believe that Judge Wilkey, like Dr. Mann, greatly exaggerates in maintaining that balancing of interests will always result in application of forum law. There does, however, seem to be an instinctive preference for application of the law of the forum to controversies with substantial connection to the forum state—for wholly private controversies (if there is such a thing) such as product liability actions as well as for the semi-private types of controversies that we have been exploring here. And if that is true, it makes forum selection, and the rules of judicial jurisdiction, more important than we had perhaps realized. It is to that subject that we turn in the next chapter.

[71] 731 F.2d at 848–9. [72] 731 F.2d at 951–2. [73] *Id.* 952.

4

Jurisdiction of Courts

A. INTRODUCTION: FOUR QUESTIONS AND A FRAMEWORK

The bases of judicial jurisdiction in civil actions are much less controversial than the subjects discussed thus far. *Actor sequitur forum rei* is the fundamental principle accepted virtually everywhere. Plaintiff follows the defendant to the latter's forum, i.e., to the defendant's domicile. Evidently jurisdiction founded on defendant's domicile is not sufficient, and the discussion here, as in other dicussions of the subject, will quickly turn to other bases, some controversial, some almost universally agreed. I want to raise four questions concerning jurisdiction of courts over non-residents.

1. The defendant's domicile seems to be the only place where no one asks, in an inquiry directed to jurisdiction, what the claim or cause of action is about. Putting aside claims concerning real property and actions arising out of family relationships—divorce, child custody, and the like—it seems that any kind of claim can be litigated at the defendant's domicile, regardless of where the events giving rise to the claim occurred.[1] In short, judicial jurisdiction on the basis of defendant's domicile—or for a corporation its principal place of business—is *general jurisdiction*, to use the term introduced in the United States by von Mehren and Trautman in the mid-1960s.[2]

Should the domicile of the defendant be the only place for general jurisdiction, as was the view of the drafters of the Brussels Convention?[3] Or should other bases of jurisdiction, such as *presence* or *doing business* in a given state, or even being personally served with process in that state, support jurisdiction in actions that have no link to the forum state, or no link to the presence or activity of the defendant in that state, as in the American, and I think the Anglo-American, view?

[1] In some instances, to be sure, a contention may be raised that the plaintiff has chosen an inappropriate forum. It is rare, however, that the defense of *forum non conveniens* will succeed at the domicile or principal place of business of the defendant.

[2] See Arthur T. von Mehren and Donald T. Trautman, 'Jurisdiction to Adjudicate: A Suggested Analysis', 79 *Harv. L. Rev.* 1121 (1966). So far as I have been able to discover, the term has not caught on outside the United States, but the concept is reflected in numerous writings, as well as in the Brussels Convention, as discussed hereafter.

[3] Convention on Jurisdiction and the Enforcement of Judgments in Civil and Commercial Matters signed at Brussels, Sept. 27, 1968. A convenient source for the Convention, as amended by the various treaties of accession, is [1990] OJ C189.

2. However one answers the first question, situations will arise where there is clearly no general jurisdiction over the defendant but sustaining jurisdiction based on a particular activity would be fair, and compelling the plaintiff either to abandon his claim or to seek out the defendant at the latter's domicile might well lead to injustice. In some instances the link between the activity and the claim is clear. If an American tourist rents a car and runs down a pedestrian crossing a street in London, there can be no doubt that the court in London will have jurisdiction in a civil claim for damages against him arising out of the accident, even if he is long back in the United States by the time the injured person files his or her lawsuit. Assuming that he was properly served with the initiating process and given adequate time to respond, there can be no objection to the jurisdiction of the English court, and a judgment resulting from the action will be enforceable in the United States (as well as throughout the European Union and elsewhere), whether or not the defendant appeared before the court or presented a defense. In other instances, the relationship between the location of the activity and cause of action will not be so clear. I want to try here to shed some light on the appropriate contours of that relationship.

3. As opportunity for jurisdiction of courts based on activity or effect in the forum state has expanded, is it still acceptable or desirable to found judicial jurisdiction on the basis of presence of property in the forum state?

4. Finally, I want to raise the question whether jurisdiction over non-resident parties is, or should be, a matter of discretion, as is the rule in England and states following the English model, or of fixed law, as is the rule—or at least the theory—in the United States and I believe in most European states.

A fair question is whether there is a unifying principle with respect to the four topics that I have selected for discussion. Does the discussion, in other words, engage international law or only separate national laws addressing similar issues? My answer, which need not be accepted uncritically, is that the subject of judicial jurisdiction is best understood within a framework of international law, without drawing a distinction, in this context, between 'public' and 'private' manifestations of that discipline. The evidence of that framework, as I see it, is threefold.

First, I believe there is a growing consensus that the exercise of judicial jurisdiction must be reasonable, and a convergence, if not yet congruence, on the elements of reasonableness in this area. Second, a considerable number of judgments of national courts have been attentive to how a decision to exercise jurisdiction over a non-resident would be acceptable abroad, i.e., whether it would be perceived as an affront to another state's sovereignty, or alternatively, whether exercise of jurisdiction would parallel the decision of foreign courts in comparable circumstances. Third, judgments against non-residents of the forum state often need to be enforced in another state. While the requirements for enforcement of foreign judgments have their own national peculiarities, as we shall see in Chapter 6, the universal rule is that judgments rendered in foreign states will be denied recognition when they fail to meet international standards of judicial jurisdiction. This is one area of international law where enforcement or enforceability is in many instances an aid to defining the rule itself.[4]

B. GENERAL VERSUS SPECIFIC JURISDICTION

General jurisdiction, to repeat, describes the authority of a court to adjudicate any claim (or any but a limited class of claims), without any requirement of a link between the claim and the forum state. A simple illustration came before the Supreme Court of Japan a decade ago in *Michiko Goto* v. *Malaysian Airline System*.[5] A Japanese businessman, resident of Aichi Prefecture near Nagoya, booked a round-trip passage in Kuala Lumpur, Malaysia, on Malaysian Airlines from Kuala Lumpur to Penang, also in Malaysia, and back to Kuala Lumpur. The return flight crashed, killing all on board, including Mr Goto, the businessman from Japan.[6] The widow and heirs of Mr Goto brought suit against Malaysian Airlines in the Nagoya District Court, demanding damages arising from non-performance of the contract of carriage.[7] Malaysian Airlines maintains a branch office as well as flight operations in Japan, but the airline moved to dismiss the suit for lack of jurisdiction, on the ground that the contract of carriage on which the suit was based was a wholly domestic contract which bore no relation to the business of its Tokyo branch. The Nagoya District Court accepted this argument and dismissed the suit. Plaintiffs appealed. How should this case be decided?

Under a concept of general jurisdiction not limited to defendant's domicile, Malaysian Airlines had a permanent establishment in Japan, i.e., it was 'present', in the English formulation, or was 'doing business', in

[4] For a somewhat similar discussion, see American Law Institute, *Restatement (Third) of the Foreign Relations Law of the United States*, Introduction to Part IV, ch. 2, 'Jurisdiction to Adjudicate' (1987).

[5] Sup. Ct., Oct. 16, 1981. I rely for this account on a paper by Kenichiro Hayashida entitled 'Jurisdiction and Applicable Law in Arbitration Cases in Japan', delivered to a Conference on International Air and Space Law held in Tokyo, June 1993. An abridged version of the paper appears in (1993) 42 *Zeitschrift für Luft- und Weltraumrecht* 250.

[6] The cause of the crash, not directly relevant to the issue we focus on here but possibly relevant at a later stage of the litigation, was a brutal hijacking on 4 Dec., 1977, which ended with the hijacker shooting the crew, followed by a crash that killed 7 crew members and 93 passengers.

[7] Since the passage had been booked in Malaysia and called only for transportation within that country, no issue arose under the Warsaw Convention for the Unification of Certain Rules Relating to International Transportation by Air of Oct. 12, 1929, 137 L.N.T.S. 11, or its amendments.

the common American formulation. Accordingly, it would be required to defend the action in Japan, at least where, as here, the plaintiffs had a good reason for bringing suit in Japan. Under a concept where general jurisdiction is limited to defendant's domicile and all other jurisdiction must depend on a link between the cause of action and the forum state,—i.e., specific or special jurisdiction—the dismissal of the action should be upheld.[8]

In the United States, I have no doubt that, *mutatis mutandis*, the action could be maintained. Thus (remembering that for most purposes jurisdiction of courts is defined by the individual states, even if the action is brought in federal court) assume the ill-fated passenger resided in the United States, and his widow chose to bring suit in New York, where Malaysian Airlines maintains an office. A motion to dismiss the suit for lack of jurisdiction would almost certainly fail, unless the airline came within the definition of a foreign state instrumentality for purposes of the United States Foreign Sovereign Immunities Act of 1976.[9] The law to be applied by the New York court would probably be the law of Malaysia,[10] but the action could go forward in New York.[11]

[8] One could make an argument that Malaysian Airlines' presence in Japan was connected with providing air transportation, that the claim was based on provision of air transportation, and that it was thus linked to defendant's presence in the forum state. Such arguments, however, have rarely succeeded. Compare the discussion of *Helicopteros Nacionales*, 53–6 *infra*.

[9] 28 U.S.C. §§ 1330, 1602–11. If Malaysian Airlines qualified as a foreign state instrumentality, only specific jurisdiction would seem to govern, and thus the suit could be sustained only with some additional link, such as purchase of the ticket in the United States. See e.g., *Barkanic* v. *General Administration of Civil Aviation of the People's Republic of China*, 822 F.2d 11 (2d Cir. 1987), upholding an action by heirs of American passengers killed aboard a domestic flight on the Chinese government-owned airline CAAC, but only because an additional nexus was found between defendant and the United States, a sales agency contract with a U.S. airline through which the decedents had purchased their tickets.

A brief investigation suggests that Malaysian Airlines is a borderline case of state instrumentality under § 1603(b) of the Foreign Sovereign Immunities Act, with 30% of its shares traded publicly and the rest owned in part by the federal Malaysian government and in part by states of what used to be called the Federated Malay States. See *Aviation Week and Space Technology* Vol. 139, No. 19, 38 (Nov. 8, 1993).

[10] See *Barkanic* v. *General Administration of Civil Aviation of the People's Republic of China*, 923 F.2d 957 (2d Cir. 1991), a later phase of the case cited at n. 9 *supra*, applying Chinese law limiting recovery to $20,000 per passenger.

[11] The relevant New York statute, N.Y. Civil Practice Law and Rules (CPLR) § 301, reads, cryptically:

> A court may exercise such jurisdiction over persons, property, or status as might have been exercised heretofore.

This is understood to refer to the leading case of *Tauza* v. *Susquehanna Coal Co.*, 220 N.Y. 259, 115 N.E. 915 (1917) in which Judge Benjamin Cardozo wrote for New York's highest court that

> the defendant corporation is engaged in business within this state. We hold further that jurisdiction does not fail because the cause of action sued upon has no relation in its origin to the business here transacted . . . The essential thing is that the corporation shall have come into the state. When once it is here, it may be served;

220 N.Y. at 268–9, 115 N.E. at 918. The reason for the peculiar reference to 'heretofore' is that the following newly enacted section, § 302, sets out a series of specific bases for jurisdiction.

If the ill-fated passenger had been a resident of the United Kingdom, and his widow or heirs brought suit in London, the same result would obtain. Malaysian Airlines maintains an office as well as flight operations in London, and so would be regarded as present and amenable to service of the initiating writ in England.[12] There would be no need to establish any connection between the claim and the airline's activity in England.[13]

The rule in Western Europe—that is among the Member States of the European Union and the EFTA states governed by the Brussels or Lugano Convention—is different. If, for instance, the decedent, a resident of the United Kingdom as in the previous example, had purchased a ticket in Barcelona from Iberia, the airline of Spain, to travel from Barcelona to Madrid, and the plane had gone down, the widow or other survivors could not maintain an action in England. Iberia is not domiciled in England, the contract of carriage in our example was not to be performed in England (see Brussels Convention, Art. 5(1)), and the harmful event did not occur in England (Brussels Convention, Art. 5(3)). The fact that Iberia has offices in England and flies regularly to several cities in the United Kingdom would make no difference, because the dispute did not arise out of the operations of Iberia's branch in the United Kingdom (Brussels Convention, Art. 5(5)).[14] The fact that it would not be nearly as burdensome for Iberia to defend in London as it would be for the widow to bring an action in Spain is equally irrelevant.[15]

Which, then, is the better rule? The rule favored by the drafters of the Brussels Convention, and favored also, for instance, by von Mehren and Trautman,[16] limiting general jurisdiction to a defendant's home base? Or the traditional Anglo-American rule, focusing on presence or establishment of some permanence or continuity, without a necessary link between the claim and the activity of the defendant in the forum state?[17] Rather

[12] See, e.g., Dicey and Morris, *The Conflict of Laws* (12th edn., Collins, 1993), Rule 24 and pp. 304–8.

[13] See, e.g., *South India Shipping Corp. Ltd* v. *Export-Import Bank of Korea* [1983] WLR 585, [1985] 2 All ER 219 (CA).

[14] For the leading case under Art. 5(5), holding that an independent standard, rather than the law of the parent corporation or the law of the forum, applies to determine the necessary permanency of the branch, see *Ets. Somafer SA* v. *Saar-Ferngas, AG*, Case 33/78, [1978] ECR 2183, [1979] 1 CMLR 49 (ECJ, Nov. 22, 1978).

[15] Jurisdiction on the basis of continuous presence of the defendant in the forum state is not listed in Art. 3 of the Brussels Convention as exorbitant, as is, for example, the English rule permitting jurisdiction on the basis of service of a writ during defendant's *temporary* presence. It is clear, nevertheless, that any basis for judicial jurisdiction not expressly authorized by the Convention is precluded as between persons domiciled in a Contracting State. See introductory sentence to Art. 3; also Report of Prof. Peter Schlosser on the Convention of Oct . 9, 1978 on the Association of Kingdom of Denmark, Ireland, and the United Kingdom of Great Britain and Northern Ireland to the [Brussels Convention] (the Schlosser Report), [1979] OJ C59/71, para. 87.

[16] See von Mehren and Trautman, n. 2 *supra*, esp. at 1177–9.

[17] See, e.g., American Law Institute *Restatement (Second) of Conflict of Laws*, § 35(3); *Restatement (Third) of Foreign Relations Law*, § 421(h) (1987).

than giving my answer, I think it is time to go back to the actual case with which we started, of the Japanese businessman killed in Malaysia.

We left the narrative at the point where the District Court in Nagoya dismissed the case for lack of jurisdiction over the defendant. The High Court of Nagoya reversed the District Court and declared the action admissible, whereupon the defendant airline appealed to the Supreme Court of Japan. I am advised that when this case reached the Supreme Court in 1981, there was no clear precedent, and that the decision of the Court in *Goto* v. *Malaysian Airlines*[18] is regarded as the leading authority on international judicial jurisdiction in Japan. The Supreme Court sustained jurisdiction. It did not distinguish, as I have done here, between general and specific jurisdiction; rather it looked at the case from an overall point of view of justice:

> Where there is no treaty or legislation with respect to international jurisdiction, international jurisdiction shall be determined pursuant to 'jori' (the principle of reasonableness and fairness) which realizes fairness between the parties, adequacy of judgement, and promptness of trial.
>
> If there is a forum under the Japanese Civil Procedure Code . . ., [for example the defendant's residence, a place of business of a juridical person, the place of performance, or the location of defendant's property], jurisdiction of the court complies with 'jori'.

Here the address of the defendant's branch in Japan (Civil Procedure Code Article 2) was sufficient.[19]

I find the decision of the Supreme Court of Japan in the *Malaysian Airlines* case quite satisfying. It is not an all-embracing acceptance of jurisdiction based on doing business or corporate presence. On the other hand it does not reject jurisdiction *a priori* when the link between the plaintiff's claim and the defendant's activity in the forum state cannot be clearly established. Unlike some of my American colleagues,[20] I am not unhappy about attention to reasonableness and fairness, in preference to rules that often do not fit. If the case has not led us to a firm conclusion on the question of general jurisdiction outside of defendant's domicile, it has, I trust, at least illustrated the problem. We return to the question of discretion in section E of this Chapter.

[18] Sup. Ct. of Japan, Oct. 16, 1981, excerpted in English in 26 *Japanese Ann. Int'l L* 122 (1983); 3 *Waseda Bull. Comp. Law* 203 (1983).

[19] Other bases of jurisdiction not here complied with would be principal office of a judicial person (Art. 4), place for performance of an obligation (Art 5), location of defendant's property (Art. 8), and place of the tort (Art. 15).

[20] See, e.g., Stephen B. Burbank, 'The World in Our Courts: Review of Gary Born, *International Civil Litigation in United States Courts*', 89 *Mich. L. Rev.* 1456, 1468–71 (1991). Linda Silberman, 'Reflections on *Burnham* v. *Superior Court*: Toward Presumptive Rules of Jurisdiction and Implications for Choice of Law', 22 *Rutgers L.J.* 569 (1991).

C. THE LINK BETWEEN THE CLAIM, THE DEFENDANT, AND THE FORUM STATE

Whether or not one accepts general jurisdiction outside the defendant's domicile, many situations will arise in which the question is whether the defendant's activity has sufficient connection with the forum state and with the claim to support jurisdiction of that state's courts. In the United States, as already mentioned, jurisdiction of courts is (with a few exceptions) determined state by state, and there have been literally hundreds of reported decisions since 1945 testing whether or not the plaintiff's claim arises out of the defendant's activity in the forum state, when that activity does not come up to the level of continuous presence or doing business, but may reach some lower threshold, for instance by signing the contract sued upon in the forum state, or perhaps conducting negotiations there for a contract signed elsewhere, or placing an advertisement in a local publication.[21] Many of these cases are similar to cases treated under Article 5(1) of the Brussels Convention, 'in matters relating to contract', though American law does not limit jurisdiction based on contract to the place of performance, as the Brussels Convention does.[22]

American jurisprudence on this subject has another complication, in that since the famous case of *Pennoyer* v. *Neff*,[23] decided in 1878, jurisdiction of courts has been a subset of constitutional law—an example which so far as I am aware no other nation has followed.[24] While the *Pennoyer* case no longer defines the boundaries of judicial jurisdiction in the United States, the declaration that the acceptability of any exercise of judicial jurisdiction is to be determined by the Due Process clauses of the United States

[21] The reason for mentioning 1945 is that that was the year the U.S. Supreme Court decided the seminal case of *International Shoe Co.* v. *State of Washington*, 326 U.S. 310 (1945), which rejected the prior concept of physical power as the basis for judicial jurisdiction in favor of a test of 'fair play and substantial justice', and in upholding jurisdiction of the courts of the state of Washington, stressed that the obligation sued on *arose out of* activities in Washington: 326 U.S. at 319–20. For a collection of the decisions flowing from this phrase and state jurisdiction statutes adopted in implementation of the phrase, see Robert C. Casad, *Jurisdiction in Civil Actions* (2nd edn., 1991).

[22] The Official *Report on the Convention on Jurisdiction and the Enforcement of Judgments in Civil and Commercial Matters* submited to governments by the drafters of the Convention (the Jenard Report), [1979] OJ C59/1 at 22–4, offers a number of explanations for rejecting the place of contracting, including the statement that a plaintiff already has a choice, in matters relating to a contract, between the courts of the state of domicile and the place for performance of the obligation in question, and the Committee of Experts considered that it would be unwise to expand the number of courts having jurisdiction.

[23] 95 U.S. 714, esp. at 722–3 (1878).

[24] For an attempt to explain how or why this happened, suggesting that Justice Field, the author of the Opinion, erroneously equated 'due process' with 'established legal proceedings', see Friedrich K. Juenger, 'American Jurisdiction: A Story of Comparative Neglect', 65 *U. Colo. L. Rev.* 1, 4–6 (1993).

Constitution[25] continues in full force.[26] As a result, (1) though most of its docket is discretionary, the U.S. Supreme Court has heard an astonishing number of cases on this subject; and (2) a number of states of the United States have decided, either by legislation or by judicial decision, that the jurisdiction of their courts extends as far as the Due Process clause of the Fourteenth Amendment of the federal constitution will permit.[27]

All this is by way of introduction to the case of *Helicopteros Nacionales de Colombia, SA* v. *Hall* (1984),[28] the first judicial jurisdiction case decided by the U.S. Supreme Court involving a foreign country defendant, which I think will serve to put the following questions in context.

First, what level of activity does it take to support the assertion of general jurisdiction over the defendant; and secondly, might some lower level of activity support assertion of jurisdiction, on the basis that even if the claim did not directly *arise from* the defendant's activity in the forum state, the defendant's activity in the forum state was *sufficiently related* to the claim to make it fair and reasonable to assert jurisdiction over the defendant?

The facts of the *Helicopteros* case were not complicated. Defendant Helicol, a Colombian corporation, provided helicopter transportation for Consorcio, a joint venture made up of three American firms with headquarters in Houston, Texas, which had contracted with the state-owned oil company of Peru to construct a pipeline from the interior of that country to the Pacific Ocean. The chief executive officer of Helicol had come to

[25] i.e., the Fifth Amendment for jurisdiction of federal courts, and the Fourteenth Amendment for jurisdiction of state courts.

[26] Dr. Mann, criticizing what he regards as excessive exercise of judicial jurisdiction by American courts, wrote:

> The root trouble is that American courts and lawyers think in terms of constitutional requirements. The decisions which have been mentioned may be in conformity with the Constitution . . . But whether they come up to the level which international law demands is an entirely different matter . . . There is much to be said for giving a negative answer.

F. A. Mann, 'The Doctrine of International Jurisdiction Revisited after Twenty Years', (1984–III) 186 *Recueil des Cours* 9 at 72. Without going into the specific lower court cases that he cites, I would say, a decade later, that Mann's assertion that international law is never alluded to by American courts in this context is no longer completely valid. See esp. *Asahi* v. *Superior Court*, discussed at 76–9 *infra*.

[27] For a statute to this effect, see, e.g., Rhode Island General Laws Annotated, § 9–5–33(a):

> Every foreign corporation, every individual not a resident of this state or his executor or administrator, and every partnership or association, composed of any person or persons, not such residents, that shall have the necessary minimum contacts with the state of Rhode Island, shall be subject to the jurisdiction of the state of Rhode Island, and the courts of this state shall hold such foreign corporations and such non-resident individuals or their executors or administrators, and such partnerships or associations amenable to suit in Rhode Island in every case not contrary to the provisions of the constitution or laws of the United States.

The California Code of Civil Procedure, in § 410.10, provides merely:

> A court of this state may exercise jurisdiction on any basis not inconsistent with the Constitution of this state or of the United States.

[28] 466 U.S. 408 (1984).

Houston to negotiate with Consorcio concerning the supply of helicopter services needed for the pipeline project, but the contract between Helicol and Consorcio had been formally signed in Peru. The contract provided that the residence of all the parties would be in Peru and that any controversies arising out of the contract would be submitted to the jurisdiction of the Peruvian courts. Consorcio was to make specified payments in U.S. dollars to Helicol's account at Bank of America in New York.

On January 26, 1976, a helicopter owned by Helicol crashed in Peru. Among the persons killed were four United States citizens employed by Consorcio; their survivors brought suit against Helicol in state court in Houston, Texas. Helicol could not just default, because judgments against it from the Texas court would have been enforceable anywhere in the United States pursuant to the Full Faith and Credit clause of the United States Constitution,[29] presumably including its bank account in New York.[30] But Helicol entered a so-called special appearance, challenging the jurisdiction of the Texas court. Helicol asserted that it was not engaged in business or present in Texas, and that the claim arose only out of activity in Peru. The trial court declined to dismiss the action, the intermediate appellate court reversed and ordered the case dismissed, and the Texas Supreme Court first affirmed the dismissal, then changed its mind and reinstated the action.[31] Eventually the case reached the U.S. Supreme Court, based on the contention that the decision of the Texas Supreme Court violated Helicol's rights under the Due Process clause of the Constitution.[32]

Have I stated all the necessary facts? Plaintiffs would say no. What about the helicopter involved in the accident? It turns out that it had been manufactured by the Bell Helicopter Company in Fort Worth, Texas, and that Helicol's entire fleet came from Bell. Further, Helicol had sent its pilots to Fort Worth to pick up the aircraft as they were completed and fly them to South America, and it had regularly sent both pilots and maintenance personnel to Bell's facility for training. Also, Consorcio's payments to Helicol were made from a Houston bank, and in one instance Helicol had directed that the payment be forwarded to a third party in Colorado.

What did any of these 'contacts' have to do with the accident in Peru? If Helicol had failed to make a payment to Bell and the manufacturer had brought suit in Texas, one could be certain that such a claim would be regarded as *arising out of* Helicol's activities in Texas; if one of Helicol's aircraft had crashed while being ferried from Texas to Colombia or Peru

[29] U.S. Constitution, Art. IV, § 1.

[30] See also text at n. 71 *infra*.

[31] *Hall* v. *Helicopteros Nacionales de Colombia, SA*, 638 S.W. 870 (Tex. 1982).

[32] It may be noted in passing that it has long been clear that the Due Process clause applies to corporations as well as to natural persons, and (for most purposes) that it applies to aliens as well as to U.S. citizens.

with an American citizen or resident on board, a claim arising out of such a crash would also probably be sustained under the Texas 'long-arm', i.e., activity-based, jurisdiction statute. So also, I think, would have been a claim for wrongful discharge on behalf of a pilot hired by Helicol in Texas, but dismissed after he had begun his service in South America.

In the actual case, however, no comparable arguments could be made. Plaintiffs accordingly sought to persuade the four courts that heard their case that when all of Helicol's contacts with Texas were added together—the negotiations with Consorcio, the purchase of helicopters, the arrangements for training of its staff, and the payments to it—they were sufficient to support general jurisdiction in Texas over Helicol. As noted, plaintiffs succeeded in persuading a bare majority of the Texas Supreme Court. They failed, however, to persuade the U.S. Supreme Court. The majority opinion by Justice Blackmun pointed out that:

> Helicol never has been authorized to do business in Texas and never has had an agent for the service of process within the State. It never has performed helicopter operations in Texas or sold any product that reached Texas, never solicited business in Texas, never signed any contract in Texas, never had any employee based there, and never recruited an employee in Texas. In addition, Helicol never has owned real or personal property in Texas and never has maintained an office or establishment there. Helicol has maintained no records in Texas and has no shareholders in that State.[33]

While 'due process' is not offended by a State's subjecting [a foreign] corporation to its *in personam* jurisdiction when there are sufficient contacts between the State and the foreign corporation',[34] here the contacts were not sufficient.

Justice Brennan, in dissent, thought that by its frequent commercial dealings in Texas, 'Helicol clearly falls within the category of nonresident defendants that may be subjected to the forum's general jurisdiction'.[35] 'It is eminently fair and reasonable', Justice Brennan argued, 'to expect Helicol to face the obligations that attach to its participation in such commercial transactions.'[36]

But Justice Brennan had another argument, one that is more interesting from our point of view. If the case must be considered under 'specific jurisdiction', he asked, why must that basis for jurisdiction be limited to a claim that formally 'arises out of' Helicol's activities in Texas?

> I believe that the wrongful-death claim filed by the respondents is significantly *related* to the undisputed contacts between Helicol and the forum. On that basis, I

[33] 466 U.S. at 411. [34] *Id.* 414.
[35] 466 U.S. at 423 (Brennan J. dissenting).
[36] *Id.* 424.

would conclude that the Due Process Clause allows the Texas courts to assert specific jurisdiction over this particular action.[37]

It is interesting to explore how this case would come out, *mutatis mutandis*, under the Brussels Convention. First, however, it is worth remarking that while *Helicopteros* is not quite like *Laker* or *Insurance Antitrust* discussed in the previous chapters,[38] in that a wrongful death action could have been maintained against Helicol in Colombia or Peru,[39] it bears some resemblance to those cases in the disparity of outcome. In the actual case in Texas, which went to trial before the appeals on jurisdiction were heard, the jury awarded $1.14 million for the death of four American men working on the pipeline. Such sums would be unheard of in Lima or Bogotá. The struggle about jurisdiction, thus, made all the difference.

Perhaps the difference would not be so great in the hypothetical set in Europe, but I believe it could be substantial as well. Suppose for Bell Helicopter we substitute Aérospatiale, a company domiciled in France which also manufactures helicopters; the employees (and their heirs) are French, and the pipeline project is in Greece. The helicopter that crashed in Greece was owned and operated by a Greek company that I will call Hellenicopt. All other facts are the same as in the actual case, but all concerned are domiciliaries of a Contracting State of the Brussels Convention. Could the families of the deceased workers successfully maintain their action against Hellenicopt in France?

Surprisingly enough, I think the answer is yes. Plaintiffs could not sustain jurisdiction under Article 5(3), the basic tort provision of the Convention, because the 'harmful event' did not occur in France. I believe that they could not succeed under Article 5(5) concerning operations of a branch, though it is interesting that the Convention uses the same term as the specific jurisdiction statutes and cases in the United States—'arising out of the operations of', which Justice Brennan, as we saw, questioned in the *Helicopteros* case.

The easier path for plaintiffs in our hypothetical would be to do what plaintiffs in the actual case did, that is to join the manufacturer as a defendant.[40] In the United States, the fact that a co-defendant, or even the partner of a defendant, is properly before the court does not provide a basis for jurisdiction over a non-resident not otherwise amenable to suit.[41]

[37] 446 U.S. at 424 (emphasis added).

[38] See Ch. 1, sect. D; Ch. 2, sect. D.

[39] See Peru: Codigo Civil, Art. 1969 (liability), Art. 2058 (jurisdiction); Colombia: Codigo Civil, Art. 2341 (liability), Codigo de Procedimiento Civil, Art. 23 (jurisdiction).

[40] In the actual case, a directed verdict was entered in favor of Bell Helicopter after trial, on the basis of evidence that the accident was caused by failure of the pilot to keep the helicopter under control and that it was flown into a tree-top fog condition: see 464 U.S. at 412, n. 6, and 426, n. 4.

[41] See, e.g., *Restatement (Second) of Conflict of Laws*, § 40 and comments thereto (1971). In England and states that follow the English model, jurisdiction on this basis is available with leave of the court under Order 11, r. 1(1)(c).

Under Article 6(1) of the Brussels Convention however, a person domiciled in a Contracting State (Hellenicopt in our example) may also be sued where he is one of a number of defendants, in the courts of the place where one of the defendants is domiciled.[42]

I have no relevant precedent from the European Court of Justice, but I do have a case from the Supreme Court of Italy, which illustrates and, I think, confirms the point. In *BV Handel- en Exploitatie Maatschappij 'Selene'* v. *Soc. Philips SpA and Others*,[43] a resident of Italy had been killed in a hotel fire in the Netherlands. His relatives sued his employer, an Italian company, in Italy (Brussels Convention, Art. 2), and joined the Netherlands company that managed the hotel. So long as there was a genuine basis for action against the Italian company, and the claims against the two defendants, even if brought under different legal theories, resulted from the same event, jurisdiction over the Netherlands company was perfectly appropriate. The fact that the plaintiffs subsequently settled with the Italian company did not deprive the court of jurisdiction over the Dutch company.

We are left, then, with the question what is 'fair and reasonable', in Justice Brennan's words in *Helicopteros*,[44] or 'consistent with international law', in the terms of our inquiry. I think we know pretty well where the gray area lies, but we do not quite know where to draw the line.

D. JURISDICTION ON THE BASIS OF PROPERTY IN THE FORUM STATE

Why should ownership of property in a given state ever be the basis for jurisdiction of a claim against the owner? If one goes backwards from enforcement to judgment to jurisdiction, the answer becomes plain: property of the defendant, particularly if one can tie it up in some way at the beginning or in the course of the litigation, gives plaintiff a strong chance of enforcement of an eventual judgment, whereas absence of property of the defendant in the forum state may require a successful plaintiff to take

[42] It is worth noting for persons not closely familiar with the Brussels Convention that the Convention is not merely an enabling treaty requiring domestic legislation to establish a stated basis for jurisdiction, but that it confers direct authority on courts of contracting states to exercise jurisdiction on the basis of the provisions in the Convention. See Jenard Report, n. 22 *supra*, 22. The idea here was to facilitate implementation of the Convention, so that states ratifying the Convention would not be required to adopt any additional measures of implementation. Only a few of the jurisdictional provisions include clauses depending on optional internal legislation, e.g., Art. 5(2) (maintenance) second clause; Art. 5(4) (civil action pendent on criminal proceedings); Art. 6a (ship liability). For a detailed explanation, see Reinhold Geimer and Rolf A. Schütze, *Internationale Urteilsannerkennung* (1983), i, 283–5.

[43] Corte di Cassazione, Sezioni unite, Nov. 6, 1975 [1976]–I Giurisprudenza Italiana, 1349; 13 Rivista di Diritto Internazionale Privato e Processuale 389, summarized in *EC Digest of Case Law Relating to European Communities*, D Series, I–6, B.2.

[44] 466 U.S. at 428.

additional steps in another forum in order to obtain satisfaction of the judgment. But if one goes forward and says talk of judgment and enforcement is premature until the exercise of jurisdiction is justified, the question becomes much harder.[45] Suppose *D*, a non-resident, maintains a bank account in Patria, or owns an apartment house there. To what extent does, or should, this fact, without more, expose *D* to suit in Patria? One answer, codified in Germany since 1877 and emulated in some dozen countries,[46] is that *D* should be amenable to suit for any amount.[47] Another answer, which has been the American law until recently, is that *D* should be amenable to jurisdiction in any action, but only up to the value of the property, with no *res judicata* effect outside the forum state. A third answer, adopted by the Brussels Convention, is that ownership of property in Patria by *D* is not an acceptable basis for jurisdiction at all, even for an action contesting ownership of the property.[48]

Again, I use the American approach of testing the question by reference to particular cases. This time, however, I want to start with Germany.

1. Germany: Some Second Thoughts

In 1975, the Republic of Nigeria embarked on a massive construction program, and made contracts with suppliers all over the world to ship cement to Lagos, its capital city and principal port. Most of the contracts called for payment by drafts drawn against letters of credit issued by the Central Bank of Nigeria. It turned out, however, that the port of Lagos did not have the capacity to receive the ships or to unload the cement, and as ships lined up in the South Atlantic Ocean, Nigeria attempted to cancel the contracts. Sellers, many of which were middlemen that had purchased the cement in order to fill the contracts with Nigeria, brought suit wherever they could against the government of Nigeria for breach of contract, and against the Central Bank for dishonor of letters of credit. In the United States and England, the litigation established important aspects of the law of claims against foreign states.[49] In Germany, a Liechtenstein company

[45] I am not here addressing suits related directly to the property in question, such as the suit by *P*, who falls on a defective stairway in an apartment house in Patria owned by *D*, a non-resident of Patria. The illustration comes from *Restatement (Second) of Conflict of Laws*, § 38(1) and comment *b* thereto, which supports jurisdiction over *D*. Apparently jurisdiction on the basis of ownership of the property clause would not be permissible under the Brussels Convention, but under Art. 5(3), jurisdiction on the basis of the place where the harmful event occurred, the same result would be achieved.

[46] See Schack, 'Vermögensbelegenheit alz Zuständigkeitsgrund' (1984), 97 *Zeitschrift für Zivilprozeß*, 46, 50–3.

[47] Germany, Code of Civil Procedure (Zivilprozeßordnung or ZPO) § 23, reproduced below.

[48] See Schlosser Report, n. 15 *supra*, para. 88.

[49] *U.S.*: *Texas Trading & Milling Corp.* v. *Federal Republic of Nigeria*, 647 F.2d 300 (2d Cir. 1981), cert. denied, 454 U.S. 1148 (1982), holding that the activity of the bank and the government came within the definition of commercial activity in the Foreign Sovereign Immunities

brought an action against the Central Bank of Nigeria under Article 23 of the Code of Civil Procedure, on the basis of accounts that the Nigerian bank maintained at the Deutsche Bank in Frankfurt. Article 23 of the Code of Civil Procedure (ZPO) reads as follows:

> Actions pertaining to property against a person having no domicile within the State may be brought before a court in whose district property of the defendant is situated, or the subject of the action is situated. Claims shall be deemed to be situated at the domicile of the debtor, and if the claims are secured, also at the place where the security is situated.[50]

The court in Frankfurt held, consistently with the modern trends and with decisions in other countries,[51] that the Central Bank of Nigeria was not entitled to immunity with regard to claims arising out of dishonor of the letter of credit. But was there any basis for bringing the action in Frankfurt, neither the domicile of the seller nor the place of payment of the letters of credit or place of performance of the underlying contracts? A leading critic of Article 23 jurisdiction thought not, and thought that this case illustrated the flaw in Article 23, in that it placed German courts in the position of adjudicating a controversy in which they had no interest.[52] The court of first instance in Frankfurt, however, was not concerned with such questions. The defendant was not domiciled in Germany; it had assets within the district where the court sat, and that was all that was required, whether or not a judgment resulting from the action would be granted international recognition.[53]

Act, and that it had sufficient connections with the United States to support jurisdiction of U.S. courts under the FSIA and the Constitution; *Verlinden BV* v. *Central Bank of Nigeria*, 461 U.S. 480 (1983), holding that claims against foreign states 'arise under' United States' law, rather than under the law of states of the United States, and thus that if there was sufficient nexus with the United States, U.S. courts could hear a suit by an alien against a foreign state or state instrumentality.

U.K.: *Trendtex Trading Corporation* v. *Central Bank of Nigeria*, [1977] QB 529 (CA), holding (prior to adoption of the State Immunity Act) that a foreign government was not entitled to immunity in respect of commercial transactions.

[50] The text in the original reads:

> Für Klagen wegen vermögensrechtlicher Ansprüche gegen eine Person, die im Inland keinen Wohnsitz hat, ist das Gericht zuständig, in dessen Bezirk sich Vermögen derselben oder der mit der Klage in Anspruch genommene Gegenstand befindet. Bei Forderungen gilt als der Ort, wo das Vermögen sich befindet, der Wohnsitz des Schuldners und, wenn die für Forderung eine Sache zur Sicherheit haftet, auch der Ort, wo die Sache sich befindet.

[51] See n. 49 *supra*.

[52] Schumann, 'Aktuelle Fragen und Probleme des Gerischtsstandes des Vermögens' (1980), 93 *Zeitschrift für Zivilprozeß* 408 at 413.

[53] *X.* v. *Central Bank of Nigeria*, Decision of Landgericht, Frankfurt, Dec. 2, 1975 (1976) 29 Neue Juristische Wochenschrift 1044. Apparently the case was settled following this decision, and no appellate decision is reported. For a collection of earlier cases decided under Art. 23, see de Vries and Lowenfeld, 'Jurisdiction in Personal Actions—A Comparison of Civil Law and Views', 44 *Iowa L. Rev.* 306, 330–44 (1959).

We know that under Article 3 of the Brussels Convention (the list of exorbitant jurisdictions), the action could not have gone forward if (other facts being the same) the defendant had been, say, the Central Bank of Italy. But beyond the Convention, was the exercise of jurisdiction on the basis of the bank account in Frankfurt exorbitant? Would it still be exorbitant if, instead of a Liechtenstein seller, plaintiff had been a German firm? Or if drafts against the letter of credit had been payable in Frankfurt? Note that by these questions, we approach more closely to some form of specific jurisdiction, i.e., to a link between the forum, the defendant, and the claim, whereas Article 23 as written and as applied by the court in the *Nigeria* case is a form of general jurisdiction, requiring neither the claim nor the defendant to have any link to the forum.

I suggested at the outset of this Chapter that there was an international law of judicial jurisdiction, though perhaps 'international climate of opinion' would have been more accurate. The German Supreme Court's response in 1991 to the questions raised about Article 23 provides a good illustration, though the facts are somewhat complicated. The action was brought in Stuttgart by M Ltd, a construction company incorporated in Northern Cyprus. It had entered into a contract in 1976 with the Libyan Directorate of Military Procurement to construct harbor works in Tripoli. The Libyan agency had agreed to make an advance payment of $37 million (one sixth of the total contract price), provided M Ltd furnished a counterguarantee to secure repayment of the advance in specified circumstances. M Ltd procured a counterguarantee from a Turkish bank, TC Ziraat Bankasi, against which M had to deposit $20 million plus additional securities. In 1979, the Libyan Directorate terminated the contract and demanded return of the advance payment. After a lengthy inquiry, TC Ziraat, the Turkish bank, paid Libya under its counterguarantee and enforced the security deposited with it by M Ltd. M contended that Libya's claims were unfounded and that the Turkish bank had wrongly paid under the counterguarantee.

When the Turkish bank refused M's demand for a return of its deposit, M brought suit. Where? Not in Turkey, where TC Ziraat had its principal office, because, according to M Ltd, it could not secure a fair trial there, since the affair had become a major political issue, including a report by a commission of inquiry whose chairman had since become Prime Minister. M first tried England, where TC Ziraat had a representative office, but that effort failed on the basis of *forum non conveniens*.[54] M did not take up the English court's suggestion that the dispute should be heard in Turkey, but instead brought suit in Germany. In fact TC Ziraat had several branches or representative offices in Germany, but since the transaction

[54] *Muduroglou Ltd* v. *TC Ziraat Bankasi* [1986] 3 WLR 606, [1986] 3 All ER 682.

was unrelated to the activity of any of these branches, that would have made no difference. What would—or at least might—be significant was that TC Ziraat had substantial assets in Germany, and M now asserted that the presence of these assets supported jurisdiction of the German courts. The court of first instance upheld jurisdiction, but the defendant appealed and, to the surprise of many observers, both the Court of Appeal (Oberlandesgericht) and the Supreme Court rejected the claim of jurisdiction.[55] While the text of Article 23 supported jurisdiction, it was necessary also to examine the international competence of the German courts. Though Article 23 was neither unconstitutional nor contrary to international law, the Bundesgerichtshof concluded that jurisdiction under Article 23 could be justified only if the cause of action had some link to the forum. The court said it need not declare what links with Germany would be sufficient to support jurisdiction under Article 23; clearly there were no such links in the present case. It seems that either the domicile of the plaintiff or origin of the claim in Germany would have supported jurisdiction under Article 23, so that Article 23 has not been rendered wholly insignificant. But where neither link is present, as in the actual case, jurisdiction of the German court could not be maintained.[56]

I think the German Supreme Court got it right, and I am impressed both by the impact of international law on its decision and by the effect that its decision has, or at least may have, in building a wider consensus.

2. The United States: A U-turn

In the United States, the rule was for a long time like that under Article 23 of the German Code of Civil Procedure, except that plaintiff was required at the outset to secure an attachment of the property in the forum on which he based jurisdiction, and that no judgment could be recovered for more than the value of the property attached.[57] In the period before the

[55] *M.* v. *T.* (1990) 36 Recht der Internationales Wirtschaft [RIW] 829, Oberlandesgericht Stuttgart, 6 Aug. 1990; 115 BGHZ 90, Bundesgerichtshof, July 2, 1991.

[56] Because the defendant bank's assets in Germany exceeded plaintiff's claim, the court did not address the question whether a judgment could be given in an amount in excess of the value of the property in the forum state. The issue can be important if defendant has assets in another state with a rule similar to Art. 23 and recognizes and enforces judgments on the basis of reciprocity. See e.g., *H. & Gen.* v. *L.*, Reichsgericht (VII. Zivilsenat), Jan. 19, 1911, 75 R.G.Z. 147, in which enforcement was granted in Germany of an Austrian judgment in an action in Austria under that country's counterpart to Art. 23 based on defendant's ownership in the forum district of four baskets of fruit. The case is discussed in de Vries and Lowenfeld, n. 53 *supra*, at 339–40.

[57] See, e.g., *Restatement (Second) of Conflict of Laws*, §§ 66–68 (now superseded as discussed below) (1971). Usually the plaintiff would be required to post security as a condition for obtaining an attachment. If defendant ultimately prevailed, he could recover out of the security any losses caused by attachment of his property; if plaintiff prevailed and defendant did not otherwise satisfy the judgment, the attached property could be sold to satisfy the judgment.

1945 decision in *International Shoe* v. *Washington*,[58] when jurisdiction of courts was believed to be founded on 'physical power' or some theoretical surrogate,[59] power over property within the forum state was often a substitute for 'power over the person' in the situations where, by today's standards, a court ought to be able to adjudicate a claim. Once jurisdiction had been firmly established on the basis of conduct by the defendant or effect caused in the forum state, within a general framework of 'fair play and substantial justice', many scholars and some judges questioned whether there was any longer any need for so-called *quasi-in rem* jurisdiction, or whether such jurisdiction could be justified on theoretical grounds.[60]

The criticism was intensified by a practice that grew up in New York and a few other states whereby an automobile liability policy taken out by a person involved in an accident was his property up to the face amount of the policy, and that property was deemed to be located wherever the insurance company was located. If the policy had been issued by a company that did business throughout the country, this meant that the defendant could be sued virtually wherever plaintiff chose to sue. Thus to take the facts of the case that gave the name to this practice, *Seider* v. *Roth*,[61] when a resident of Quebec collided on a highway in Vermont with a car driven by plaintiff, a domiciliary of New York, the New York Court of Appeals held that the Quebecker could be sued in New York, on the basis that he carried liability insurance issued by the Hartford Insurance Company, which did business all over North America, including New York. That was clearly stretching the limits of *quasi-in rem* jurisdiction, and it could easily have been stopped either by judicial decision or by legislation, on numerous grounds.[62] But before that happened,[63] as it turned out, the whole structure of property-based jurisdiction in the United States collapsed in rather surprising fashion.

[58] See n. 21 *supra*.

[59] The oft-quoted phrase of Justice Holmes 'the foundation of jurisdiction is physical power': *McDonald* v. *Mabee*, 243 U.S. 90 at 91 (1917) was never taken literally, and indeed Justice Holmes continued:

> No doubt there may be some extension of the means of acquiring jurisdiction beyond service or appearance, but the foundation should be borne in mind.

Jurisdiction over a person on the basis of domicile was generally accepted, even when the defendant was temporarily absent from the forum state, see, e.g., *Restatement of Conflict of Laws* §§ 47, 59 (1934); Austin W. Scott, *Fundamentals of Procedure in Actions at Law* (1922), 38, 41, though the Supreme Court did not formally so hold until 1940, in *Milliken* v. *Meyer*, 311 U.S. 457 (1940).

[60] See, e.g., Paul Carrington, 'The Modern Utility of Quasi in Rem Jurisdiction', 76 *Harv. L. Rev.* 303 (1962); also the concurring opinion by Judge John Gibbons in *Jonnet* v. *Dollar Savings Bank of the City of New York*, 530 F.2d 1123, 1130–43 (3d Cir. 1976).

[61] 17 N.Y.2d 111, 269 N.Y.S.2d 99, 216 N.E.2d 312 (1966).

[62] See, e.g., David Siegel, 'Jurisdiction ad Infinitum: New York's "Rem" Seizure of the Insurance Policy for Jurisdiction in Accident Cases' (1971) 20 *Int'l & Comp. L.Q.* 99; Maurice Rosenberg, 'One Procedural Genie Too Many or Putting *Seider* Back Into Its Bottle', 71 *Colum. L. Rev.* 660 (1971).

[63] As it eventually did: *Rush* v. *Savchuk*, 444 U.S. 320 (1980).

Shaffer v. *Heitner*[64] was a so-called derivative shareholder's action, whereby the shareholder of a corporation brings a claim on behalf of the corporation against officers or directors, charging malfeasance or breach of duty to the corporation. The corporation in question was incorporated, like many American companies, in the state of Delaware, but it had its principal office in Arizona; the alleged misconduct had taken place in Oregon. However, under Delaware law, the shares of a Delaware corporation are deemed to be situated in that state. Plaintiff asserted that defendants owned shares in the corporation, that these were located in Delaware and could be attached (sequestered) under Delaware law, and that nothing further was required to support jurisdiction over the defendants. The Supreme Court of Delaware upheld jurisdiction on this basis over the directors and officers of the corporation.

When the case reached the United States Supreme Court, that court could have held, as Justice Brennan, whose dissent we followed in *Helicopteros*, would have done, that a suit by shareholder of a Delaware corporation alleging misconduct by its officers or directors is an action *related* and not *unrelated* to the forum, and that it is not unreasonable or unfair to require the corporation's officers and directors to answer for their conduct in the state of incorporation.[65] Alternatively, it could have held that the trouble with the Delaware law was that it imposed an artificial situs on corporate shares, when neither their owners nor the share certificates were located in Delaware. In the event, however, the Supreme Court went much further. It held that all assertions of state court jurisdiction would be evaluated according to the standard set forth in *International Shoe* v. *Washington*,[66] and that that standard was not met when jurisdiction was asserted solely on the presence of defendant's property in the forum state unrelated to the plaintiff's cause of action. The Court understood that it was making a major change, overturning a century of history.[67] But the majority concluded that:

> The fiction that an assertion of jurisdiction over property is anything but an assertion of jurisdiction over the owner of the property supports an ancient form without substantial modern justification. Its continued acceptance would serve only to allow state court jurisdiction that is fundamentally unfair to the defendant.[68]

The Supreme Court left open situations where the claim is directly related to the property whose presence is asserted as the basis for jurisdiction, as in the hypothetical case mentioned earlier, where the plaintiff is injured

[64] 433 U.S. 186 (1977).
[65] 433 U.S. 219 at 117–28.
[66] N. 21 *supra*.
[67] See Linda J. Silberman, '*Shaffer* v. *Heitner*: The End of an Era', 53 *N.Y.U.L.Rev*. 33 (1978).
[68] 433 U.S. at 212.

as the result of a defect in the staircase of an apartment house owned by a non-resident defendant.[69] More important, in what has become a famous footnote among American litigators, the Court said that:

> Once it has been determined by a court of competent jurisdiction that the defendant is a debtor of the plaintiff, there would seem to be no unfairness in allowing an action to realize that debt in a State where the defendant has property, whether or not that State would have jurisdiction to determine the existence of the debt as an original matter.[70]

Thus, to come back to the *Helicopteros* case, if the plaintiffs had succeeded in their *in personam* action in Texas, they could have enforced their judgment against the defendant's bank account in New York, and also against any unpaid debt from Consorcio or other clients of Helicol in the United States.[71] They could not, after *Shaffer* v. *Heitner*, have proceeded initially in New York on the basis of Helicol's bank account in that state. In contrast to the apparent situation in Germany after *M Ltd*, the domicile of plaintiffs in the United States would make no difference in this context.

It may surprise readers accustomed to view the United States as the champion of exorbitant jurisdiction to learn that in this respect it has retreated as far as the contracting states of the Brussels Convention have retreated *inter se*, and substantially farther than, for instance, Germany has done *vis-à-vis* non-Convention domiciliaries.[72]

3. England: New Horizons

In 1975 a Panamanian company, Mareva Compania Naviera SA, time-chartered its vessel, the *Mareva*, to another Panamanian company, International Bulkcarriers, SA, for a voyage from Rotterdam to the Far East

[69] See n. 45 *supra*. In fact, a survey of efforts of this kind shows that in the decade and a half since the decision in *Shaffer* v. *Heitner*, not more than 15 of such cases have been reported. See Michael B. Mushlin, 'The New Quasi in Rem Jurisdiction: New York's Revival of a Doctrine Whose Time has Passed', 55 *Brooklyn L. Rev.* 1059 (1990). For three interesting, but not typical, cases in which jurisdiction on the basis of the presence of property was maintained where the property and the claim were in some way related, see A. Lowenfeld, *International Litigation and Arbitration* (1993), 244–7.

[70] 433 U.S. at 210–11, n. 36.

[71] This is so because for most purposes, apparently not disturbed by the decision in *Shaffer* v. *Heitner*, a debt from *B* to *A* is regarded (i) as property of *A*, and (ii) situated where *B* is domiciled or present. See generally, A. Lowenfeld, 'In Search of the Intangible: A Comment on *Shaffer* v. *Heitner*', 53 *N.Y.U.L.Rev.* 102 (1978).

[72] With the expansion of the European Community (Union) and the extension of the ambit of the Brussels Convention through the largely identical Lugano Convention of Sept. 16, 1988, Austria, Denmark, Norway, Sweden, and Switzerland have had to give up property-based jurisdiction *inter se*. I am not informed whether any of these states have followed the German Supreme Court in requiring some link to the forum before sustaining such jurisdiction in suits against persons not domiciled in one of the contracting states of the Brussels/Lugano Convention, but one may assume that, if a case like *M Ltd* were to arise in one of these states, the issue would be raised.

and back. Bulkcarriers subchartered the vessel to India on a voyage charter. India paid the freight as provided in the subcharter to a bank account in London maintained by Bulkcarriers, but after paying two instalments to the owner out of that bank account, Bulkcarriers stopped paying. The owner, Mareva SA, thereupon brought suit against Bulkcarriers in London, serving its agents in London and also applying for leave to serve out of the jurisdiction pursuant to Order 11 of the Rules of the Supreme Court, England's device for exercising jurisdiction over non-residents in specified circumstances.[73]

If these events had taken place in the United States and, say, New York had been substituted for London, the shipowner would almost certainly have sought to attach Bulkcarriers' account in the (New York) bank as security for its claim.[74] After the *Shaffer* case, such an attachment would not have conferred jurisdiction on the court, but if a plausible basis for jurisdiction were shown, for instance that Bulkcarriers was engaged in business in New York or had contracted to supply services in the state, the order of judicial attachment would normally have been granted *ex parte*, subject to confirmation of an *inter partes* proceeding if the defendant contested.[75] But the practice of foreign attachment had not developed in England as it had in the United States, either for jurisdiction or for security, and attachment of Bulkcarriers' London bank account was not available to Mareva.[76] Mareva's lawyers, however, had another idea.

Mareva applied, *ex parte*, to the High Court for an injunction to restrain disposal of the assets of Bulkcarriers on deposit in the London bank. The High Court granted the injunction, but because the judge who heard the application was not sure that he had the authority to do so, he ordered that the injunction run only until 5 p.m. on the date of issue, the idea being that this gave sufficient time to take the question up to the Court of Appeal.

The case made it to the Court of Appeal in time, and that court held that it was 'just and right' that the injunction be continued.[77] The nominal defendant was Bulkcarriers; but the injunction was served on the bank which held Bulkcarriers' deposit, and which now was prohibited from paying money out of the account. Thus was born, on June 23, 1975, a new device, which soon became known as the Mareva injunction.[78]

[73] See sect. E(1) *infra*.

[74] See New York Civil Practice Law and Rules (CPLR), § 6201, incorporated into federal practice through Rule 64 of the Federal Rules of Civil Procedure.

[75] See N.Y. CPLR §§ 6211, 6223.

[76] For a brief summary of the prior English practice, see Silberman, n. 67 *supra*, 53 *N.Y.U.L.Rev.* at 40–2 and sources there cited.

[77] *Mareva Compania Naviera SA* v. *International Bulkcarriers SA* [1975] 2 Lloyd's Rep. 509 (CA).

[78] The discussion here is focused on England. The Mareva injunction has also been introduced into most of the countries that use the English system as its model, including Canada, Australia, and New Zealand, and also Hong Kong, Malaysia, Nigeria, and Singapore.

To be precise, the Mareva injunction is not a basis for jurisdiction: some basis for jurisdiction of the English court other than presence of defendant's assets must be shown before the injunction can be issued. But if a plausible basis for jurisdiction of the English court can be shown (remembering that the procedure begins *ex parte*), the Mareva injunction as it has developed offers a powerful incentive for litigating in England.[79]

It was originally believed that Mareva injunctions were available only to restrain removal or dissipation of assets situated in England. Further, it was originally assumed that a Mareva injunction would be granted only in connection with an action pending or about to be filed in England. And in the *Mareva* case itself, there was clear connection between the account subjected to the injunction and the plaintiff's claim. In a series of cases in the late 1980s, all of these possible limitations on Mareva injunctions were cast aside.

The first case in the series, *Babanaft International Co. SA* v. *Bassatne*,[80] arose out of a judgment of the High Court in London, issued in an action in favor of a Panamanian company represented by an English liquidator, against the shareholders, officers, and directors of the company. The defendants were two brothers characterized by the Court of Appeal as 'unusually peripatetic in their life style and elusive in the way they do business and hold assets'. Both were nationals of Lebanon; one resided mainly in Switzerland, the other in Greece, and, to quote Lord Justice Kerr, 'all "their" assets appear to be held in the names of a large network of companies incorporated in many countries in which they or members of their families hold bearer shares'.[82]

On the day after the judgment was issued in the principal case for some 15 million dollars, the plaintiff applied for an injunction (i) precluding defendants from dealing with any of their assets worldwide, and (ii) ordering disclosure by defendants of their assets wherever situated and oral examination of the defendants in relation to their assets. After at first declining to grant a Mareva injunction with respect to external assets of defendants, the judge granted the injunction and defendants appealed. Clearly this was in some sense extraterritorial jurisdiction. But was it exorbitant? The Court of Appeal upheld the injunction, but in order to avoid 'exorbitant assertion of extraterritorial jurisdiction over third parties',[83] it limited the order to the defendants themselves. Thus no third

[79] For an unusual illustration, in which the wife of a Saudi Arabian citizen domiciled in Spain employed a Mareva injunction in connection with a divorce action, see *Ghoth* v. *Ghoth* [1992] 2 All ER 920 (CA). The case is discussed in detail in A. Lowenfeld, 'Injunctions Across National Frontiers: A Tale of Two Cities', 3 *Am. Rev. Int'l Arbitration* 3 (1992).

[80] [1990] Ch. 13; [1989] 2 WLR 232 (CA).

[81] At 22 (Ch.), 237 (WLR).

[82] *Ibid.*

[83] [1990] Ch. at 28 (Kerr LJ), 43–4 (Nicholls LJ); [1989] 2 WLR at 243 (Kerr LJ), 257 (Nicholls LJ).

parties would be bound by the order, and the notice of the High Court's order given by plaintiffs to forty-seven banks and other institutions believed to hold assets of the defendant outside England was ordered revoked. Since some of the recipients of the notice, for instance Banque Nationale de Paris, had branches in London, and others were in fact foreign branches of London banks, the Court of Appeal reasoned that, without the limitation, the order might have improper extraterritorial effect, in that some of the institutions might well be reluctant to risk violating the order for fear of being subject to contempt of court proceedings in England.

The next case, *Republic of Haiti* v. *Duvalier*,[84] arose out of an attempt by the government of Haiti that succeeded Jean-Claude (Baby Doc) Duvalier to recover some $120 million alleged to have been looted by the Duvalier family from the public treasury. Duvalier had fled to France with his wife and mother, and the principal action was pending in the Tribunal de Grande Instance in Grasse, in southern France, near the Duvalier château. In the English proceeding, the government of Haiti asserted that the Duvalier family had used English solicitors to hold and conceal property belonging to the Republic. Haiti did not claim that all the assets in question were actually situated in England, but it alleged that the London solicitors had knowledge of, access to, and control over the assets. The Republic sought an order (i) restraining the Duvalier family from removing from England or dealing with any assets in England; (ii) requiring defendants by their London solicitors to permit inspection of documents and answer questions on the location of their assets, wherever situated; and (iii) thereafter serving the defendants out of the jurisdiction. The High Court granted the order; the Court of Appeal modified the order by adopting the 'Babanaft proviso' concerning the effect on third parties outside England, except that the exclusion of binding effect on third parties would apply 'unless the order is enforced by the courts of the states in which any of the defendants' assets are located'.[85] The Court wondered whether such an addition to the Babanaft proviso was necessary, since if a foreign court made an order on its own it would not need to enforce the order of the English court but, as Lord Justice Staughton wrote, the revised formulation 'may encourage the courts of other countries to enforce the English order, and if it has that effect it is in my opinion desirable'.[86]

In the third case in this series, *Derby & Co. Ltd* v. *Weldon No. 1)*, [87] plaintiffs, members of the Philipp Bros. and Salomon commodity houses, brought suit against two executives of an affiliated English company, who,

[84] [1990] 1 QB 202; [1989] 2 WLR 261 (CA).
[85] At 217–18 (QB), 274 (WLR).
[86] *Ibid.*
[87] [1990] Ch. 48; [1983] 2 WLR 276 (CA).

according to plaintiffs, had diverted some £34 million of assets from the English company to a Hong Kong company and ultimately to their own benefit. Plaintiffs did not have a judgment, and they could not, as in *Haiti*, be said to be 'tracing' assets, but they sought an order freezing defendants' property within and outside of England. The High Court judge granted a Mareva injunction only as to assets in England, but ordered defendants, who resided in England, to make full disclose as to their world-wide assets. On appeal, the Court of Appeal affirmed as to the order to make full disclosure, but reversed as to the limited character of the restraint, i.e., it applied the Mareva injunction to defendants' assets wherever situated. In place of the Babanaft proviso, plaintiffs offered and the court accepted an undertaking that, before they applied to a foreign court to enforce the order, they would first seek leave from the English court. The court in that event would presumably consider the law of the foreign country in question before granting or denying leave.[88]

As noted at the outset of this discussion, technically the Mareva injunction does not, in contrast to pre-*Shaffer* 'foreign attachment' in the United States, provide the basis for assertion of jurisdiction.[89] Mareva assumes that there is a basis for jurisdiction over the defendant, though in many instances the injunction is issued together with an *ex parte* order permitting service on a non-resident outside of the United Kingdom.[90] The defendant may move to set aside service—i.e., to challenge the judicial jurisdiction, but meanwhile his assets are under restraint. There is no requirement that

[88] In a related case naming two companies incorporated respectively in Luxembourg and Panama, *Derby & Co. Ltd* v. *Weldon (Nos. 3 and 4)* [1990] Ch. 65 at 87, [1989] 1 W.L.R. 412 at 429 (CA), the Court of Appeal again reformulated the Babanaft proviso, to read:

> in so far as this order purports to have any extraterritorial effect, no person shall be affected thereby or concerned with the terms thereof until it shall be declared enforceable or be enforced by a foreign court and then it shall only affect them to the extent of such declaration or enforcement unless they are [a person to whom the order is addressed or persons subject to the jurisdiction of the court].

Lord Donaldson, MR, said 'This seems to me to meet any charge that the court is seeking to exercise an exorbitant jurisdiction . . . and to avoid any argument based on circularity': at 84 (Ch.), 426 (WLR).

[89] It should also be noted that the Mareva injunction is not an attachment or arrest, though it has some similarity with those devices. Thus the applicant does not become a secured creditor by obtaining a Mareva injunction, and if eventually the assets under restraint are executed on, the applicant does not, by virtue of the Mareva injunction, have priority over other creditors.

[90] It is worth observing that Mareva injunctions do not fall within the exorbitant jurisdiction provisions of the Brussels Convention, because they are regarded as provisional measures falling under Article 24, which states:

> Application may be made to the courts of a Contracting State for such provisional, including protective, measures as may be available under the law of that State, even if, under this Convention, the courts of another Contracting State have jurisdiction as to the substance of the matter.

The effect of a Mareva injunction in another state party to the Brussels Convention is not settled. See Lawrence Collins, 'The Territorial Reach of Mareva Injunctions', (1989) 105 *Law Quarterly Rev.* 262 at 293–4, repr. in Collins, *Essays in International Litigation and the Conflict of Laws* (1994), 189.

plaintiff be a resident of the United Kingdom, as in the recent judicial modification on jurisdiction under Article 23 in Germany, and there is no necessary link between the assets placed under restraint and the plaintiff's claim.[91]

The applicant for the injunction must have a 'good arguable case', but he need not be a judgment creditor or demonstrate a high likelihood of success on the merits. Most important, third parties—typically banks but also brokers, jewelers, art dealers, or others holding assets of the defendant—will be served with copies of the injunction, and at least if they are present in England, they will be bound by it. We have not yet seen the working out of the compromise developed in the *Babanaft*, *Haiti*, and *Derby* cases, whereby the defendant is ordered not to withdraw or dispose of any assets world-wide and to make full disclosure, but the custodians outside of the United Kingdom are not liable for carrying out the defendant's withdrawal orders. In the one case with which I am familiar, the New York head office of a securities firm declined to honor payment or withdrawal orders from its client in Spain while a Mareva order against the client which had been served on its branch in London was outstanding.[92]

We have, I submit, come almost full circle from the first chapter, and arrived at a frontier where three aspects of jurisdiction meet. The Mareva injunction shows that the effort to divide jurisdiction into three separate categories—prescription, enforcement, and adjudication—is a useful starting point, but clearly not the end of analysis. I want in the last part of this Chapter to add one more element to the mix—the question of rules *v.* discretion.

E. JURISDICTION BY LEAVE OR BY RIGHT

A priori one might think that jurisdiction of courts ought to be the subject of clear rules. True, once the bases of jurisdiction move beyond defendant's domicile, particular facts may well be determinative—where was the contract concluded, where was an injury sustained, where was the obligation in question to be performed. In some instances the facts may be in controversy, and the lawyer cannot assure the litigant concerning the outcome of

[91] In *Mercedes-Benz AG* v. *Leiduck* (PC) [1995] 3 WLR 718, [1995] 3 All ER 929 24 July 1995, the Privy Council decided that a Mareva injunction is not available in support of an action pending elsewhere than in the court asked to issue the injunction, when the underlying cause of action has no connection with the forum where the injunction is sought and there is no basis for jurisdiction over the target of the injunction other than presence of his assets. The decision, on appeal from Hong Kong, seems not to disturb the *Haiti* case, n. 84 *supra*, because that case involved judicial assistance under Art. 24 of the Brussels Convention to another state party to that Convention, but that point was not clear as the present volume went to press.

[92] See n. 79 *supra*.

that controversy. But if the facts bearing on jurisdiction of the court are clear, it ought to be possible to say 'yes, the court has jurisdiction over Defendant *X* in respect of this claim', or 'if you wish to pursue that claim against Defendant *Y*, you will need to proceed in another forum'.

In theory, this is the American view, and also the view of most European countries, reflected in the Brussels Convention and in the respective civil codes or codes of civil procedure. It is not the view with respect to actions against non-residents in England and the countries following the English model.

1. The English Model

Order 11 of the Rules of the Supreme Court, promulgated in 1883 and amended several times since then, sets forth in Rule 1(1) a series of heads of jurisdiction (or to be precise, bases for permission to serve the defendant outside of the forum state), but all dependent on leave of the court. Rule 4(2) of Order 11 states that '[n]o such leave shall be granted unless it shall be made sufficiently to appear to the Court that the case is a proper one for service out of the jurisdiction under this order.[93] What does that mean?

It has long been said that if there is any doubt whether one of the stated heads of jurisdiction is applicable, the doubt is to be resolved in favor of the defendant.[94] It quite clearly does not mean that leave should be granted only in circumstances where, if the facts were reversed, an English court would recognize the judgment of a foreign court.[95] It has recently been stated in the House of Lords that the basic criterion for exercising jurisdiction pursuant to Order 11 is whether the English forum is a *forum conveniens*, i.e. whether it is the most appropriate forum for resolving the controversy before the court.[96] I am not sure the reported cases bear out these statements.

In *Coast Lines Ltd* v. *Hudig & Veder Chartering NV*,[97] for instance, an

[93] In a number of jurisdictions following the English model, including New Zealand, several states of Australia, and several provinces of Canada, prior leave to serve a non-resident defendant abroad is not generally required, but the court's discretion is nevertheless involved when the defendant moves to set aside service. For a discussion with citations, see *Kuwait Asia Bank E.C.* v. *National Mutual Life Nominees Ltd* [1990] 3 WLR 297 at 310–15, [1990] 3 NZLR 513, 524–9 (PC) (New Zealand).

[94] See Dicey and Morris, *The Conflict of Laws* (12th edn., Collins, 1993), 317; Cheshire and North, *Private International Law* (12th edn., North and Fawcett (eds), 1992), 208; and sources there cited.

[95] See Cheshire and North, 207; also the statement by Lord Reid in *Indyka* v. *Indyka* [1969] 1 AC 33 at 58: 'Comity has never been the basis on which we recognize or give effect to foreign judgments.'

[96] *Spiliada Maritime Corp.* v. *Cansulex* [1987] AC 460 at 480–2 (*per* Lord Goff of Chieveley). It seems, however, that in a case brought under Order 11, plaintiff bears the burden of persuasion, whereas in a case in which defendant seeks dismissal on grounds of *forum non conveniens*, the burden of persuasion falls on the defendant.

[97] [1972] 2 QB 34 (CA).

English shipowner, Coast Lines, had chartered its English flag vessel to a Dutch charterer, Hudig & Veder, on a voyage charter to pick up cargo in Rotterdam and carry it to Ireland. The cargo was damaged at sea, apparently due to unseaworthiness of the vessel. The shipowner admitted liability to the owner of the cargo, but sought to bring suit in England against the Dutch charterer, on the basis of a clause in the charter party (i.e., the contract between owner and charterer) relieving the owner of liability for unseaworthiness of the vessel.

Among the heads of jurisdiction set out in Order 11 is that the claim is based on a contract 'which . . . is by its terms, or by implication, governed by English law'.[98] Such a basis is, I am quite sure, not acceptable in the United States,[99] and it is not specified (and therefore impermissible) under the Brussels Convention.[100] But the United Kingdom had not yet become a party to the Brussels Convention, and it was on this basis that the English shipowner brought its action for indemnification against the Dutch charterer. The Master gave leave to 'serve out', and the High Court judge rejected the motion to set aside the service. Eventually, the case reached the Court of Appeal.

The trouble, however, was that nothing in the charter party said anything about application of English law, and the object of the contract was to carry cargo between the Netherlands and Ireland. Thus in order to uphold its jurisdiction, the court had first to find that English law governed the contract, and then to decide whether the discretion to grant leave had been properly exercised.

It turned out that the negotiations leading up to the contract had been conducted by telephone and telex between the charterer in Rotterdam and a broker acting for the shipowner in the United Kingdom. The charter party had been drawn up in Rotterdam on a standard form, and had been signed there by the charterer on behalf of both parties, with a copy mailed to the broker. The charterer had issued a bill of lading in Rotterdam.

So far nothing indicates links to England. But the ship was registered in England and the owner was English. To Lord Denning, putting these two facts into the scales on one side, the Dutch connections on the other, 'you

[98] Currently Order 11, r. 1(1)(d)(iii).

[99] See, e.g., *Hanson* v. *Denckla*, 357 U.S. 235 at 253 (1958), pointing out that while the connections of the parties and the transaction with the forum state might be sufficient to justify application of that state's law, they were not sufficient to support jurisdiction of the forum state under the Due Process clause. Whether the judgment of a foreign state based only on Order 11, r. 1(1)(d)(iii) or analogous provisions would be recognized in the United States has not been decided, so far as I know. In some instances a court in the United States might conclude, e.g., that defendant had sufficiently engaged in business in the forum state so that that state's exercise of jurisdiction did not violate U.S. standards of due process, although the specific basis for the assertion of jurisdiction was not within those standards. See, e.g., *Bank of Montreal* v. *Kough*, 430 F.Supp. 1243 (N.D.Cal. 1977), affirmed, 612 F.2d 467 (9th Cir. 1980).

[100] See n. 15 *supra*.

find they are equal . . . So as a last resort, you take the law of the flag, which is English law.'[101] But to decide on this basis not only the 'proper law', in the English formulation, but also the jurisdiction of the English court is pretty thin. The law of the flag, in fact, was not Lord Denning's last resort. Plaintiff contended that if it were required to litigate in the Netherlands, the Dutch court would be required to apply the Hague Rules, and these would overcome a stipulation whereby a shipowner is exonerated from liability for unseaworthiness; under English law, in contrast, the exoneration clause would be given effect, because the Hague Rules do not apply to charter parties. 'That', Lord Denning says, 'I think is important.'

> In the maritime law of this country—and I believe of all other maritime countries—it is an accepted principle that a contract is, if possible, to be construed so as to make it valid rather than invalid . . . A stipulation must be construed *ut res magis valeat quam pereat*. Applying [the maxim] here, the exemption clause in the charterparty is valid by English law, but invalid by Netherlands law. This is a pointer to English law as the proper law of the contract.[102]

With all respect, I find this reasoning unpersuasive. I had always thought that the principle of validation expressed in the Latin maxim had to do with the formation of contracts, not with the question of whether particular clauses in a contract will be honored—particularly an exoneration clause.[103] Lord Denning and his colleagues bolster their argument by asserting that they might not grant leave to serve out of the jurisdiction if Netherlands courts were free to make an independent choice of the proper law: since those courts are constrained by a statutory command to apply the Hague Rules, a law which (with respect to charter parties) 'is contrary to the general understanding of commercial men, . . . I do not think we should send the English owners to the Netherlands courts.'[104] Interestingly enough, Lord Denning says he knows that if the charterer defaults, the judgment of the English court will not be enforceable in the Dutch courts.[105] That is not his problem, however.

It seems to me that this case is wrongly decided, and draws into question the proposition stated by Dicey and others[106] that in doubtful cases the decision should be against the exercise of judicial jurisdiction. Moreover, I think nothing is gained by the kind of statement made by Lord Justice Stephenson, concurring in *Coast Lines*, that though he is tempted to say that the court's discretion to grant leave ought to be exercised only in plain

[101] [1972] 2 QB at 44.

[102] *Ibid.*

[103] See, e.g., Albert Ehrenzweig, 'Contracts in the Conflict of Laws', 59 *Colum. L. Rev.* 973, 992–5 (1959); Ole Lando, 'The Conflict of Laws of Contracts: General Principles', 189 *Recueil des Cours* 225 at 392 (1984–VI).

[104] [1972] 2 QB at 45. The same point is made by Megaw, LJ at 48–9.

[105] *Id.* 45.

[106] See text at n. 93 *supra*.

cases, 'these temptations ought to be resisted', because the discretion exercised by the lower court in accordance with Order 11 'is unfettered except by comity, convenience and the justice of the case'.[107]

In suggesting that the *Coast Lines* case was wrongly decided, I am not suggesting that there should be no discretionary element in determining the jurisdiction of courts. I do suggest, however, that the kind of discretion exercised in determining whether a case belongs in a given forum is not the kind of discretion that depends on the trial court's assessment of the demeanor of the parties or witnesses, or of the circumstances surrounding the litigation. When an appeals court concludes with a statement that 'in any event we should not overturn the exercise of discretion by the lower court', I suspect it has run out of arguments.

A more attractive example of working within Order 11 was *Mackender* v. *Feldia AG*,[108] decided by the Court of Appeal a few years before *Coast Lines*. A Lloyd's insurance syndicate had issued a policy to three affiliated European dealers in diamonds and other precious stones. The contract was made in London, thus satisfying one of the stated bases for jurisdiction under Order 11, but the policy contained a clause designating the courts of Belgium as the exclusive forum, and stating that it was governed by Belgian law. One of the insured's representatives was robbed in Naples, and the diamond dealers claimed under the policy. The Lloyd's underwriters rejected the claim on the basis that the diamond dealers made a practice of smuggling gems into Italy. The underwriters claimed that if this fact had been disclosed they would not have issued the policy, and they sought a declaration of non-liability from the English court, on the ground that the contract, including the forum selection clause, was void for illegality.

One High Court judge granted leave *ex parte* to serve out, and a second High Court judge, after an *inter partes* hearing, affirmed that decision. The Court of Appeal, however, reversed. Whatever are the facts of the case and the ultimate validity of the contract, Lord Denning said, the forum selection clause 'still stands, and is a strong ground why discretion should be exercised against leave to serve out of the jurisdiction'.[109]

To the argument that the Court of Appeal should not interfere with the exercise of discretion by the two High Court judges, Lord Justice Diplock (as we then was) pointed out that the issues in question were issues of law—whether the forum selection clause covered the matter in controversy and whether the defense of illegality would be cognizable by the Belgian courts. Having decided that the judge had been wrong on both points,

107 [1972] 2 QB at 51.
108 [1967] 1 WLR 619 (CA).
109 [1967] 2 QB at 598, [1967] 2 WLR at 123.

'[t]hat entitles us in this court to exercise our discretion *de novo* unfettered by the way in which the judge exercised his'.[110]

I want to mention briefly one more English case, and then focus on an important recent decision of the United States Supreme Court. The English case, *Roneleigh Ltd* v. *MII Exports Inc.*,[111] arose out of a sale of scrap steel by a New Jersey corporation f.o.b. New York to an English company, for shipment to Turkey.[112] Plaintiff, the English buyer, alleged that the steel did not meet the contract specifications, and applied to the master for leave to serve the defendant at its headquarters in New Jersey. The master granted leave under Order 11, rule 1(1)(d)(i), i.e. on the basis that the contract had been made in England, and defendant was served at its headquarters in New Jersey. When the application to set aside was refused, defendant appealed to the judge, pointing out that it had no connection with the United Kingdom other than doing business with an English customer. The judge thought the question where this case should be tried was closely balanced:

> With one qualification I have come to the conclusion that this is a case where the proceedings should be stayed because on the whole it is more appropriate that they should be litigated in the defendant's jurisdiction than in the plaintiff's courts.
>
> But the one qualification is this: it is common ground that if the plaintiff is successful in New Jersey, he will have to pay all his own costs. The claim is for about $250,000. I take the view that this is a case where the plaintiff would be placed at a substantial personal or juridical disadvantage in litigating in New Jersey by reference to the costs.

Accordingly, the judge announced that he would stay the action in England if the defendant would give an undertaking to pay plaintiff's costs of proceeding in New Jersey in accordance with English practice, so that if plaintiff prevailed defendant would pay plaintiff's legal fees rather than plaintiff having to pay a contingent fee to its lawyer based on a percentage of the award. Defendant refused to give the undertaking, and so the master's order was upheld.

The American defendant appealed to the Court of Appeal from the order upholding service out of the jurisdiction, and plaintiff argued that the condition proposed by the judge was an improper exercise of discretion, since it took into account something that should not be taken into account. Lord Justice Nourse, in the Court of Appeal, said:

[110] [1967] 2 QB at 604, [1967] 2 WLR at 128.

[111] [1989] 1 WLR 619 (CA).

[112] Under an f.o.b. port of export contract, seller is obligated to load the goods on board a ship designated by buyer, with payment of the freight for the account of buyer. Title passes to buyer either when the goods are loaded or at the latest when the bill of lading is tendered to buyer or buyer's agent.

I do not think that it is open to this court to say that [the judge] was not entitled to conclude . . . both that the costs advantage from litigating here was made out and that it ought to tip the balance against proceedings in New Jersey.[113]

Lord Justice Butler-Sloss had doubts about taking litigation costs into account, and thought that the proposal for the undertaking on costs was inappropriate:

I would not like to suggest that, where other factors are clearly in favor of the case going to one of the American jurisdictions, the cost factor should be determinative. But there were other factors in this case in favor of the plaintiff [concerning the travel of witnesses from Turkey and from England to the United States] . . . I for my part cannot say that the judge was plainly wrong.[114]

Either way, the case remained in England.

I have doubts about this case too. Is the English rule on legal fees so superior as to tip the scales in favor of retaining jurisdiction in a case that really belongs somewhere else?[115] Note again that this head of jurisdiction depends on a legal determination—where the contract was made—that may not be obvious,[116] and note also that this basis for jurisdiction is excluded by the Brussels Convention, which provides for special jurisdiction in suits arising out of a contract only at the place of performance.[117] At all events, I do not think that this case, any more than the ship charter case, justifies deference to the lower court judge who upholds his own jurisdiction.[118]

[113] [1989] 1 WLR at 624.

[114] *Id.* 624–5.

[115] It is ironic that here plaintiff prefers the English 'loser pays' rule, rather than the American rule under which each party pays its own lawyer and plaintiffs may (not must) make a contingent fee arrangement. I had always believed that the English rule favored defendants, while the American rule favored plaintiffs; apparently this plaintiff was very confident that it would prevail.

[116] The report of the case makes no mention of how the conclusion was reached that the contract was made in England. One cannot tell whether the conclusion was based on the fact that negotiations were conducted in England, or was based on the 'mailbox rule'—contract effective upon *dispatch* of acceptance—see *Adams* v. *Lindsell*, 1 B. & Ald. 681, 106 ER 250 (KB, 1818), or alternatively, on the place of *receipt* of a telex, see *Entores Ltd* v. *Miles Far East Corporation* n. 8 *supra*.

[117] Brussels Convention, Art. 5(1). For explanation of why the place of contracting was rejected as a permissible forum by the drafters of the Convention, see n. 22 *supra*, summarizing the Jenard Report on this point.

[118] For the most recent discussion of the elements of discretion under Order 11, see *Seaconsar Far East Ltd* v. *Bank Markazi Jomhouri Islami Iran* [1994] 1 AC 438, [1993] 3 WLR 756 (HL(E)). In a long speech by Lord Goff of Chieveley, the House of Lords rejects the idea put forward in several earlier cases that the stronger the claim on the merits, the weaker need be the connections with the forum and vice versa; the House also rejects the proposition that plaintiff must establish a 'good arguable case' in order to obtain leave to serve out, in favor of a standard that there is a serious issue to be tried. Interestingly enough, the House also rejects as a significant factor the pendency in England of related litigation between the same parties.

2. The American Model

It is appropriate to conclude this discussion with the second important case to come before the United States Supreme Court involving jurisdiction of an American court over a foreign country defendant, *Asahi Metal Industry Co.* v. *Superior Court*.[119] I had a small, but perhaps not insignificant, part in this case as counsel to two British trade associations who submitted a brief as *amicus curiae*.

The case arose out of a motorcycle accident on a highway in California. The original plaintiff was a Mr Gary Zurcher, who was riding on a Honda motorcycle with his wife when he lost control of his machine and crashed into a tractor. Mr Zurcher was severely injured and his wife was killed in the accident. Mr Zurcher alleged that the accident was caused by a sudden loss of air and an explosion in the rear tire of the motorcycle, and he brought suit in state court in California against various defendants, including Dunlop, which had manufactured the tire; Honda, which had manufactured the motorcycle; and Cheng Shin, a Taiwanese company that had manufactured the inner tube. Cheng Shin in turn filed a 'cross complaint', seeking indemnification from its co-defendants and from Asahi Metal Industry Co., a Japanese company that had supplied valve assemblies for installation on Cheng Shin's tubes. Asahi was served with process in Japan via the Hague Service Convention.[120]

Asahi did not challenge the manner of service, but it moved to quash the service on the ground that it was not subject to the jurisdiction of the California court. Asahi said that it had no offices, property, or agents in California, solicited no business, made no sales, did not advertise or maintain spare parts in California, in short that it had done nothing to subject itself to the jurisdiction of the California courts. Cheng Shin replied that Asahi has 'purposefully availed itself of the benefits' of California law,[121] by regularly supplying valves to Cheng Shin, knowing that the latter was selling tubes containing the valves to California.

Unlike *Helicopteros*, the assertion here was of *specific jurisdiction*—i.e. that Asahi had made the valve involved in the accident. As in *Helicopteros*, the various levels of the state court were divided. The court of first instance rejected the challenge to jurisdiction, the Court of Appeal sustained the challenge, and the Supreme Court of California reversed, i.e. it reinstated the action. Meanwhile, Mr Zurcher, who never claimed against

[119] 480 U.S. 102 (1987).

[120] Convention on the Service Abroad of Judicial and Extrajudicial Documents in Civil or Commercial Matters, signed at The Hague, Nov. 15, 1965, 20 U.S.T. 361, 658 U.N.T.S. 163.

[121] The quotation comes from *Hanson* v. *Denckla*, 357 U.S. 235 at 251 (1958), a case holding that Delaware trust companies could not be subjected to the jurisdiction of the courts of Florida, where the settlor and beneficiary of Delaware trusts was domiciled.

Asahi, had settled with Cheng Shin and the other defendants. Thus what was left was Cheng Shin's claim for indemnity or contribution against Asahi. The California Supreme Court said the dismissal of Mr Zurcher from the suit had 'no bearing on the propriety of California's exercise of jurisdiction over Asahi'.[122]

When I first learned about this case after the U.S. Supreme Court granted review, I wondered about that remark. Was it really correct that, for purposes of jurisdiction over the Japanese maker of a sub-sub-component,[123] it did not matter whether the adversary was another foreign party in the production chain or an injured and bereaved citizen of the forum state? That did not seem reasonable to me, and therefore (since by then I was well along in the work on the *Restatement*) it did not seem right.[124]

Moreover, reading the decisions of the various California courts plus the first round of submissions to the U.S. Supreme Court, it occurred to me that all the discussion was in terms of the previous decisions of the U.S. Supreme Court, with no attention to the international law aspect of the case.[125] Judging by the briefs, the case might as well have involved a tube manufacturer in Oregon and a valve manufacturer in Idaho, rather than a dispute between a Taiwanese and a Japanese company. That, too, did not seem right to me, though it was probably consistent with American doctrine, which for purposes of judicial jurisdiction, usually treated states of the Union as if they were independent sovereigns.

Third, and most pertinent to our present discussion, the California courts had treated the *Asahi* case under the traditional American doctrine that there either is jurisdiction over a defendant or there is not—the light switch is either on or off. That doctrine had been modified to a significant extent with the recognition of specific or activity-based jurisdiction, but where, as here, the claim could be clearly stated to arise out of an injury in the forum state, the light switch analogy held. Either the defendant had reached a level of minimum contacts with the forum by participating in the stream of commerce and thus 'purposefully availing itself' of the benefits of the law of the forum, or it had not. Perhaps because I had become familiar with the more flexible English approach, I thought the light switch

[122] *Asahi Metal Industry Co. Ltd* v. *The Superior Court of Solano County*, 39 Cal.3d 35 at 52, n. 9; 702 P.2d 543 at 552; 216 Cal. Rptr. 385 at 395 (1985).

[123] Valve for tube for tire for motorcycle.

[124] See *Restatement (Third) of the Foreign Relations Law of the United States (1987)*, § 421(1):

> A state may exercise jurisdiction through its courts to adjudicate with respect to a person or thing if the relationship of the state to the person or thing is such as to make the exercise of jurisdiction reasonable.

The formulation borrows from the *Restatement (Second) of Conflict of Laws* (1971), §§ 24 and 56, which in turn was based on *International Shoe Co.* v. *State of Washington*, 326 U.S. 310 at 319–20 (1945).

[125] Compare the observation of F. A. Mann, quoted in n. 26 *supra*.

was the wrong analogy; perhaps the house lights in a theater, which can be slowly made dimmer or brighter, would be a more suitable metaphor.

My associates and I raised these points in our *amicus curiae* brief, I believe to good effect, though I must confess that not all of my American academic colleagues agreed.[126]

In the Supreme Court there was a four–four split on whether Asahi had entered the 'stream of commerce' sufficiently to subject itself to the jurisdiction of the California court.[127] But eight of the nine Justices saw that the case was not about Oregon and Idaho. Justice O'Connor, writing for the Court, said:

> Certainly the burden on the defendant in this case is severe. Asahi has been commanded by the Supreme Court of California not only to traverse the distance between Asahi's headquarters in Japan and the Superior Court of California in and for the County of Solano, but also to submit its dispute with Cheng Shin to a foreign nation's judicial system. The unique burdens placed upon one who must defend oneself in a foreign legal system should have significant weight in assessing the reasonableness of stretching the long arm of personal jurisdiction over national borders . . .
>
> The procedural and substantive interests of other nations in a state court's assertion of jurisdiction over an alien defendant will differ from case to case. In every case, however, those interests, as well as the Federal Government's interest in its foreign relations policies, will be best served by a careful inquiry into the reasonableness of the assertion of jurisdiction in the particular case.[128]

Further, the assertion of the California Supreme Court that the state had an interest in protecting its consumers by ensuring that foreign manufacturers comply with the state's safety standards was unpersuasive, because the dispute before it had nothing to do with compensation for the injured California plaintiff:

> The dispute between Cheng Shin and Asahi is primarily about indemnification rather than safety standards. Moreover, it is not at all clear at this point that California law should govern the question whether a Japanese corporation should indemnify a Taiwanese corporation on the basis of a sale made in Taiwan and a shipment of goods from Japan to Taiwan.[129]

[126] See, e.g., the articles by Burbank and Silberman cited at n. 20 *supra*.

[127] The ninth Member of the Court, Justice Stevens, preferred not to decide a point that was not necessary to the Court's decision.

[128] 480 U.S. at 114, 115.

[129] *Id.* 114. Only Justice Scalia, who thought that Asahi had not had the required minimum contacts with the forum state, declined to join this section of the opinion; he gave no reason, but other opinions of his, notably in the later domestic case of *Burnham* v. *Superior Court of California*, 495 U.S. 604 (1990), which sustained jurisdiction on the basis of service on a defendant temporarily present in the forum state, suggest that he was uncomfortable with a reasonableness standard that took into account the factors set out in Justice O'Connor's opinion for the court.

It remains to be seen whether the decision in *Burnham* will be applied if the person served

The inference, I believe, is that if for some reason, Mr Zurcher needed Asahi in the law suit—for instance if no settlement had been reached and Asahi's evidence was required, or if Cheng Shin had become bankrupt—the case might have come out the other way. As it stood, however, considering the international context, the heavy burden on the alien defendant, and the slight interests of the plaintiff and the forum State, the exercise of personal jurisdiction by a California court over Asahi in this instance would be unreasonable and unfair.[130]

I believe the decision by the U.S. Supreme Court in the *Asahi* case is correct, and I think it can serve to introduce an overall summary of the discussion of judicial jurisdiction in the international arena.

F. SUMMARY: JUDICIAL JURISDICTION AND REASONABLENESS

I think the attempt to establish rigid rules for the exercise of judicial jurisdiction is doomed to fail, as it fails for the exercise of jurisdiction to prescribe. But, as with jurisdiction to prescribe, I believe that a consensus is emerging about the relevant criteria, so that courts can exercise judgment acceptable by their own states' standards and by those of the international community. I believe the cause of action matters, the alternate *fora* matter, the reasonable expectations of the parties matter, the layers in a product liability suit between the defendant and the end-product matter. Thus I believe that it was correct for the Japanese court to assume jurisdiction over *Malaysian Airlines* in the suit by the Japanese widow, but it would not have been appropriate for that court to assume jurisdiction in a suit by an insurance company that had insured cargo damaged during the flight from Penang to Kuala Lumpur. The *Helicopteros* case is somewhat harder, but I would have sustained jurisdiction in the action brought by the widows, because I think it would not be unreasonable to aggregate all of the defendant's activities in the United States, and I think that the suit by the widows is sufficiently related to those activities to make it reasonable for the helicopter company to defend their claim in the United States.[131] Likewise, while I agree with so much of the U.S. Supreme Court's decision in *Shaffer*

while temporarily present in the forum state is domiciled in a foreign country. For the position, with which I agree, that exercise of 'tag jurisdiction' over foreign country defendants is unreasonable, and 'simply exorbitant', see Peter Hay, 'Transient Jurisdiction, Especially Over International Defendants: Critical Comments on *Burnham* v. *Superior Court of California*', 1990 *U. Ill. L. Rev*. 593, 601–3.

[130] 480 U.S. at 116.

[131] My friend and colleague, Professor Silberman, criticizing the result in *Asahi*, suggested that 'assertions of jurisdiction may be invited on subjective notions even in the absence of minimum contacts': Silberman, n. 20 *supra*, 22 *Rutgers L.J.* at 581. Without conceding her point that such an outcome 'is certain to cause mischief', my response with reference to *Helicopteros*

v. *Heitner* as rejects jurisdiction on the basis solely of the presence of property in the forum state, I think it not unreasonable to require the directors of a company organized under the laws of the forum state to answer in that state for their official actions. I am pleased that the German Supreme Court has begun to limit jurisdiction based solely on the presence of defendant's property in the forum state; when jurisdiction under ZPO Article 23 comes before that court again, I would hope that the court takes the next step and asks whether assumption of jurisdiction is reasonable even if plaintiff is domiciled in Germany or the action can be said to have arisen in that country. I like the English formulation requiring the court to ask itself whether the particular case is a proper one for exercise of its jurisdiction, but I am not wholly comfortable with the attention of the English courts at the jurisdiction stage to the merits of the case, or with the link between jurisdiction under Order 11 and Mareva injunctions.[132] I think the Brussels Convention, while correct in the catalogue of jurisdictional bases it condemns in Article 3, is somewhat too limited in the bases of jurisdiction that it expressly permits. I think there is often justification for general jurisdiction, and also for certain other bases that are not expressly condemned but not permitted, such as jurisdiction on the basis of the place of making of a contract.

I realize that in supporting discretion and reasonableness, I seem to be inviting litigation about litigation. So far as I can see, however, litigation about judicial jurisdiction has been a favorite indoor sport in all states. Even if the questions here discussed do not lead to international incidents or diplomatic protests, I am pleased that the rôle of international law is increasingly acknowledged by courts in deciding cases of this kind. Once again I reject the sharp distinction between public and private international law, and content myself with defining international law as a set of standards to which states adhere or ought to adhere.

is that the criterion of reasonableness leads to aggregation of contacts within the [United States] forum, so that the minimum level is achieved and Professor Silberman's anxiety is, at least in that case, not justified.

[132] Thus an initial leave to serve out, granted under Order 11, can support a Mareva injunction; even if the defendant prevails on a motion to set aside service, plaintiff can appeal that decision, meanwhile maintaining the world-wide freeze on defendant's assets.

5

National Jurisdiction and the Multinational Enterprise*

I want in this Chapter to focus on the special case of the multinational corporation as the object of both of the subjects that we have been discussing thus far—jurisdiction to prescribe and jurisdiction to adjudicate. In many ways the multinational enterprise has been the dominant institution in the international economy, at least since World War I. Yet, to a surprising degree, the law has not kept up with reality. While there is an enormous body of legislation, judge-made law, and commentary in all the industrial states concerning the governance of corporations, nearly all such law was developed in a private law context, before the wave of regulation, taxation, labor law, environmental controls, and other forms of governmental intervention familiar today; moreover, nearly all such law was developed with a view to a single firm operating out of a single state, owned by shareholders who might or might not also be managers but were not other corporations. The modern multi-layered, multinational enterprise, in which dozens or even hundreds of firms are linked through common ownership or control, has not been the focus of company law in any state. The question that I want to address here is the extent to which responsibility—substantive and procedural—can or should be attributed to multinational enterprises for obligations of member companies under national laws.

Ideally, the answer to this question would be decided uniformly in all states. There is no such uniform law, and it may be premature to speak even of an emerging consensus. Nevertheless, I believe some instructive precedents can be presented, and some useful suggestions can be made, both concerning substantive principles of law and concerning the source of law to be applied when the parent corporation is established in one state and the subsidiary or the obligation in question is centered in another state. Once again, we find ourselves in the gray area between public and private international law.

* Some of the material in this chapter is drawn from the present author's Report on behalf of the Fifteenth Commission of the Institut de Droit International, 66th Session, Milan, 1993, published in Vol. 65–I *Annuaire de l'Institut de Droit*, 191–326 (1993). The conclusions here expressed, however, are only those of the author, and not necessarily those of the Institut.

A. THE MULTINATIONAL ENTERPRISE

The typical multinational corporation is well known. It comprises a group of companies operating under common ownership or control, usually (though not always) for a common purpose or in related economic sectors, usually (though again not always) employing a common trade mark or trade name, sometimes with local variations. The names of the important multinational corporations are known the world over—Shell and Exxon (Esso), Nestlé and Philip Morris, General Electric and Siemens, Mercedes-Benz and Ford, Fiat and General Motors, Mitsubishi and Mitsui, Philips and Unilever, and so on. The leading American scholar on the subject, Dean Phillip Blumberg, reports that in 1982, the 1,000 largest American industrial corporations had an average of forty-eight subsidiaries each. Mobil Oil Corporation, perhaps an extreme example, operated in sixty-two different countries through 525 subsidiaries. British Petroleum operated through more than 1,000 subsidiaries, and Unilever (British/Dutch) through more than 800. Nestlé, based in Switzerland, operated in more than sixty countries with 600 subsidiaries.[1]

In some instances the subsidiaries conduct truly separate businesses, and outsiders may not even know that they belong to a particular group; in most instances, however, the subsidiary is a part of an integrated activity conducted under direction of common management. Usually the parent company is identified with a single country—Siemens with Germany, Philips with the Netherlands, Ford with the United States, and so on; in some instances, notably Royal Dutch/Shell and Unilever, the top of the pyramid is located in more than one country. It is no longer as typical as it was formerly that top management will come from the same country, or even share the same mother tongue. In some multinational corporations, management is rotated among the members of the group, and a member of the parent company's board of directors sits on the board of important subsidiaries; in other multinational corporations, senior management and boards of directors of subsidiaries are kept separate. The one defining element of a multinational enterprise is that the investing public relates to the large group of companies—through shares purchased and sold, capital contributed and dividends received, management supported or replaced—at one level only, i.e. at the level of the parent company. All the other relationships among members of group, even though they may cross frontiers and time zones and language changes, are essentially internal, within the enterprise as a whole.[2]

[1] Phillip I. Blumberg, *The Law of Corporate Groups*, iv, p. xli (1989). See also, e.g., Hadden, 'Inside Corporate Groups' (1984) 12 *J. Soc. L.* 271, reporting on a study of five large corporate groups with headquarters in Great Britain.

[2] Compare the following description by Chief Justice Warren Burger, speaking for the U.S.

B. A BRIEF DOSE OF THEORY

More than twenty years ago in a pioneering article, Professor Detlev Vagts wrote that 'the present legal framework has no comfortable, tidy receptacle for [the multinational enterprise]'.[3] That conclusion is still true, notwithstanding a vast amount of thinking about the multinational enterprise—in the United Nations, in the Organization for Economic Co-operation and Development, in the European Community, and in academic and professional circles around the world. The question remains whether, for legal (as contrasted with economic) purposes, a multinational enterprise is simply an aggregation of corporations organized under the laws of various states, or whether a multinational enterprise may or should in some circumstances be treated as having distinct legal characteristics.

1. The Corporate Entity Theory

The conceptual basis of the modern business corporation is deceptively simple. Whether created pursuant to a grant from the sovereign or by a contract among the organizers registered with a public authority, a business corporation is in all states a juridical person. Accordingly, it is entitled to hold property, to enter into contracts, to sue and be sued, to enjoy rights and be subject to duties, and to engage in such activities as are covered by its foundation document and not prohibited by law. The rules for management of corporations and for relations among shareholders, officers, directors, and supervisory authorities differ in detail from state to state.[4] But under the law of virtually all countries, corporations organized for commercial purposes are aggregations of capital represented by shares of stock which can be freely transferred and traded, and the corporation may—so long as it remains solvent—continue in existence without limit of time.

The assets of a corporations are separate from those of its shareholders, and the shareholders are not liable for the obligations of the corporation

Supreme Court, in a case raising the question whether a parent and its subsidiary could conspire together in violation of U.S. antitrust laws:

> A parent and its wholly owned subsidiary have a complete unity of interest. Their objectives are common, not disparate; their general corporate actions are guided or determined not by two separate corporate consciousness, but one. They are not unlike a multiple team of horses drawing a vehicle under the control of a single driver.

Copperweld Corp. v. *Independence Tube Corp.*, 467 U.S. 752 at 771 (1984).

[3] Vagts, 'The Multinational Enterprise: A New Challenge for Transnational Law', 83 *Harvard L. Rev.* 739, 740 (1970).

[4] For instance some states permit and others prohibit bearer shares; some states provide for a single board of directors and others prescribe a two-tiered structure of supervision (*Vorstand* and *Aufsichtsrat*); and some states have active regulatory commissions that require periodic reports while other states provide for only minimal regulation so long as a corporation remains solvent.

beyond the capital that they have contributed (or agreed to contribute) through purchases of shares. The key question is whether a given firm or association is or is not incorporated. If it is not—for example if it is a 'branch' of another corporation—its beneficial owners may be held liable for its debts. If it is, then it has a separate legal identity, and all the attributes of corporate existence, including limited liability. As stated by the British House of Lords in the famous *Salomon* case,[5] in which creditors of what was essentially a one-person company sought to pursue their claims against the owner of 20,001 of the 20,007 shares, '[e]ither the limited company was a legal entity or it was not. If it was, the business belonged to it and not to Mr. Salomon . . . [I]t is impossible to say at the same time that there is a company and there is not.[6]

Of course it is well understood today that the original description of a corporation as an association of a number of persons for a common object no longer fits the reality of industrial or financial corporations, in that the typical public shareholder, though in theory a member of the corporation, is in economic reality a mere supplier of capital on which he hopes for a return, without any effective control over the corporation itself.[7] On the other hand, the passive investor can normally divest himself of relationship with the corporation by the simple act of selling his shares, without thereby removing any capital from the corporation.

The separation between the shareholders and managers strengthens the case for limiting the liability of the investor/shareholder, for it would be unfair to charge a shareholder with liability for an obligation incurred by the corporation wholly beyond his or her control. Moreover, as raising capital from the public through sale of shares depends to a significant extent on the transferability of the shares, any potential risk for subsequent purchasers beyond the cost of their investment might well impair the marketability of shares and even the functioning of stock exchanges. Thus the theory of the corporation as a self-contained legal entity and the concept of limited liability for shareholders fit together well with the objective of encouraging economic activity by facilitating the mobilization of capital—the original stated purpose of the law of corporations.

The immunity of shareholders from liability for obligations of corporations has not, of course, been absolute. It is understood in most countries that, when the corporate form is used to defraud third parties or when the corporation in question is a 'mere *alter ego*' or 'puppet' of another person or firm, with no independent decision-making authority in its nominal

[5] *Salomon* v. *A. Salomon & Co. Ltd* [1897] AC 22 (HL(E)).

[6] *Id.* at 31 (*per* Halsbury LC).

[7] See, e.g., L. C. B. Gower *et al.*, *Principles of Modern Company Law* (4th edn., 1979), 9–10. Gower in turn points to the pathbreaking American book by A. A. Berle and G. C. Means, *The Modern Corporation and Private Property* (1933).

managers, the corporate form may be disregarded and liability may be imposed on the shareholder.[8] But disregard of the corporate form usually depends on a finding of fraud or abuse, and ultimately on a conclusion that the corporation in question is not entitled to the protection of the form of doing business that it has chosen. Such cases are not a rejection of the entity theory of the corporation, though in many instances they illustrate unhappiness with that theory on the part of courts.

2. The Corporate Enterprise Theory

It is evident that the theory of the corporate entity, and the description of the typical passive investor/shareholder does not fit the corporate group or multi-tiered enterprise. Whether the group of related corporations is confined to a single state or, as is common, the separate subsidiaries reflect not only different functions within the enterprise but also different areas of operation, it is quite unrealistic to describe the subsidiary corporation as a self-contained entity, to think of the investor/shareholder as a member of the general public, or to be concerned about the marketability of the subsidiary's shares on a stock exchange. An emerging doctrine, not yet fully articulated or universally accepted, rejects the narrow focus on individual corporate entities. Instead it focuses on the enterprise as a whole with respect to at least some of the many aspects of the legal relations among parent and subsidiary corporations and of the relations of units of the enterprise with non-members, public and private.[9] As Blumberg writes in the General Introduction to his multi-volume work on *The Law of Corporate Groups*:[10]

> this change reflects a growing unwillingness on the part of courts and legislatures to continue to accept the traditional view of the law of the corporation when it no

[8] See, e.g., *Int'l Encyclopedia of Comparative Law*, xiii, ch. 3, Part IV, 'The Corporate Entity and Its Disregard' (Buxbaum); also L. C. B. Gower *et al.*, *Principles of Modern Company Law* (4th edn., 1979), ch. 6 'Lifting the Veil'; Phillip I. Blumberg, *The Law of Corporate Groups: Substantive Law* (1987), Part II, 'The Limits of Limited Liability'; Cohn and Simitis, '"Lifting the Veil" in the Company Laws of the European Continent' (1963) 12 *Int'l & Comp. LQ* 189; Dobson, '"Lifting the Veil" in Four Countries: The Law of Argentina, England, France and the United States' (1986) 35 *Int'l & Comp. LQ* 839.

[9] The only state that has adopted the enterprise doctrine ('Konzernrecht') by statute appears to be the Federal Republic of Germany, in the Aktiengesetz 1965, §§ 15–22, 291–338. A draft along similar lines was introduced into the French National Assembly in 1978 and widely discussed—the so-called 'Proposition Cousté', Projet de loi (Assemblée Nationale) No. 236, May 17, 1978, repr. in K. Haupt (ed.), *Groups of Companies in European Laws* (1982) ii, 296. The Advance Draft of a Ninth Council Directive concerning Groups of Companies, EC Doc. XI/593/75, first released in 1975 and now apparently postponed indefinitely, would build on the concept of corporate enterprise as a whole. See, generally, Immenga, 'Abhängige Unternehmen und Konzerne im Europäischen Gemeinschaftsrecht' (1984) 48 Rabels Zeitschrift für Ausländisches und Internationales Privatrecht 48.

[10] N. 1 *supra*. The introduction is repeated (with small variations) in each of the five volumes making up this work. The quotation here is taken from the 1987 volume on *Substantive Law*, pp. xxxiv, xxxvi.

longer corresponds to the reality of the modern business enterprise in a complex industrialized international society. Where constituent corporations of a group are collectively conducting a single business of an integrated enterprise, . . . particularly where issues of substantive liability are not involved,[11] entity law is in the process of collapse. Where, however, substantive liability is at stake and the traditional conceptual view of the separate legal personality of the corporation is strengthened by the principle of limited liability of shareholders, as in cases involving the attempted imposition on one affiliate of a corporate group of liability for the torts or contracts of another affiliate of the group, entity law still retains much of its vigor . . .

Such concern with limited liability greatly strengthens judicial respect for the separate personality of each corporate entity, and judicial disregard of entity occurs only in exceptional circumstances. The occasions for the exceptional disregard of entity typically have been determined on a case-by-case basis, yielding hundreds of irreconcilable decisions and constituting the much criticized jurisprudence of 'piercing the corporate veil.' Wreathed in metaphor, 'piercing the corporate veil' fails to provide a workable framework for analysis, but still largely prevails.[12]

C. CHOOSING BETWEEN ENTITY AND ENTERPRISE: SOME ILLUSTRATIONS

I do not believe that it is necessary to choose for all purposes between the entity theory and the enterprise theory. I do believe, however, that an appreciation of the enterprise theory and acceptance of its consequences by the international community in suitable circumstances can contribute to a desirable *rapprochement* between the perceptions of the general public and the solutions of the legal system, and, not infrequently, to the overall goal of fairness and justice. The question, of course, is what circumstances are suitable.

Once again, I want to present some examples.

1. Oil Spill in the English Channel: The *Amoco Cadiz*[13]

In the evening of March 16, 1978, the M/V *Amoco Cadiz*, a VLCC ('very large crude carrier') bound fully laden from the Persian Gulf to Rotterdam,

[11] For instance in matters of civil procedure, rights in bankruptcy, and application of national regulatory programs.

[12] '*Piercing* the corporate veil' is the American formulation; '*lifting*' is the more common English usage. Professor Gower suggests that, etymologically, 'mask' might have been a better metaphor than 'veil', since 'persona' is derived from the name for a mask worn by a player in the Greek theater: Gower, n. 7 *supra*, at 112, n. 1.

[13] This account is based largely on the opinion of the U.S. District Court in *In re Oil Spill by the Amoco Cadiz off the Coast of France on March 16, 1978*, 1984 A.M.C. 2123 (N.D. Ill. 1984); and Bartlett, 'In re Oil Spill by the Amoco Cadiz—Choice of Law and a Pierced Corporate Veil Defeat the 1969 Civil Liability Convention', 10 *The Maritime Lawyer* 1 (1985).

ran aground in French territorial waters off the coast of Britanny, some twelve hours after her steering gear failed in a heavy storm. The members of the crew were rescued by helicopter. The ship itself could not be saved, however: its hull ripped open and the vessel broke in two, spilling its entire cargo of about 1.6 million barrels of oil over about 215 kilometers of the northwest coast of France.

It did not take long for the injured parties, including coastal property owners, municipalities, and the French Republic (as well as the insurers of the cargo) to file claims arising out of the oil spill, alleging negligent operation as well as faulty design of the supertanker.[14] Nor was there much doubt that someone would be liable for the damage done. The questions were who would be liable, whether various regimes limiting liability would be applicable, and whether the party found liable would have the resources to pay such claims as were allowed.

The *Amoco Cadiz* was a Liberian flag ship with Monrovia as its home port, though there is no showing that she had ever called at that port. The registered owner was Amoco Transport Co., a Liberian corporation with its principal place of business in Hamilton, Bermuda, which had purchased the ship from Amoco Tankers Company, another Liberian company. Amoco Tankers had contracted for construction of the ship with Astilleros Españoles, SA, a Spanish corporation with its principal place of business in Madrid and its shipyard in Cadiz.[15] Both Transport and Tankers were wholly-owned subsidiaries (through intermediate companies) of the Standard Oil Company (Indiana), a corporation organized under the laws of Indiana that had its principal place of business—i.e. group headquarters—in Chicago, Illinois. Still another subsidiary of Standard of Indiana, Amoco International Oil Company ('AIOC'), a corporation organized under the laws of Delaware with its principal office in Chicago, had actually proposed the purchase of the *Amoco Cadiz*, and had worked with Astilleros on the design, construction, and maintenance of the *Amoco Cadiz* and her sister ships. AIOC was in fact the operator of the vessel on the fateful voyage. The voyage was on a time charter to Shell International Petroleum Company Ltd; two other affiliates of the Shell group were listed as the owners of the crude oil on board and still another affiliate of the Royal Dutch/Shell group, Petroleum Insurance Limited, had insured the cargo and later became a claimant as subrogee after it had paid off the cargo owners. There is no evidence of any relationship of ownership or control between the Amoco parties and the Shell parties, though of course they did business with one another regularly.

[14] The *Amoco Cadiz* was indeed a very large ship—1,095 feet long with a carrying capacity of 230,000 deadweight tons and a draft, when fully laden, of 65 feet.

[15] Not all of these companies were organized for the occasion, or even for the twentieth century oil business. Astilleros, in fact, had built the three ships used by Christopher Columbus on his first voyage—the *Niña*, the *Pinta*, and the *Santa Maria*.

The various French parties could, of course, have brought suit in France. Such an action would, however, have come up against the International Convention on Civil Liability for Oil Pollution Damage of 1969,[16] which provided for recovery only from the registered owner of the vessel—here probably from Amoco Transport—and limited recovery to about $180 (133 SDRs) per vessel ton, or $18.9 million (14 million SDRs) per incident, whichever was less.[17] France and Liberia, but not the United States, were parties to the Civil Liability Convention. Also, the French parties evidently concluded that their chances of reaching the enterprise as a whole, including the parent company, were substantially better—both procedurally and substantively—in the United States. Accordingly, the French parties all brought suit in the United States, and the various actions (as well as a limitation proceeding brought by Amoco Transport) were consolidated before Judge Frank J. McGarr in the U.S. District Court for the Northern District of Illinois in Chicago. The defendants were Standard, the parent company; AIOC, the operator; Transport, the owner; an employee of AIOC; and Astilleros, the builder of the vessel. The allegations included faulty construction of the vessel, faulty navigation, inadequate maintenance, failure to send a distress signal early enough, and errors in an attempt by a salvage tug to tow the ship to safety.

Interestingly the French parties, including the Republic itself, urged the application of American law, arguing that France was merely the 'purely fortuitous' place of injury whereas 'the culpable conduct of Standard and AIOC was centered almost exclusively in the United States and specifically in Chicago'. Thus, the plaintiffs urged that the 'outmoded and obsolete *lex loci* rule' should be rejected. Counsel for the Standard/Amoco parties agreed that United States law was applicable to most of the issues but argued that the Convention should be applied to the question of whether AIOC could be held liable, urging the court to accommodate the relevant policy of the foreign state (i.e. the Convention in France) in its choice of law decision.

The question of the law to be applied to the issue of enterprise liability is

[16] 973 U.N.T.S. 3, 9 Int'l Leg. Mats. 45 (1970) signed at Brussels Nov. 29, 1969, entered into force June 19, 1975. The figures given here reflect a 1976 Protocol, which converted the former damage limits, expressed in Poincaré francs, to Special Drawing Rights of the International Monetary Fund.

[17] This account is not meant to be an authoritative interpretation of the Civil Liability Convention. In the *Amoco Cadiz* case, the judge said, obiter, that the Convention only applied to suits against the vessel's owner, and did not govern suits against parent corporations of the owner: 1984 A.M.C. at 2190–1. He also considered that the Convention only covered strict liability and not liability for negligence or unseaworthiness. It is not clear that these interpretations are correct. Bartlett, in the article cited at n. 13 *supra*, concludes that an interpretation that neither brings a parent corporation within the Convention's limits nor excludes parent corporations of a vessel owner from liability renders the limitation provision of the Convention worthless: 10 *The Maritime Lawyer* at 22.

not free from doubt. In this action in tort, if the forum is the state of the seat of the parent corporation and that state's law imposes liability on the enterprise, it seems to me that that state's law should be applied, even if the law of the place where the harmful event occurred would impose liability only on the subsidiary. If, on the other hand, the law of the state of injury imposed liability on an enterprise theory, I do not believe that the law of the state of incorporation or principal place of business should provide a shield.[18]

Judge McGarr eventually held that French law applied, on the ground that the damages were sustained in French territorial waters or on the coast of France:

> [T]he substantive law applicable to such claims would therefore have been French law if it had been proved different from that of the United States. However, it was not proved different. Claimants Côtes du Nord, in open court, stipulated that United States law applied, and claimants Bretagne-Angleterre-Irlande, et al. made no objection.[19]

In the result, the court applied U.S. law.

In general, the old English rule that foreign law is deemed to be like the law of the forum[20] is not followed in the United States; here, however, it had the effect of a kind of *post hoc* party autonomy, strengthened by the irony of the French government opting for United States law and in effect rejecting the convention that it had recently adopted.

With the interesting, but in the end not dispositive, choice of law question put aside, the real question, for present purposes, was whether Standard, the parent company, could be held liable. The court first held AIOC, the ship's operator (but not registered owner) liable on several counts of negligence, failure to assure construction of a seaworthy vessel, and failure to have a redundant steering system or other means of controlling the rudder if the hydraulic system failed.[21] Second, the court held Transport, the nominal owner, liable for failure to carry out a series of non-delegable duties relating to seaworthiness, crew training, and operating the vessel. 'Transport presented no evidence which would tend to establish its freedom from privity or knowledge of AIOC's negligence and of the conditions which resulted in the grounding of the vessel.'[22]

[18] Readers familiar with American writing on conflicts of law will recognize the influence here of Professor David Cavers. See, in particular, Cavers, *The Choice of Law Process* (1965), ch. VI, 'Principles of Preference Exemplified: Torts'. So far as I know, Cavers never discussed his principles of preference in the context of multinational corporations.

[19] 1984 A.M.C. at 2189.

[20] See Dicey and Morris, *The Conflict of Laws* (11th edn., Collins, 1987), Rule 18(2). I am pleased to note that the current edition of that work does not repeat that rule, pointing out that 'this mode of expression has given rise to uneasiness in certain cases': Dicey and Morris, *The Conflict of Laws* (12th edn., 1993) 238.

[21] 1984 A.M.C. at 2191–3.

[22] *Id.* 2193–4.

The critical question concerned Standard, the parent company and 'deep pocket'—which at the time ranked No. 12 on the Fortune List of the World's Largest Industrial Corporations. In significant part the court regarded the question as a factual one. To summarize many pages of findings, none of the defects in design, construction, maintenance, crew training, or operation could be attributed directly to Standard: AIOC was in fact the 'parent' which actually arranged for and conducted these activities even when they were nominally conducted by Transport or Tankers. The decision to purchase the vessel, however, was made by Standard's board of directors on recommendation of AIOC, most of the legal documents concerning the *Amoco Cadiz* were drafted by an attorney in Standard's legal department; the decision as to which company in the Standard family would own the vessel, including the sale from Tankers to Transport, was apparently made by Standard on the basis of reports of its accounting, tax, and legal departments; and the president of AIOC was a member of Standard's board of directors and reported to Standard's president and chairman. No single fact, it seems, was decisive. Taken together, however, the court concluded:

> As an integrated multinational corporation . . ., Standard is responsible for the tortious acts of its wholly owned subsidiaries and instrumentalities, AIOC and Transport.
>
> Standard exercised such control over its subsidiaries AIOC and Transport that those entities would be considered to be mere instrumentalities of Standard. Furthermore, Standard itself was initially involved in and controlled the design, construction, operation and management of the *Amoco Cadiz* and treated that vessel as if it were its own.[23]

Accordingly, Standard was held liable to the full extent of recoverable damages, jointly and severally with the companies that had owned and operated the vessel, Transport and AIOC.[24]

I believe this decision was correct, not just as a matter of American law but, I would submit, as a matter of international law. While there is no suggestion of fraud in the way Standard Oil/Amoco organized its global production/shipping/marketing operations, there is no justification for limiting the liability in tort of the enterprise as a whole toward parties that

[23] 1984 A.M.C. at 2194.

[24] Some six years and many hearings and inquiries later, the court issued its final damage award. The sum was approximately $160 million, far below the $1 billion originally claimed, but still about 12 times the amount that could have been awarded under the Civil Liability Convention and probably substantially more than the assets of Amoco Transport Co. Of the sum awarded, approximately $100 million went to the French government for clean-up costs, $30 million to the Shell interests for the value of the crude oil, and the remainder to the private French interests, including hotel keepers and oyster growers.

in no way had a prior relationship with the enterprise or any of its units.[25] I would hope the same result would have been achieved if the tanker had been owned, controlled, and operated by the Total/Compagnie Française des Pétroles group and the accident had occurred off the coast of Maine, either by application of United States law or by application of French law.[26] A different result might be correct in regard to claims by parties to contracts with the shipping company or by holders of a ship mortgage, who are able to protect themselves by proper risk analysis, insurance, or guarantees from the parent company or another unit of the multinational enterprise.

2. Insolvency in Argentina: The *Swift/Deltec* Case[27]

Compañía Swift de la Plata SA Frigorifíca was the largest meatpacking firm in Argentina and a major exporter from that country. Cía Swift was the largest of a number of Argentine subsidiaries of the Chicago-based Swift & Co., which since the last quarter of the nineteenth century had been a leader in packing and shipping meat in refrigerated ships and rail cars. Swift & Co. had been acquired in the 1960s by the Deltec group, based in Canada. Cía Swift was a wholly-owned subsidiary of Deltec Argentina, SA, which in turn was a subsidiary of Deltec Banking Corporation Ltd, a Canadian corporation wholly owned by Deltec International Corporation Ltd, a corporation organized under the laws of Canada with its headquarters in the Bahamas.

By 1970, when we pick up the story, Cía Swift had been unprofitable for many years: it had ceased paying dividends in 1962, and had ceased paying interest on intra-group debt in 1967. Deltec now sought to sell Cía Swift to Argentine purchasers, and apparently in order to make itself more marketable Cía Swift petitioned the Commercial Court of Buenos Aires for a *convocatoria*, i.e. for a summoning of creditors with a view to working out a court-approved reorganization or *concordato*. After a court-appointed referee found Cía Swift to have assets of 556 million pesos and debts of 143 million pesos, 86 per cent of the creditors concurred in a proposed

[25] I believe it is not irrelevant, and indeed instructive, that when, 11 years later, the tanker *Exxon Valdez* ran aground in Prince William Sound, Alaska, also causing massive environmental damage, the Exxon Corporation never raised the issue of separate ownership or operation of the vessel by its subsidiaries, though the ship was owned by Exxon Shipping Company, and the cargo that spilled belonged to Exxon Company, USA.

[26] See, e.g., *SA Saint Gobain Vitrage et al.* v. *Soc. Fabbrica Pisana SpA et al.*, 1987 Rec. Dalloz Sirey 41 (Cour d'Appel Versailles 17 Sept. 1986); Juris-Classeurs, *Sociétés*, vi, Fasc. 165–1, ¶¶ 52 *et seq.*; Weissberg and Moissinac, 'Piercing the Corporate Veil in France', 1987 *Int'l Financial L. Rev.* No. 7, 33 (July 1987).

[27] This account is based on M. Gordon, 'Argentine Jurisprudence: The *Parke Davis* and *Deltec* Cases', 6 *Lawyer of the Americas* 320 (1974); M. Gordon, 'Argentine Jurisprudence: *Deltec* Update', 11 *Lawyer of the Americas* 43 (1979); Phillip Blumberg, *The Law of Corporate Groups: Bankruptcy Law* (1985), § 17.16; and the judicial decisions cited.

concordato, which would have provided for payment in full of all of Cía Swift's debts over a four-year period, with interest at 12 per cent *per annum*. However, a creditor with a claim for US$4,000 opposed the *concordato*, and the court rejected it. More significant, the court decreed Cía Swift to be in bankruptcy, rejected the claims of other members of the Deltec group, and declared that the liabilities of Cía Swift extended to all other members of the Deltec group world-wide, on the basis of a 'unified structure' of the organism which makes Cía Swift one of the prolongations of a multinational enterprise. The federal government was designated as receiver/liquidator.

On appeal by Deltec International and other members of the group, the Court of Commercial Appeals affirmed the order of bankruptcy, but set aside the ruling extending liability to the group, essentially on the ground that the other members of the group had not had their day in court.[28]

Cía Swift appealed the bankruptcy decree to the Argentine Supreme Court; the government of Argentina (since 1973 under Peronista control) opposed the appeal and sought reinstatement of the first court's ruling. The Supreme Court did reinstate the Commercial Court's decision, on the basis that 'the companies forming the so-called "Deltec Group" comprise, insofar as the bankruptcy is concerned, a unified socio-economic entity with the bankrupt company':[29]

> It is of no interest . . . to delve into history nor to analyze in detail the interrelationship to which the Referee refers. It is sufficient to point to the existence of a group of companies with their seat in this country and abroad whose shares—practically in their totality—remain the property of the entities which form the group, and to their direct and indirect linkages, ultimately resulting in control by Deltec International. This is clearly evident . . . in the Prospectus of Deltec International to its shareholders and in [International's] Report and Balance Sheet . . . It is also evident in Deltec International's communication to its shareholders relative to the *convocatoria*, in which that company refers to the fact that the financial arrangements of 'our' company Swift de la Plata in Argentina failed and that 'we' are forthwith addressing ourselves to the pertinent Argentine tribunal to seek a *convocatoria*—Deltec repeatedly refers to 'its subsidiaries,' to 'our property,' etc. Swift, 99% of whose shares Deltec International owns, is listed as one of the above; also listed are many other companies in Argentina and abroad, owned either directly or indirectly through other subsidiaries. By way of example . . . Swift is one of the subsidiaries which, directly or indirectly, controls [four other named Argentine companies] . . . Also, e.g., more than 80% of Swift's sales have been to entities of the 'group,' including the totality of the sales of cooked and frozen meats; and [various shifts of debts, credits and guarantees among members of the group].

[28] 15 J.A. 368, 146 La Ley 612 (June 6, 1972).

[29] *Compañía Swift de la Plata, SA Frigorífica s/convocatoria de acreedores*, 286 Fallos de la Corte Suprema 257 at 273, 151 La Ley 516 at 520 (1973).

> . . .
>
> [T]he varied legal forms used by different fractions of the group . . . should not produce a result in which only one of the fractions (Swift) . . . should be the only entity affected by the judicial decision under review. The [Supreme] Court has declared 'that excessive reliance on juridical traditionalism is one of the most serious obstacles to economic expansion and social justice.' Accordingly, the rationale of the law must not be confused with formal juridical ritualism so as to replace substantive justice.[30]

Does this decision go too far? I think it does. When a contractual obligation is entered into by a company with adequate disclosure of its corporate form and capital structure, the argument for looking through the corporate form, it seems to me, is much reduced. One can understand the frustration of a court that sees one part of a corporate group seeking to avoid its debts while other parts remain solvent, particularly when the creditors are local and the group is centered elsewhere. One may also sympathize with a court that gives priority to claims of outsiders as compared to claims by affiliates. In the actual case, however, it was not the debtor who had sought relief in bankruptcy, and the imputation of liability to a large group of companies having no connection with or obligations to Argentine parties cannot be supported. If Cía Swift de la Plata had put into circulation tainted meat that had caused a massive outbreak of botulism among consumers in Argentina, one could support an effort of the Argentine courts to see that compensation to the victims were made available, if necessary from affiliates abroad. In the commercial context of the *Swift/Deltec* case, however, the decision of the Argentine courts seems unjustified. Though, as spelled out in the next chapter, I am generally in favor of expanded recognition of foreign judgments, I agree with the decision of a New York court not to recognize the judgment of the Argentine court when a marginally related case came before it.[31]

[30] 151 La Ley at 518–9. The translation follows Gordon, n. 27 *supra*, with some slight modifications.

[31] In that case, Deltec Banking Corporation, a Canadian member of the Deltec group, brought suit against an unrelated Argentine company on a promissory note calling for payment in New York. The Argentine company moved to dismiss the action on the ground that the plaintiff company had been declared bankrupt in Argentina, so that the defendant could not legally make payment to it in New York, or if it did that the payment would not discharge the debt in favor of the receiver in Buenos Aires. The New York court rejected the motion to dismiss, saying:

> It is well-settled that New York courts are not required to recognize foreign judgments which come in conflict with prevailing concepts of justice and fairness. The determination that plaintiff is bankrupt because it is one segment of a chain of corporations, one of which is insolvent, may under our laws amount under certain circumstances to confiscation of property.

Deltec Banking Corporation v. *Companía Italo-Argentina de Electricidad, SA*, 171 N.Y.L.J. 18, col. 1 (Sup. Ct. N.Y. Cty. Apr. 3, 1974), aff'd mem. 46 A.D.2d 847, 362 N.Y.S.2d 391 (1st Dept. 1974), 68 Am. J. Int'l L. 741 (1974).

It is interesting to note that the principles of the *Deltec* case were enacted into the Argentine Foreign Investment Law shortly after the decision of the Supreme Court, making foreign affiliates of multinational enterprises liable for the obligations of their Argentine companies[32]—apparently the only statute of its kind anywhere in the world.[33] When the Peronista regime was ousted in 1976, that law was quickly repealed, and replaced by a new Foreign Investment Law reflecting the entity theory of corporate liability.[34]

3. Plant Closure in Belgium: The *Badger* Case[35]

Badger Belgium NV was a unit of a world-wide construction and engineering firm, engaged in building plants for the chemical, petroleum, pharmaceutical, fertilizer, and similar industries. At the head of the group was The Badger Company, Inc., founded in 1949 with headquarters in Cambridge, Massachusetts. Badger USA in turn, was owned by the Raytheon Corporation, a major company specializing in electronics and defense-related equipment,[36] which had become a conglomerate by acquiring not only Badger, but companies engaged in such disparate activities as manufacturing home appliances and publishing textbooks. At the relevant time, in the mid-1970s, Badger had establishments in three states of the United States and twelve nations outside the United States, and about 2,000 employees world-wide. About half of the Badger group's earnings came from its foreign operations.

Badger came to Belgium when Esso expanded its refinery in Antwerp in 1956. The business gradually expanded, and by 1976 Badger Belgium had just under 250 employees, primarily white-collar workers and professionals, based in Antwerp. The shares of Badger Belgium were almost 100 per cent owned by Badger USA; its chairman was an Englishman, and important decisions, such as whether to bid on a given project and how much, were usually made for Badger Belgium by BV Badger in The Hague, which in turn received instructions from the parent company in the United States.

Thus far the story is typical of many medium-sized multinational enterprises, though perhaps because of the proximity of its sister company in the Netherlands the management of Badger Belgium had somewhat less

[32] Argentina: Law No. 20,557 of Nov. 7, 1973, Art. 31, Legislacion Argentina No. 87, 70 at 74 (Dec. 1973); (1973) 12 Int'l Leg. Mats. 1489.

[33] See Phillip I. Blumberg, *The Multinational Challenge to Corporation Law* (1993), 189.

[34] Argentina: Law No. 21,382 of Aug. 13, 1976, Art. 20, Legislacion Argentina, No. 118, 76 at 83 (Aug. 1976); (1976) 15 Int'l Leg. Mats. 1364.

[35] Much of this account is drawn from R. Blanpain, *The Badger Case and the OECD Guidelines for Multinational Enterprises* (1977).

[36] Raytheon produced, *inter alia*, the Patriot anti-missile missile that became famous in the Gulf War of 1991 for its ability to destroy Iraqi 'Scud' missiles.

authority than usual. However, at some time in 1976 it was decided—probably at group headquarters in Massachusetts but in any event at multinational level—that the Belgian operation of Badger was not sufficiently successful to be kept going. Throughout the summer and fall of 1976, discussions were held about a possible merger with another Belgian company, but no solution materialized. Badger USA confirmed that it would not supply additional capital; on December 23, 1976 the employees were told that efforts to sell the company had failed and that the plant would be closed in the near future.

On January 12, 1977, Badger Belgium filed a petition with the Antwerp Commercial Court seeking a composition of creditors. Two days later, on Friday, January 14, 1977, some 250 employees of Badger Belgium received registered letters stating that their services were no longer needed, effective immediately. Employees would be paid through the end of the month, plus accumulated leave time.

Badger Belgium's notice to its employees, however, was inconsistent with Belgian labor law, which made elaborate provision for laid-off workers. The Belgian law required advance notice prior to any termination, and in principle consultation.[37] The term of notice varied according to a complicated formula, depending on the employee's salary, years of employment, age, and skills, with a minimum of three months and a maximum as long as two years. If the employee was not permitted to work during the statutory term of the notice, he or she was nevertheless entitled to be paid at full salary plus benefits. In addition, severance pay was due in two categories, one based on years of employment, the other on the employee's age. These payments were due even if the employee found other work immediately. Badger estimated that the payments would amount to an average of 16 months' pay of $23,000 per employee.

Altogether, Badger Belgium NV was liable for about BFr. 250 million (about $6.25 million) in employee compensation and benefits. But on February 17, 1977, just over a month after the notices had gone out, Badger Belgium was declared bankrupt, with net worth of no more than BFr. 108 million or about $2.8 million. Badger BV, its sister company in The Hague, an hour and a half away, was not bankrupt; neither was its parent, Badger USA, let alone its grandparent, Raytheon. Moreover, Badger Belgium was not in arrears in payments to ordinary trade creditors or to other Badger companies. In brief, the bankruptcy was essentially a function of the lay-off and severance obligations imposed by Belgian law. But Badger USA announced that it did not regard itself liable for the debts of Badger Belgium, and that it would not make the required severance payments.

Belgian trade unions, as well as the press and the Belgian government,

[37] Loi relative à l'indemnisation des travailleurs licenciés en cas de fermeture d'entreprises, June 28, 1966 [1966] Pasinomie 351.

took the position that these obligations should be imputed to the Badger group as a whole, which had made its investment in Belgium subject to all aspects of Belgian law—concerning exit as well as entry. Badger, on the other hand, took the position that the severance obligations were solely obligations of Badger Belgium, and should be treated in the same way as debts of all other firms whose liabilities exceeded their assets. The spokesman of the Badger group pointed out that in none of the other bankruptcies of Belgian companies in recent years had pressure been put on the shareholders to pay the debts of the insolvent companies; indeed Belgium maintained a national fund, financed by payroll taxes, to pay the severance obligations of closed companies (up to a stated maximum) when the employer failed to do so. 'Is it', Badger asked, 'because the major shareholder of Badger Belgium is a multinational company that it is being attacked?'

The answer, of course, was 'yes'. The attack took the form not only of a law suit in Belgium against Badger Belgium, Badger Netherlands, Badger USA, and Raytheon, but of mailings to shareholders of the parent companies, and representations to the American Ambassadors in Belgium and the Netherlands, asserting that 'this action of one multinational American company . . . will harm not only Badger's and Raytheon's reputation, but also affect the so far good reputation of other American multinational companies established in the Benelux.' For both sides, the issue was one of principle.

The decisive forum turned out to be the OECD, and in particular the Committee on International Investment and Multinational Enterprises created to oversee the Guidelines for Multinational Enterprises attached to the OECD's 1976 Declaration on International Investment and Multinational Enterprises. The OECD Guidelines are not a treaty, nor a code subscribed to by either states or companies. Still, the Declaration and Guidelines reflect an effort by the Western industrial states to come to terms with the phenomenon of multinational enterprises; perhaps they could be described as 'soft law'.[38] The Badger case was to be the first test of the Guidelines.

Though a suggested provision calling for review by the Committee of individual cases had been rejected when the Declaration and Guidelines were being drafted, the Committee agreed to place the issue raised by the Badger case on its agenda, and to permit the Belgian Secretary of State for Regional Economy to make an oral presentation at a meeting on March 31, 1977. The Committee responded to the Minister's presentation that it was not a tribunal and had no mandate to reach conclusions on the conduct of individual enterprises. Thus it did not deal with the merits of the Badger case, and indeed the company's name was hardly mentioned in the day-

[38] See, e.g., I. Seidl-Hohenveldern, 'International Economic "Soft Law"' (1979) 163 *Recueil des Cours* 165, 180.

long meeting. But the Committee accepted the facts as submitted by Belgium 'as an illustration which could help to clarify the meaning of a text the Committee itself had negotiated some months ago'.

In fact, the text of the Guidelines was not clear. On the one hand, paragraph 6 of the Guidelines on Employment and Industrial Relations read:

> Enterprises should, within the framework of law, regulations and prevailing labour relations and employment practices in each of the countries in which they operate
>
> . . .
>
> (6) in considering changes in their operations which would have major effects upon the livelihood of their employees, in particular in the case of the closure of an entity involving collective lay-offs or dismissals, provide reasonable notice of such changes . . . and cooperate with the employee representative and appropriate governmental authorities so as to mitigate to the maximum extent practicable adverse effects.

This text suggested that Badger had not done all it should have done in terms of discussion and notice, but did not address the issue of holding a parent liable for severance obligations in the case of bankruptcy of the subsidiary.[39] For its part Badger could point to Preambular Paragraph 9 of the Guidelines, which says:

> The guidelines are not aimed at introducing differences of treatment between multinational and domestic enterprises; wherever relevant they reflect good practice for all. Accordingly, multinational and domestic enterprises are subject to the same expectations in respect of their conduct wherever the guidelines are relevant to both.

While Badger should have given more notice, as local firms would have done, the national treatment principle reflected in paragraph 9 also might be understood to suggest there should be no imposition of liability on foreign shareholders that would not be imposed on domestic shareholders. On the one hand, there appeared to have been no instance in Belgium of imposition of liability on shareholders of a bankrupt corporation; on the other hand, the Belgian government asserted that there had been no case of a bankruptcy to avoid severance pay as prescribed by law.[40] Moreover, the principle of limited liability, in Belgium's view, could only be accepted

[39] Moreover, the Guideline on Employment and Industrial Relations, like all the Guidelines, is written as a recommendation—'Enterprises should . . .' and Preambular Para. 6 specifically states that observance of the Guidelines 'is voluntary and not legally enforceable'.

[40] Professor Pierre van Ommeslaghe suggests (without citation to precedent or written law) that Belgian courts would probably permit recourse to a foreign parent company's resources when that company had abandoned its Belgian subsidiary to 'une faillite sans gloire', but doubts whether a judgment along these lines would be enforceable abroad, particularly in the United States. Van Ommeslaghe, 'Les groupes de sociétés et l'expérience du droit belge', in Klaus Haput (ed.), *Groups of Companies in European Laws* (1982), 59 at 91.

in situations where the company in question had the capacity to make independent decisions. It would be wrong to apply the principle to shield a company whose decisions were not its own but were made elsewhere.

The official publication of the OECD, in reporting on the meeting of the Committee, said only:

> The discussion within OECD permitted all interested parties—governments, the unions and the companies involved—to cooperate and to pursue their dicussions with a clearer understanding of what each is expected to do according to recognized international standards.

Within a week of the OECD meeting, however, senior officials of the Badger group were meeting with the Belgian government officials and union leaders. For Badger, it turned out that the principle of limited liability receded in importance if a financial settlement could be worked out; for the Belgian parties, if the principle of responsibility of the multinational enterprise for plant closings could be established, one could negotiate about the amounts due to the employees. Agreement was eventually reached on a formula under which all the assets of Badger Belgium were applied to the severance payments, and Badger USA contributed an additional sum of BFr. 20 million (roughly $500,000)—about 15 per cent of the initial claims. It was understood that the employees of Badger Belgium had priority over all other claimants, and that the parent company assumed no liability for other debts of Badger Belgium. One point on which Badger insisted and the Belgian parties agreed was that those employees who had been transferred to Badger companies in other countries were removed from the list of employees eligible for payments under the Belgian law.

How should this case be judged? The claims for severance pay by employees of the subsidiary fall somewhere between claims arising out of a disaster, as in the case of the *Amoco Cadiz* (or in the hypothetical outbreak of botulism in Argentina) and the commercial claims in *Swift/Deltec*. On the one hand, the claimants had a prior relationship with the corporation, and, it is fair to assume, had access to information about the capital structure and financial condition of their employees. On the other hand, it was not unreasonable for the employees in accepting their employment with a member firm of an international group (as well as for the government in permitting establishment of the subsidiary in the first place) to expect the enterprise to be committed to complying with local law, including labor law. One cannot fault the Belgian government for taking the side of the employees, and for urging the U.S. government to put pressure on Badger USA/Raytheon to resolve the matter. Surely the American parent company was wise to reach a settlement, rather than standing on a principle that in the actual case had little appeal. It is worth repeating, however, that Badger USA assumed no liability for any other obligations of Badger

Belgium; ordinary trade obligations, presumably, would be processed through the local bankruptcy court, without recourse to the parent corporation.

4. United Nations Sanctions against Rhodesia[41]

The issue of responsibility of the parent or the group for the activities of a subsidiary can run down as well as up. The *Rhodesia* case does not come out of the law reports, but it was very much in the news, particularly in the United Kingdom and the United States, about two decades ago.

On November 11, 1965, the government of Southern Rhodesia, until then a self-governing colony within the British Empire, issued a Unilateral Declaration of Independence. Since the government represented only the white settlers—some 4 per cent of the population—the British Parliament immediately passed a law declaring that 'Southern Rhodesia continues to be a part of Her Majesty's dominions, and that the Government and Parliament of the United Kingdom have responsibility and jurisdiction as heretofore for and in respect of it'.[42] Both the General Assembly and the Security Council of the United Nations condemned UDI,[43] and not a single country recognized Rhodesia (as it now called itself) as an independent state.

Great Britain promptly initiated a program of economic sanctions, designed to bring down the government by denying export markets for the products of Rhodesia and depriving Rhodesia of assorted supplies. Within a year, the United Nations Security Council adopted 'Selective Mandatory Sanctions',[44] and by 1968 the Security Council adopted Comprehensive Mandatory Sanctions,[45] designed to stop all trade in and out of Rhodesia.

In some ways, Rhodesia was well equipped to withstand an economic boycott. Rhodesia had the most diversified economy in Africa apart from South Africa, and its principal exports, non-ferrous metals, wheat, sugar, and tobacco, were in world-wide demand and could be disguised as to place of origin, if buyers did not inquire too closely. Rhodesia had plentiful supplies of hydro-electric power and coal; its one economic vulnerability was that it had no indigenous sources of oil, and neither did its friendly neighbor, the Republic of South Africa. From the beginning, the principal focus of the program of sanctions against Rhodesia, both by Britain and by

[41] For a more detailed description of this topic, focusing on the problems of economic sanctions in general, see A. Lowenfeld, *Trade Controls for Political Ends* (2nd edn., 1983), 425–535 plus Documents Supplement.

[42] U.K. Southern Rhodesia Act 1965, 1965 c.76, s. 1.

[43] GA Res. 2024, Nov. 11, 1965, 20 UN GAOR Supp. 14 55, UN Doc. A/6014 (1966); SC Res. 216, Nov. 12, 1965, 20 UN SCOR Res. & Dec. 1965, 8.

[44] SC Res. 232, Dec. 16, 1966, 21 UN SCOR Res. & Dec. 1966, 7 (1966).

[45] SC Res. 253, May 29, 1968, 23 UN SCOR Res. & Dec. 5 (1968).

the United Nations, was to deny to Rhodesia its supplies of petroleum and petroleum products.[46]

Prime Minister Wilson predicted in January 1966 that the measures taken by the British government (even before mandatory United Nations sanctions were in place) would bring an end to the rebellion 'within a matter of weeks rather than months'.[47] In fact the white minority government of Rhodesia held out for more than fourteen years. It finally gave in not because its supplies of oil ran out, but because an increasingly violent guerilla war sapped the will of the government leaders to continue the struggle. Indeed, fuel rationing, which had been imposed by the Rhodesian government just after UDI, was repealed in 1971, and consumption of petroleum products in Rhodesia almost doubled from its pre-UDI level in the decade and a half of UDI.[48]

Prior to UDI, five companies had supplied Rhodesia's needs for petroleum products—Shell Rhodesia (39.1 per cent), BP/Rhodesia (12.9 per cent), Mobil Oil Southern Rhodesia (20 per cent), Caltex Oil Rhodesia (20 per cent), and Total Rhodesia (8 per cent).[49] Each of these companies was incorporated under the laws of Southern Rhodesia, and each was 100 per cent owned, via intermediate entities, by the major international oil company whose name it bore. Different subsidiaries of the same multinational companies supplied more than 90 per cent of the petroleum needs of South Africa. Early in 1966 the major international oil companies, at parent company level, entered into an understanding with the British and American governments that they would not supply oil to the breakaway colony, and a recently built pipeline from Beira in Mozambique to a jointly-owned refinery in Rhodesia ceased to operate at the close of 1965. But shortly after UDI the Rhodesian government created a new semi-secret state purchasing agency GENTA, and GENTA constructed several distribution centers in South Africa for overland supplies to Rhodesia. Apparently oil for Rhodesia was supplied by Shell (Middle East) through the Shell/BP refinery in Durban, South Africa, to Shell/BP Marketing (South Africa), a company owned by Royal Dutch-Shell and British Petroleum but controlled by local (South African) directors. Marketing, in turn, sold refined products to numerous customers in South Africa, including GENTA, which transported the products to Rhodesia by truck or rail. Once in Rhodesia,

[46] See SC Res. 217, Nov. 20, 1965, para. 8, 20 UN SCOR Res. & Dec. 1965, 8; SC Res. 221, Apr. 9, 1966, 21 UN SCOR Res. & Dec. 5; SC Res. 232, Dec. 16, 1966, para. 2(f); U.K.: The Southern Rhodesia (Petroleum) Order 1965, S.I. 1965 No. 2140, Dec. 17, 1965, amended S.I. No. 2168, Dec. 24, 1965.

[47] Commonwealth Prime Ministers' Meeting in Lagos, Nigeria Jan. 1966, Final Communiqué. Cmnd. 2890, 5 (1966).

[48] See the *Bingham Report*, cited at n. 52 *infra*, 217, para. 14.4 (xxxiii).

[49] Shell and BP conducted many operations in southern Africa jointly, and their respective subsidiaries were owned through a jointly-owned holding company, the Consolidated Petroleum Company incorporated in the United Kingdom.

the products were sold by GENTA to Shell/BP Marketing (Rhodesia), a company now under Rhodesian control, which distributed the gasoline and other products at retail. The Mobil, Caltex, and Total groups also furnished supplies in similar transactions, so that the pre-UDI proportions in the Rhodesian market were maintained, but no direct link could be established between crude supplies in South Africa and product sales in Rhodesia.[50]

For some years this chain of supplies, though disclosed in the press and official reports,[51] went on without attracting much public attention. In the mid-1970s, however, a series of exposés, Congressional hearings in the United States, and eventually a major independent inquiry—the Bingham Commission—ordered by the British foreign secretary, brought out the facts in elaborate detail,[52] to the considerable embarrassment of the British government.[53]

At parent company level, in London, New York, San Francisco, and Paris, management maintained that it knew nothing of the activities in question. The officers of Shell, Mobil, etc. said that they had no contact with or control over Shell Rhodesia, Mobil Oil Rhodesia, etc., and that their subsidiaries in South Africa, though wholly owned, had no control over the destination of their products once these products had been sold to independent purchasers in South Africa. A growing number of critics believed corporate headquarters must know what was going on, had probably planned it (possibly even in advance of UDI), and in any event were responsible for the activities of their subsidiaries and subordinates. In England, the maverick British multinational company Lonrho, which had owned the Beira-Umtali pipeline that operated for less than a year, brought suit against Shell and BP, alleging conspiracy to breach the British sanctions orders and otherwise to supply or agree to supply petroleum to Rhodesia.

[50] The description here is based on reports in the *Sunday Times*, London, Aug. 27, 1967, 9, cols. 1–8; Sept. 3, 1967, 2, cols. 3–8. Similar reports appeared in the press and academic studies throughout the decade 1966–76, as well as in reports of the UN Committee on Sanctions established pursuant to Security Council Resolution 253.

[51] See n. 50 *supra*.

[52] U.K. Foreign and Commonwealth Office, *Report on the Supply of Petroleum and Petroleum Products to Rhodesia* (London, 1978), 296. The inquiry was conducted by T. H. Bingham, Q.C. (now Sir Thomas Bingham, Master of the Rolls) and S. M. Gray, a chartered accountant, on appointment from Dr. David Owen, Secretary of State for Foreign and Commonwealth Affairs.

[53] For instance, when Prime Minister Callaghan traveled to Zambia early in 1977 to enlist the support of that country's leader in a proposed settlement of the Rhodesia crisis, he was met by a sharp attack from President Kenneth Kaunda about the breach of sanctions, questioning whether Zambia could continue to maintain diplomatic relations with Great Britain. Callaghan replied in a handwritten letter to 'Dear Kenneth':

> I am shocked and astonished that you should not only say but apparently believe that I have been cheating you for years . . . over the matter of oil sanctions . . . Kenneth, you must understand, if I have evidence about sanctions-breaking then that evidence will be followed up and, if it is possible to bring the culprits to book, then that will happen.

Quoted in Martin Bailey, *Oilgate, The Sanctions Scandal* (1979) at 66.

As the failure of the oil embargo became apparent, anti-UDI and anti-apartheid groups in Great Britain, the United States, and at the United Nations spoke of massive conspiracy.[54] For the governments and their legal advisers, the issue was more complicated, involving both the relation among parent companies and subsidiaries and the question of extraterritorial jurisdiction.

The United Kingdom initially made its embargoes applicable to

(a) citizens of the United Kingdom ordinarily resident in the United Kingdom;
(b) citizens of Southern Rhodesia;
(c) corporations incorporated or constituted under the law of the United Kingdom or the law of Southern Rhodesia,

wherever the contravention takes place.[55]

Later, the scope of the prohibitions was changed to apply also to British citizens or subjects who were not ordinarily resident in the United Kingdom. Consistently with the British tradition, corporations not organized under the laws of the United Kingdom or Southern Rhodesia, including subsidiaries of companies organized under the laws of the United Kingdom, were clearly not covered. In the United States, the typical sanctions and embargo orders, including the Foreign Assets Control Regulations (directed to mainland China, North Korea and North Vietnam),[56] Cuban Assets Control Regulations,[57] and later the Iranian Assets Control Regulations[58] had all been directed (with minor changes in wording) to:

(1) Any citizen or resident of the United States;
(2) Any person actually within the United States;
(3) Any corporation organized under the laws of the United States or any state of the United States; *and*
(4) Any partnership, association, corporation or other organization, *wheresoever organized or doing business* which is owned or controlled by persons specified in (1), (2), or (3).[59]

With respect to Rhodesia, however, the U.S. government followed the lead of the British government, and replaced the underlined text in its regulations implementing sanctions against Rhodesia by the words 'organized

[54] See, e.g., Center for Social Action of the United Church of Christ, *The Oil Conspiracy* (1979); M. Bailey, *Oilgate, The Sanctions Scandal* (1979), as well as successive Reports of the UN Security Council Committee established in Pursuance of Res. 253 (1968) Concerning the Question of Southern Rhodesia, 32 UN SCOR Spec. Supp. No. 2, Vol. II, 299 (1977), 33 UN SCOR Spec. Supp. No. 2, Vol. I, 294 (1978) *et seq.*

[55] See, e.g., The Southern Rhodesia (Petroleum) Order 1965, art. 1(2) (Dec. 17, 1965, amended Dec. 24, 1965); The Southern Rhodesia (Prohibited Exports and Imports) Order 1966, art. 1(4) (Jan. 20, 1966); The Southern Rhodesia (Prohibited Trade and Dealings) Order 1966, arts. 2(6), 4(2), 6(6) (Dec. 23, 1966).

[56] 31 C.F.R. Part 500.

[57] 31 C.F.R. Part 515.

[58] 31 C.F.R. Part 535.

[59] See 31 C.F.R. § 500.329; § 515.329; § 535.329 (emphasis supplied).

under the laws of, or having its principal place of business *in Southern Rhodesia*'.

Of course regulations of this kind are difficult to understand, even for lawyers. What the public understood was pictures of Shell and Mobil service stations in Rhodesia pumping fuel, and memoranda that began to be leaked by disgruntled employees disclosing communications between officers and different companies in the respective groups, sometimes speaking openly about supplies to Rhodesia, sometimes speaking in codes that suggested an effort to conceal but were not difficult to place in context.

The critics had two avenues of attack against 'sanctions busting'. As to the multinational enterprises, even if it was true that only the American and British members of the group could be made subject to the jurisdiction of the United States and the United Kingdom, it was inconceivable that corporate headquarters, including citizens of the United States and the United Kingdom, did not have it in their power to find out about the supply of oil to Rhodesia by their subsidiaries and to put a stop to it. For instance, a brochure put out by an activist group that was reproduced both in Congressional and United Nations documents said:

> It is hard to imagine that the sanctions breaking activities of Mobil (South Africa) were unknown to its board; after all, they involved business worth tens of millions of dollars, which would normally be reported on and evaluated at board meetings. And with three U.S. citizens who are or have been directors of Mobil (South Africa) and very senior executives within Mobil (U.S.A.), it is difficult to see how Mobil (U.S.A.) could be said not to know of the sanctions-breaking activities of its subsidiary.[60]

Mobil responded at a Congressional hearing that there had been no violations of U.S. law either by Mobil Rhodesia, which was not prohibited from marketing inside Rhodesia products it purchased from GENTA, or by Mobil South Africa, which was not prohibited from selling non-U.S. origin products to anyone, including persons in Rhodesia. Moreover, Mobil's efforts to find out more about what its South African affiliates might have known about the destination of their products were frustrated by South African law, which made it a crime to transmit outside of the country information which would prejudice the security interests of South Africa. 'It seems clear', Mobil's spokesman told a skeptical Congressional committee, 'there is nothing further which Mobil can do to resolve the matter, which involves matters of national policy required to be handled on a government-to-government basis.'[61]

The other avenue of attack, heard both in Britain and in the United

[60] *The Oil Conspiracy*, n. 54 *supra*, 31.

[61] *South Africa–U.S. Policy and the Role of U.S. Corporations*, Hearings before Subcomm. on Africa of Senate Comm. on Foreign Relations, 94th Cong., 2d Sess., 357–77 (Sept. 17, 1976).

States, as well as in the sanctions committees of the United Nations, was to question the policies of the governments directly. If it was true that Mobil and Shell and BP were not technically liable, should not the laws and regulations be changed? Should the United States regulations, for instance, have been drafted as its other economic sanctions regulations had been to include the phrase 'and any . . . corporation or other organization wheresoever organized or doing business, which is owned or controlled by [U.S. corporations]'? Should the regulations have required parent companies, as controlling shareholders and overall managers, to direct their subsidiaries to obey the embargoes? Should some kind of duty of inquiry be imposed on top level management, so that the parent company could not say, as Shell and Mobil did, that it could do nothing about their subsidiaries' policies of non-disclosure?

On the one hand, the resolutions of the United Nations Security Council had not spoken to the issue: the requirements ran to 'any activities by [member states'] nationals or in their territories'.[62] On the other hand, since the sanctions had been implemented pursuant to 'decisions' taken by the Security Council under Article 41 of the United Nations Charter binding on all states pursuant to Article 25 of the Charter, there ought not—at least in theory—to be the kind of conflicts that had arisen when the United States had sought to apply its embargoes against China and Cuba to foreign subsidiaries of American companies, contrary to the policies of Canada, Great Britain, France, and other countries.[63]

Most fundamentally, had the failure in the Rhodesia crisis of the oil embargo—and of sanctions generally—demonstrated that major multinational enterprises had slipped their moorings from national control?

No final decisions came out of the investigations into the failure of the oil embargo. The Bingham Report was critical of Shell and BP, and also of the British government, but it did not recommend either prosecution or revision of the sanctions regulations. In the United States, the Treasury Department also conducted an investigation and issued a report, which did not quite exonerate Mobil but did not accuse it either of breach of the regulations or of having known of breaches by its subsidiaries.[64]

Given that the sanctions against Rhodesia were based on a unanimous decision of the United Nations Security Council, an argument based on private international law in favor of deference due to the law of the state where the subsidiaries were established—here South Africa—would seem to be trumped by the public international law that makes decision of the

[62] See, e.g., S.C. Res. 253 of May 29, 1968 para. 3.

[63] See, e.g., Corcoran, 'The Trading with the Enemy Act and the Controlled Canadian Corporation', 14 *McGill L.J.* 174 (1968); see also, generally, Lowenfeld, *Trade Controls for Political Ends*, n. 41 *supra*.

[64] U.S. Treasury, *Treasury Investigation of Charges Made Against the Mobil Oil Corporation* (mimeograph released May 12, 1977).

Security Council binding on all states. But it seems that private commercial law—i.e. respect for the formalities of corporate organization—prevailed, to the mystification of the general public and charges of hypocrisy from civil rights groups and African states opposed to UDI.

To me, it is clear that if the world is serious about economic sanctions or embargoes—whether against Serbia or Iraq today, against North Korea tomorrow, Iran or Libya in the past decade, or Rhodesia in the 1970s—the proposition that a multinational enterprise is nothing more than separate corporations that happen to have the same name but operate under different legal regimes cannot stand, either under the national law of the seat of the parent corporation or under the operative provisions of resolutions of the United Nations Security Council. It may be worth adding that during the world-wide anti-apartheid movement directed against South Africa in the 1980s, none of the multinational corporations targeted with divestment initiatives and boycotts for their activities in South Africa said to an aroused public, 'We are not doing business in South Africa, that is only Kodak South Africa Pty., or General Motors South Africa, Pty., or Philips South Africa, Pty.' Clearly the public, including university students, pension funds, parliaments, and consumers, had no patience or understanding for such legalisms.

D. THE SEARCH FOR A PRINCIPLE

It is evident that no single generally acceptable rule of public international law emerges either from the theoretical foundations of company law or from the cases here discussed. Nor is it possible to find refuge in a universal rule of private international law, such as a rule that would look always to the law applicable at the place of the challenged activity, or one that would look always to the law applicable at the place of incorporation of the parent company. It may be worth trying, however, to borrow from the techniques of modern conflicts of law in order to make some statements of a normative character, formulated in terms of presumptions and principles of preference.

1. The starting point for analysis of the liability for obligations of a corporation is the presumption that the shareholders are not liable beyond the capital that they have contributed (or undertaken to contribute). This presumption can virtually never be overcome with regard to shareholders from the general public[65]; it *can* be overcome when the shareholder is another corporation holding all or substantially all the stock of the corporation in question, or the stock is distributed among members of the same corporate family.

[65] Exceptions are cases of fraud and special laws in some states concerning the organization of banks and insurance companies that provide for calls on the shareholders for additional capital in certain situations of insolvency.

2. The more a person dealing with a corporation can be expected to inquire about the organization and capitalization of the corporation in question, the weaker is the claim to penetrate beyond that corporation to engage the responsibility of a parent or affiliate. Thus, generally, the presumption of limited liability should not be overcome with respect to claims arising out of commercial relationships. Conversely the presumption of limited liability is weakest with respect to claims arising out of torts—and in particular out of mass disasters.

3. There is no necessary additional presumption against attributing liability to members of a corporate group because the source of the asserted obligation is in public or administrative law. Thus obligations of a public law character, such as requirements that issuers of securities or operators of financial institutions make disclosure regarding their worldwide activities and assets, may ordinarily be imposed both by the state of establishment of a subsidiary and by the state of the parent corporation. Both the state of the parent corporation and states where a subsidiary is established may impose taxes on the activity of the subsidiary, though ordinarily the effect of such overlapping jurisdiction is ameliorated by double tax conventions or provision in national law for foreign tax credits.

4. Regulation by one state in respect of the activity of a corporate parent, subsidiary, or other member of a multinational group is often not in the first instance extraterritorial, because enforcement is typically directed to the member of the group established in the territory of the regulating state.[66] However, the effect of national regulation of a multinational enterprise may well be multinational—i.e. extraterritorial, and states are required to consider the potential or actual effect on other states of their exercise of regulatory jurisdiction.

5. The fact that imposition of liability on one member of a corporate group for the activity of another member of the group has effect in another state with a different substantive rule concerning the activity in question does not *a priori* render it unlawful. We are back to the subject with which this volume began—the scope and limitations of jurisdiction to prescribe. That suggests that there is an obligation to avoid conflict if possible, but not that all difference in legal rules is equivalent to the kind of conflict which calls for application of the territorial preference. I would also suggest that the case for deference to the law and policy of the state of incorporation is stronger (i.e. the interest necessary to overcome the presumption against imposing liability must be greater) when the state of incorporation is also the state of the activity at issue, as contrasted with a 'flag of convenience' state of incorporation. This point will come back in Chapter 7, addressed to the problems of transnational discovery. Before leaving the

[66] The U.S. pipeline sanctions of 1981–2 were an exception, in that foreign subsidiaries of U.S. companies were held directly liable for violating U.S. controls. See Ch. 2 at n. 25.

subject of the multinational corporation however, one more subject merits a brief discussion, which will serve also as a bridge to the next chapter.

E. JUDGMENTS AGAINST A MULTINATIONAL CORPORATION OR THE PARENT COMPANY

Suppose a court in Xandia, where a member of the corporate group SuNatCo is established, issues a judgment directed not only to the subsidiary SuNatCoXan, but also to the Group as a whole, including specifically SuNatCo, the parent company with seat in Patria. Suppose, for instance, the *Badger* case had not been settled, and the Belgian court had issued a judgment in favor of the employees' union directed not only against Badger Belgium but also against Badger USA. Or suppose the litigation arising out of the wreck of the *Amoco Cadiz* had been carried out in France and a judgment had been entered not only against Amoco Transport, the vessels' registered owner, but also against Standard Oil (Indiana), the parent company of the Amoco/Standard group. Should such judgments be enforced in Patria?

For present purposes, to be explored further in the next chapter, assume that SuNatCo has been properly served with initiating process, and that it has been afforded adequate opportunity to respond, to retain local counsel, and to participate in the proceeding in Xandia. But when the judgment of the Xandian court comes to be enforced in Patria, SuNatCo defends on the ground that

(i) the Xandian court did not have jurisdiction to adjudicate claims against it; and
(ii) the obligations on which the judgment is based were incurred only by its subsidiary SuNatCoXan, and that any effort to impose on it the obligations of SuNatCoXan or to enforce against it a judgment arising out of those obligations is contrary to international law and to the public policy of Patria.

What should be the response of the Patrian court?

One answer would be to reject all recognition and enforcement in these circumstances, on both of the grounds raised by SuNatCo. I believe that answer would be wrong. Another answer would be to say that if under the principles that we have been discussing Xandia was justified in imposing obligations on SuNatCo—i.e. that Xandia had jurisdiction to prescribe—then there should be a presumption that Xandia had jurisdiction to adjudicate as well and the judgment should be recognized and enforced. I believe that answer, too, is not quite right. On reflection, while the criteria for evaluating jurisdiction to prescribe and jurisdiction to adjudicate are similar, I believe a better answer for the Patrian court (as well as earlier for the Xandian court) is to make an independent inquiry on each question. Considerations concerning allocation of judicial competence—both general and specific—are not the same as those concerning ultimate responsibility. There may well be instances in which adjudicatory jurisdiction over a parent company is available to a state, but prescriptive jurisdiction over an activity in another state ought not to be exercised, and other situations in which prescriptive jurisdiction may be exercised—for instance through embargoes or blacklists—while judicial jurisdiction is not available. Thus any conclusion or presumption that jurisdiction to adjudicate and jurisdiction to prescribe are coterminous could well lead to serious misunderstanding.[67]

I believe the best response for the Patrian court would be to conduct an independent inquiry on both issues, in conformity, if possible, with the norms proposed in the preceding Chapters. What should be avoided, however, is any *a priori* rejection of the judgment of the Xandian court on the ground of separate incorporation of the subsidiary from that of the parent or other member of the corporate group.[68]

[67] Moreover, in a litigation context, which in our example would arise in Xandia, the issue of jurisdiction to adjudicate needs to be decided early in the controversy, while the question of jurisdiction to prescribe, i.e. to hold the parent or affiliated company liable, can often be decided only after lengthy inquiry. Neither decision should be viewed as preempting or determining decision of the other issue, though some of the same factors—for instance degree of control over a subsidiary by a parent, and representations by the entity to the outside world—may well be applicable to both issues. In addition, as the *Amoco Cadiz* case illustrates, while lifting the corporate veil for purposes of ultimate responsibility may well be appropriate, the most suitable forum for reaching that decision may be a court at the parent company's principal place of business, which has the best opportunity of probing the intra-enterprise relationships.

[68] A resolution substantially consistent with the views here expressed was adopted at the 67th Session of the Institut de Droit International in Lisbon, 1995. The text of the resolution appears in Vol. 66–II of the Annuaire of the Institut.

6

Recognition and Enforcement of Judgments

A. INTRODUCTION: STATING THE PRINCIPLE

Should judgments be purely territorial, with no effect outside the rendering state? I did not believe anyone today would take that position, until I learned that, absent a treaty, that is the law in as generally enlightened and internationalist countries as the Netherlands, Norway, and Austria.[1] Clearly, the better view, if not yet the view required by international law, is that at least some judgements from some other states ought to be recognized and enforced, to establish the security of contracts, promote commercial dealings, and generally further the rule of law among states that are interdependent as well as independent.

The framers of the American Constitution believed that requiring recognition and enforcement—full faith and credit was their term—of judgments of one state of the United States in all the other states was essential to establishing what they called a 'more perfect Union' out of what were, and to some extent still are, separate sovereign states.[2] The framers of the European Community, long before their successors aspired to the word 'Union', believed that it was essential to creating a common market that its members agree on conditions under which judgments rendered in one Member State would be recognized and enforced in all the other Member States. From this decision, recorded in Article 220 of the Treaty of Rome, came what we now know as

[1] *Austria*: Exekutionsordnung, §§79–85; Fasching, *Lehrbuch des österreichischen Zivilprozessrechts* (1984), ¶ 1511.

Netherlands: Code of Civil Procedure, Art. 421(1). For the statement that in practice Netherlands courts do often recognize foreign judgments, even when they are not required to do so, see Kokkini-Iatridou and Verheul, 'Recognition and Enforcement of Foreign Judgments in Civil and Commercial Matters', in Netherlands Reports to Twelfth International Congress of Comparative Law (1987), 189.

Norway: Act of Aug. 13 1915 relating to judicial Procedure in Civil Cases, §§167–8, *Norges Lover 1685–1983* (1984), 591.

[2] See U.S. Constitution, Art. IV, § 1:

> Full Faith and Credit shall be given in each State to the public Acts, Records, and judicial Proceedings of every other State.

See also the Preamble to the U.S. Constitution:

> We the People of the United States, in Order to form a more perfect Union, establish Justice, insure domestic Tranquility ... and secure the Blessings of Liberty to ourselves and our Posterity, do ordain and establish this Constitution for the United States of America.

the Brussels Convention, which—improving both on the American model and on the mandate in Article 220—addresses both jurisdiction of courts and judgments. But what about recognition and enforcement of judgments among states that maintain friendly and respectful relations with one another but do not wish to form a more perfect union or indeed any union? What about, for instance, enforcement of judgments among all states, omitting only those whose judicial systems are manifestly unfair or corrupt?

Putting aside for the moment the important problem of disputes about jurisdiction and the consequences of judgments by default, I would posit a general principle that two parties to a legal dispute should have one opportunity, and one opportunity only to resolve their dispute in a court of law. If one party is dissatisfied with the result, some kind of vertical recourse should be—and nearly always is—available, typically appeal to a higher judicial instance in the state in which the original judgment was rendered. Horizontal recourse—i.e. a trial of the merits of the dispute before the courts of another state—should be discouraged, if not totally precluded.

This rather bland statement of the principle of *res judicata* may seem too obvious to be worth discussing. But note that I have not placed any qualifications on the principle:

—I have not limited my statement to controversies of a 'civil or commercial character'. I have not, for instance, excluded judgments in disputes concerning succession to the estate of a decedent, or judgments of divorce, or decrees concerning custody of a child, or judicial settlements of a bankruptcy.

—I have not stated that both parties to the controversy must be private persons: thus I have not excluded judgments for taxes or civil penalties.

—I have not said anything about judgments alleged to have been procured by fraud.

—I have not said anything about indirect effects of judgments, such as issue preclusion, claim preclusion, or estoppel.

—I have not said anything about injunctions and similar orders of a court directing the respondent to do something, or refrain from doing something, other than making a payment.

—Finally, I have not said anything about the public policy of the state asked to recognize a judgment of another state. In particular, I have not mentioned such issues as punitive damages, multiple damages, award of counsel fees, and similar elements of judgments dear to the hearts of lawyers in some states but abhorrent to lawyers in other states.

Perhaps the mere mention of these issues suggests that the principle as first stated is too broad, and that *res judicata* across national frontiers is acceptable only subject to a number of exclusions, limitations, and qualifications. I would propose the opposite inference. My point of departure is that among basically like-minded states—i.e. among democratic states with judiciaries independent of political control—the principle is correct as stated; it is the exceptions that have too long been accepted uncritically, and have not been adequately tested against the principle.

B. UP FROM THE BASICS

We need not spend much time on the basics. At a minimum, if Xandia is prepared to recognize foreign judgments at all, it will recognize a judgment rendered by a court in Patria in, say, an action brought by a Seller against a Buyer for the purchase price of goods that Seller asserts it delivered pursuant to a contract with Buyer. For purposes of this most elementary example, assume that both Seller and Buyer are subject without controversy to judicial jurisdiction in both states, and that Buyer participated in the lawsuit in Patria.[3] If Seller obtains a judgment in its favor in Patria and that judgment is not satisfied, Seller can secure judicial enforcement of that judgment in Xandia, without having to prove the underlying claim a second time. Buyer will be precluded from asserting in the Xandia proceeding that the goods were defective, or that the payment was not yet due, or that the invoice was incorrect. Correspondingly, if Seller loses in Patria, the judgment in favor of Buyer will be recognized in Xandia, and Seller will be precluded from making a second attempt to collect the purchase price.

All this is easy—too easy. But before we leave this paradigm case, it is worth pondering that we have skipped over a number of possible objections.

(1) *Do the nationalities of Seller and Buyer matter?* The answer should be no; recognition and enforcement of judgments has nothing to do with nationality, whether the parties are individuals or juridical persons.[4]

(2) *Do the domiciles of Seller and Buyer matter?* Again the answer should be no. We know that the domicile of the defendant may affect the jurisdiction of the Patrian court, and also the application of international treaties, such as the Brussels and Lugano conventions. But assuming that jurisdiction is not an issue, there is no reason why the parties' domicile should matter either.[5]

(3) *Should it matter that Patria was a common law country and Xandia a civil law country, or vice versa?* Certainly not.

[3] For more on the issues of judicial jurisdiction, see sect. D *infra*.

[4] We may leave aside for present purposes extraordinary situations, such as might arise if economic sanctions were applicable in Xandia against certain nationals. Thus if in 1993 the Seller who prevailed in Patria were a national of Iran and Xandia was the United States, enforcement of the Patrian judgment might be barred under the Iranian Assets Control Regulations, 31 C.F.R. §§ 535.201 *et seq*.

[5] It is worth remarking that under the UN Convention for the Recognition and Enforcement of Foreign Arbitral Awards of 1958, 330 U.N.T.S. 3 (the New York Convention), only the place of the arbitration is dispositive. If that place is in a state party to the Convention, an award is enforceable (subject to very limited defenses) in all other contracting states, regardless of the state of domicile or nationality of the parties to the arbitration, and regardless of whether such state is a party to the Convention.

(4) *Should it matter that the action in Patria was tried to a jury while that could not have been the case in Xandia, or vice versa?* Again, my answer is certainly not, though, as we shall see, not everyone agrees.

(5) *Should it matter that different rules of evidence or modes of proof were applied in Patria from those applicable in Xandia?* Again the answer is certainly not, given some basic common characteristics of the litigation process, such as an opportunity for each side to make its presentation, to be assisted by counsel, and to summon witnesses.

It is worth quoting from the famous case of *Hilton* v. *Guyot*,[6] decided by the United States Supreme Court just 100 years ago. As is well known, in the end the U.S. Supreme Court did not grant enforcement to the judgment of a French court in favor of a French citizen against an American citizen, on the now substantially obsolete ground of lack of reciprocity.[7] But in the course of an elaborate survey of international law and practice the court said:

> It is ... objected that in these courts one of the plaintiffs was permitted to testify not under oath, and was not subjected to cross-examination by the opposite party, and that the defendants were, therefore, deprived of safeguards which are by our law considered essential to secure honesty and to detect fraud in a witness; and also that documents and papers were admitted in evidence, with which the defendants had no connection, and which would not be admissible under our own system of jurisprudence. But it having been shown by the plaintiffs, and hardly denied by the defendants, that the practice followed and the method of examining witnesses were according to the laws of France, we are not prepared to hold that the fact that the procedure in these respects differed from that of our own courts is, of itself a sufficient ground for impeaching the foreign judgment.[8]

I think that is right. It is certainly the law in the United States, and I believe there is substantial, if not complete, international agreement on this question, and on all of the questions raised thus far.

The questions gradually get more difficult:

(6) *Does it matter what law the Patrian court applied?* Once more, going back to the initial principle, the answer should be no. The Patrian court may have applied Patrian law, whereas if the initial action had been brought before a Xandian court, that court would have applied Xandian law. Or the Patrian court may have declared that it was applying Xandian law, but misunderstood that law. Either way, if one believes in the recognition and enforcement of judgments, these decisions—errors if you will—by the Patrian court should

[6] 159 U.S. 113 (1895).

[7] For an explanation of why the condition of reciprocity, though not formally overruled, is considered obsolete and inoperative, see, e.g., *Restatement (Third) of the Foreign Relations Law of the United States*, § 481, comments (*a*) and (*d*) and Reporters' Note 1 (1987).

[8] 159 U.S. at 204–5.

not affect the validity of the judgement in Xandia. If the losing party wished to challenge the correctness of the decision, it should have appealed to a higher instance in Patria, and not attempted to make its challenge in connection with recognition or enforcement in Xandia. Even if the contract between the Seller and Buyer contained a clause selecting Xandian law but the Patrian court had disregarded or rejected it, I think that the judgment should not be denied recognition.

Not everyone may agree at this point. For instance under French law (for judgments not falling under the Brussels/Lugano Conventions), if the Patrian court had applied Patrian law under circumstances where a French court in the position of Xandia would have applied French [Xandian] law and the outcome would have been substantially different, the French court would not, as I understand it, recognize or enforce the Patrian judgment.[9] But I am pleased to confirm that errors of law, including choice of law, are not among the bases for refusal of recognition under the Brussels Convention,[10] or under § 4 of the Uniform Foreign Money/Judgments Act in force in about half the states of the United States;[11] or under the grounds for refusal of enforcement of judgments under English law.[12] I had thought that at least since 1986 this was the rule in Germany as well,[13] but I am not so sure.[14]

I want to raise the level of difficulty one more step, remembering that we are still addressing the easy case of a dispute between two private parties about payment of the purchase price in a sales transaction.

(7) Suppose Seller asserted in the action in Patria that because Buyer did not make payment of the purchase price when due, Seller was unable to pay its supplier, who thereupon cut off all shipments to Seller. Seller sought and was awarded consequential damages by the Patrian court, i.e. not only the purchase price plus interest, but also compensation for profits lost on other sales and indemnification for claims brought against Seller by the supplier. In Xandia, the only recovery for failure to pay for the goods would have been the purchase

[9] See *Munzer* v. *Munzer-Jacoby*, Cass. Jan. 7, 1964, [1964] II Semaine Juridique 13590 (1969) 91 Journal du Droit International (Clunet) 302. But if the Patrian court had applied French law, but misunderstood it, that would probably not be a ground for non-enforcement of the judgment. See, e.g., Pierre Mayer, *Droit International Privé* (5th edn., 1994), 259 and sources there cited.

[10] See for an express statement, *Report on the Convention on Jurisdiction and the Enforcement of Judgments in Civil and Commercial Matters* (the Jenard Report) [1979] OJ C59/1 at 44.

[11] See 13 Uniform Laws Annotated, 261 *et seq*. As of year-end 1995, 25 states, including the major commercial states of California, Illinois, New York, Pennsylvania, and Texas had adopted the Act, and its provisions were in general applied by other states in the United States as well. See *Restatement (Third) of Foreign Relations Law*, n. 7 *supra*, §§ 481–482.

[12] See Dicey and Morris, *Conflict of Laws* (12th edn., Collins, 1993), Rule 41, 499–503.

[13] See Zivilprozessordnung (ZPO), § 328(1)3 as amended; Reinhold Geimer, *Internationales Zivilprozessrecht* (1987), ¶ 2263.

[14] See the discussion of the *P. & Co* v. *T.* case, 131–2 *infra*.

price plus interest.[15] *May Xandia now reject the judgment of the Patrian court, or reduce it by the amount in excess of the elements of damages that a Xandian court would have awarded?* Again I say no, though I think some of the problematics with recognition and enforcement of judgments have begun to emerge. Indeed, such a proposal, addressed to tort damages, was seriously discussed in the late 1970s by representatives of the United States and the United Kingdom, attempting to revive their stalled negotiations of a judgments convention.[16]

This brief escalation from the simplest case has demonstrated, I think, that the subject of transnational effect of judgments is not nearly as easy as the initial principle suggests, and that the consensus is not nearly at the level required to sustain fulfilment of the principle. Nevertheless, I want to explore whether the consensus can be pushed further in the direction of the initial principle in three areas, and then to raise some questions about the agenda for a judgments convention looking beyond Western and Central Europe.

C. THE SURPRISINGLY NARROW LIMITS OF RECOGNITION PRACTICE

The Brussels Convention on Jurisdiction and the Enforcement of Judgments is expressly limited to 'civil and commercial matters', defined to exclude not only criminal matters, but the status or legal capacity of natural persons, rights in property arising out of a matrimonial relationship, wills, and succession; also bankruptcy and analogous proceedings; and revenue, customs, and administrative matters (Art. 1).[17] The 1971 Hague Convention on the Recognition and Enforcement of Foreign Judgments in Civil and Commercial

[15] Compare the UN Convention on Contracts for the International Sales of Goods (1980) (Vienna Convention), Art, 74, providing for 'damages . . . equal to the loss, including loss of profit', with United States, Uniform Commercial Code, §§ 2–209, 2–210, limiting damages to the purchase price plus 'incidental damages', which include expenses of reselling but not loss of profits.

[16] The draft of the proposed Convention between the United Kingdom and the United States for the Reciprocal Recognition and Enforcement of Judgments in Civil Matters was published by the British government in Cmnd. 6771 (1977), and also in 16 *Int'l Leg. Mats.* 71 (1977). Proposed Art. 8A, not there published but discussed in various versions for several months, read:

> Where the respondent establishes that the amount awarded by the court of origin is greatly in excess of the amount, including costs, that would have been awarded on the basis of the findings of law and fact established in the court of origin if the assessment of that amount had been a matter for the court addressed, the court may, to the extent then permitted by the laws generally applicable in that court to the recognition and enforcement of foreign judgments, recognize and enforce the judgment in a lesser amount.

A slightly different version of proposed Art. 8A appears as an addendum to P. M. North, 'The Draft U.K./U.S. Judgments Convention: A British Viewpoint', 1 *Nw. J. Int'l L. & Bus.* 219 at 239 (1979).

[17] The Convention also excludes arbitration, on the persuasive ground that other conventions, notably the New York Convention, n. 5 *supra*, cover the subject.

Matters, which has not been widely adopted, contains substantially the same exclusions, as do numerous bilateral judgments conventions.[18] The United States has no treaties with any other country concerning recognition or enforcement of judgments, but the Uniform Foreign Money-Judgments Recognition Act[19] also is directed only to judgments granting or denying recovery of a sum of money, and expressly excludes 'judgments for taxes, a fine or other penalty, or a judgment for support in matrimonial or family matters'.[20] Why is recognition practice so limited? Putting aside family matters, which often have different jurisdictional bases and which are gradually being dealt with in other conventions,[21] why are huge areas of civil litigation excluded from the scope of international recognition?

1. Death

One can understand that, in their initial effort to secure approval of a convention, the drafters of the Brussels Convention, and of the 1971 Hague Judgments Convention, wished to avoid controversial issues that might derail their projects. But the reasons for the underlying controversies, in my submission, are not persuasive a quarter century later. The Jenard Report on the Brussels Convention, for instance, quotes an opinion rendered by the International Union of Latin Notaries that it would be desirable to facilitate the recognition and enforcement of judgments in matters related to succession, but that it was essential first to unify the rules of conflict of laws.[22] I am not at all sure that this is the correct sequence. Granted that both the substantive rules with respect to succession and the relevant conflict of laws rules are different in different states. Some states protect or prefer the children, others the surviving spouse, and the levels of reserved shares or elective shares vary from state to state; also some states look to the domicile of the decedent, others to nationality, and these terms are themselves subject to definition and interpretation. All of this suggests that succession to property of decedents is a fertile field for litigation, typically between surviving spouses and children, especially children of a prior marriage. But if reduced litigation, consistency of results, and finality are worthwhile goals, recognition practice should, it seems to me, be encouraged, not avoided or postponed to some distant era of substantive harmonization.

Once again I have a case, or rather two related cases, one from France, the other from New York.

[18] See e.g., Convention between the United Kingdom and Canada, Apr. 24, 1984, Art. II: UK: Cm 306; Treaty between the Federal Republic of Germany and Israel of July 20, 1977, Art. 4.

[19] See n. 11 *supra*.

[20] Uniform Foreign Money-Judgements Recognition Act, § 1(2). § 7 makes clear, however, that the Act does not prevent the recognition of a foreign judgement in situations not covered by the act.

[21] See, e.g., The Hague Convention of Oct. 25, 1980 on the Civil Aspects of International Child Abduction.

[22] Jenard Report, n. 10 *supra*, at 11.

The decedent, Mr Aristide Lanari, was an Italian national domiciled at the time of his death in France, where he had resided with his second wife, Roberta, an American citizen. Among other assets he had kept funds in a bank in New York in a joint account with his wife. When he died, Roberta, the surviving spouse, requested the bank to turn over the balance of the account to her. Before the bank could do so, Mr Lanari's daughter by his first marriage, Maria Elena, notified the bank that she claimed the funds, as the heir of her father under the applicable French law. Maria Elena immediately brought suit in Nice, seeking a declaration that various transfers by her father during his lifetime were disguised gifts in violation of French law. Further she contended that joint accounts that her father had opened in foreign banks, including the one in New York, did not confer any rights on Roberta, but should be returned to the estate, out of which Maria Elena was entitled to her *légitime* or forced share. Shortly thereafter, Roberta, the widow, brought suit in New York against the bank seeking turnover of the account, and Maria Elena intervened in that suit.

Thus parallel actions were in progress in two states, with essentially the same parties, and with no doubt about judicial jurisdiction in either proceeding.

For the New York courts, the issue was complicated, because under one recent precedent joint bank accounts should be assimilated to trusts and governed by the law of the situs,[23] while under another slightly later precedent a decedent could not by choosing New York law or placing his assets in New York avoid the restrictions applicable at his domicile on freedom to reduce the inheritance of specified family members.[24] It might have been possible to choose between the two precedents, because the first one involved an *inter vivos* disposition, the second a testamentary disposition. But such a distinction, though often made in American cases, was not inherently persuasive.[25] Moreover, it could have led to an inconsistent result with the French action, which had meanwhile proceeded to judgment in favor of the daughter, both in the court of first instance in Nice and the Court of Appeal in Aix-en-Provence.[26] Accordingly, in *Watts* v. *Swiss Bank Corporation*,[27] the New York Court of Appeals (the state's highest court) treated the case as a judgments case. No treaty or statute compelled this result. But the court wrote:

[23] *Wyatt* v. *Fulrath*, 16 N.Y.2d 169, 264 N.Y.S.2d 233, 211 N.E.2d 637 (1965).

[24] *Estate of Clark*, 21 N.Y.2d 478, 288 N.Y.S.2d 993, 236 N.E.2d 152 (1968)

[25] Compare *Restatement (Second) of Conflict of Laws*, § 269 (wills governed by law applicable at testator's domicile) with § 270 (*inter vivos* trust generally governed by settlor's designation or place of administration of trust), criticized by the present writer in A. Lowenfeld, '"Tempora Mutantur ..."—Wills and Trusts in the Conflicts Restatement', 72 *Colum. L. Rev.* 382 (1972).

[26] *Maccoun/Watts* v. *Lanari/Meyer*, Cour d'Appel, Aix-en-Provence, Oct. 22, 1964. So far as I know, the decision is not published in a French reporter. An edited version in English appears in A. Lowenfeld, *Conflict of Laws: Federal, State, and International Perspectives* (1986), 342, along with the New York case under discussion, cited in n. 27 *infra*.

[27] 27 N.Y.2d 270, 317 N.Y.S.2d 315, 265 N.E.2d 739 (1970).

> Under principles of comity the courts should give full effect to a judgment rendered by a French court of competent jurisdiction. Recognition will not be withheld merely because the choice of law process in the rendering jurisdiction applies a law at variance with that which would be applied under New York choice of law principles. It is concluded that no contravention of public policy sufficient to justify nonrecognition has been demonstrated by the appellants.[28]

I think the New York court reached the right result and by the correct path. It avoided inconsistent outcomes, and achieved *pro tanto* a unity of succession. It is true that the result does not avoid forum shopping to some extent, and possibly a race among courts. It is also true that one can make up variations on the *Lanari* case that complicate the problem further, for instance if litigation had been going on at the same time in Italy, the state of the decedent's nationality. But the decision demonstrates what the questions raised earlier only suggest. It does make a difference whether a party has only a *claim*, which may be decided under various substantive laws, or a *judgment*, which ought to carry with it at least a presumption that it will be recognized in other states.

While there may be areas in which drafting and securing agreement on a treaty will continue to be difficult,[29] my message would be that (assuming regularity of jurisdiction) the absence of a treaty or statutory requirement to recognize a given judgment should not be regarded as an argument against recognition. Further, a presumption in favour of recognition should apply in matters of succession to the same extent as in the transaction between seller and buyer with which the Chapter started, regardless of the substantive law or the choice of law that would have been applied by the second state had it decided the underlying litigation.

2. . . . and Taxes

More than 200 hundred years ago, Benjamin Franklin wrote to a friend (in French): 'In this world nothing is certain but death and taxes'.[30]

Franklin was clearly correct. While different states take different approaches to all kinds of legal issues–from property to trade to family matters to labor relations—there is no real country on earth that does not collect taxes. In contrast to exchange controls, export restrictions, antitrust decrees, and similar regimes that may be imposed by one state but be contrary to the public policy or *ordre public* of another, taxes are universal. And while some kinds of

[28] 27 N.Y.2d at 279, 317 N.Y.S.2d at 321, 265 N.E.2d at 744–5.

[29] For this writer's suggestions about such a treaty, see Lowenfeld, 'Thoughts about a Judgments Convention: A Reaction to the von Mehren Report', 57 *Law & Contemp. Probs.* No. 3, 289 (Summer 1994).

[30] Letter to Jean-Baptiste Le Roy, 13 Nov. 1789. The complete passage read:

> Our Constitution is in actual operation; everything appears to promise that it will last; but in this world nothing is certain but death and taxes.

The Writings of Benjamin Franklin (Albert Henry Smyth ed., 1907) x, 68.

taxes are unusual, the basic formulas for imposition of taxes—on income, on property, and on transfer of property—are accepted almost everywhere. Moreover, most industrial and many developing countries are parties to treaties for the avoidance of double taxation and for cooperation among national tax authorities. Why then should judgments for taxes be regarded as out of bounds when it comes to recognition and enforcement?

The leading case, *Government of India* v. *Taylor*,[31] involved an English company that had operated the electric tramway system in Delhi. Seeing that India was about to become independent, the company had sold its assets to the government. The Indian government paid the purchase price, which was promptly remitted to England. Thereafter the Indian government, in accordance with an amendment to its tax law, imposed a capital gains tax on the proceeds of the sale. The company contested the tax and secured a reduction, but it did not pay the tax and removed all its assets from India. The Government of India obtained a judgment for the tax from the relevant court, and sought to collect the amount due by an action in England against the liquidator of the company. Having lost in the lower courts, the Indian government eventually appealed the case to the House of Lords, which unanimously rejected the appeal.

Viscount Simonds said he was 'greatly surprised' that this suit had been brought, though he admitted that the history and origin of the rule barring such a suit, 'if it be a rule', are not easy to ascertain.[32] Lord Keith, drawing on an opinion (in fact a concurrence) by Judge Learned Hand in the United States,[33] put forward the explanation that a tax claim should not be enforced without some scrutiny, and since such scrutiny by the court of the second state might embarrass the claimant state, there should be no enforcement at all.[34] To me a simple answer would be that claimant judgment creditor was apparently willing to risk a certain embarrassment, for instance a check by the court where enforcement is sought whether the tax was discriminatory, or whether it had been imposed with impermissible retroactivity, or whether the taxpayer had been given the opportunity to contest the assessment. To deny the claim in order to spare embarrassment to the claimant seems odd, to say the least. Lord Somervell, conceding that 'there is no decision binding on your Lordships' House', said there are 'many propositions for which no express authority can be found because they have been regarded as self-evident to all concerned.'[35] He conceded further that the initial burdens of investigating a tax claim will normally have disappeared once the claim has been reduced to a judgment. Still, '[t]he principle remains. The claim is one for a tax.'[36]

It seems to me that a rule that cannot be explained except on the basis that it is surprising that someone would think to challenge it, that it is self-evident, that the challenging party might be embarrassed, and that there is

31 [1955] AC 491.
32 [1955] AC at 503.
33 *Moore* v. *Mitchell*, 30 F.2d 600, 604 (2d Cir. 1929)
34 [1955] AC at 511.
35 [1955] AC at 514.
36 *Ibid.*

no significant difference between a claim and a judgment, does not stand on very strong foundations.[37]

I was not able to persuade the American Law Institute that the rule should be the reverse, for there had been a recent decision of a U.S. Court of Appeals in a similar case,[38] rejecting an attempt by British Columbia to enforce a judgment for a logging tax in an American court, which is no more persuasive than *India* v. *Taylor* except that it could cite a Canadian case that had declined enforcement of an American tax judgment on the authority of *India* v. *Taylor*.[39] I was, however, able to persuade the Institute to approve a section in the *Restatement* which said in 'black letters':

> Courts in the United States are not required to recognize or to enforce judgments for the collection of taxes, fines or penalties rendered by the courts of other states,[40]

followed by a Comment that states 'No rule of United States law or of international law would be violated if a court in the United States enforced a judgment of a foreign court for payment of taxes or comparable assessment that was otherwise compatible with the standards [for recognition and enforcement of foreign country judgments]'.[41]

I would hope that international practice, and any new treaty that might come out of the Hague Conference or elsewhere, would move at least as far as the *Restatement* did in 1987, and keep open the possibility of reversing the presumption completely.[42]

3. Breaking Through the Public Law Taboo

In my Hague Lectures of 1979,[43] one of the cases I criticized was *Schemmer* v. *Property Resources Ltd*,[44] decided by the High Court of Justice in England in 1974, and to my regret not appealed. In that case a receiver appointed by the U.S. District Court in New York on motion of the Securities and Exchange Commission sought the assistance of the English court in freezing funds on

[37] Compare Viscount Simonds, in discussing the challenge, 'My Lords, these seem to me frail weapons with which to attack a strong fortress': [1955] AC at 506.

[38] *Her Majesty the Queen in Right of Province of British Columbia* v. *Gilbertson*, 597 F.2d 1161 (9th Cir. 1979).

[39] *United States* v. *Harden*, 1963 S.C.R. 366, 41 D.L.R. 2d 721 (Sup. Ct. Canada 1963).

[40] *Restatement (Third) of Foreign Relations Law*, § 483.

[41] *Id.*, Comment *a*; see also Reporters' Note 2 and sources there cited.

[42] It is worth mentioning a recent decision of an intermediate state court in Florida, which enforced an order of an English court for amounts owed after defendant's conviction for fraudulent evasion of value-added tax, *Bullen* v. *Her Majesty's Government*, 553 So.2d 1344 (Fla. Dist. Ct. App. 1989).

[43] A. Lowenfeld, 'Public Law in the International Arena: Conflict of Laws, International Law and Some Suggestions for their Interaction' (1979–II) 163 *Recueil des Cours* 311. I refer here to the discussion at 412–17.

[44] [1975] Ch. 273; [1974] 3 WLR 406.

deposit in London banks. The purpose of the application was to save what could be saved for thousands of investors who had been defrauded by Robert Vesco, by then a fugitive from the United States, who had somehow secured control of the IOS empire previously controlled by Bernard Cornfield. The receiver had discovered that some $40 million had been deposited in London by Bahamian companies controlled by Vesco, and he sought an order from the High Court restraining transfer of these assets while their ownership and origin could be traced to Vesco group.[45]

Rather than viewing the action brought by the receiver as one seeking co-operation among friendly states to defend against massive international fraud, Mr Justice Goulding in the High Court saw the action as one for the enforcement of a foreign judgment. That would be acceptable if the principles for recognition and enforcement here urged were accepted. The 'judgment' of the U.S. Court did not meet Mr Justice Goulding's standards, however; one of the companies alleged to hold funds in London had not been a named defendant in the New York proceeding. Further, the judge went through an elaborate inquiry into the origins and purposes of the United States Securities Exchange Act of 1934,[46] concluding that it was a penal statute and as such unenforceable outside the United States.[47] It followed that the receiver appointed by the U.S. court on motion of the federal agency stood in the shoes of the agency, thus had to be considered a public officer, and therefore his application could not be granted. In other words, because plaintiff represented the interest of a foreign state, that interest could not be granted any support by the English court. I thought that was quite wrong, and suggested further that such attitudes only encouraged the United States in its sometimes excessive resort to unilateral exercise of jurisdiction over transnational activities.

I am happy to report that there has been a substantial change of attitude in the past few years, not only in England, but in France, Switzerland, and other countries that have come to appreciate the opportunities, and the dangers, of international fraud. Particularly in the field of securities regulation, a web of co-operation, formal and informal, has in significant measure replaced the emphasis on national sovereignty reflected in cases such as *Schemmer* v. *PRL*. A full report on this development would require a whole volume, and would stray very far from the topic of recognition of judgments.[48] I do want, however, to summarize the case of Eddie Antar, to show how much progress has been

[45] Note that the events here described took place shortly before the invention of the Mareva injunction described in Ch. 4, sect. D(3).

[46] 15 U.S.C. § 78a *et seq*.

[47] [1975] Ch. at 282–8, [1974] 3 WLR at 409–15.

[48] For a useful and comprehensive account of recent developments by the three members of the staff of the U.S. Securities and Exchange Commission, see Michael D. Mann, Joseph G. Mari, George Lavdas, *Developments in International Securities Law Enforcement and Regulation* (1994).

made since the Vesco affair in addressing common interests rather than excessive concern about sovereignty.[49]

Eddie Antar was known to persons in the greater New York area for many years as the principal owner of the 'Crazy Eddie' chain of discount electronics stores, and sponsor of zany advertisements on local television stations. It turned out, however, that for several years Antar systematically falsified the financial records of the Crazy Eddie chain, greatly overstating the firm's earnings and understating its debts. On the basis of these false representations, Crazy Eddie sold some $60 million in shares to the public, in violation of numerous provisions of the U.S. securities laws. When the SEC moved against Eddie Antar and his associates in 1989 in federal court in New Jersey seeking injunctions and disgorgement of the proceeds of the stock sale, Antar failed to appear and apparently transferred the bulk of his assets abroad.

The U.S. District Court entered an order enjoining Antar from violating the securities laws. As in the *Vesco* case, the court appointed a receiver, and it ordered Antar to turn some $52 million over to the receiver. While Antar remained in hiding, the SEC obtained a civil judgment against him for some $72 million.

Should such a judgment be enforceable abroad? Mr Justice Goulding, who had decided the *Schemmer* case, would say no. In the 1990s, however, Mr Carella, the receiver appointed by the U.S. court on motion of the SEC, did much better. First, in response to a request by the SEC under a 1988 Memorandum of Understanding, the Commission des Valeurs Mobilières du Québec froze funds deposited by Antar in a bank in Montreal, and thereafter Mr Carella, the receiver, brought a civil action in the District Court of Quebec to enforce the judgment of the U.S. District Court. The Quebec court entered judgment in favor of the receiver, and pursuant to that judgment the Canadian bank transferred more than $1 million from an account controlled by Antar to the receiver.[50]

The Commission and the receiver brought similar actions in Switzerland, Israel, and England, and all were successful. The Court of First Instance in Geneva, ordering some $40 million held in bank accounts in that city, expressly held that the U.S. judgment sued on was a civil and not a penal or administrative judgment, and that entry of its own judgment against Antar on the basis of the American judgment was not against Swiss *ordre public*.[51] In

[49] This account draws on the publication cited in the previous footnote, as well as on a series of Litigation Releases issued by the SEC in the period Sept. 6, 1989–April 15, 1994, all entitled *Securities and Exchange Commission* v. *Eddie Antar et al.*

[50] See SEC Litigation Release No. 13649 (May 25, 1993).

[51] *Carella* v. *Antar*, Geneva, Tribunal de Première Instance, Apr. 12, 1994. Interestingly enough, after close of the oral hearing, counsel for Antar sought to introduce a copy of the English judgment in the *Schemmer* case, n. 44 *supra*, but the Geneva court declined to accept it. On the issue of public policy or *ordre public*, the court wrote:

> The public policy exception should be interpreted restrictively, particularly when the matter concerns rights definitively acquired abroad through legal proceedings. A

January 1994, the High Court in London issued a similar judgment against Eddie Antar in the amount of almost $90 million.[52] The fact that, meanwhile, a grand jury in New Jersey had indicted Eddie Antar, that he had been extradited from Israel to face the charges, and that he had been found guilty on seventeen counts of securities fraud, mail fraud, and conspiracy to commit racketeering did not change the outcome of the efforts to enforce the civil judgments, which were brought for the benefit of investors who had been defrauded.

It would be premature to conclude from this one episode that the public law taboo has been eliminated in the context of international judgments practice.[53] I am pleased, however, to see that the taboo looks less impregnable than before. I would hope that the next time courts are faced with the public law argument in other contexts, for instance in connection with judgments for taxes, this breakthrough in four countries will be seen as an important example.[54]

D. THE QUESTION OF JURISDICTION: CHOICE OF LAW AND *RES JUDICATA*

Thus far the discussion of recognition of judgments has proceeded on the assumption that the first forum clearly had jurisdiction over the defendant. It goes without saying that no legal system would regard an *in personam* judgment rendered by a foreign forum binding on a party over whom that forum did not have jurisdiction.[55] There is no comparable consensus, however,

> refusal to recognize such judgments in Switzerland would create limping judgments. For this reason the exception of Swiss public policy may be invoked only if the contradiction with Swiss public perception of law and morals is grave. In other words, recognition constitutes the rule which may be cast aside only for very good reasons.

[52] See SEC Litigation Release No. 13958 (3 Feb., 1994).

[53] For instance, in *United States of America* vs. *Inkley*, [1989] QB 255, [1988] 2 WLR 304 (CA), a British subject had been charged with fraud in the United States, and then released on bail. He had been permitted to go to England for a month to attend his father's funeral, but he failed to return for his court appearance and the U.S. government obtained a civil judgment in Florida in the amount of his appearance bond plus interest. When the U.S. government sought to enforce that judgment by suit in England, the High Court judge entered judgment in favor of the United States, but the Court of Appeal reversed and dismissed the action on the ground that the action was in substance, if not in form, execution by the United States of its public law, citing *inter alia*, *Government of India* v. *Taylor* and *Schemmer* v. *PRL*.

[54] It is worth pointing out that the Commission of the European Communities has announced that it will study the possibility of extending the scope of the Brussels Convention to competition cases assigned to administrative courts, and has expressed its view (without citation) that competition judgments of national courts are already governed by the Convention where they are handed down in cases of a civil or commercial nature: *Notice on Co-operation between National Courts and the Commission in Applying Articles 85 and 86 of the EEC Treaty* [1993] O-J C39/6 at para 44.

[55] Perhaps this statement is too broad without a more precise definition of *in personam* judgment than is here offered. Certainly an *in rem* judgment may cut off title claims of a person not within the jurisdiction of the rendering court if the *res* was within the

concerning the effect in the forum where recognition is sought of a determination in the first forum concerning its own jurisdiction.

At least two propositions necessary for the present discussion emerged from the exploration of judicial jurisdiction in Chapter 4. First, there is a broad consensus concerning the acceptable bases for judicial jurisdiction, beginning with the defendant's domicile and including also such links or contacts as the place of injury in a claim in tort, the place of performance of a contract, and so on. Secondly, there are some differences in the accepted bases of jurisdiction; the interesting ones for present purposes are not the exorbitant ones, but rather what one might consider the gray areas accepted in some but not all states, such as place of making of a contract, doing business in the forum state when the claim did not arise out of that business, or being a partner to a person over whom the court clearly has jurisdiction. A third proposition, or perhaps corollary would be a better term, is that many questions of judicial jurisdiction in particular cases depend on factual, or mixed legal/factual, determinations. Should such determinations be regarded as binding outside the rendering state? Putting the question differently, is a decision in exercise of *compétence de la compétence*, which in the first instance every court possesses, itself entitled to recognition in other fora? Should there be a distinction, for this purpose, between factual determinations, such as whether *X* was defendant's agent, and legal conclusions, such as whether defendant's contacts with the rendering state were sufficient to support the court's jurisdiction?

Perhaps the most instructive (if not the most scientific) way to put the question is to ask how one should advise a defendant established or domiciled in Xandia who is served—I will assume properly served—with process in a lawsuit initiated in Patria. There is some basis for assertion of jurisdiction by the Patrian court, but also some basis to question that jurisdiction. Should the defendant appear in Patria to challenge the court's jurisdiction, or should he default?

My favorite illustration for pedagogic purposes involves two widely separated states of the United States, but the facts are easily adapted to the international arena. Essentially, the *White Lumber Sales* case[56] is the paradigm 'simplest case' with which the Chapter started,[57] except that, in contrast to the initial case, here judicial jurisdiction was a major issue. Continental Forest Products, the plaintiff, was an Oregon corporation engaged in the lumber business. White Lumber Sales was a Florida corporation also engaged in the lumber business, and the two companies had known one another from prior dealings.

In the transaction that gave rise to the litigation, White, the Florida buyer,

jurisdiction, and various types of legal proceedings concerning annulment, divorce, child custody, adoption, and the like may have similar effect. It is understood that proceedings of this kind are not embraced in the present discussion.

[56] *State ex rel. White Lumber Sales, Inc.* v. *Sulmonetti*, 242 Or. 121, 448 P.2d 571 (Sup. Ct. Oregon 1968).

[57] See 111 *supra*.

asked Continental by telephone for a price quotation on twenty carloads of plywood to be manufactured to specifications that White would supply, to be delivered to a designated site in Georgia. Continental, the Oregon seller, consulted its suppliers and gave a quotation to White which White accepted, also by telephone. Subsequently the order was confirmed in writing, and Continental shipped the first three carloads. White paid for the first carload, but then notified Continental that the plywood was too thin to conform to the specifications. White withheld further payments and gave notice of cancellation of the contract. Following further telephone calls and correspondence, Continental brought suit—in Oregon. The suit claimed (i) the purchase price for the second and third carload; (ii) damages for losses incurred in manufacturing the plywood not shipped; and (iii) further damages for breach of the contract to deliver the remainder of the twenty carloads. Jurisdiction over the buyer was asserted on the basis of an Oregon statute conferring jurisdiction on the Oregon courts as to any cause of action arising out of the 'transaction by defendant of any business within this state'.[58]

How should White, the Florida company with no other links to Oregon, respond to this suit? One option for the Florida buyer would be to make no appearance at all. If the litigation continued, it is reasonable to expect that hearing only from plaintiff, the Oregon court would find that it had jurisdiction, and that the court would enter judgment for the seller. We cannot be sure that it would award all the elements of damages sought by the seller,[59] but absent any contrary evidence it would almost certainly find that the goods shipped conformed to the specifications in the contract.

If Buyer did not pay, Seller could bring an action on the judgment in Florida, in reliance on the Full Faith and Credit Clause of the United States Constitution,[60] and the implementing legislation passed by the Congress in 1790 and only slightly changed since that time.[61] Buyer could not, in Florida, contest or 'relitigate' the quality of the goods shipped: that issue would be said to be 'merged' into the judgment of the Oregon court.[62] (A European would say looking into the quality of the goods would be *révision au fond*.) But the question of *jurisdiction* of the Oregon court would not merge into the judgment, and since it had not previously been examined in a contested proceeding, that question could now be contested by defendant/judgment debtor. The Florida court (state or federal) could make its own determination as to where the contract had been concluded, where (if it were relevant to jurisdiction) title to the plywood had passed or was supposed to pass, and whether or not the prior dealings between the parties were linked to the transaction that gave

[58] Oregon revised Statutes, § 14.035(1)(a).

[59] See n. 15 *supra*.

[60] See n. 2 *supra*.

[61] Act of May 26, 1790, c. XI, 1 Stat. 122, presently 28 U.S.C. § 1738

[62] See American Law Institute, *Restatement (Second) of Judgments* § 18 and Comments thereto (1982).

rise to the lawsuit. If the corresponding Florida statute would not have conferred jurisdiction on Florida courts in comparable circumstances, however, that would not justify rejection of the Oregon judgment, because the overall standard is a national constitutional standard. To be precise, if the Oregon court's assertion was consistent with the Due Process clause of the U.S. Constitution, it would violate the Full Faith and Credit clause of the Constitution for the Florida court to deny recognition and enforcement to the Oregon judgment.[63]

A second option for the Florida buyer would be to contest the jurisdiction of the Oregon court in Oregon. That, of course, would impose some burden on the buyer—hiring a lawyer several thousand miles away, possibly litigating in an unfriendly forum. But if Buyer persuaded the Oregon court that it did not have jurisdiction, either under the Oregon statute or under the federal Constitution, that would be the end of the case; if it failed in its jurisdictional challenge, Buyer could do what it could not do under the first option—present a defense on the merits.[64]

Could Buyer present its jurisdictional challenge in Oregon, and if that failed, withdraw from further participation in the case? It could do so, but having participated in a jurisdictional challenge in Oregon, it would be bound by the result of that challenge. Whether or not Buyer participated further in the Oregon proceeding, if Seller brought suit on the judgment of the Oregon court in Florida, Buyer would have no defense. Buyer not only had had the opportunity to challenge the jurisdiction of the Oregon court, but had taken advantage of the opportunity, and was bound by the result.[65] Buyer could not, in the American idiom, have 'two bites at the apple'.

Thus to come back to the question of how one should advise White Lumber

[63] For instance, one of the leading decisions of the U.S. Supreme Court on so-called 'long-arm jurisdiction', *McGee* v. *International Life Insurance Co.*, 355 U.S. 220 (1957), arose from refusal by the courts of Texas to enforce the judgment of a California court against an insurance company established in Texas, on the ground that the insurance company's contacts with California were insufficient to support jurisdiction over it. The Supreme Court held that assertion of jurisdiction by the California Court had not violated the Due Process clause, and therefore that the Texas courts' refusal to recognize and enforce the judgment had violated the Full Faith and Credit Clause.

[64] Indeed, if the motion to dismiss the action for lack of jurisdiction, or to quash service outside the forum state, failed in the court of first instance, the defendant could preserve its challenge for an eventual appeal, while presenting its defense on the merits. Recall that in the *Helicopteros* case discussed in Ch. 4, the challenge to jurisdiction was heard by the appellate courts in Texas and by the U.S. Supreme Court only after trial of the action and a verdict by the jury. See Ch. 4, 46 *supra*.

[65] The principal decision of the U.S. Supreme Court confirming this statement is *Baldwin* v. *Iowa State Traveling Men's Association*, 283 U.S. 522 (1931). There is no Supreme Court decision applying this ruling in an international context, but a leading decision by a federal court of appeals gives strong indication that the principle of *res judicata* will be applied to jurisdictional determinations of foreign courts as well, *Somportex Limited* v. *Philadelphia Chewing Gum Corporation*, 453 F.2d 435 (3d Cir. 1971), cert. denied, 405 U.S. 1017 (1972).

Sales when it is served with initiating process, if there is a significant chance to prevail on the merits, good advice would be to appear in the Oregon court and raise both the jurisdictional challenge and a defense based on the quality of the plywood.[66] If White Lumber Sales has no assets in Oregon and its defense on the merits seems weak, it should probably stay out of the Oregon courts and wait to raise its jurisdictional challenge in an enforcement proceeding in Florida.[67]

How does this case look on the international stage? In the variations that follow, the facts remain the same, but the locations change.

In Variation I, Seller is still in Oregon, but Buyer is in England. Under a decision of the English Court of Appeal in 1976, *Henry* v. *Geoprosco International Ltd*,[68] the result would be the same as in the United States, that is if the Buyer had challenged the jurisdiction of the Oregon court and lost, it would be bound by that decision and a subsequent judgment of the Oregon court in favor of Seller would be enforceable in England. But *Henry* v. *Geoprosco* was strongly criticized in England,[69] and when the United Kingdom came to adopt legislation putting the Brussels Convention into effect, Parliament reversed the decision in the *Henry* case. Under sections 32 and 33 of the Civil Jurisdiction and Judgments Act 1982,[70] defendant could move in Oregon to dismiss the action for lack of jurisdiction, or make a motion to stay the action pending arbitration, or move to dismiss on grounds of *forum non conveniens*, and if such motion were unsuccessful, defendant could withdraw from further participation, secure in the knowledge that if plaintiff seller sought to enforce the resulting judgment in England, the judgment would not be enforced.[71]

[66] There is no longer any doubt in the United States that a jurisdictional challenge can be combined with a substantive defense, so long as the jurisdictional challenge is raised before or at the same time as the defense on the merits. See, e.g., Federal Rules of Civil Procedure, Rule 12(b) and (h).

[67] In the actual case, White Lumber Sales did make its jurisdictional challenge in Oregon. The Supreme Court of Oregon sustained jurisdiction. The majority wrote:

> Obviously, the convenience of both parties could not be equally served by giving each a wholly free choice of the forum in which to conduct litigation of the type involved here. On the other hand, a defendant has no greater claim to preferred treatment than has a plaintiff. So long as the defendant is not compelled to defend himself in a distant state with which he has had no relevant connection, he cannot be said to have been denied either fair treatment or substantial justice. We are entitled to assume that buyers are as likely to receive justice in the courts of the states in which they choose to do business as in the courts of the states in which they choose to maintain their principal offices,

252 Or. at 127, 448 P.2d at 574. Thereafter the case went to trial and appeal, with the result that Buyer's claim of non-conformity of the first shipment was upheld, but its claim of justification to cancel the entire contract was rejected and damages were awarded to the Seller: *Continental Forest Products Inc.* v. *White Lumber Sales, Inc.*, 256 Or. 460, 474 P.2d 1 (1970).

[68] [1976] QB 726 (CA).

[69] See, e.g., Lawrence Collins, '*Harris* v. *Taylor* Revived' (1976) 92 LQR. 268, repr. in Collins, *Essays in International Litigation and the Conflict of Laws* (1994) at 313.

[70] *United Kingdom*: 1982 c.27.

[71] See Dicey and Morris, *The Conflict of Laws* (12th edn., Collins, 1993), 479–82. Just

In Variation II, the Buyer is still in England, but the Seller is now established in Germany. Accordingly a dispute between the Seller and Buyer will be subject, both as to jurisdiction and as to recognition and enforcement of judgments, to the Brussels Convention. Suppose Seller now brings an action in Germany, relying on Article 5(1) of the Convention, asserting that the place of performance of the contract was Germany, where Seller was to cause the plywood to be made up and loaded onto railroad cars. Buyer wishes to contend that the place of performance was the place of delivery, or possibly that a clause in its purchase order selected another forum.

Buyer can make these contentions, but it has no choice about where to make them. Under the Brussels Convention, the only place to raise a jurisdictional challenge would be in Germany, and the decision of that court would be final. We now know, notwithstanding the ambiguous wording of Article 18 of the Convention, that Buyer could join a defense on the merits to the jurisdictional challenge;[72] it could not, by declining to participate in the German action, preserve the right to challenge the jurisdiction of the German proceeding in an enforcement proceeding in England.[73] Moreover, if the jurisdiction of the German court depended on a question of law or conflict of laws, such as where title is deemed to pass, the determination of that point by the German court would be conclusive, not reviewable either in an English court or by the European Court of Justice.[74]

In Variation III, Seller remains in Germany, but Buyer is back in Florida. Seller brings suit in Germany, asserting jurisdiction on the basis that it was the place of payment, or, say, on the basis that the local court in the Seller's district was specified in its order confirmation. Buyer has grounds—but not wholly irrefutable grounds[75]—for challenging the jurisdiction of the German court, and no assets in Germany. The answer turns out to be the same as in the

what constitutes participation is not clear. Probably taking part in discovery while continuing to reiterate objection to jurisdiction would not be regarded as submission for purposes of s.33 of the UK Act; if following denial of a motion to dismiss by the court of first instance defendant put in a defense on the merits, even though it preserved its right to appeal on the issue of jurisdiction, as in *Helicopteros*, n. 64 *supra*, it seems that the right to challenge the jurisdiction of the first court in an enforcement action in England would have been lost.

[72] See *Etablissements Rohr SA* v. *Ossberger*, Case 27/81 [1981] ECR 2431, [1982] 3 CMLR 29 (ECJ, Oct., 22 1981); *Elefanten Schuh GmbH* v. *Jacqmain*, Case 150/80, [1981] ECR 1671, [1982] 3 CMLR 1 (ECJ. June 24, 1981).

[73] See Brussels Convention, Art. 28. It is worth pointing out that under Art. 20 of the Convention, if the defendant makes no appearance, the court where the action is brought is required on its own motion to determine whether the defendant has been properly served and whether the jurisdiction on which the action is based is consistent with the Convention.

[74] See *Industrie Tessili Italiana Como* v. *Dunlop AG*, Case 12/76 [1976] ECR 1473, [1977] 1 CMLR 26 (ECJ, Oct. 6, 1976).

[75] For instance, e.g., an assertion that jurisdiction of the German court had been asserted on an exorbitant basis, such as under ZPO, § 23. See Ch. 4, sect. D(1).

original case, with Seller in Oregon, Buyer in Florida. If Buyer contests the jurisdiction of the German court, it will be bound by the result;[76] if it makes no appearance in Germany and the German court issues a judgment in favour of Seller, Buyer will not be able to relitigate the quality of the plywood or the damages owed to Seller, but it will be able to challenge the jurisdiction of the German court before the Florida court (again state or federal) before which recognition and enforcement are sought.

Thus we have three models—determination of judicial jurisdiction only in the first forum (F–1) (the Brussels model); determination of jurisdiction in either F–1 or F–2 at the option (for purposes of enforcement) of the defendant (the American model); and the opportunity for defendant to seek determination of jurisdiction in both *fora* (the English model when the Brussels Convention does not apply). I have thought a good deal about which of these models is the most desirable. Among like-minded states bound by treaty, I think the Brussels Convention approach is the most desirable; as the European Community or Union keeps expanding and the Brussels/Lugano Conventions with it, small doubts may creep in. The American model is a reasonable compromise, it seems to me, between competing considerations. The argument in favor of this approach is that if F–2 respects F–1 on a question of liability or damages, why should it not show the same level of respect on issues of jurisdiction, such as where a contract was made or was to be performed, or whether or not *X* was the agent of the defendant, when the determination has been made in an adversary proceeding? Of course this approach assumes an impartial judicial system in F–1, and a rough consensus about the bases of judicial jurisdiction. I do not think, however, precise congruence is required.[77] The English model, as I see it, reflects a level of distrust of foreign *fora* that should not be encouraged.[78]

[76] See *Restatement of Foreign Relations Law*, § 482, Comment *c*, as well as the *Somportex* case, n. 65 *supra*.

[77] For instance, suppose F–1 provides for jurisdiction over partners of a firm engaged in activity in that state; a defendant in the United States duly served on this basis (e.g. pursuant to U.K. Order 11, r.1(1)(c)), makes a conditional or special appearance in F–1, asserting that he was not a partner of the local defendant. The F–1 court, after hearing, determines that the American was a partner of the local defendant, and sustains jurisdiction over him. I believe that a court in the United States should, and probably would, enforce a resulting judgment in accordance with § 7 of the Uniform Foreign Money-Judgments Recognition Act, n. 20 *supra*, even though jurisdiction on the basis of partnership with a defendant over whom F–1 clearly has jurisdiction is not ordinarily a recognized basis for jurisdiction in the United States.

[78] I made substantially the same point some years ago in a review essay on the 11th edition of *Dicey*, pointing out also the irony of the 1982 legislative change in the United Kingdom, which moved simultaneously to the first model *vis-à-vis* its treaty partners in the European Community, and to the third model *vis-à-vis* the rest of the world. See A. Lowenfeld, 'Conflict of Laws English Style: Review Essay', 37 *Am. J. Comp. L.* 353, 361–9 (1989). It is worth pointing out that *Henry* v. *Geoprosco*, the case adopting the second model that was reversed by the Civil Jurisdiction and Judgment Act, involved a judgment from the Canadian province of Alberta, whose jurisdictional rule was based on the English order 11. Since the *Henry* case, Canada and the United Kingdom have concluded a Convention on the Reciprocal Recognition and Enforcement of Judgments in

E. AMERICAN JUDGMENTS ABROAD: FOUR ENFORCEMENT CASES IN GERMANY

In June, 1994, the Hague Conference on Private International Law convened a Special Commission on Jurisdiction and the Enforcement of Judgments, to explore whether an attempt should be made to craft a world-wide judgments convention.[79] I have some doubt whether the world is ready for such a convention, and I hope that governments do not settle on a draft too narrow in coverage and too broad in exceptions. Since most of Europe is already united in the Brussels/Lugano system of recognition and enforcement of judgments, the key to a wider convention is clearly adherence of the United States. In fact the United States, or at least the Private International Law section of the State Department's Office of Legal Adviser, has expressed an interest in such a convention. I want to conclude this chapter with brief descriptions of four cases in which judgments of American courts were sought to be enforced in Germany, and the frustrations that the successful plaintiffs in the United States encountered. On the one hand, I think these cases demonstrate what the United States—clearly the most hospitable country to foreign judgments[80]—has to gain from a judgments convention. On the other hand, if a judgments convention cannot provide for recognition and enforcement of these cases, it is not, in my view, worth presenting to governments.

1. A Routine Tort Case

The first case, *Solimene* v. *B. Grauel & Co.*,[81] arose from a rather routine product liability case, brought by a woman worker in an electronics plant, whose wrist was caught in a machine that she thought she had turned off as she bent down to pick up something that had fallen to the floor. She brought suit in Superior Court in Massachusetts against the manufacturer, a German company, alleging negligent design and breach of warranty. The manufacturer

Civil and Commercial Matters, UK Treaty Series No. 10 (1986), Cm. 306. Whether a judgment rendered by the court of a Canadian province following assumption of jurisdiction under a counterpart of Order 11 could be registered, or a defendant who entered a conditional appearance in, say, Alberta, would be given a second chance to challenge the jurisdiction of the first forum, is not clear to me.

[79] See Hague Conference on Private International Law, Annotated Checklist of Issues to be Discussed at the Meeting of the Special Commission on Jurisdiction and Enforcement of Judgments, drawn up by the Permanent Bureau, Prel. Doc. No.1, May 1994.

[80] See, e.g., Charles Platto and William G. Horton (eds.), *Enforcement of Foreign Judgments Worldwide* (2nd edn., 1993). The present author, together with Prof. Linda Silberman, contributed the American report to this compendium.

[81] (1989) 35 Recht der Internationalen Wirtschaft (RIW), (Landgericht Berlin, June 13, 1989). English versions of this and the two following cases, translated and edited by the present writer, appear in A. Lowenfeld, *International Litigation and Arbitration* (1993), 440–50.

participated in all stages of the litigation—pleading, discovery, trial, and post-trial motions.

On the basis of evidence that plaintiff had to have an operation five weeks after the accident and that even after the operation she continued to have pain and impaired function, the jury awarded $275,000 in damages, plus interest at 12 per cent. Defendant moved for direct appeal to the highest state court; that motion was granted, but in a fourteen-page opinion, the Supreme Judicial Court of Massachusetts upheld the judgment entered on the jury's verdict.[82] The manufacturer did not pay, and the injured worker was forced to seek enforcement of the judgment at the defendant's seat in Berlin. By now, fourteen years after the accident, the judgment came to about $483,999, including interest from the date the action was filed. Is there any reason why this judgment should not be enforced?

The Berlin court conceded that the Massachusetts court had jurisdiction; that the reciprocity required by the Code of Civil Procedure[83] was assured; and that there was no requirement in this case of equivalence between German and foreign law. But . . .

The judgment of the court of the first instance, for which enforcement was sought did not contain a written statement of reasons. 'There is no general statement', the Landgericht wrote, 'of the way fault on the part of the defendant was determined or what circumstances were considered concerning the role played in the accident by both parties.'[84] Moreover, 'no statement explains the level of damages awarded.'

Of course juries render verdicts, not 'reasoned judgments', and the Landgericht noted that the absence of written grounds for a judgment is not by itself a violation of German *ordre public*. But, the court said, 'the resulting lack of clarity is to be charged to the plaintiff as the prevailing party.'[85]

In fact one can tell a good deal about the case from the appellate opinion. What emerged, as the Berlin court saw it, was 'that the breach of duty on the part of the defendant was inferred from the fact of the injury'. 'This', the Landgericht wrote, 'corresponds to American jurisprudence', but not to the 'basic norms of German law concerning liability and insurance', which would require proof of a defect in the product.[86] The Landgericht concluded:

[82] *Solimene* v. *B. Grauel & Co. KG*, 399 Mass. 790, 507 N.E.2d 662 (1987).

[83] Zivilprozessordnung (ZPO) § 328(1)5.

[84] 35 RIW at 989.

[85] *Ibid.*

[86] According to the opinion of the Supreme Judicial Court of Massachusetts, plaintiff offered two theories of design defect supported by expert testimony, one involving placement of the switch controlling the machine, the other involving the oscillating arm that pinned and injured plaintiff's wrist. The jury did not indicate which theory it accepted, and the appellate court, quoting Massachusetts precedents, held that there is no requirement that plaintiff point out the exact way the accident happened, as long as she sustains her burden of proving that there was a greater probability than not that the accident was caused by a design for which the manufacturer was responsible: 399 Mass. at 797, 507

Therein lies a violation of German *ordre public* .... If it were to prevail in the Federal Republic of Germany, it would lead to serious impairment of the right to property of the defendant and of its right to organize and carry out its business. .. Further basis for a violation of German *ordre public* results from the height of the original award of damages of US $275,000. This amount far exceeds the amounts that would be payable in a comparable case in Germany. The constituent elements of the amount are neither explained nor can they be understood.[87]

To me, without even quoting other objections of the Berlin court to the Massachusetts judgment,[88] there is no room in judgments practice among friendly states for this attitude. Whatever one may think of the American law of torts, or the jury system, or contingent fees, it is clear that there was nothing special about this case, no discrimination because defendant was a foreigner, no new or unexpected theory that was unfairly applied to defendant.[89] It is fair to add that the judgment of non-enforcement was rendered by a court of first instance, that the case was apparently settled pending appeal, and that it does not represent the settled jurisprudence of the Bundesgerichtshof. Still, it shows an attitude toward foreign judgments—or perhaps only toward American judgments—quite inconsistent with what we have been saying here.[90]

2. Debt to a Broker

The second case, which I will call *P & Co.* v. *T*[91] is a decision of the Supreme Court of the Federal Republic, involving a German citizen, T, who opened a margin account with a New York brokerage house for the purpose of trading in cocoa futures. As a result of a drop in the price of cocoa, T suffered sharp losses. The brokerage firm issued a margin call, and when that was not answered, it closed out T's account, leaving a debit balance of some $73,000. When T failed to settle the account, the brokerage firm, P & Co., brought suit in federal court in New York. The suit resulted in a judgment in favor

N.E.2d at 667. Thus the statement by the German court that American law is satisfied with a mere inference of defect, is not borne out by the *Solimene* case.

[87] 35 RIW at 389.

[88] For instance, objections concerning the calculation of interest; concerning the failure to reduce the award to account for contributory fault on the part of the plaintiff; and concerning the pre-trial discovery procedure.

[89] For criticism of this decision by a German scholar currently teaching at an American university, making substantially the same points here made, see Joachim Zekoll, 'Zur Vollstreckbarkeit eines US-amerikanischen Schadensurteils' (1990) 36 RIW 302.

[90] I was not pleased by the suggestion of an American lawyer writing for a German journal that the *Solimene* case be used as a negotiating device by German manufacturers sued in the United States, the point being that the greater the difficulty for an American plaintiff in collecting on an American jury verdict in Germany, the lower the sum for which he might be prepared to settle. See Peter Heidenberger, 'Vollstreckbarerklärung von U.S. Jury-Urteilen' (1991) 37 RIW 599.

[91] Bundesgerichtshof VIII Civ. Sen., June 4, 1975 (1975) 28 Neue Juristische Wochenschrift (*NJW*) 1600.

of P & Co. for about $100,000 including interest and costs; when T did not pay, P & Co. sought to enforce its judgment at T's domicile in Frankfurt.

What objection can there be to enforcing this judgment? Again, there was no jurisdictional objection, and no problem with the requirement of reciprocity. Yet P & Co. failed at all three levels of the German courts.

It turned out that in Germany, claims arising out of futures contracts are treated like gambling debts, and are not enforced. Germany also has futures markets, but in order to participate in such markets, a permanent resident of Germany must be registered as a merchant engaged in futures trading or banking or be admitted to a stock exchange. T was not so registered or qualified. Of course T had not engaged in trading on a German futures market, and P & Co. was not suing on a claim but on a judgment. Never mind. Section 61 of the Stock Exchange Law applies to trades conducted outside as well as inside Germany, and this rule of German conflict of laws breaks through the normal rule of *locus regit actum*:

> The appellant fails to understand that the protective intent of the German legislature ... would be frustrated by recognition of ... a judgment arising out of futures trading conducted abroad. Just as the defences contained in the Stock Exchange Law concerning futures and margin trades may be raised before German courts under § 61 with respect to claims arising from such trades outside Germany, these defences must be given effect in an action to enforce a foreign judgment arising out of such claims.[92]

I would not accept the first part of the last sentence quoted as a matter of choice of law. For me, a trade on a New York exchange is governed by New York or United States law, on a London exchange by English law, and so on—even, I would have thought, with respect to capacity. For present purposes, however, the fault lies in the second part of the sentence. Recognition and enforcement practice will get nowhere, if the distinction between a claim and a judgment is not kept firmly in mind.

3. A Counterclaim

The third case, also decided by the Bundesgerichtshof, is perhaps the most surprising of all. *A.C. Inc.* v. *F. & J.*[93] was again our paradigm case. Seller in Germany supplied two machines to Buyer, which had its place of business in New York. Buyer paid the purchase price for the first machine, but withheld the last instalment of $3,975 of the purchase price of $35,500 for the second machine. When Seller sued for payment of the last instalment in a New York court, Buyer asserted that the machines were defective and counterclaimed for $35,000 for repairs needed to make the machines operative. Seller sought a

[92] 28 NJW at 1601.

[93] 52 BGHZ 31 (Bundesgerichtshof, VIII Civ. Sen., Mar. 26, 1969).

stay of the counterclaim and did not address the merits. The New York court dismissed the Seller's action and gave judgment for Buyer on the counterclaim for $42,000, including interest and costs. It was this judgment that Buyer sought to enforce in Germany.

Believe it or not, the enforcement action was rejected by all three German courts that considered it. Although Seller had selected the forum in its initial action, the German courts held that the New York courts lacked jurisdiction. The reasoning was as follows: Seller's order confirmation contained a clause providing for arbitration under the rules of International Chamber of Commerce; when Seller brought an action in court and Buyer responded in that action rather than moving for a stay pending arbitration, the agreement to arbitrate lapsed. That, said the German Supreme Court, brought the printed conditions of sale back into effect, rather like a previous will that becomes operative after a later will is revoked. The conditions of sale provided for exclusive jurisdiction of the court at Seller's principal place of business, i.e. Germany. What about the fact that Seller had initiated the litigation in New York? The Bundesgerichtshof said:

> The Plaintiff [Buyer] is not unreasonably disadvantaged if it is unable to resort to jurisdiction based on the existence of a counterclaim, since defendant [Seller] acted in the interest of the plaintiff when—for whatever reason—it brought its action for the purchase price in New York at plaintiff's domicile, and not in Nürnberg. Plaintiff may not, however, take additional advantage of this accommodation, so that the defendant for its part becomes subject to jurisdiction at plaintiff's domicile. He who gives a little finger is not required to give the whole hand.[94]

Not only did the court not enforce the judgment of the New York court, it expressly declined to recognize the factual findings of that court concerning the defective condition of the machines. The New York judgment was treated as of no effect at all, and Seller's failure to respond to the counterclaim was treated as a default on the issue of jurisdiction, entitling it (as in the American model) to raise the jurisdictional challenge *de novo* in the second forum.

I make no pretence to expertise in the fine points of German civil procedure. But I think there is something wrong with permitting a party to bring suit in a forum, and then to avoid enforcement of a judgment rendered by that forum on a counterclaim based on precisely the same issue as was raised in the initial action.

4. Damages: Special, General, and Punitive

The most recent decision on the subject of foreign judgments by the German Supreme Court, one may hope, reflects a change in attitude.[95] The case arose

[94] 52 BGHZ at 36.

[95] *G.D.S.* v. *E.S.*, 118 BGHZ 312 (Bundesgerichtshof, IX Civ. Sen. June 4, 1992). For

out of an action in California for sexual abuse of a boy not yet 14 years old, which resulted, as the jury found, in long-term psychological damage to the boy. The jury awarded and the California court upheld $100,000 for future psychiatric treatment, $50,000 for accommodation in a home for disturbed children; $200,000 for 'anxiety, pain, and suffering'; and $400,000 for 'exemplary and punitive damages'—a total of $750,000. After civil and criminal proceedings in California, the defendant, a dual citizen, moved back to Germany without payment of the judgment. Enforcement proceedings were, accordingly, initiated in Düsseldorf.

The Landgericht granted full recognition to the judgment, including interest at 10 per cent according to California law. The Court of Appeal (Oberlandesgericht) accepted the award of the California court to the full extent of damages allocated to psychiatric treatment and other special care—$150.000;[96] it reduced the award for pain and suffering from $200,000 to $70,000; and it denied punitive damages completely. Thus instead of $750,000 the court of appeal allowed $220,000 plus 25 per cent thereof (i.e. $55,000) for attorney's fees, which it called the recognizable part of the punitive damages award. The appeals court made no award for interest. Both sides appealed.

Punitive damages are not a peculiar American phenomenon,[97] but both in frequency and in amount, it is punitive damages awarded by American juries and sustained by American courts that cause the most controversy.[98] The

an interesting commentary, see Harald Koch and Joachim Zekoll, 'Zweimal amerikanische "punitive damages" vor deutschen Geichten' [1993] 5 *IPRax* 288.

[96] Even this was an issue, because under German law sums for future treatment would be released only as the expenses were actually incurred. The Supreme Court, affirming the Court of Appeals, held that this difference between German law and the law that gave rise to the judgment did not rise to the level of contravention of German *ordre public*: 118 BGHZ at 327–32.

[97] See, generally, *Encyclopedia of Comparative Law*, xi, *Torts*, ch. 8 (Stoll), International Consequences of Liability: Remedies' at § 8–107–116.

[98] It is worth observing that the controversy is not limited to foreign countries. Numerous attempts have been made—thus far not successfully—to persuade the U.S. Supreme Court that punitive damages violate the due process, double jeopardy, cruel and unusual punishment, or other clauses of the U.S. Constitution. See, e.g., *Browning-Ferris Industries of Vermont, Inc.* v. *Kelco Disposal, Inc.*, 492 U.S. 257 (1989); *Pacific Mutual Life Insurance Co.* v. *Haslip*, 499 U.S. 1 (1991) and the many lower court decisions and commentaries there cited. The Supreme Court did write in the *Haslip* case, however, that

> One must concede that unlimited jury discretion—or unlimited judicial discretion for that matter—in the fixing of punitive damages may invite extreme results that jar one's constitutional sensibilities ... [G]eneral concerns of reasonableness and adequate guidance from the court when the case is tried to a jury properly enter into the constitutional calculus.

499 U.S. at 18.

In *Honda Motor Co. Ltd* v. *Oberg*, 114 S.Ct 2331 (1994), the Supreme Court remanded to the state courts of Oregon a judgment on a jury verdict including punitive damages of $5,000,000 arising out of an accident in a three-wheeled 'all terrain' vehicle, on the ground that an amendment to the Oregon Constitution precluding judicial review of the size of award of damages in excess of the loss suffered by the injured party seems to give expression to the public's sense of outrage over defendant's conduct, when it is deliberate or in reckless disregard of the risks incurred.[99] If one accepts punitive damages at all, the behavior of a prolonged sexual child molester is a suitable case. The question here, however, is whether a country that does not know punitive damages in its own system should, must, or may not enforce a judgment of a foreign court that provides for such damages.

Should the German court grant enforcement of the California judgment without any deduction, as the court of first instance had done? Or should a judgment tainted by the award of punitive damages in an amount of more than half the total award, be denied any enforcement, as defendant contended? Could one adopt a middle ground, striking punitive damages from the enforceable award while otherwise preserving the integrity of the judgment for enforcement purposes?

The Bundesgerichtshof chose the third alternative—the middle ground. First, it reversed the decision of the Court of Appeal to reduce the amount awarded for pain and suffering. The California measure of damages might be more expansive than the German measure of damages would be, but this difference did not affect German *ordre public* in an unacceptable way;[100] moreover, there was no basis for the court from which recognition and enforcement is sought to go into the allocation of damages between the injured party and the attorney, whether on the basis of a contingent fee arrangement or otherwise. As to the award of punitive damages, however, though they are clearly civil in nature, in that the award is made to the injured party, not to the state, they are incompatible in German law with the state monopoly of proceedings leading to punishment and the special procedural safeguards connected with such proceedings. The court rejects the suggestion that possibly acceptable elements of the punitive damages award—such as sums for lawyers' fees or for injuries not otherwise compensated—be separated out; punitive damages are rejected in their entirety for purposes of

punitive damage awards deprives defendants of the safeguards against arbitrary deprivation of property required by the Due Process clause of the federal Constitution.

Also, as these lines were written (spring 1995), a major effort to impose a ceiling on punitive damages in product liability (and possibly in medical malpractice) cases was being considered in the U.S. Congress, as part of the Republican 'Contract with America'. See H.R. 10, 104th Cong., 1st Sess. (1995). Whatever the fate of this legislation, which also seeks to curb contingent fees and to introduce a 'loser pays' principle with regard to lawyers' fees, the evidence is clear that discontent with the American legal system prevails in the United States as well as in foreign states where American judgments are sought to be enforced.

[99] See, generally, W. Page Keeton *et al.*, *Prosser and Keeton on the Law of Torts* (5th edn., 1984), 9–15.

[100] Compare the proposal to permit just such an inquiry made in the course of the unsuccessful negotiation of a judgments convention between the United States and the United Kingdom, n. 16 *supra*.

enforcement. But the court also rejects the contention that because the judgment included punitive damages, it should be rejected *in toto*.

I think this is a sound result, a reasonable compromise. I am hopeful that the Supreme Court's message in this case will eliminate, or at least reduce the frequency of, decisions such as the decision of the Berlin court with which this section began, which denied enforcement because the jury did not give its reasons or the damages appeared excessive to the German court.

* * *

Altogether, I think it is fair to say that the consensus on recognition and enforcement of foreign judgments is much thinner than it is for jurisdiction of courts, and perhaps even than it is for jurisdiction to prescribe. I would hope that if states renew the effort to develop a multilateral judgments convention—whether under the auspices of the Hague Conference on Private International Law or otherwise[101]—they do not grasp prematurely for an international convention that would lock in too narrow a consensus and would limit developments in the directions that I have suggested. If, for instance, the drafters of a convention were not prepared at the outset to go beyond final money judgments in 'civil and commercial matters', I would hope that they would at least include a provision that said:

> Nothing in this Convention precludes any contracting state from recognizing
> [injunctions issued by courts in other contracting states];
> [judgments of courts in other contracting states
> —for payment of taxes or civil fines;
> —in proceedings arising out of bankruptcy;
> —in proceedings concerning the estate of decedents]; ... and so on,

coupled with a commitment to reconvene within a stated period to consider whether some or all of these subjects should be included in the affirmative obligation to recognize and enforce judgments of other contracting states.

[101] See G. Droz and A. Dyer, 'The Hague Conference and the Main Issues of Private International Law for the Eighties', 3 *Nw. J. Int'l L. & Bus.* 155, 174–80 (1981).

7

Discovery Across National Frontiers

A. INTRODUCTION TO THE *JUSTIZKONFLIKT*

As the preceding chapters have shown, there has been no lack of controversy in regard to jurisdiction to prescribe, jurisdiction to adjudicate, and recognition of judgments across national frontiers. Still, no aspect of international litigation has caused as much friction as the issue of discovery.[1] And more, I think, than any other focal points of controversy, the controversy over discovery is not one pitting the common law against the civil law, but rather one pitting the United States of America against the rest of the world. England, for instance, including both the courts and Parliament, has been in the forefront of resistance to American-style discovery, which is in many ways quite different from discovery in England.[2] In this regard, the aphorism attributed to George Bernard Shaw about America and England—two countries divided by a common language—is clearly correct.

I want to try to explore here at least some of the ingredients in this controversy. There seem to be three strands to the conflict. I will try in this and the following chapter to weave them together, but I think it is important to recognize them as separate strands. What all elements of the conflict have in common is a desire by the United States—litigants, governments, and courts—for disclosure, particularly of documents, and resistance to such disclosure by everyone else.

Roughly speaking, the conflicts can be divided into (i) purely civil litigation, primarily product liability actions, in which American plaintiffs allege injury caused by defective products made abroad—automobiles, airplanes, or machines—and seek to use American-style discovery to find out the facts that could establish a defect in the product; (ii) public law litigation alleging conduct that is deemed unlawful in the United States but in one way or another is condoned or protected by foreign countries—cartels of various kinds, shipping conferences, and the like; and (iii) public law litigation in which no country defends the underlying conduct, such as drug trafficking or United Nations sanctions-busting, but countries in varying degrees defend their 'turf', including in particular the secrecy

[1] Compare to the same effect, *Restatement (Third) of the Foreign Relations Law of the United States*, § 442, Reporters' Note 1.

[2] See, e.g., Julius Byron Levine, *Discovery: A Comparison between English and American Discovery Law and Reform Proposals* (1982).

of banking records. The relative perceptions on many of these subjects have been changing a good deal—clearly in the direction of United States law, though not all the way. The European Community and its Member States, for instance, now recognize liability for product defects, but not, generally, punitive damages; antitrust, once a monopoly of the United States, is now well understood in the European Community, but not private actions and certainly not treble damages. Perhaps the most striking change over the past three decades has been acceptance in all the major financial centers of the concept of securities fraud, including insider trading and misrepresentation in offering or registration statements. This change, demonstrated in a number of memoranda of understanding or co-operation agreements among the principal enforcement agencies, leads me to some hope that there is a possibility for progress (if not full reconciliation) in the more general subject of fact-gathering across national frontiers.

A few points should be made clear at the outset. First, the conflict about discovery is in many ways a surrogate conflict reflecting a more general discontent among foreign parties coming into contact with the American legal system. Some of the complaints directed against American discovery are really aimed at expansive concepts of jurisdiction—to prescribe and to adjudicate; at juries generous with other people's money; at antitrust suits in general and treble damages in particular; and at developments in the law of product liability that often make recovery by injured parties easier than it would be in the state where the product was manufactured.

Second, while the overall approach of American civil litigation—in favor of disclosure rather than secrecy—is generally accepted in the American legal community, and while the concept that each party is responsible for the proof of its own case is not analogized to the privilege against self-incrimination, as some German writers have done,[3] there is a good deal of discontent in the United States with the current practice of discovery, and there is a continuous re-examination of the discovery rules, both state and federal. When some changes were introduced to the discovery rules for federal courts in 1980 but major revision was deferred, Justice Powell, joined by two other members of the U.S. Supreme Court, dissented from adoption of the amendments by the Court, on the ground that the amendments 'fall short of those needed to accomplish reforms in litigation that are long overdue':

> Delay and excessive expense [Justice Powell continued] now characterize a large percentage of all civil litigation. The problems arise in significant part, as every judge and litigator knows, from abuse of the discovery procedures available under the [Federal] Rules.[4]

[3] See, e.g., Rolf A. Schütze, 'Die Anerkennung und Vollstreckbarerklärung US–Amerikanischer Zivil Urteile die nach einer pre-trial-discovery ergangen sind, in der Bundesrepublik Deutschland', in *Festschrift für Ernst C. Stiefel* (1987), 697 at 702.

[4] 446 U.S. 997 at 99–100.

Third, while foreign persons engaged in litigation in the United States often perceive requests for disclosure or inspection as excessive or exorbitant, it is clear to me that the American lawyers making such requests are not being intrusive particularly into the affairs of foreign parties: they are just doing what comes naturally in their domestic practice. I am not suggesting that some of these requests are not exorbitant or intrusive. We will come to that question. I am saying only that the discovery requests encountered by foreign parties in American courts are not discriminatory or anti-foreign or anti-international law.

In drafting the relevant section of the *Restatement*,[5] the Reporters tried to raise a cautionary flag, that is to say 'doing what comes naturally' is not always acceptable in cases with significant foreign elements, which may include cases with a party domiciled or established abroad, evidence located abroad, or activity conducted abroad— in other words all the cases we have considered throughout these essays. The *Restatement* urges that, in contrast to the typical American practice, the judge in such cases should become engaged in the discovery process early on, with a view to minimizing the prospect of conflict, for instance by ordering discovery requests to be more narrowly framed, or by asking whether there are alternative sources for particular information. Most difficult, the *Restatement* endeavours to build a bridge between the universally accepted proposition that matters of procedure are governed by the *lex fori*, and the equally accepted proposition that primary activity (as contrasted with litigation activity), including record keeping and reliance on confidentiality, is generally governed by the *lex loci*.[6]

I cannot report that the result of these endeavours has been everywhere accepted or fully successful. I do believe that both American and foreign litigators are more sensitive to the issues than they were a decade ago, and more aware that 'national treatment' is not always good enough. I hope that these essays can contribute to growing understanding of what Professor Schlosser and others have called a *Justizkonflikt*—a conflict about justice between the United States and Europe.[7] I think the place to start is with a small dose of comparative law. I focus on the American model, with occasional (and I hope accurate) remarks about similarities and differences with other models.

[5] What became § 442 in the final version of the *Restatement* was first published as § 420, in *Tentative Draft No. 3 of the Restatement* (1982); a revised version was published as § 437 in *Tentative Draft No. 6* (1985), and a further revision was published as § 437 in *Tentative Draft No. 7* (1986).

[6] *Restatement (Third) of the Foreign Relations Law of the United States*, § 442 (1987), reproduced in Ch. 8, sect. D(1) *infra*.

[7] See Peter Schlosser, *Der Justizkonflikt zwischen den USA und Europe* (1985); also Walther Habscheid (ed.), *Der Justizkonflikt mit den Vereinigten Staaten von Amerika* (1986).

B. FACT GATHERING IN CIVIL LITIGATION: THE AMERICAN MODEL AND SOME COMPARISONS

Discovery, broadly defined, is the process that takes place between completion of pleadings (i.e. submission of complaint and answer or counter-claim) and the beginning of the trial. As in England but not in Continental Europe in civil cases, the trial is supposed to be a consecutive presentation of evidence, first on behalf of plaintiff, thereafter on behalf of defendant, typically by oral testimony and by submission of documents and physical evidence, all in 'open court' with a judge presiding over the proceedings.[8] At the close of presentation of evidence, lawyers may 'sum up', i.e. present closing arguments focusing on the evidence, and thereafter the judge (nearly always a single judge) either submits the case to the jury with instructions, or if there is no jury, takes the case under advisement for his or her own decision.[9] In brief, though the burdens of proof are different, a civil trial in the United States proceeds very much like a criminal trial familiar from films and television. Once the trial begins, there is no further time to gather evidence. The time for assembling facts, locating documents, retaining experts, and finding witnesses is before trial—i.e. the period of discovery. Here is one fundamental difference between American and continental procedure, which I think has led to much of the controversy in the context of the Hague Evidence Convention, as explored in the next chapter.

In principle, which may be changing, discovery is to be conducted by the lawyers, without intervention of the court. Lawyers address requests for information to their adversaries (as well as to non-parties, as we shall see). Lawyers quarrel about the extent to which requests are permissible and the extent to which requests have been complied with, and it is possible to apply to the court (i) for a protective order limiting or deleting a discovery request; and (ii) for sanctions against a non-complying person. With some exceptions,[10] judges do not participate in discovery. In contrast to the practice in continental Europe, discovery in the United States (as in England) is not regarded as a judicial or even an official function—another difference that has in the past led to some misunderstandings on both sides of the Atlantic.

How do American lawyers assemble the facts? It is not true, as is sometimes supposed, that first the plaintiff files suit, then the lawyer rummages through

[8] I speak here only of plaintiff and defendant. Where more parties are involved, there are inevitable variations from the standard pattern, not significant for present purposes.

[9] In certain situations, the judge may also take the case away from the jury by 'directing a verdict' if he concludes that a reasonable trier of fact could reach only one verdict on the basis of the evidence presented. See, e.g., Federal Rules of Civil Procedure, Rule 50. This power is important in the context of the relation between judge and jury, but is not pertinent to the present discussion.

[10] In some cases, judges will become involved, typically by appointing a referee or designating a magistrate to supervise discovery and make rulings as they are requested.

the adversary's file to build a case. Normally, plaintiffs and their counsel have a good grasp of the necessary facts before they file suit, and they recite many of these facts (in their version, of course) in the complaint or statement of claim.[11] It is true, however, that if plaintiff was injured by a machine, or while being attended in a hospital, or in a transportation accident, he or she may allege a design defect or negligence and use discovery to learn exactly what went on in the hospital while the patient lay on the operating table, or how the machine was built or how many other times it failed. Thus there is no doubt that the discovery process changes the legal position of the parties—generally in favor of plaintiffs—in that it enables them to establish claims that they could not establish without some access to information in control of defendants.[12] Such discovery is most valuable in medical malpractice and product liability actions, but it is also useful (and sometimes decisive) in actions for commercial fraud, antitrust and unfair competition, and insider trading and other securities-related cases.

Non-Americans are often surprised to learn of two further aspects of American discovery. First, discovery is not limited to parties. Anyone with discoverable information can be requested, and if necessary, required, to make it available, by oral deposition under oath and by production of documents or other evidence.[13] The 'I don't want to get involved' syndrome will not work in the face of determined counsel. In principle, this is contrary to English practice, though in personal injury actions since 1981 third party

[11] Under Rule 11 of the Federal Rules of Civil Procedure and some but not all state rules, an attorney filing a pleading must sign it, and the signature constitutes 'a certificate . . . that to the best of the signer's knowledge, information, and belief formed after reasonable inquiry it is well grounded in fact and is warranted by existing law or a good faith argument for the extension, modification, or reversal of existing law.'

Violation of this rule may subject both the lawyer and the client to sanctions.

[12] Discovery is not a one-way street, however. For instance under Federal Rule 35 and comparable rules in most states, defendant in a personal injury action can cause plaintiff to be examined by a physician designated by the defendant, and defendants can use all the devices of discovery to learn about the prior physical condition, work record, and earnings of the plaintiff. Also, in some of the most famous cases, for instance the *Westinghouse* case discussed hereafter, defendants have used discovery to support a defense or counterclaim.

[13] Non-parties who do not respond voluntarily may be subpoenaed. In federal courts the jurisdiction to issue a subpoena runs throughout the state in which the court is located and to an area within a 100-mile radius of the place where a deposition or document production is to take place. If a non-party from whom discovery is sought resides beyond this range, the party seeking discovery obtains a subpoena from the federal district court within the jurisdiction (or within the 100-mile bulge) where the person resides. The subpoena may be issued by the clerk of court or an attorney authorized to practise in the court where the action is pending or the deposition or production is to be made. In some states of the United States, it is necessary to show 'special circumstances' or the likelihood that the non-party from whom discovery is sought will not be available at trial. Different states have different rules about out-of-state depositions, including, in some instances, the requirement of a court order and appointment of a 'commissioner' to take the deposition. See, e.g., New York CPLR, Rules 3108, 3113(a). In practice, these requirements do not impose serious impediments to discovery from non-parties within the United States.

discovery is now available upon application to the court, in some instances even before commencement of the action.[14] Under French law, as I understand it, a non-party can be required to give evidence and to produce documents, but only by the judge. A party can apply to the judge for such an order, but it will be granted only if the documents or other evidence are identified with precision.[15] There is no comparable authority for civil litigation in Germany whereby a non-party can be required to give evidence or produce documents.

Second, the information requested in discovery need not be admissible in court, and it need not be limited to the claim or defense of the party seeking discovery, but may extend as well to the claim or defense of any other party. While Lord Diplock's characterization of American discovery as a 'wide-roving search for any information that might be helpful'[16] is somewhat exaggerated, it is not far off the mark. Under the Federal Rules of Civil Procedure, discovery extends to 'any matter, not privileged, which is relevant to the subject matter involved in the pending action' (Rule 26(b)).[17] Moreover,—a point particularly galling to the English, as we shall see—information may be requested even if the party making the request does not know that the information exists or cannot describe it with specificity. Thus, for instance, a request for all correspondence or memoranda of meetings between the defendant and *X* in a given time period would ordinarily not be regarded as too broad in American litigation. Critics of American discovery always speak abut 'fishing expeditions'.[18]

[14] *U.K.*: Supreme Court Act 1981, c. 54, s. 34(2) and (3) (after commencement of action) s. 33(2) (pre-action discovery). Discovery of third parties is also possible in some other situations, to discover the name of an unknown wrongdoer: see *Norwich Pharmacal Co.* v. *Customs and Excise Commissioners* [1974] AC 133. For a convenient summary of discovery in English practice, see Stuart Sime, *A Practical Approach to Civil Procedure* (1994), chs. 20–22.

It is worth mentioning that devices to get around the prohibition of document discovery from non-parties are beginning to grow up in England, blurring the distinction between 'evidence' and 'discovery'. For example, it appears to be possible in some instances to issue a *subpoena duces tecum* that requires a non-party to appear 'at trial' on a given date with specified documents, coupled with an artificial trial date well before the parties are actually ready to try the case. This practice was upheld by the Vice-Chancellor in *Khanna* v. *Lovell White Durant* [1994] 4 All ER 267, on the ground that it enabled parties to study the documents in preparation for the actual trial, thus obviating the need to grant a continuance once the trial proper has begun.

[15] See *France*: Nouveau Code de Procédure Civile, Arts. 138–141.

[16] *British Airways Board* v. *Laker Airways Ltd* [1984] 3 WLR 413 at 419, [1985] AC 58 at 78.

[17] Some state rules have slightly narrower formulations of the scope of discovery. See, e.g., New York Civil Practice Law and Rules (CPLR) § 3101(a):

> There shall be full disclosure of all evidence material and necessary in the prosecution or defense of an action, regardless of the burden of proof.

In English practice, as I understand it, such discovery as is permitted—i.e., *inter partes* and limited third party discovery, n. 14 *supra*, is also not restricted to matters admissible in evidence, but 'fishing' is not permitted. See Sime, n. 14 *supra*, ¶ 20.3.

[18] The first use of that term in connection with American discovery appears to have been by Lord Goddard CJ in *Radio Corporation of America* v. *Rauland Corporation* [1956] 1 QB 618 at 649, quoted with approval by Lord Diplock in *Rio Tinto Zinc Corporation* v.

The U.S. Supreme Court, in the leading case on discovery under the Federal Rules, rejected that attack:

> No longer can the time-honored cry of 'fishing expedition' serve to preclude a party from inquiring into the facts underlying his opponent's case. Mutual knowledge of all the relevant facts gathered by both parties is essential to proper litigation. To that end, either party may compel the other to disgorge whatever facts he has in his possession.[19]

It is not necessary to list here all the discovery devices available to the litigants. The two that cause the most controversy in international litigation are requests for oral depositions and requests to produce documents and to permit inspection of tangible things, including, for example, assembly lines in a factory. An oral deposition, also called an examination before trial or EBT, is like a dress rehearsal for a courtroom appearance. The witness (whether a party, employee, or officer of a party, or a non-party) appears accompanied by counsel, and is examined under oath by the party that called him, with a shorthand reporter recording all the questions and answers. This is followed by 'cross-examination', 're-direct', 're-cross', and so on until no more remains to be said. Only the judge is absent.[20] Objections to questions are noted, and either the witness answers subject to objection, or, if his counsel directs him not to answer, the question remains unanswered. So far as I know, no other country routinely provides for such examinations, except in some maritime actions or other situations where a potential witness will be unavailable to the court because of absence, illness, or old age.

Documents produced through discovery may be introduced into evidence at trial by either party, subject to the normal rules of evidence. Any relevant answer to an interrogatory or statement made in a deposition by a party (or generally by agents of a party) may be introduced at trial by the opposing party; the record of a deposition by a non-party may generally not be introduced unless the deponent has died or (in federal practice) lives or works

Westinghouse Electric Corporation [1978] AC 547 at 609, [1978] 2 WLR 81 at 87. Actually the critique by English courts of 'fishing expeditions' did not originate with comments on litigation originating in the U.S. For example, in a 1936 English case, seller sued buyer for the balance of the purchase price of some Indian miniatures, and buyer defended on the ground that the miniatures were fakes: *Rofe* v. *Kevorkian* [1936] 2 All ER 1334 (CA). Buyer proposed an interrogatory to seller asking 'whence and from whom and upon what date' seller had obtained the objects: *id.* at 1337. The interrogatory was disallowed as 'in the nature of a fishing interrogatory, trying to get, for the purpose of the defendant's case, evidence which he has not already got': *id.* For this and similar examples, see P. Langan and L. Henderson, *Civil Procedure* (3rd edn., 1983).

[19] *Hickman* v. *Taylor*, 329 U.S. 495 at 507 (1947). It is fair to add that the quoted statement is qualified later in the same paragraph, and indeed in the *Hickman* case itself, the discovery request by plaintiff's counsel for the notes of defendant's lawyer after interviewing survivors of a shipwreck was held to go beyond the authorization in the Rules.

[20] As mentioned in n. 10 *supra*, in rare cases a magistrate or referee may preside, and make on the spot rulings subject to later challenge.

more than 100 miles from the court; if a person who gave a deposition testifies at the trial, his or her deposition may be introduced to contradict or impeach the trial testimony. More important, according to the reformers who introduced the present system of discovery into American practice with adoption of the Federal Rules of Civil Procedure in 1938, is that, as discovery progresses, each party knows more and more of the strength of its position and that of its adversary. A claimed advantage of the system is that this shared knowledge leads to settlements that would not have been possible without discovery. On the other hand, the effect of discovery American-style is to delay the time between the joinder of issue and the beginning of the trial, and it unquestionably increases the costs of litigation, sometimes massively so. It is not unusual in important cases to have two large law firms (or even more if there are additional parties) employ twenty lawyers per side solely on discovery and pre-trial motions. Thus, quite apart from the information unearthed, discovery is a major element in the system which, in the words of Lord Diplock 'seems to any English lawyer strange and, indeed, oppressive upon defendants'.[21] Obviously the English are not alone in this perception.

I must say, however, that while I am far from a whole-hearted defender of the American discovery system, I have sometimes been equally astonished by other countries' outlook on the search for truth. For instance, a much cited case in which the German Supreme Court discussed the propriety of procuring information from an adversary involved a conflict about an inheritance.[22] The decedent had made a will in favor of the defendant, and plaintiff, the decedent's daughter, sought to reclaim a portion of the bequest on the ground that the bequest cut into her reserved share. The defendant sought to interrogate plaintiff concerning gifts she may have received from the decedent. To an American lawyer, this would be a routine discovery request, not even worth arguing about. To the German courts, the request was regarded as an attempt at an *Ausforschungsbeweis*, because the defendant had not indicated specifically that he had information about such gifts—he just thought that it was not unlikely that a father had made gifts to his daughter. In the actual case, the Supreme Court reversed the Court of Appeal, which had refused the defendant's request, not on the ground that the interrogation should have been permitted, but on the ground that plaintiff seeking to assert her reserved share had a duty on her own to disclose gifts she had received from the decedent. Thus in the end, the outcome may not have been unjust, as I thought when I read the first few paragraphs of the decision, often quoted in the literature.[23] The case does suggest, however that sensitivity that apparently had its origin in cases when plaintiff in

[21] *British Airways Board* v. *Laker*, n. 16 *supra*.

[22] Bundesgerichtshof, III Civ. Sen. May 4, 1964, (1964) 17 Neue Juristische Wochenschrift 1414.

[23] See e.g., 'Schütze, n. 3 *supra*; Schlosser, 'Internationale Rechtschilfe und rechtsstaatlicher Schutz von Beweispersonen' (1981) 94 *Zeitschrift für Zivilprozess* 369 at 377–8.

a paternity action would be asked, without any foundation, with whom other than the defendant she had had sexual intercourse in the relevant period[24] has been carried rather too far.

Professor Schütze, co-author of the leading multi-volume German work on recognition of judgments,[25] urges that American discovery that he classifies as *Ausforschung* is contrary to German public policy to such an extent (i.e. 'manifestly incompatible with the fundamental principles of German law'[26]) that a judgment rendered by a foreign (read American) court following such discovery should be denied recognition and enforcement.[27] Thus, suppose in the controversy between the beneficiary under the will and the daughter, the beneficiary lives, say, in Boston, and the daughter brings her action in a Massachusetts court. The Massachusetts court (state or federal) will apply German substantive law on the basis of the domicile of the decedent,[28] but will apply the *lex fori* on matters of procedure and evidence.[29] Defendant's counsel makes the routine discovery request, asking the daughter to disclose all substantial gifts she received from her father during his lifetime. As I understand Professor Schütze, if she refused to provide the required information and her claim was thereafter struck out and judgment was entered for defendant,[30] he would permit her to litigate the claims again in Germany, where the beneficiary might well have assets, because the Massachusetts judgment would be disentitled to recognition. If she complied with the discovery request, but only under protest (or perhaps under court order when the motion to strike the request was denied), I think Schütze would come out the same way, that is he would deny recognition to the Massachusetts judgment.[31]

In my view such an attitude is quite unjustified, and feeds the attitude of some American lawyers—remember that the *Justizkonflikt* goes both ways—that the rest of the world is engaged in a conspiracy of concealment. American discovery is often oppressive, intrusive, expensive, time consuming; it does, however, aim to bring out the truth. I do not think that American-style discovery is a violation of due process, basic principles of law, or international human rights.

[24] The court in the case under discussion itself mentions this situation; see also Abbo Junker, *Discovery im deutsch-amerikanischen Rechtsverkehr* (1987) 323.

[25] Geimer/Schütze, *Internationale Urteilsanerkennung* (1983–4).

[26] ZPO § 328(I)(4).

[27] Schütze, *Festschrift für Stiefel*, n. 3 *supra*, 703–5; also Note to the sexual abuse case discussed in Ch. 6, sect. E(4) (1993) 39 RIW 139 at 141. I did not find a comparable statement in the Geimer/Schütze treatise.

[28] Cf. *Restatement (Second) of Conflict of Laws*, §§ 263, 265 (1971).

[29] *Id.*, §§ 122, 138.

[30] See 147 *infra* for more on the sanctions for non-compliance with discovery under American law.

[31] I hasten to add that I have not found quite this hostility to American discovery reflected in other German scholarly writings, though it does come through in other instances, such as the *Solimene* decision discussed in Ch. 6, sect. E(1).

C. AMERICAN DISCOVERY ACROSS NATIONAL FRONTIERS: *INTERHANDEL* AND BEYOND

Thus far we have only sketched the background of American discovery practice, without focusing on the location of the information to be discovered. What if the information is located in a foreign country but the party that controls it is present before the court? Further, what if the documents in question are subject to a rule of non-disclosure in the country where they are located? And still further, what if there is reason to believe the documents were placed in that country expressly to conceal them from American courts and authorities? Or the country adopted non-disclosure laws precisely to attract such business or to thwart American investigators?

Altogether it is quite an exciting story, though as we shall see none of the principal participants emerges covered with glory.

1. The *Interhandel* Case

Once again I begin with the leading case decided by the United States Supreme Court. The case is formally entitled *Société Internationale pour Participations Industrielles et Commerciales, SA* v. *Rogers*,[32] but is generally known as the *Interhandel* case—the same company, and in fact the same dispute, as the case by that name that came before the World Court.[33] A bit of background is necessary, which would have been familiar in the early post-war years, but has probably now receded in public consciousness. One of the principal engines of the German war machine and also a principal employer of slave labour during World War II was I. G. Farben, itself a conglomerate of several important German chemical companies. Among Farben's holdings prior to the war was an 89 per cent share of a major American chemical and photographic supply company, General Aniline and Film, makers of Ansco film and numerous other products. Prior to outbreak of the war, I. G. Farben organized a Swiss company, I. G. Chemie, also known as Société Internationale or Interhandel, to hold the shares of GAF and other external assets of Farben.[34] Soon after the United States entered World War II, GAF was vested by the U.S. government as enemy property, on the basis that it was owned by or held for the benefit of I. G. Farben, an enemy national, through

[32] 357 U.S. 197 (1958).

[33] *Interhandel Case (Switzerland* v. *United States)* (Preliminary Objections), judgment of Mar. 21, 1959, [1959] ICJ Rep. 6. See n. 38 *infra*.

[34] For a brief account of the rise of I. G. Farben and its American subsidiaries, General Aniline Works and Agfa-Ansco Corporation, and of the assignment of the shares to I. G. Chemie or Interhandel, see Kelly, 'United States Foreign Policy: Efforts to Penetrate Bank Secrecy in Switzerland from 1940 to 1975', 6 *Cal. Western Int'l L.J.* 24, esp. at 225–7 (1976). For more detail, see J. Dubois, *The Devil's Chemists* (1952); T. Fehrenbach, *The Swiss Bankers* (1966).

the Swiss company, Interhandel. When the war ended, Interhandel brought suit in the U.S. District Court for the District of Columbia for return of the shares of GAF, worth about $100 million. Interhandel alleged that it was an independent Swiss company and—not having been an enemy national—was entitled to return of its property. There was no doubt that Interhandel and its predecessor companies had been organized by I. G. Farben. The question before the American court was whether Farben's ownership had been terminated before the war or had merely been concealed.

The United States government, defendant in the action, challenged Interhandel's claim of ownership of GAF, and asserted that in any event it was affected by 'enemy taint' by virtue of its intimate connection with I. G. Farben. At an early stage of the litigation—here we come to our issue—the United States government moved under Rule 34 of the Federal Rules of Civil Procedure for an order requiring Interhandel to make available for inspection and copying a large number of banking records of a private bank in Basel, Sturzenegger & Cie. The United States asserted that the documents were in the control of plaintiff within the meaning of Rule 34 because Sturzenegger and Interhandel were substantially identical, and further that the documents sought would demonstrate the true ownership of the stock of GAF.

The District Court granted the motion, notwithstanding the plaintiff's assertion that it was unable to comply with such an order, because disclosure of the documents would constitute a violation of Article 273 of the Swiss Penal Code prohibiting economic espionage, and Article 47 of the Swiss Banking Law, relating to secrecy of bank records. The United States government thereupon moved for sanctions under Rule 37(b) of the Federal Rules of Civil Procedure. That rule, which we have not discussed up to now, provides for several sanctions, including a finding of fact by the court adverse to the non-complying party, striking a claim or defense by the non-complying party, and dismissing the action or granting a default judgment. In this case, the United States asked for dismissal. Meanwhile, the Swiss Federal Attorney took symbolic possession of the records, thus confirming the Swiss government's position that disclosure of the records would violate Swiss law.

Before ruling on the motion, the U.S. district judge appointed a Special Master to investigate and report (a) on the nature of the Swiss laws alleged to block compliance with the production order, and (b) on plaintiff's good faith in seeking to achieve compliance with the court's order. The Special Master came back with a report favorable to plaintiff on both points: the Swiss government had acted in accordance with its established law;[35] and the plaintiff had shown good faith in its efforts to comply with the production order. There was no evidence, the Master reported, of collusion between

[35] Art. 47 of the Swiss Banking Law was adopted in 1934, Loi Fédérale sur les Banques et les Caisses d'Espargnes (Bundesgesetz über die Banken und Sparkassen) of Nov. 8, 1934.

plaintiff and the Swiss government in the seizure of the papers. The District Court confirmed the Master's findings, but nevertheless granted the motion to dismiss the action pursuant to Rule 37(b) of the Federal Rules of Civil Procedure. Swiss law, the court said, did not furnish an adequate excuse for plaintiff's failure to comply with the production order, since foreign law could not be invoked to justify disobedience to orders entered under the law of the forum, and since the records not produced might well prove crucial to the outcome of the case.[36] The Court of Appeals affirmed,[37] but the Supreme Court granted review.[38]

The case was a hard one for the Supreme Court, because plaintiff's property had been seized by the government without compensation, and the Fifth Amendment of the United States Constitution states that no person shall be deprived of property without due process of law. Only a fully defensible conclusion that plaintiff was tainted as an enemy in time of war could justify retention of the property, and it was difficult to reach such a conclusion on the basis of a sanction for non-compliance with a discovery order. The U.S. government tried to repeat the assertion that Interhandel had 'deliberately courted legal impediments' to disclosure, words that became important in several later cases. Here, however, the Special Master had expressly found that Interhandel had acted in complete good faith. Accordingly, failure to satisfy the discovery order could not be attributed to any fault on its part, and dismissal of the action was not appropriate.

Thus when the U.S. Supreme Court came down with its decision in June of 1958, Swiss secrecy laws, backed by the threat of prosecution, prevailed over the American discovery order.

> The findings below, and what has been shown as to petitioner's [i.e. Interhandel's] extensive efforts at compliance, compel the conclusion on this record that petitioner's failure to satisfy fully the requirements of this production order was due to inability fostered neither by its own conduct nor by circumstances

[36] *Société Internationale* v. *McGranery*, 111 F. Supp. 435 (D.D.C. 1953).

[37] *Société Internationale* v. *Brownell*, 243, F.2d 254 (D.C. Cir. 1957).

[38] It is worth noting that in Oct. 1957, after the Court of Appeals had affirmed dismissal of the action but before the Supreme Court granted review, the government of Switzerland filed suit against the United States in the International Court of Justice, seeking a declaration that the United States was under an obligation to restore the assets of Interhandel to that company, or in the alternative, to order the dispute submitted to arbitration under a 1931 treaty. The United States challenged the jurisdiction of the ICJ on several grounds, among them that the company had not exhausted the local remedies available in U.S. courts. Evidently, if the Supreme Court had not granted certiorari or if it had subsequently upheld the dismissal of the action, the claim that local remedies were still available to Interhandel could not have been sustained. None of this, however, is stated in the opinion of the U.S. Supreme Court, which focuses on the discovery issues, as discussed hereafter.

In the event, in Mar. 1959, well after the U.S. Supreme Court had issued its decision, the World Court ruled (by 9–6) that it did not have jurisdiction because the litigation in the United States was still in progress: [1959] ICJ Rep. 6, esp. at 26–30.

within its control ... [T]he findings below establish that the very fact of compliance by disclosure of banking records will itself constitute the initial violation of Swiss laws ...

In view of the findings in this case, the position in which petitioner stands in this litigation, and the serious constitutional questions we have noted [i.e. concerning the taking of property without just compensation], we think that Rule 37 should not be construed to authorize dismissal of this complaint because of petitioner's noncompliance with a pretrial production order when it has been established that failure to comply has been due to inability, and not to willfulness, bad faith, or any fault of petitioner.[39]

The Supreme Court went on to say, however, that it was not suggesting that Interhandel would profit through its inability to tender the records called for. Plaintiff retained the ultimate burden of proof, and it might be that 'in the absence of complete disclosure by [Interhandel], the District Court would be justified in drawing inferences unfavourable to [Interhandel] as to particular events'.[40]

In fact, the litigation went on for several more years, and was ultimately resolved by a court-approved sale of GAF, with 30 per cent going to Interhandel (whoever owned it), and the remainder to the U.S. Treasury.[41]

Every subsequent American decision concerning transnational discovery—civil, criminal, or administrative—has used the *Interhandel* case as its point of departure, with different parties and courts emphasizing different aspects of the decision.

2. The *City Bank* Case

The first important test of the meaning of the *Interhandel* case came some ten years later, not in a civil case, but in connection with a subpoena issued by a federal grand jury. A grand jury, under United States law, has authority to require the attendance of any person to give evidence, and, if so directed, to produce documents and other objects, all subject to supervision of the court.[42]

United States v. *First National City Bank*[43] arose out of an investigation of an alleged world-wide quinine cartel, even as several hundred thousand young

[39] 357 U.S. at 210–12.

[40] *Id.* at 212–13.

[41] See *Wall St. Journal*, Mar. 4, 1963, 3, col. 1; Apr. 1, 1963, 14, col. 5; Oct. 15, 1963, 30, col. 1; Apr. 16, 1964, 6, col. 2; also *Société Internationale v. Kennedy*, 231 F. Supp. 132 (D.D.C. 1964).

[42] As it has developed in American jurisprudence, a grand jury made up of a group of lay persons—usually 23—is charged with investigating wrongdoing, and if it finds probable cause, handing up indictments as requested by a public prosecutor. A brief description of the history and function of the American grand jury appears in A. Lowenfeld, *International Litigation and Arbitration* (1993) 670–3. For a more detailed description and analysis, see M. Frankel and G. Naftalis, *The Grand Jury: An Institution on Trial* (1977); S. Beale and W. Bryson, *Grand Jury Law and Practice* (2 vols. 1986, plus supplements).

[43] 396 F.2d 897 (2d Cir. 1968).

Americans were being sent to Southeast Asia, where they were exposed not only to enemy fire, but to malaria. Among the targets of the grand jury's investigation was the well known German pharmaceutical company Boehringer. Boehringer maintained accounts with Citibank, both in New York and in Frankfurt, and the bank was served with a subpoena requiring it to produce any documents relating to transactions in the name or for the benefit of Boehringer. Citibank complied with the subpoena with respect to documents located in its New York office, but refused to produce any documents held in the Frankfurt office or even to state whether there were such documents, on the ground that to do so would be contrary to German law.

It turned out, however, that there was no German counterpart to the Swiss bank secrecy law. There was a general policy of confidentiality of banking records, but no specific criminal penalties were attached to that policy, and even civil liability was not clear—the expert witnesses differed—in the event the bank acted under compulsion of a foreign (i.e. here an American) court. Boehringer had not sought to enjoin disclosure, and the German government had expressed no support for Citibank's assertion that production of the documents would violate an important public policy of Germany. Moreover, the German Penal Code prohibited disclosure of secrets acquired in the course of exercising the profession of physician, dentist, pharmacist, lawyer, accountant, and tax consultant, but not banker,[44] and the Code of Criminal Procedure authorized priests, midwives, and publishers, among others, to refuse to give evidence, but also said nothing about bankers.[45]

Altogether, this case was significantly different, as the Court of Appeals saw it, from *Société Internationale* v. *Rogers*. Citibank was ordered to produce the documents, on penalty until compliance of a fine of $2,000 a day and commitment of its vice-president handling the matter to jail for up to sixty days. Citibank complied.[46]

D. DISCOVERY AND THE FOREIGN COMPULSION DEFENSE

One lesson from the *Interhandel* case was that the way to stand up to American discovery requests would be to enact laws making it unlawful for citizens or residents of the enacting state to comply with such requests. This lesson was reinforced not only by the *First National City Bank* case, in which German law turned out not to be firm enough to overcome a United States grand jury

[44] *Germany*: Strafgesetzbuch, § 300, repealed 1974.

[45] *Germany*: Strafprozessordnung, § 53.

[46] For a follow-up on the quinine cartel, including an indictment, a civil antitrust case, and a damage case in the United States, plus a major case in the European Community, see Wilbur L. Fugate, *Foreign Commerce and the Antitrust Laws* (4th ed. 1991), i, 312–3, and sources there cited; also *ACF Chemiefarma NV* v. *Commission*, Case 41/69, [1970] ECR 661 (ECJ July 15, 1970).

subpoena, but also by a series of cartel cases, including the *Nylon*,[47] *Light Bulb*,[48] and *Swiss Watchmakers*[49] cases, in which foreign parties and foreign conduct had been found to violate U.S. law, but the United States had refrained from enforcement of their decisions in respect of foreign conduct by foreign parties in the face of foreign laws or court orders, under what became known as the foreign government compulsion doctrine.[50] Numerous states now adopted what became known as blocking statutes, all designed, using differing techniques, to endow their citizens and companies with the foreign government compulsion defense if they should become targets of discovery orders emanating from U.S. courts or agencies.

1. The Rise of Blocking Statutes

The first such statute, the Ontario Business Records Protection Act,[51] was enacted in 1947 in response to an order of a federal court in New York directed to Canadian subsidiaries of a New York corporation to produce documents located in Canada for use by a grand jury investigating a possible violation of the Sherman Antitrust Act with respect to newsprint.[52] When the United States Department of Justice investigated the alleged international petroleum cartel in the early 1950s, the governments of Great Britain, the

[47] See *United States* v. *International Chemical Industries*, 105 F.Supp. 215 (S.D.N.Y.) ordering the British Company ICI to permit imports of nylon into the United Kingdom, followed by *British Nylon Spinners Ltd* v. *Imperial Chemical Industries* [1953] 1 Ch. 37, ordering ICI to perform its contract to give an exclusive license to BNS; no action was taken thereafter by the United States as prevailing plaintiff or by the U.S. District Court to enforce the U.S. judgment or to punish ICI for not obeying it, on the ground that, as U.S. District Judge Ryan had written:

> No provision of this judgment shall operate against I.C.I. for action taken in compliance with any law of any foreign government or instrumentality thereof, to which I.C.I. is at the time being subjected, and concerning matters over which, under the law of the United States, such foreign government or instrumentality thereof has jurisdiction.

[48] See *United States* v. *General Electric Co.*, 115 F.Supp. 835 at 878 (D.N.J. 1953), decreeing that the Netherlands company Philips shall not be in contempt of the judgment of the U.S. court for doing anything outside of the United States which is required, or for not doing anything outside of the United States which is unlawful, under the laws of the state in which Philips or any other subsidiaries may be incorporated.

[49] Compare *United States* v. *Watchmakers of Switzerland Information Center*, 1963 CCH Trade Cas. ¶ 70,600 (S.D.N.Y. 1962), holding various agreements among Swiss makers of watches and watch parts destined for the American market unlawful, with *id.*, 1965 CCH Trade Cas. ¶ 71,352 (S.D.N.Y. 1965) sustaining most of the practices previously ruled unlawful because in the interval the practices had been made subject of mandatory governmental regulations.

[50] For a concise statement of this doctrine and the principal incidents of its application in the United States, see *Restatement (Third) of the Foreign Relations Law of the United States*, § 441 and the Comments and Reporters' Notes thereto (1987).

[51] Ontario Rev. Stat., c. 54.

[52] See *In re Grand Jury Subpoena Duces Tecum Addressed to Canadian International Paper Company*, 72 F.Supp. 1013 (S.D.N.Y. 1947).

Netherlands, France, and Italy issued orders prohibiting the removal of documents, and subsequently the Netherlands enacted permanent legislation prohibiting compliance with any measures or decisions of any other state regarding regulation of competition.[53]

In the early 1960s, the U.S. Federal Maritime Commission launched a series of investigations into alleged discriminatory and anticompetitive activities of international shipping conferences. Under the Shipping Act of 1916,[54] the FMC and its predecessor agencies were authorized to grant antitrust immunity to ocean carriers and had nearly always done so with respect to international shipping conferences, in return for filing of various reports, records, and tariffs. Now, under prodding from the U.S. Congress, the Commission sought to find out what was really going on beneath the cloak of immunity, whether, for instance, outbound freight from the United States was being charged more than inbound freight, and whether shippers were being coerced not to employ independent, i.e. non-conference, carriers. The Commission's investigative demands were still a different kind of American discovery, neither criminal nor civil, but issued under several sections of the Shipping Act authorizing regulatory agencies to require firms subject to their regulation to furnish a variety of records, both in the context of routine regulation such as approving rate filings and in the context of investigations into alleged violations.[55] The range of jurisdiction sought to be exercised by the Federal Maritime Commission is a serious question, but belongs in Chapters 1 or 2, under Jurisdiction to Prescribe.[56] For present purposes, what is noteworthy is that these investigations provoked a series of diplomatic protests, followed by a wave of blocking statutes—in Great Britain, Germany, France, Norway, Belgium, Sweden—for the most part focused specifically on the shipping investigations but adaptable to other discovery requests as well.[57]

[53] The Netherlands Economic Competition Act of June 28, 1956, amended by Act of Nov. 14, 1958, Art. 39.

[54] 46 U.S.C. § 801 *et seq*.

[55] See Shipping Act of 1916, §§ 21, 27, 46 U.S.C. §§ 820, 826.

[56] For more on the FMC investigations and the jurisdictional conflicts they generated, see, e.g., A. Chayes, T. Ehrlich, and A. Lowenfeld, *International Legal Process* (1968) ch. VI; May, 'The Status of the Federal Maritime Regulation under Principles of International Law', 54 *Georgetown L.J.* 794 (1966); Lowenfeld, "'To Have One's Cake ...' The Federal Maritime Commission and the Conferences', 1 *J. Maritime Law & Commerce* 21 (1969). For the story of one such investigation, involving the FMC, several foreign governments, and two U.S. Courts of Appeals, see A. Lowenfeld, *International Litigation and Arbitration* (1993), 'The Ludlow Litigation', 700–8.

[57] *Great Britain*: The Shipping and Commercial Documents Act 1964, c. 97; *Federal Republic of Germany*: Federal Maritime Shipping Act of May 14, 1965, Art. 11, [1965] II BGBl. 833, 835; *France*: Law 68–678 of July 26, 1968 Relating to the Transmission of Documents and Information to Foreign Authorities in the Area of Maritime Trade, [1968] J.O. 7267. [1968] B.L.D. 438; *Norway*: Act of June 16, 1967, Power for the King to Forbid Shipowners to Give Information, etc., to Foreign Authorities, 1685–1985 Norges Lover at 1726 (1986). *Belgium*: Law of Mar. 27, 1969, concerning the Regulation of Marine Transport, [1969] Bull. Usuel des Lois et Arrétés No. 723 at 500, amended to include Air Transport, June 21, 1977 [1976] *id*. No. 1490 at 1075 supplemented by Royal

A third round of blocking statutes was provoked in the mid-1970s, as news gradually spread of a world-wide uranium cartel. As the United States Department of Justice, private litigants, and several committees of Congress sought to obtain information about the extent and effect of the cartel, all of the countries concerned,—Australia, Canada, France, Great Britain, and South Africa—adopted further blocking statutes or implementing regulations.[58] Again, some of these statutes were narrowly focused on uranium or atomic energy; others, including the French and British acts, were of general application. Some, such as the French statute, seemed to be automatically effective 'except when international treaties or agreements provide otherwise';[59] others, such as the British Protection of Trading Interests Act, depended on invocation of measures by the relevant minister.[60] All of these statutes, it is fair to say, represent the opposite of what I have been groping for—throughout this volume, in the work of the *Restatement*, and indeed throughout my professional career. Rather than accommodation, reasonableness, balancing of interests, 'comity' if you will, blocking statutes are invitations to an international game of 'chicken',[61] with the outcome not always predictable. I want to tell briefly

Decree of Feb. 6, 1979, [1979] *id.* No. 464 at 319; *Sweden*: Ordinance Regarding Prohibition in Certain Cases for Shipowners to Produce Documents Concerning the Swedish Shipping Industry. [1966] Svensk Författningssamling No. 156, at 411.

[58] *Australia*: Foreign Proceedings (Prohibition of Certain Evidence) Act 1976, Austl. Acts No. 121, amended by Foreign Proceedings (Prohibition of Certain Evidence) Amendment Act 1976, Austl. Acts No. 202, replaced by Foreign Proceedings (Excess of Jurisdiction) Act 1984, Austl. Acts No. 3; *Canada*: Uranium Information Security Regulations, Prov. Can. Stat. 1976–2368, Stat. O. & R. 76–644 (Sept. 21, 1976), replaced by Prov. Can. Stat. 1977–2923, Stat. O. & R. 77–836 (Oct. 13, 1977), in implementation of the Atomic Control Act 1970, s. 9, Can. Rev. Stat. c. A–19, Foreign Extraterritorial Measures Act, Stat. Can. 1984, c. 49; *France*: Law 80–538 of July 16, 1980 Relating to the Communication of Economic, Commercial, Industrial, Financial or Technical Documents or Information to Foreign Natural or Legal Persons, [1980] J.O. 1799, English version with commentary, 75 Am. J. Int'l L. 382 (1981); *Great Britain*: Protection of Trading Interests Act 1980, c. 11, ss. 1–4; *South Africa*: Second General Law Amendment Act No. 94, 1974, § 2, 12 Stat. S. Africa 602.

For a collection of blocking statutes in English, see A. V. Lowe, *Extraterritorial Jurisdiction* (1983) 79–143. The British and French blocking statutes (as well as the Swiss Banking and Business Secrecy Laws) are reproduced in the Documents supplement to the present author's book, n. 42 *supra*.

[59] *France*: Law 80–538, Arts. 1, 1 *bis*.

[60] *Great Britain*: Protection of Trading Interests Act, ss. 1 and 2. Recall that this Act was invoked in connection with the antitrust action brought by the receiver of Laker Airways against British Airways and others in the U.S. District Court in Washington. The order of the Secretary of State to British Airways not to give discovery in the American action was an important factor in the decision of the English Court of Appeal to enjoin continuation of the action by Laker, but both the reasoning and the result were rejected by the House of Lords. See Ch. 1, 11–14

[61] For those not familiar with this term or with the game, 'Chicken' is defined as follows:

> A trial of valor in which two persons drive cars at each other down the middle of the road, the first to swerve aside being designated as 'chicken'.

R. L. Chapman, *American Slang* (1989).

one story about the use (or abuse) of a blocking statute that I have told in print before but that is not widely known or reflected in the law reports, and then address three of the major controversies in this continuing conflict of laws—taking these words literally, and not as a synonym for an important branch of international law.

2. The Ampicillin Litigation[62]

In March 1970, the U.S. Department of Justice filed a civil antitrust complaint, alleging that the Bristol-Meyers Company, an American firm, and the Beecham Group Ltd, a British firm with an American subsidiary, had conspired to restrain and monopolize the trade in ampicillin and other semi-synthetic penicillin products. Soon a number of private actions were joined to the principal action, on behalf of forty-three states of the United States, several cities, including New York and Philadelphia, and numerous private and charitable hospitals, wholesale and retail druggists, consumer groups and competitors. The United States government sought compensatory damages in its capacity as purchaser of ampicillin for its hospitals and the armed services, as well as injunctive relief, including compulsory licensing under United States patents alleged to have been improperly obtained or misused in furtherance of the conspiracy between Bristol-Meyers and Beecham; the non-federal plaintiffs sought treble damages for the amount of alleged overcharges attributable to the conspiracy.

As is standard practice in cases of this kind, plaintiffs made a wide-ranging demand for documents and defendants resisted; eventually the discovery request came before Chief Judge Sirica of the U.S. District Court for the District of Columbia, in a hearing concerning sanctions pursuant to Rule 37 of the Federal Rules of Civil Procedure, the same rule that had been the focus of the *Interhandel* case. The judge granted the request, and ordered the defendants, including Beecham, to produce the information and documents requested, regardless of where they were located.

Plaintiffs believed that Beecham applied to the Secretary of State for Trade and Industry for an order under section 2 of the Shipping Contracts and Commercial Documents Act,[63] the forerunner of the Protection of Trading Interests Act. Beecham, conscious of the discussion in *Interhandel* about courting impediments and good faith, submitted an affidavit denying that it had sought an order under the Act. The judge seems to have believed plaintiffs, but he made

[62] This account is adapted from an account by the present author in 'Sovereignty, Jurisdiction and Reasonableness: a Reply to A. V. Lowe, 75 *Am. J. Int'l L.* 629 (1981), in reply to an article by Professor A. V. Lowe, defending and praising adoption of the PTIA by the United Kingdom. Lowe, 'Blocking Extraterritorial Jurisdiction: The British Protection of Trading Interests Act, 1980', 75 *Am. J. Int'l L.* 257 (1981). A somewhat shorter version of the same story also appears in my book, n. 42 *supra*, at 710–13.

[63] See n. 57 *supra*.

no finding to this effect. In any event, the British minister, Sir Geoffrey Howe, issued an order under the Act. There is no way to know whether the minister examined the discovery request, asked himself whether or not it was reasonable, and whether real harm would be caused by the requested disclosure—not to just Beecham but to Britain. Was he, in other words, defending a genuine interest of his government, or was he protecting turf—British sovereignty in some abstract sense? All the order says is that the documents requested by an Order of the U.S. District Court or some of them:

> are not within the territorial jurisdiction of the United States ... and that the requirement, so far as it relates to documents in the United Kingdom and to information compiled from such documents, constitutes an infringement of the jurisdiction which, under international law, belongs to the United Kingdom.

Accordingly, the Minister directed that Beecham 'shall not comply with the said requirement'.[64]

'Very well', Judge Sirica said, 'I will respect the order of the British government; Beecham is absolved from any liability for contempt for failure to comply with the discovery order'. However, he issued an order indicating that he was about to make findings of fact adverse to the position taken by Beecham. Beecham said it had not made agreements with Bristol-Meyers, the documents concerning the relation between the companies had not been produced, and thus the inference would be drawn that such an agreement existed.

Whether or not Beecham had initiated the minister's interest in the case, the blocking order now appeared more hazardous than beneficial to its cause. Accordingly, Beecham petitioned the minister to release it from the prohibition against furnishing the documents. Inability to make the disclosures, Beecham's Managing Director wrote to the minister, 'might seriously jeopardize Beecham's ability to win the litigation which it believes it should otherwise be able to do'. The minister, as the London *Times* put it, 'relented', except with respect to confidential communications between Beecham and the British government.[65]

Eventually a consent judgment was entered against Beecham, providing for substantial damages and injunctive relief; in addition, and evidently as a condition of the settlement, Beecham agreed to have its employees informally interviewed and deposed for use in the litigation against Bristol-Meyers, which was continuing.[66]

[64] Direction by the Secretary of State for the Department of Trade and Industry under s. 2 of the Shipping Contracts and Commercial Documents Act 1964, Dec. 5, 1972. The order was published in the BNA Antitrust and Trade Reporter, Jan. 9, 1973 at A–5. For other sources and texts of some of the communications mentioned, see my comment in the *American Journal of International Law*, n. 62 *supra.*

[65] *The Times* (London), Sept. 17, 1973, 24, cols. 3–4.

[66] See *United States* v. *Bristol-Meyers Co.*, 82 F.R.D. 655, 659 (D.D.C. 1979).

I have three observations on the *Ampicillin* case. First, one can never really know whether a litigant is 'courting an impediment' from a foreign government. Even if Beecham wrote a letter for the record to the minister urging that the British government not issue a prohibitory order, suspicion remains, as it did with the court in this case, about what went on in the minister's club, on the golf course, or even in a telephone call. I do not suggest that the blocking statutes should be automatic; I only point out that discretion of this kind does not breed confidence.

Second, the concern for the principles of international law recited by the minister as required by the statute seems to have receded fairly quickly once he was advised that non-disclosure might hurt the 'client' more than disclosure. It is worth noting that, when the Protection of Trading Interests Act superseded the Shipping Contracts and Commercial Documents Act, the required finding by the minister that the foreign discovery order 'constitutes or would constitute an *infringement of the jurisdiction which, under international law belongs to the United Kingdom*'[67] was replaced by a required finding that the foreign order 'infringes the jurisdiction of the United Kingdom *or is otherwise prejudicial to the sovereignty of the United Kingdom*'.[68] I still do not like it, but at least it does not purport to state international law.[69]

Third, I would much rather have a discovery request from state *A* scrutinized by a court in England, or any other state *B*, than by a minister, who has other priorities, other values. I am reinforced in that view by the holding of the House of Lords (if not the Court of Appeal) in the *Laker* case.[70] Whether current arrangements for international judicial assistance, notably the Hague Evidence Convention, are adequate for cases such as *Ampicillin*, is explored in Chapter 8. The awkwardness of mixing politics with legal proceedings in the context of transnational discovery context is illustrated—perhaps better than anywhere else—in the notorious Uranium Cartel litigation.

[67] *UK*: Shipping Contracts and Commercial Documents Act 1964, s. (1)(b).

[68] *UK*: Protection of Trading Interests Act 1980, s. 2(2)(a).

[69] I do like the statement of Justice La Forest of the Supreme Court of Canada, in holding unconstitutional a blocking statute of the Province of Quebec, relied on by defendants in resisting a discovery request in an action brought in British Columbia by a cancer victim who alleged injury from products containing asbestos manufactured, *inter alia*, by defendant companies in Quebec:

> The whole purpose of a blocking statute is to impede successful litigation or prosecution in other jurisdictions by refusing recognition and compliance with orders issued there. Everybody realizes that the whole point of blocking statutes is not to keep documents in the province, but rather to prevent compliance, and so the success of litigation outside the province that the province finds objectionable. This is no doubt part of sovereign right, but it certainly runs counter to comity. In the political realm it leads to strict retaliatory laws and power struggles. And it discourages international commerce and efficient allocation and conduct of litigation.

Hunt v. *Lac d'Amiante du Québec* [1993] 4 S.C.R. 289 at 327–8 summarized in 88 *Am. J. Int'l L*. 532 (1994).

[70] See Ch. 1 sect. D.

E. ANOTHER GLOBAL LITIGATION: THE *URANIUM* CASE

The first chapter in this volume addressed the *Laker* litigation, which opened up many of the issues explored in more detail in the succeeding chapters. I want here to contrast the *Laker* case with another litigation that took place on both sides of the Atlantic Ocean, but turned, at least on the surface, on conflicting views of discovery. The case, or rather the cases, are well known, having to do with the world-wide uranium cartel that came to light in the 1970s, but I think it will be illuminating to place the litigation in the framework that we have been constructing throughout this volume.

1. Background: Westinghouse's Predicament

Nuclear energy for the purposes of electric power generation was slow to develop in the United States. Until 1950, the U.S. Atomic Energy Commission was the only purchaser of uranium, the basic fuel for nuclear reactors, and in the following eight years the price of uranium was regulated by the AEC at about $8 per pound. The Westinghouse Electric Corporation, a major manufacturer of electric generators using nuclear energy, sought to encourage electric power companies to purchase its generators and nuclear fuel assemblies by promising to supply uranium to its customers at fixed prices (tied to an inflation index) of between $6 and $10 per pound over a twenty-year period. Westinghouse was not a uranium producer, but it relied on purchases in the market, which had been relatively stable for the previous decade. By 1973, however, the price had risen by 20 per cent, by 1975 the price stood at $22 per pound, and by the end of 1975, the price had reached $42 a pound.

In September 1975, Westinghouse gave notice to its customers—fourteen American and three Swedish electric utility companies—that it would be unable to fulfill its supply contracts, on the ground, it said, that to carry out the contracts would be 'commercially impracticable'. This was a reference to § 2–615 of the Sales Article of the Uniform Commercial Code applicable in all states of the United States, entitled 'Excuse by Failure of Presupposed conditions'.[71] Westinghouse's notice said that it had secured only about 15 million pounds, as compared to the 79 million pounds for which it was committed, and it proposed to allocate that amount among its customers.

[71] U.C.C. § 2–615 reads in pertinent part as follows:

> Except so far as a seller may have assumed a greater obligation . . .:
>
> (a) Delay in delivery or non-delivery in whole or in part by a seller . . . is not a breach of his duty under a contract for sale if performance as agreed has been made impracticable by the occurrence of a contingency the non-occurence of which was a basic assumption on which the contract was made or by compliance in good faith with any applicable foreign or domestic governmental regulation or order.

Paragraphs (b) and (c) require the seller to give reasonable notice to buyer, and where appropriate, to allocate limited supplies in a fair and reasonable manner.

All the companies so notified rejected Westinghouse's proposal, and all filled suit against Westinghouse in various courts in the United States, as well as in Sweden. Thirteen of the actions were transferred for pre-trial purposes to the U.S. District Court in Richmond, Virginia, and eventually ten of these actions were retained for trial before Judge Robert Merhige. Westinghouse's exposure was in excess of $2 billion, if it could not establish a defense of 'commercial impracticability'. While no one knew for certain what 'commercial impracticability' meant—it was one of the innovations in the Uniform Commercial Code that had not yet been definitively construed[72]—Westinghouse's defense would surely be strengthened if it could be shown that the situation giving rise to its predicament was truly unforeseeable. A criminal conspiracy would presumably qualify as an unforeseeable circumstance.

2. Finding out about the Cartel: The Search for International Judicial Assistance

Shortly after the litigation against Westinghouse began, a previously little known environmentalist group in Australia called Friends of the Earth came upon some documents disclosing the existence from 1972 on of a world-wide cartel designed to manage the supply and price of uranium. The participants in the cartel included British, French, Australian, South African, and Canadian companies, many of them belonging to several multinational corporations. Whether the cartel was tolerated, inspired, or required by the governments of the countries where the companies were established later became a major matter of controversy. For Westinghouse, the existence of the cartel and its impact on the price rise in the United States might well be an escape from the liability that threatened its very existence.

It seemed from the documents found by Friends of the Earth that one of the pivotal members of the uranium cartel was the Rio Tinto Zinc group, a multinational enterprise whose parent RTZ was incorporated in England. In the action before Judge Merhige in Virginia, Westinghouse sought discovery from RTZ, including documents and testimony of its officers. Westinghouse also went on the offensive, by bringing a civil antitrust action in federal court in Chicago, seeking damages of $2 billion, trebled. Meanwhile, the U.S. Department of Justice began to investigate the uranium cartel, and in June 1976 a grand jury was convened in the District of Columbia to look into possible criminal violations. A committee of the U.S. Congress also launched an investigation.[73]

Meanwhile, as mentioned in the preceding section, Australia, Canada, France, and South Africa either adopted or reinforced laws designed to protect

[72] Nearly two decades later, this is still true. For a searching but inconclusive analysis, see Sheldon W. Halpern, 'Application of the Doctrine of Commercial Impracticability: Searching for the "Wisdom of Solomon"', 135 *U. Pa. L. Rev.* 1123 (1987).

[73] See *International Uranium Supply and Demand*, Hearing before Subcomm. on Oversight and Investigations of House Comm. on Interstate and Foreign Commerce (374 pages inc. documentary app.), 94th Cong., 2d Sess. (1976).

against discovery emanating from the United States.[74] It is significant that none of these governments, at least initially, announced publicly that they believed in restricting the production or raising the price of uranium as a matter of public policy, or even that a uranium cartel existed.[75] The announced policy was simply to keep American investigators out of the affair.

The United Kingdom did not adopt uranium regulations, and indeed it had recently adopted legislation to implement the Hague Evidence Convention and in general to make international judicial assistance easier.[76] In October 1976, on application of Westinghouse, Judge Merhige issued Letters Rogatory addressed to the High Court in London seeking that court's assistance in the *Westinghouse* case.[77] In particular, the Letters Rogatory sought a court order requiring the testimony before a U.S. consul in London of seven individuals connected with RTZ, and the production of documents identified in a fourteen-page schedule. Judge Merhige, evidently made aware of the English attitude toward 'discovery', wrote in his letter to the High Court:

> It has been shown to us that justice cannot be done ... without the testimony which is intended to be given in evidence at the trial of the actions of [the named persons] nor without the production of certain documents in the possession of RTZ, ... such testimony being related to the existence and terms of various agreements, arrangements, or concerted practices between RTZ and [other named companies].[78]

A Master in the High Court ordered the individuals named to testify and ordered RTZ to produce the requested documents for inspection and copying. The prospective witnesses and RTZ appealed to a judge, and the Master's orders were confirmed. On further appeal, the Court of Appeal essentially upheld the orders giving effect to the Letters Rogatory. Lord Denning, Master of the Rolls, 'blue-pencilled' certain of the document requests as too broad, because they contained such phrases typical in American discovery requests as 'and also all memoranda, letters, or other documents', but he wrote that 'it is both our duty and our pleasure and our power under the [Evidence] Act of 1975 to assist the American court, so far as we properly can.'[79]

[74] See 153 *supra*.

[75] In September 1976, after investigations had begun in the United States and Canada had issued its Uranium Information Security Regulations, n. 58, *supra*, the Canadian Minister of Energy did issue a Press Release and Background Paper stating that Canadian producers had entered into a marketing arrangement among non-U.S. producers 'with the approval and in some cases, at the specific request of the federal government'. See *Westinghouse Electric Corporation and Duquesne Light Company, Application to enforce Letters Rogatory*, 16 O.R. (2d) 273 at 280–4, 78 D.L.R. (3d) 3 at 10–14 (Ontario High Ct. 1977).

[76] *U.K.*: Evidence (Proceedings in Other Jurisdictions) Act 1975, c. 34.

[77] Similar letters went to courts in Australia and Canada.

[78] Reproduced in *Re Westinghouse Electric Corporation Uranium Contract Litigation MDL Docket No. 435* [1977] 3 WLR 430 at 435–6, [1977] 3 All ER at 707–8.

[79] [1977] 3 WLR at 436, [1977] 3 All ER at 707–8.

3. Private Becomes Public

It looked as if international judicial assistance was working. Soon, however, the plot thickened. The prospective witnesses claimed that they were relieved from testifying by the privilege against self-incrimination. They were British subjects domiciled in England, but no charges against the individuals had been or were likely to be brought against them under English law. Could these witnesses testifying in London claim the rights accorded to witnesses in the United States under the famous Fifth Amendment to the American Constitution? The answer to that question was not obvious: the Hague Evidence Convention (in Article 11) adopts a principle of preference under which a person required to give evidence may refuse to do so if he has a privilege under the law of either the requesting or the requested state, but the request from the court in Virginia in the *Westinghouse* case had not technically been submitted pursuant to the Convention. I think with ordinary privileged communications, such as between a doctor and patient or a bank and its client, the privilege should be defined by the law where the communication is made. Thus, for instance, if an intra-company memorandum involving corporate legal staff is not privileged in the state where it is made, it should not be privileged for purposes of U.S. discovery, unless it was made in connection with a proceeding in the United States.[80] But the privilege against self-incrimination is different, and one can well understand that the English Court of Appeal held that the witnesses could claim the privilege under American law.

For the English court to rule on whether answers to the questions put in Westinghouse's request implicated the privilege against self-recrimination might require rather detailed understanding of the United States antitrust laws, which the English court did not have and was probably not anxious to acquire. The Court of Appeal made the interesting suggestion that the U.S. judge fly over to London,[81] and Judge Merhige did so. Apparently an American judge conducting a hearing in London did not offend British sovereignty. The judge ruled that the privilege did indeed apply to the English witness who had appeared before him at the American Embassy in London.[82]

RTZ itself could not claim a self-incrimination privilege under American law because that privilege (unlike other aspects of the Fifth Amendment such as the Due Process clause and the Just Compensation clause) is not available to corporations. RTZ persuaded the Court of Appeal, however, that it could claim the privilege under English law because it might be subjected to

[80] Accord *Restatement (Third) of Foreign Relations Law*, § 442, Comment *d*; *Restatement (Second) of Conflict of Laws* (1988 Suppl.), § 139.

[81] [1977] 3 WLR at 445, [1977] 3 All ER at 716 (Roskill LJ).

[82] See Robert Merhige, 'The Westinghouse Uranium Case: Problems Encountered in Seeking Foreign Discovery and Evidence', 13 *Int'l Lawyer* 19 (1979); also *In re Westinghouse Electric Corporation Uranium Contract Litigation M.D.L. No. 235 (No. 2)* [1977] 3 WLR 492, [1977] 3 All ER 717 (CA).

penalties under the competition articles of the Treaty of Rome. Thus far Westinghouse's quest for evidence had not been accomplished. But it seemed as if the courts of the two countries—a U.S. District Judge in Virginia and three levels of the English judiciary—were co-operating closely. The plot, however, thickened further.

Immediately following Judge Merhige's ruling that the officers of RTZ were entitled to claim the privilege against self-incrimination, a Deputy Assistant Attorney General in the United States Department of Justice wrote a letter to the judge, then still in London, stating that the deposition of certain employees of RTZ was required for the grand jury investigation of the uranium industry. 'We . . . believe', the letter said, 'that the depositions taken pursuant to the letters rogatory . . . might well be the sole opportunity for our grand jury to obtain information vital to its investigation.' The Department gave assurances that the witnesses' testimony would not be used against them as a basis of criminal prosecution in the United States, either directly or indirectly. Judge Merhige, however, refused to order the witnesses to testify on the basis of this informal communication. 'My view of the matter', he wrote later, 'was to accord the British witnesses every benefit of the doubt, and every opportunity to protect their legal rights.'[83]

The privilege against self-incrimination, of course, is an ancient privilege in the common law tradition, going back at least to the revulsion against the Courts of Star Chamber and High Commission in seventeenth-century England and more generally to opposition to the inquisitional style of adjudication of ecclesiastical courts in England and on the European continent.[84] But since 1970, the United States Criminal Code has contained a provision, 18 U.S.C. § 6002, authorizing a court, government agency, or committee of Congress to require a person to testify or give other information, in return for a grant of immunity with respect to that testimony.[85] A further provision, § 6003, states that a court of the United States *shall* issue an order under § 6002 when the Attorney General (or one of his principal deputies) certifies that in his judgment 'the testimony or other information from such individual may be necessary to the public interest'.

The United States Attorney General himself now wrote a letter to Judge

[83] Merhige, n. 82 *supra*, at 25.

[84] See, generally, Leonard W. Levy, *The Origins of the Fifth Amendment: The Right Against Self-Incrimination* (1968), esp. at 329–32.

[85] Just how far this immunity extends has been a subject of continuing controversy. Before Colonel Oliver North gave testimony to Congress under a grant of immunity in the Iran-Contra affair, the Independent Counsel recorded his documentary evidence concerning North, and he and his staff certified that they had not listened to or read the testimony given to Congress. Thereafter North was tried and convicted of several offenses, but the conviction was overturned on appeal, on the ground that some of the witnesses who had testified against North in his trial might have seen his testimony on television, and thus their testimony might have been tainted: *United States* v. *North*, 920 F.2d 940 (D.C. Cir. 1990).

Merhige requesting an order under §§ 6002 and 6003 on the basis that the testimony of the officers of RTZ was necessary in the public interest. Attorney General Griffin Bell wrote that ordinarily the Department of Justice has a 'firm policy against seeking such orders in private litigation'; the circumstances of this case, however, were 'most extraordinary', because of the importance of the case, because the witnesses were outside the reach of the American courts, and because 'it is highly unlikely that their testimony could be obtained through existing arrangements for law enforcement cooperation between the United States and the United Kingdom'.[86] Thereupon Judge Merhige, stating that he had no discretion in the matter, ordered the RTZ officers to give testimony or to respond to questions propounded pursuant to the Letters Rogatory, subject to full testimonial or use immunity.

It is fair to ask what led the United States Attorney General to the conclusion that it is 'highly unlikely' that testimony–evidently for use of the grand jury in Washington–could be secured by co-operation between the American and British governments. The Hague Evidence Convention would probably not work, because the function of the grand jury could not be fitted within 'civil or commercial matters'. But why should two friendly countries not co-operate in other—even possibly criminal—matters? I believe Attorney General Bell may have been unwise to write his letter, or in any event not to have been much more careful in drafting it. But he was probably correct in his conclusion. It was not just that the grand jury had a criminal investigation function, or that the questions to be put to RTZ and its officers might be too 'wide-roving' in British eyes. The underlying allegations, whether presented by Westinghouse or by the United States government, concerned activity outside the United States having a price and supply effect within the United States. Back, in brief, to extraterritorial jurisdiction and the dreaded 'effects doctrine'. As far as is known, the United States Justice Department did not even attempt to gain co-operation of the British government, quite apart from any support which that government might or might not have given to the uranium producers.

But to return to the main plot, the posture of the case at this stage was that the English Court of Appeal had ordered the individual officers of RTZ to testify, subject to their privilege against self-incrimination under United States law. That privilege had now been removed for purposes of the *Westinghouse* case by order of the U.S. court, leaving the order to testify standing. One week after Judge Merhige issued his order, the first of the RTZ witnesses appeared at the United States Embassy in London. However, the witness still declined to answer the questions put to him, on the ground that he wished to appeal to the House of Lords. The other witnesses and RTZ joined the appeal, and

[86] The full text of Attorney General Bell's letter is reproduced in *Rio Tinto Zinc.* v. *Westinghouse Electric Corp.*, [1978] AC 547 at 630, [1978] 2 WLR 81 at 106–7 (Viscount Dilhorne).

Westinghouse cross-appealed from the decision upholding RTZ's claim of privilege under European Community law.

It would be interesting to know how these appeals would have fared before the House of Lords without any additional element. But another unforeseen—if not unforeseeable—event now took place. The United States Attorney General had introduced the 'public interest' of the United States into the controversy, and that attracted an equal and opposite response from the British Attorney General:

> [T]he intervention of the United States Government followed by the grant of the order and immunity ... shows that the execution of the letters rogatory is being sought for the purposes of the exercise by United States courts of extra-territorial jurisdiction in penal matters which in the view of Her Majesty's Government is prejudicial to the sovereignty of the United Kingdom.[87]

Unlike the *Laker* case a few years later, here the Law Lords, already doubtful about aiding these American discovery requests,[88] found the intervention of the Crown to be decisive. Lord Wilberforce wrote:

> My Lords, there is no doubt that, in deciding whether to give effect to letters rogatory, the courts are entitled to have regard to any possible prejudices to the sovereignty of the United Kingdom; that is expressly provided for in art. 12(b) of the Hague Convention. Equally, that in a matter affecting the sovereignty of the United Kingdom the courts are entitled to take account of the declared policy of Her Majesty's Government is in my opinion beyond doubt. Indeed, this follows as the counterpart of the action which the United States Government has taken ... [I]f public interest enters into this matter on one side, so it must be taken into account of on the other; and as the views of the executive in the United States of America impel the making of the order, so must the views of the executive of the United Kingdom be considered when it is a question of implementing the order here. It is axiomatic that in anti-trust matters the policy of one state may be to defend what it is the policy of another state to attack.
>
> The intervention of Her Majesty's Attorney-General establishes that quite apart from the present case, over a number of years and in a number of cases, the policy of Her Majesty's Government has been against recognition of United States investigatory jurisdiction extra-territorially against United Kingdom companies. The courts should in such matters speak with the same voice as the Executive; ... they have, as I have stated, no difficulty in doing so.[89]

[87] [1978] AC at 616, [1978] 2 WLR at 93–9. For longer summaries of the submission on behalf of the Crown, see [1978] AC at 589–95.

[88] Lord Wilberforce, for instance, wondered whether instead of 'blue pencilling' by the Court of Appeal, the request should not have been stricken altogether, on the ground that it was 'so far in the nature of "fishing" that, even though a portion of it can be salved it ought to be rejected out of hand': [1978] AC at 610–11, [1978] 2 WLR at 88.

[89] 1978 AC at 616–17, [1978] 2 WLR at 94. See, to the same effect, [1978] AC 630–1, [1978] 2 WLR 107–8 (Viscount Dilhorne); [1978] AC 639–40, [1978] 2 WLR 114–16 (Lord Diplock).

Thus at the end of the day a good deal of law had been made, about the Evidence Convention, about blue-pencilling requests for evidence, about information sought 'for trial' and not just for 'pre-trial discovery', and about the 'public interest', but Westinghouse obtained no information confirming the existence of the cartel. Westinghouse was not through, however; there was still the action in Chicago.

4. The *Westinghouse* Case in a Domestic Setting: Can Balancing be Avoided?

Even as Westinghouse's requests for use in the Virginia litigation were making their way through the English courts, the antitrust litigation in the Northern District of Illinois, where Westinghouse was the plaintiff, was also caught up in battles over discovery, with the added complication that nine of the twelve foreign defendants, including several members of the RTZ group, made the decision not to appear at all.[90] To the annoyance of the U.S. courts, these firms—four were incorporated in Australia, two in Great Britain, two in South Africa, and one in Canada—presented their challenges to both adjudicatory and prescriptive jurisdiction through briefs of their government as *amici curiae*.[91] A number of the defendants that did appear pleaded foreign government compulsion and the act of state doctrine, but particularly with respect to Canada the documents that defendants said would establish these defenses were located abroad and were themselves subject to blocking statutes or regulations. Eventually, Westinghouse moved for orders compelling production of these documents pursuant to Rule 37 of the Federal Rules of Civil Procedure, the same rule that had been at issue in *Interhandel* and *City Bank*, and again in *BSI*, discussed in the next section.

Once again the parties argued about whether, as Westinghouse contended, the discovery order was solely a matter of American law or, as the defendants contended, the issue was one of international law or comity that required the court to balance the competing interests.[92] Balancing, as we have seen, has

[90] In re *Uranium Antitrust Litigation, Westinghouse* v. *Rio Algom Ltd. et al.*, 480 F.Supp. 1138 (N.D. Ill. 1979).

[91] In the appeal from the decision of Judge Marshall and the resulting order discussed below, the U.S. Court of Appeals for the Seventh Circuit wrote:

> In the present case the defaulters have contumaciously refused to come into court and present evidence as to why the District Court should not exercise its jurisdiction. They have chosen instead to present their entire case through surrogates. Wholly owned subsidiaries of several defaulters have challenged the appropriateness of the injunctions, and shockingly to us the governments of the defaulters have subserviently presented for them their case against the exercise of jurisdiction. If this Court were to remand the matter for further consideration of the jurisdictional question, the District Court would be placed in the impossible position of having to make specific findings with the defaulters refusing to appear and participate in discovery. We find little value in such an exercise.

In re Uranium Antitrust Litigation, 617 F.2d 1248 at 1255–6 (7th Cir. 1980).

[92] See 480 F.Supp. at 1148–9.

its advocates and its detractors, both in the United States and abroad.[93] In a passage quoted frequently by the opponents of balancing, Judge Prentice Marshall, who presided over the action in Chicago, wrote:

> Aside from the fact that the judiciary has little expertise, or perhaps even authority, to evaluate the economic and social policies of a foreign country, such a balancing test is inherently unworkable in this case. The competing interests here display an irreconcilable conflict on precisely the same plane of national policy. Westinghouse seeks to enforce this nation's antitrust laws against an alleged international marketing arrangement among uranium producers, and to that end has sought documents located in foreign countries where those producers conduct their business. In specific response to this and other related litigation in the American courts, three foreign governments have enacted non-disclosure legislation which is aimed at nullifying the impact of American antitrust legislation by prohibiting access to those same documents. It is simply impossible to judicially 'balance' these totally contradictory and mutually negating actions.[94]

The judge concluded that he had the power to issue a production order against eleven resisting defendants, but went on to ask whether he should exercise his discretion to do so. In thinking through the question, the judge, as I see it, did in effect balance the competing interests—the strength of the Congressional policies which formed the basis for plaintiff's action, i.e. the antitrust laws; whether the documents requested were crucial to the determination of a key issue in the litigation; the degree of intensity in the foreign country's non-disclosure laws—altogether not very different from the criteria set out in the *Restatement* a few years later. 'On balance' concluded the judge who would not balance, 'the issuance of Rule 37(a) orders is required.'[95] But he postponed imposition of sanctions under Rule 37(b), while denying defendants' motion for summary judgment based on foreign sovereign compulsion and the act of state doctrine.

> The order will serve to declare Westinghouse's right to the discovery it seeks, thereby framing the competing interests of the United States and the foreign governments on a plane where the potential moderation of the exercise of their conflicting enforcement jurisdictions can be meaningfully considered. We do not seek to force any defendant to violate foreign law. But we do seek to make each defendant feel the full measure of each sovereign's conflicting commands, so that, in the words of Chief Judge Kaufman of the Second Circuit, it now
>
>> 'must confront ... the need to "surrender to one sovereign or the other the privileges received therefrom" or, alternatively a willingness to accept the consequences.'[96]

[93] Recall Judge Wilkey's disparagement of balancing in the American phase of the *Laker* litigation, Ch. 3 at nn. 70–1.

[94] 480 F.Supp. at 1148.

[95] *Id.* at 1154–5.

[96] 480 F.Supp. at 1156, quoting from *United States* v. *First National City Bank*, sect. C(2) *supra.*, also quoted in the *BSI* case, at n. 106 *infra*.

It appears that by postponing his ruling on sanctions, Judge Marshall hoped to induce the parties to settle, and in the first three months of 1981 they did so.[97]

F. BANKS IN THE MIDDLE

Some years ago I met a man at a meeting in New York who introduced himself to me as the manager for North America of one of the major Swiss banks. As we walked out of the meeting toward my bus stop, I asked him if I could open an account through him with the home office of his bank. He said he would have to know a few things about me. I said that was easy: I lived in New York in a house that I owned, I was a tenured professor at a major university, I was married with two grown children, and I had no unusual debts or habits. He said that if this all checked out there would be no problem, but there was a $25,000 minimum. That would be harder, but I nodded and I asked if I could trade on the New York Stock Exchange through the account. He said, 'Of course', but there would be an extra commission—one to his bank, and another one to the New York broker that carried out the trades. Why then might I (or anyone else living in the United States) want to enter into such an arrangement? He shrugged his shoulders. Not his problem. Just then my bus came, and we never finished the conversation.

The question I want to raise here is whether the banker should be interested in why I might want to pay a double commission to trade on the United States stock market via Zurich or Geneva or Basel. If I were a drug dealer, the banker would reject the account; but if I were contemplating a divorce and wanted to hide assets from my wife, he would say that was no concern of his. What if I wanted to avoid U.S. taxes? Or if I thought I had the inside track on a big merger, and wanted to do some fast insider trading? Consider, in looking at the next few cases, how the banker should answer. Is there, to put the question

[97] See *Wall St. Journal*, Jan 13, 1981, 14, col. 2 (Getty); Jan. 30, 1981, 2, col. 2 (Gulf); Feb. 26, 44, col. 2 (Kerr-McGee); Mar. 10, 18, col. 3 (Utah and United Nuclear); Mar. 18, 6 col. 1 (RTZ group and Anglo-American). In each case Westinghouse recovered some money, but far short of the amount claimed, to a total of about $100 million. Some settlements included a promise by the energy companies to assume a portion of Westinghouse's obligations to supply uranium to the utilities. Of particular relevance here, all the settlements included an agreement by Westinghouse not to disclose documents furnished in discovery.

Westinghouse also reached out-of-court settlements in the *Uranium Contracts Litigation* before Judge Merhige that had given rise to the English proceedings. In a related litigation, also before Judge Merhige, in which Westinghouse sought to rely on the defense of commercial impracticability to avoid an obligation to remove and reprocess spent nuclear fuel, the court's effort to promote a settlement was unsuccessful, and eventually Westinghouse was held liable. See *In re Westinghouse Electric Corporation Uranium Contracts Litigation*, 517 F.Supp. 440 (E.D. Va. 1981); *Florida Power and Light Co.* v. *Westinghouse Electric Corporation*, 597 F.Supp. 1456 (E.D. Va. 1984), both discussed in Halpern, n. 72 *supra*, at 1148–54.

differently, some duty of inquiry on banks, or should banks, even banks offering special shelter, be treated like the post office, which is expected to deliver the mail, and not to read it?

1. The *Banca della Svizzera Italiana* Case[98]

In the last week of February 1981, the management of Joseph E. Seagram & Sons, Inc. decided to make a tender offer for the stock of St Joe Minerals Corporation, a New York company traded on the New York Stock Exchange. On March 9, Seagram's Board approved the plan and set the price of the tender offer at $45 per share; the public announcement of the offer was to be made on March 11, two days later. At the time St Joe's stock was selling at about $30 per share.

On March 10, more than 1,000 call options in the securities of St Joe were purchased on the Philadelphia Stock Exchange, each carrying the right to purchase 100 shares of stock. When the tender offer was announced on the following day, the options were liquidated, and whoever had made the purchase had made an immediate profit of $1.4 million. If he had acted on inside information, as seemed likely, the person who made this profit had also violated §§ 10(b) and 14(e) of the United States Securities Exchange Act of 1934.[99] The question was, who was this person? The broker who handled the option transaction said it had acted for Banco della Svizzera Italiana (BSI), a Swiss bank with its principal office in Lugano and a subsidiary in New York. BSI told the Securities and Exchange Commission that it had acted for a client, but that Swiss law—the same provisions invoked in *Interhandel*[100]—prohibited it from disclosing the client's name.

Consider this case as a conflict of laws problem: should United States law apply, on the ground that the transaction at issue had been carried out in Philadelphia and New York? Or should Swiss law apply, on the ground that the law governed the relation between BSI and its client? Should it matter whether the client was a domiciliary or citizen of (a) the United States; (b) Switzerland; or (c) some third country?

For the SEC, these questions were easy. Its mandate is to guard the integrity of American stock markets, and any action that threatened that integrity had to be investigated and (upon proper proof) punished. If possible, unlawful profits must be recaptured.[101] In the case of the St Joe options, the SEC moved immediately to secure a temporary restraining order freezing the assets of BSI on deposit at a New York bank, and brought suit in federal district court in

[98] Adapted from a comment by the present author in 15 *Review of Securities Regulation* 942 (Mar. 24, 1982).

[99] 15 U.S.C. § 78j(b), § 78n(3).

[100] i.e., Art. 47 of the Federal Law Relating to Banks and Savings Banks of Nov. 8, 1934, and Art. 273 of the Penal Code, generally known as the Business Secrecy Law.

[101] Recall the Eddie Antar case, Ch. 6. sect. C(3).

New York against BSI as well as 'Certain Purchasers of Call Options'. Various skirmishes took place before Judge Pollack (the same judge who had ordered enforcement of the subpoena against City Bank in the quinine cartel case), and the amount of assets of BSI frozen was reduced to restrain only the transfer of shares of St Joe and a sum sufficient to cover the alleged improper gains plus costs. But BSI did not disclose the name of its client, and so far as appears it made no attempt to secure a waiver of the secrecy laws from the Swiss government (if indeed such a waiver is ever possible).[102]

Eventually the SEC grew impatient. In August, it submitted a series of interrogatories to BSI, which were not answered. In October, the SEC asked Judge Pollack to impose sanctions against BSI, including a fine of $50,000 per day; an order to BSI to cease any further trading on United States securities markets; and an order holding BSI liable as agent for an undisclosed principal and striking any defenses that it might have.

As this case was going on, my colleagues and I were early in our work on what became *Restatement (Third) of Foreign Relations Law*, and I remember wondering where the BSI case fit in. We had drafted what became § 441, essentially recognizing the foreign government compulsion doctrine,[103] and a separate section—§ 442 in the final version[104]—which took a somewhat different position in regard to disclosure and blocking laws, on the ground that questions of evidence and disclosure were more related to litigation than to primary activity, and hence the balance of interests—while still required—came out closer to the law of the forum. In which category did the *BSI* case belong?

At a hearing on November 6, Judge Pollack indicated that he was ready to impose the sanctions requested by the SEC. Quoting from § 40 of the previous Restatement,[105] the judge said that he had weighed the competing interests of the two states, that the Swiss Attorney General had said only that waiver was not possible without the depositor's consent but had not expressed the kind of support to non-disclosure that it had given in *Interhandel*, and that the interests of the United States in enforcing its securities laws were clearly stronger than the interests of Switzerland in non-disclosure. Moreover, the judge concluded that the bank had acted in bad faith, in that it had deliberately courted the impediment that it was now asserting, by invading the American securities market knowing that it would be relying on the non-disclosure laws of Switzerland.

[102] My understanding from Swiss counsel is that it is not possible to obtain a waiver of Art. 47 from the government; only the bank's customer may waive bank secrecy. As for Art. 273 of the Penal Code, since its aim is to protect vital Swiss interests, even the private person in possession of the secret may not be able to disclose it, if, for instance, a trade secret is deemed vital to Swiss national security. As discussed in the next section, however, some arrangements were later worked out to prevent the secrecy laws from being used to cover criminal activity.

[103] See text at nn. 47–50 *supra*.

[104] Reproduced in Ch. 8, n. 52 *infra*.

[105] *Restatement (Second) of the Foreign Relations Law of the United States* (1965).

The bank [the judge said, quoting from *City Bank*] must confront the choice to surrender to one sovereign or the other, the privilege received therefrom ... or alternatively a willingness to accept the consequences.[106]

On November 12, BSI made its choice. One of BSI's managers submitted a detailed affidavit, stating the client's name, the time and manner of the transactions, and the amounts involved. The affidavit stated that it was made on the 'advice of Swiss legal counsel based on delivery to BSI of waivers duly executed by its client'. It turned out that the client was one Giuseppe Tome, and the purchase had been made in his own name and in the name of some Panamanian companies that he controlled. Tome was an Italian citizen residing in Switzerland who had previously represented various American brokerage houses in Europe and had had both personal and business relations with the Chairman of Seagram. The orders to purchase and then to liquidate the options had been placed by telephone from New York to BSI's office in Geneva.[107]

Thus the SEC had prevailed in the game of chicken. There was no occasion for BSI to be punished for violating Swiss law, because Mr Tome had consented to disclosure of his name and the names of the Panamanian companies. What pressures BSI put on Mr Tome to give his consent is not known.

2. The *Bank of Nova Scotia* Cases

The Bank of Nova Scotia is a major multinational bank, with headquarters in Canada and over 1,200 offices, branches, and agencies in some forty-six countries. Notwithstanding its name, the Bank of Nova Scotia's home office is in Toronto; more important for present purposes, the bank maintains an office in Miami, Florida, and also maintains offices or branches in the Bahamas and in the Cayman Islands. The Bahamas has been an independent state since 1973; the Cayman Islands are a British colony, but with certain legislative powers of their own, subject to limited veto from London. Both the Bahamas and the Cayman Islands have sought to attract banking business with promise of favorable tax regimes and bank secrecy. At the time relevant to the two Bank of Nova Scotia cases here described, both the Bahamas and the Cayman Islands had adopted bank secrecy legislation in substantially similar form.

[106] The judge read his opinion on Nov. 7, 1981; a somewhat revised version was released for publication after the events described in the next paragraph.

[107] Thereafter, Judge Pollack published his formal decision, establishing his opinion as a precedent, and withdrawing the sanctions against BSI: *SEC* v. *Banca della Svizzera Italiana*, 92 F.R.D. 111 (S.D.N.Y. 1981). Some $2 million standing in the name of BSI remained frozen as security for the liability of Tome and his tippees. Eventually the SEC won a judgement against Tome, his tippees, and the Panamanian companies. Tome did not return to the United States, but the frozen funds were used to satisfy a final judgment in favor of the SEC. See *SEC* v. *Tome*, 638 F.Supp. 596 (S.D.N.Y. 1986), aff'd, 833 F.2d 1086 (2d Cir. 1987), cert. denied sub nom. *Lombardfin S.p-A* v. *SEC*, 486 U.S. 1014 (1988).

(a) Bank of Nova Scotia I

The first case[108] began in September 1981 with a subpoena issued by a United States grand jury that was conducting a narcotics investigation in Miami.[109] The subpoena, served on the manager of the Miami agency of Bank of Nova Scotia, directed the Bank to turn over records of a customer of the Bank at its branch or branches in the Bahamas. The Bank declined to produce the documents requested without the consent of its customer or an order of the Bahamian court, on the ground that compliance with the subpoena would violate the Bank and Trust Companies Regulation Act of the Bahamas.[110] Section 10 of the Act provides that:

> No person who has acquired information in his capacity as director, officer, employee or agent of any [licensed bank] . . . shall, without the express or implied consent of the customer concerned, disclose to any person any ... information relating to the identity, assets, liabilities, transactions, [or] accounts of a customer except ... when [the bank] is lawfully required to make disclosure by any court of the competent jurisdiction within The Bahamas, or under the provision of any law of The Bahamas.

Violation of this provision is punishable by a fine of up to 15,000 dollars, imprisonment for up to two years, or both. Bank of Nova Scotia took the position before the U.S. court in Miami that, as a foreign corporation engaged in business both in the United States and in the Bahamas, it obeyed United States law in the United States and Bahamian law in the Bahamas; here, as in *Interhandel*, the law where the accounts were kept should provide a defense to the order for disclosure. How should this case progress?

Should Bank of Nova Scotia be advised, for instance, to seek an order from the Grand Court of the Bahamas permitting it to make the disclosure request? Does it, or should it, have an obligation to do so? And if it did make such an application, on what basis, if ever, should the Bahamas court grant permission to make the disclosure?

The Bank submitted an affidavit from a Bahamian lawyer to the effect that an order permitting disclosure could be obtained only if the Bahamian court were satisfied that the subject of the grand jury investigation was a crime under Bahamian law and not, for example, an investigation concerning tax evasion. The United States government—or to be precise the Assistant United States Attorney in charge of the case in Miami—took the position that a subpoena issued on the authority of a duly constituted grand jury stood on its own, and did not have to be justified, least of all before a foreign court intent on

[108] *United States* v. *Bank of Nova Scotia I*, 691 F.2d 1384 (11th Cir. 1982), cert. denied, 462 U.S. 1119 (1983).

[109] For a brief description of the functions of a grand jury and its subpoena powers, see text at n. 42 *supra*.

[110] Statute Law of The Bahamas, Vol. VII. ch. 287 (Rev. edn., 1988).

preserving its country's rôle as a secrecy haven. Moreover, the more the prosecutor disclosed to the Bank and to the foreign court about the investigation, the more the target of the investigation might learn, enabling him to cover his tracks or to leave the country before the investigation was concluded and an indictment could be issued. Accordingly, the U.S. government refused to make a showing that the documents sought were relevant and necessary to the grand jury's investigation.[111]

In this posture the Bank declined to apply to the Bahamas court for permission to comply with the subpoena, and maintained its refusal to make disclosure without permission. The U.S. District Court in Miami upheld the subpoena, and when the Bank still refused to comply held the Bank in contempt, subject to a fine of $500 per day until compliance. The Bank appealed, arguing that enforcing the subpoena would violate due process under the *Interhandel* case, and urging that the court balance the competing interests of the United States and the other concerned country, as called for by the 1965 *Restatement of Foreign Relations Law* (§ 40) and also by the new *Restatement*, then in draft form.[112] The Court of Appeals rejected all these arguments:

> The bank has failed to bring itself within the holding of *Société Internationale* [*Interhandel*]. The district court found the Bank had not made a good faith effort to comply with the subpoena . . . The Bahamian government has not acted to prevent the Bank from complying with the subpoena. Finally the Bank is not being denied a constitutionally required forum to recover confiscated assets.[113]

To the contention by the Bank that the United States government 'could avoid rather than provoke disrespect for the sovereignty of a friendly nation' by applying for an order of judicial assistance through diplomatic channels, the court answered:

> The judicial assistance procedure does not afford due deference to the United States' interests. In essence, the Bank asks the court to require our government

[111] Quite apart from the international issues, there had been a controversy among Courts of Appeals in the United States about what showing needed to be made in support of a grand jury subpoena, with some courts requiring some showing of relevance of requested documents to an investigation properly within the grand jury's jurisdiction, and other courts holding that such a showing was required only if respondent could demonstrate harassment or abuse by the prosecutor. In *Bank of Nova Scotia I* the Court of Appeals took the latter view, as did the U.S. Supreme Court several years later, on the ground that the grand jury's function was to ascertain whether probable cause exists, and thus could not be required to make a showing of probable cause in advance: *United States* v. *R. Enterprises, Inc.*, 498 U.S. 292 (1991).

[112] *Restatement (Revised) of Foreign Relations Law*, § 420, Tent. Draft No. 3 (1982), which with some changes became § 442 in the final version of the *Restatement*, as quoted in Ch. 8, n. 52.

[113] 691 F.2d at 1389. The last sentence refers to the issue, peculiar to the *Interhandel* case, where the person directed to make disclosure is not only a party, as contrasted with the intermediary, but is claiming that its assets have been taken by the government without just compensation. See 148 *supra*.

to ask the courts of the Bahamas to be allowed to do something lawful under United States law. We conclude such a procedure to be contrary to the interests of our nation and [to] outweigh the interests of the Bahamas.[114]

Bank of Nova Scotia applied for review to the Supreme Court, and when review was denied it made further motions, until the United States government moved for and the district court granted an increase in the fine from $500 to $25,000 per day until compliance. On the following day, Bank of Nova Scotia produced all the documents listed in the subpoena. The government of the Bahamas took no action against the Bank.

(b) Bank of Nova Scotia II

Even before the United States Attorney in Miami had secured compliance in the first case (but after the United States government had prevailed in the Court of Appeals), he tried the same technique again. Another grand jury, another investigation, another target, but once again the bank in the middle was Bank of Nova Scotia, and once again the manager of the Bank's Miami office was served with a subpoena calling for documents located abroad, this time in the Cayman Islands, as well as in the Bahamas.[115] Once more the Bank appeared before the grand jury without the documents, once more it filed a motion to quash the subpoena on the ground that compliance would violate the laws applicable where the documents were located, and once more the U.S. District Court in Miami denied the motion to quash and ordered the Bank to produce the documents. But having been chastised in the first case—and indeed found not to be in good faith within the teaching of *Interhandel*—because it had not sought permission to disclose from the relevant authority, Bank of Nova Scotia now made application to the Grand Court of the Cayman Islands for permission to make the disclosure required by the United States subpoena.

One might ask how the Grand Court, or the Attorney General of the Cayman Islands, should respond to such an application. For example, would the criteria proposed by the *Restatement* be suitable for consideration by the Cayman Islands court? Would the application be viewed more favourably if the U.S. court had tested the subpoena against the *Restatement* criteria? Correspondingly, if the Caymans court applied the *Restatement* criteria or some analogous approach, would its judgment be likely (or more likely) to be respected in U.S. courts?

None of these reflections are apparent in the actual case. The Attorney General of the Cayman Islands opposed the application of the Bank, and the Grand Court denied it. Moreover, the Caymans court issued an order directing

[114] 691 F.2d at 1391.

[115] S. 3 of the Confidential Relationships (Preservation) Law of the Cayman Islands, Law 16 of 1976, 4 Cayman Islands Gazette No. 20, 1976, read substantially like the corresponding Bahamas law quoted at n. 110 *supra*.

Bank of Nova Scotia not to comply with the subpoena. Now the Bank could not only plead foreign law as precluding compliance with the subpoena, but it had a foreign judgment to prove it, and at least an argument that the judgment was entitled to recognition by a court in the United States.[116]

The District Court in Miami was not impressed. It held another hearing, but it ordered the Bank to comply and, when the documents were still not produced, the court found the Bank in contempt. When counsel for the Bank asked for a finding that it had acted in good faith, the court took the opportunity to hold the opposite, and imposed a fine for contempt of $25,000 per day until full compliance.

The Bank again appealed, and at this point *amicus curiae* briefs were submitted on behalf of the Cayman Islands, the United Kingdom, and Canada.[117] If, as in *Bank of Nova Scotia I*, the court were going to weigh interests, the Cayman Islands government wanted to stress its strong interest—that is its interest in creating a banking industry in a territory with few other resources. Canada stressed the importance of multinational corporations, and their obligation to comply in each state with the law of that state.[118] The United Kingdom brief renewed the attack on exercise of 'extraterritorial jurisdiction' by the United States. Most significant, as it turned out, the Bank now produced a 'Gentlemen's Agreement', an exchange of letters between the Acting Governor of the Cayman Islands and the United States Consul General in Jamaica following the decision in *Bank of Nova Scotia I*, which set out a procedure for processing requests by the United States for information protected by the Cayman Islands confidentiality law.

Faced with all this new material, the Court of Appeals remanded the case to the District Court.[119] The District Court held another hearing, permitted the *amici* to have their say, but did not change its mind. The Bank once again appealed. By now, its fine had reached $1,825,000.

In its second consideration of *Bank of Nova Scotia II*, the Court of Appeals wrote a long opinion, but in the end it upheld the order to produce the documents, the finding of lack of good faith on the part of the Bank, and the finding of contempt.[120] The court now was willing to balance competing interests, as

[116] Of course the parties were not the same in the Cayman Islands as in the United States, and the law on the recognition given to injunctions issued by foreign courts is far from settled. See Ch. 4, sect. D(3). Still, one would think that a judgment of a foreign court could not simply be ignored, and that disregard of a foreign judgment is more of an affront to a foreign state than refusal to apply the foreign state's law.

[117] The present writer represented Canada in this appeal and in subsequent proceedings in *Bank of Nova Scotia II*. As with respect to other cases discussed in this volume in which I had a part, the effort here is to present the case as objectively as possible, and the views expressed are in no way attributable to the Government of Canada.

[118] Recall Ch. 5, especially the *Badger* case described in sect. C(3).

[119] *In re Grand Jury Proceedings, United States* v. *The Bank of Nova Scotia*, 722 F.2d 657 (11th Cir. 1983).

[120] *United States* v. *Bank of Nova Scotia II*, 740 F.2d 817 (11th Cir. 1984), cert. denied, 469 U.S. 1106 (1985).

spelled out by the respective governments, but the United States interest in combatting the narcotics trade outweighed the Cayman Islands interest in bank secrecy. As for the argument that it was unfair to require the Bank to choose between conflicting commands, the court wrote:

> The Bank has voluntarily elected to do business in numerous foreign host countries and has accepted the incidental risk of occasional inconsistent governmental actions. It cannot expect to avail itself of the benefits of doing business here without accepting the concomitant obligations.[121]

The 'Gentlemen's Agreement', as the court read it, was not a binding enforceable agreement, 'but rather an experimental and tentative alternative for the production of documents':[122]

> We have previously recognized [the court concluded] that international friction is provoked by enforcement of subpoenas such as the one in this case [citing *Bank of Nova Scotia I*]. But under our tripartite form of government federal courts remain open to the legislative and executive branches for assistance if matters such as this have international repercussions.[123]

Here, of course, the executive branch of the United States government had not come in to urge the court to moderate the effect of judicial action—quite the contrary. Accordingly, the rôle of the grand jury was upheld and the contempt finding and fine were confirmed. In the end, the banking records were turned over to the grand jury.[124]

G. A BETTER WAY

Could any lessons be drawn from cases such as *Banco della Svizzera Italiana* and *Bank of Nova Scotia*?

On one side the United States, through the Securities and Exchange Commission and the use of grand juries, had acted like a bully. Whether or not the courts accepted the obligation to balance competing interests, as the *Restatements* called for, there was a good deal of truth to the observation of two Canadian commentators:

> Each of the factors [set out in the *Restatement*] appears to be reasonable, but there is no assurance that they will be applied reasonably. The *Restatement* is flawed because its subjects a national interest of one country to the judgment of a U.S. court . . .

[121] 740 F.2d at 828.
[122] *Id.* 829–30.
[123] *Id.* 832.
[124] As in *Bank of Nova Scotia I*, the U.S. Supreme Court denied review, notwithstanding the urging of the Canadian, British, and Cayman Islands authorities: *Bank of Nova Scotia* v. *United States*, 469 U.S. 1106 (1985).

> We expect that a U.S. court, whether under the *Restatement* or otherwise, would always find the U.S. interest in enforcement of its criminal law must take priority over the interest of a small state in ensuring for its own public policy reasons, the confidentiality of a banking transaction.[125]

In fact not all cases came out like the *BSI* and *Bank of Nova Scotia* cases. In *United States* v. *First National Bank of Chicago*,[126] decided between the *Bank of Nova Scotia* cases, a different U.S. Court of Appeals, relying on the *Restatements*, reversed a district court judgment that had directed a bank in Chicago to disclose records of named depositors at its branch in Athens.[127] Still it was true that an enforcement officer focusing on a particular case could usually persuade himself—and usually a court as well—that the case at hand was supremely important, and that interests of the United States in sound international relations or progressive development of international law were hard to define, let alone to weigh. Even enforcement officials, however, when contemplating the long run, began to think there must be a better way.

On the other side, it was becoming increasingly apparent that bank secrecy was being abused. In Switzerland certainly, and to a lesser extent in the Caribbean, it was an uncomfortable position for the governments to be expending their resources, and their good relations with the United States, to protect persons engaged in insider trading, narcotics trafficking, and money laundering. The *BSI* and *Bank of Nova Scotia* cases, I believe, were a watershed in bringing the various participants in this phase of the conflict over American discovery to look for a better way.

In principle, the 'better way' was not difficult to figure out. On one side, the United States should abandon its unilateral reliance on subpoenas, court orders, and sanctions; on the other, the secrecy states should abandon their absolute prohibition on disclosure, when stated elements of wrongdoing are credibly alleged and the allegations and documents requested can be reviewed by their own designated authorities. Of course, such an arrangement could be worked out only if there was general agreement by the secrecy states that what the United States sought to punish (whether in civil or criminal proceedings) was reprehensible conduct not worthy of protection, and agreement by the United States that acts not viewed by the secrecy states as sufficiently reprehensible—notably tax evasion—would not be subject to either unilateral or bilateral efforts to procure evidence located abroad. To some extent, if such arrangements could be worked out, banks might lose some business; they would be relieved, however, from situations such as occurred in *BSI*, *Bank of*

[125] Serge April and Jonathan Fried, 'Compelling Discovery and Disclosure in Transnational Criminal Litigation—a Canadian View', 16 *N.Y.U. J. Int'l Law & Pol.* 961 at 967–8 (1984).

[126] 699 F.2d 341 (7th Cir. 1983).

[127] The Court of Appeals distinguished *Bank of Nova Scotia I* on the basis that it was dealing with an Internal Revenue summons, not a grand jury subpoena, and that the depositors were actually living in Greece, rather than just using the branch as a secrecy haven.

Nova Scotia, and earlier in *City Bank*, to mention only the cases here discussed.[128]

1. United States–Switzerland

Shortly after the *BSI* case was decided, Swiss and American delegations began consultations leading to a memorandum of understanding (MOU) 'to establish mutually acceptable means for improving international law enforcement co-operation in the field of insider trading'. Several years previously, the two countries had entered into a formal Treaty on Mutual Assistance in Criminal Matters,[129] but because that treaty covered only offenses that were crimes in both countries and Switzerland had not then made insider trading a crime, the treaty often was ineffective in insider trading cases.[130] The Swiss government was now willing to declare that securities transactions making use of material non-public information, while 'not yet' punishable under Swiss law, is considered dishonorable, and could be made subject to arrangements for mutual assistance in law enforcement. Switzerland and the United States accordingly entered into a provisional arrangement—the MOU[131] and an attached Convention XVI among members of the Swiss Bankers Association—whereby, in return for an undertaking by the United States not to resort to unilateral sanctions under Rule 37 of the Federal Rules of Civil Procedure (as under *Interhandel*, *City Bank*, and *BSI*), a request from the SEC credibly alleging serious violation of U.S. insider trading laws making use of Swiss banks would be referred to a three-member Commission of Inquiry established by the Swiss Bankers Association. If the Commission of Inquiry confirmed that the thresholds regarding volume and price of the challenged transaction had been met, the bank accounts in question would be frozen (up to the amount of the alleged profits and potential liability), the customer would be informed and given the opportunity to be heard, and the records would be sent to the Commission of Inquiry. The Commission, in most circumstances, would forward the documents to the Swiss Department of Police, which in turn would forward them to the SEC. The SEC undertook to use the information thus obtained only in connection with the particular investigation described in the request.

The details of the MOU and the Bankers Convention XVI are beyond the

[128] For other cases of this kind, see *Restatement (Third) of Foreign Relations Law*, § 442, Reporters' Notes 7–10 (1987); Peter S. Honegger, 'Amerikanische Offenlegungspflichten' in *Konflikt mit Schweizerischen Geheimhaltungspflichten* (1986), 69–72.

[129] 27 U.S.T. 2019; T.I.A.S. 8302; 1052 U.N.T.S. 61; SR [RO] 0.351.933.6, entered into force Jan. 3, 1977.

[130] See the Decision of the Federal (Supreme) Court of Switzerland in the *Santa Fe* case, 109 BGE 1b 47 (Jan. 26, 1983), repr. in abridged form in English in (1983) 22 Int'l Leg. Mats. 785.

[131] Memorandum of Understanding between Switzerland and the United States signed at Washington, Aug. 31, 1982, repr. in (1983) 22 Int. Leg. Mats. 1.

scope of this volume;[132] in any event the 1982 MOU has since been replaced as the result of adoption of an amendment to the Swiss Penal Code that makes insider trading punishable to substantially the same extent as in the United States,[133] so that requests by the SEC for assistance can now be dealt with under the Treaty for Mutual Assistance in Criminal Matters.[134] The lesson for present purposes is that it proved possible to replace unilateral assertion by the United States of jurisdiction to extract disclosure from Swiss banks engaged in business in the United States by a co-operative arrangement: the screening function is exercised by Switzerland, the requested state, both to require specific and justified requests, and to give the account holder the opportunity to raise his objections to disclosure before Swiss authorities (including the Supreme Court), but the information indicating wrongdoing is not permanently sheltered.

2. United States–Cayman Islands

In *Bank of Nova Scotia II*, as described earlier, one of the arguments made by the Bank and by the *amici* was that the United States should have proceeded by resort to the 'Gentlemen's Agreement' between the Acting Governor of the Cayman Islands and the United States Consul General.[135] The response of the U.S. Attorney, accepted by the U.S. courts, was that the agreement did not impose an obligation on either side, and thus could not serve to oust the authority of a grand jury subpoena. Following *Bank of Nova Scotia II* and similar cases,[136] the British government, on behalf of the Cayman Islands, made another effort to reach an agreement with the United States concerning disclosure of information. The United States government was willing to explore the possibilities, provided that there were not too many loop-holes or possibilities of delay. For the Cayman Islands, which by now held offices of over 500 banks, 360 insurance companies, and 16,000 companies

[132] For further information, see, e.g. Roger Zäch (ed.), *Litigation of Business Matters in the United States and Legal Assistance* (1984) pts. III and IV, also Michael Mann, Joseph G. Mari, George Lavdas, *Developments in International Securities Law Enforcement and Regulation* (1994) 58–63. Similar MOUs were subsequently negotiated by the SEC with counterpart agencies in Japan, Canada, Brazil, the Netherlands, France, Mexico, Norway, United Kingdom, Argentina, Spain, Italy, Chile, and Australia. See Mann *et al.* 63–73.

[133] *Switzerland*: Penal Code, Art. 161, as amended by Federal Law of Dec. 18, 1987, effective July 1, 1988, SR[RO] 1988 966, 967.

[134] n.129 *supra*. A further Exchange of Notes of Nov. 10, 1987 made clear that though the MOU would expire when the amendment to the Penal Code entered into effect, the SEC could still obtain and use information under the Treaty, whether or not criminal action was contemplated. See also (1988) 27 Intl'l Leg. Mats. 480. A still further exchange of notes of Nov. 3, 1993 expanded the scope of assistance available between Swiss authorities and the United States to cover securities-related offenses not falling under the definition of insider trading: SR [RO] 0.351.933.65.

[135] See 173–4 *supra*.

[136] e.g., *United States* v. *Ghidoni*, 732 F.2d 814 (11th Cir. 1984), cert. denied, 469 U.S. 932 (1984); *Doe* v. *United States*, 487 U.S. 201 (1988).

overall—and a population of just 23,000 persons[137]—it was important not to be branded a haven for the narcotics trade. Bank secrecy, its representatives believed, had many other uses that were not—or were not perceived to be—criminal, including avoidance of exchange controls, avoidance of taxes, and management of various kinds of multinational enterprises. If these could be preserved against attacks from the United States, the Islands were prepared to remove the protection of bank secrecy from narcotics traffickers.

Again the solution was first a formal interim Letter Agreement,[138] in the form of supplemental agreement to the Single Convention on Narcotic Drugs of 1961,[139] followed some years later by a formal Treaty on Mutual Assistance in Criminal Matters, concluded between the United States and the United Kingdom, modeled on the United States–Swiss treaty but limited to the Cayman Islands, and later extended to other British colonies in the Caribbean (but not to the United Kingdom itself).[140] The requested party (i.e. the Cayman Islands) undertook to obtain and transfer to the U.S. Attorney General documents sought in a criminal investigation, in return for an undertaking by the requesting party (i.e. the United States) not to enforce any compulsory measure, including a grand jury subpoena, calling for production of documents located in the territory of the requested party. In the interim Letter Agreement, the obligation of the requested state was limited to narcotics offenses; in the formal treaty, as in the Swiss–United States treaty, the scope was broadened to include securities fraud, money laundering, tax fraud (but not tax evasion), and any offense punishable by more than one year in prison by both states.

* * *

These two agreements do not, of course, bring to an end the *Justizkonflikt*, even with Switzerland and the Caribbean bank havens.[141] However, they

[137] See Ian Paget-Brown, 'Bank Secrecy and Criminal Matters: The Cayman Islands and U.S. Cooperative Development', 20 *Case Western Res. J. Int'l L.* 369 (1988).

[138] Exchange of Letters of July 26, 1984 between the Government of the United Kingdom and the Government of the United States of America concerning the Cayman Islands and the Matters Connected with ... Any Narcotics Activity referred to in the Single Convention on Narcotic Drugs 1961.

[139] 18 U.S.T. 1407, T.I.A.S. 6298, 520 U.N.T.S. 204.

[140] Treaty concerning the Cayman Islands relating to Mutual Assistance in Criminal Matters, signed at Grand Cayman, July 3, 1986, entered into force Mar. 19, 1990. The text is reproduced in (1987) 26 Int'l Leg. Mats. 536.

[141] The most acrimonious debate over disclosure between the United States and Switzerland (at least since *Interhandel*) concerning Marc Rich & Co., did not end until Nov. 1984. That story, too long to set out here, is told in some detail in my book *International Litigation and Arbitration* (1993) 796–804. For a somewhat different account, omitting the episode in which a paralegal from one of the law firms retained by Marc Rich attempted to transport two steamer trunks full of Marc Rich documents to Switzerland aboard a Swissair flight which was stopped from take-off at the last minute by the tower at New York's Kennedy International Airport, see Honegger, n. 128 *supra*, at 51–60.

demonstrate, I submit, that the more the focus is shifted to the purpose—often a common purpose—of a search for information and away from emphasis on 'the vital role of the grand jury'[142] or the 'sovereign rights' to maintain bank secrecy,[143] the better are the chances for reaching a reasonable accommodation. A fair question is whether the technique worked out in connection with criminal or quasi-criminal conduct can be adapted to civil litigation, where there may well be less consensus on substance than there is with regard to securities fraud or money laundering. This question leads directly to the next chapter, devoted to the Hague Evidence Convention.

[142] Compare *United States* v. *Bank of Nova Scotia I*, 691 F.2d at 1387, *United States* v. *Bank of Nova Scotia II*, 740 F.2d at 832.

[143] See, e.g. Kurt M. Hoechner, 'A Swiss Perspective on Conflicts of Jurisdiction', 50 *Law & Contemp. Prob.* No. 3, 271 at 273 (1987).

8

More on Discovery: The Hague Evidence Convention

A. BACKGROUND AND OVERVIEW OF THE CONVENTION

In the preceding chapter, after a somewhat abstract discussion of fact-finding in American litigation, the cases used to illustrate the controversies over transnational discovery were all based on some kind of public law, from enemy property to antitrust to securities regulation to tax evasion and the drug trade. In this Chapter, addressed to the Hague Evidence Convention,[1] we come back to the first strand of the *Justizkonflikt*, American private tort litigation, primarily based on liability for injuries caused by products alleged to be defective. Such litigation nearly always depends on some sort of fact-finding directed to the design and manufacture of the product. As the United States, which had been net exporter until the early 1970s, became a massive importer of automobiles and machinery, and European-made aircraft began to be involved in accidents in the United States, the Hague Evidence Convention took on increasing importance, viewed by some as an aid in procuring information located abroad, by others as a shield against disclosing such information.

The Evidence Convention is, of course, not limited to product liability litigation, and indeed it seems to work best in quite different types of cases—procurement of birth and marriage certificates, wills, other routine items. The question is whether it helps or hinders collection of evidence in situations where one side has an incentive to block disclosure and production.

It is often forgotten that the initiative for the Hague Evidence Convention came largely from the United States,[2] which had recently adopted unilaterally a highly liberal set of provisions concerning international judicial assistance.[3] Having become a member of the Hague Conference on Private International

[1] Convention on the Taking of Evidence Abroad in Civil or Commercial Matters, signed at The Hague, Mar. 18, 1970, 847 U.N.T.S. 231. As of year-end 1995, the Convention had 26 parties, including the United States and all Member States of the European Community except Belgium, Greece, and Ireland.

[2] See Memorandum of the United States with Respect to the Revision of Chapter II of the 1954 Convention on Civil Procedure, Conférence de la Haye, Actes et Documents de la Onzième Session, iv, 15 (1968).

[3] Pub. L. 88–619, 78 Stat. 995 (1964) adopting *inter alia* 28 U.S. Code § 1696 (Service in Foreign and International Litigation); § 1782 (Assistance to Foreign and International Tribunals); § 1783 (Subpoena of Person in foreign Country).

Law only in 1964.[4] the United States took an active part in preparation of the Tenth Session of the Hague Conference,[5] which produced the Hague Service Convention. That Convention, reflecting international recognition that there were a good many situations in which states had judicial jurisdiction over parties not present in the forum state, had developed a fairly simple method of transmitting initiating process from the court where the action was brought via a central authority in each contracting party to the person being sued. At the following session of the Hague Conference, even before the Service Convention had entered into force, the United States took the lead (with an American lawyer in private practice as Rapporteur) in drafting a Convention on the Taking of Evidence, basically using the same format as the Service Convention. In place of the prior cumbersome practice of resort to letters rogatory, which usually required the participation of two foreign ministries and sometimes two ministries of justice as well, without any obligation of compliance with a request for assistance, the Hague Evidence Convention was to provide a simple method of transmitting Letters of Request prepared on a standard form directly from the court in state *A*, where an action was pending, to a central authority (usually a bureau in the Department of Justice) of state *B* where the evidence was located. The Central Authority would serve the request on the person whose testimony or documents were required, with appropriate instructions. If the witness did not appear voluntarily or did not produce the required documents or other evidence, Article 10 of the Convention provided that 'the requested authority shall apply the appropriate measures of compulsion', i.e. that the request would be treated in the same manner as a summons or comparable instrument issued by a court in state *B*. Thereafter the Central Authority in state *B* would send the record back to the court in *A* for use in that court. The Convention said (in Article 12) that execution of a Letter of Request in due form could be refused only for limited specified reasons,[6] but not 'on the ground that under its internal law the State of execution [of the Request] claims exclusive jurisdiction over the subject matter of the action or that its internal law would not admit a right of action on it.'

In his report to the Senate urging approval of the Evidence Convention,

[4] For a history of the Hague Conference and the belated participation in its work by the United States, see Nadelmann, 'The United States Joins the Hague Conference on Private International Law (A History with Comments)', 30 *Law & Contemp. Probs.* 291 (1965). See also G. Droz and A. Dyer, 'The Hague Conference and the Main Issues of Private International Law for the Eighties', 3 *Nw. J. Int'l Law & Bus.* 155, 162–70 (1981).

[5] Convention on the Service Abroad of Judicial and Extrajudicial Documents in Civil or Commercial Matters, signed at The Hague, Nov. 15, 1965, 658 U.N.T.S. 163.

[6] The grounds specified are (a) that in the State of execution the execution of the Letter of Request does not fall within the functions of the judiciary, and (b) that the State addressed considers that its sovereignty or security would be prejudiced by executing the request.

President Nixon wrote: 'This convention is a significant step forward in the field of international judicial cooperation.'[7]

Secretary of State Rogers, in his Letter of Submittal of the Convention, reported that the United States delegation considered that the Convention is a 'major contribution to the elimination of formal and technical obstacles to securing evidence abroad in a form that is usable in the court where the action is pending', and celebrated the leadership of the United States in the field of international judicial assistance already manifested by enactment of the U.S. statutes on judicial assistance and its early ratification of the Hague Service Convention.[8] Beyond the particular subject of taking evidence, the two Hague Conventions on Judicial Assistance[9] were thought to be a blend of the common law and the civil law traditions, combining in the present context the formal and official function of taking of proof in the civil law manner with the lawyers' initiative in the common law manner. This is illustrated, for instance, in Article 9 of the Convention, which provides that the judicial authority of state *B*, the requested state, shall apply its own law as to the methods and procedures to be followed, but will follow a request of the court in state *A*, the forum state, that a special method or procedure be followed, unless this is incompatible with state *B*'s internal law. Thus, for example, if a witness is to be interrogated in Germany for use in an American court, his answers can be taken down in shorthand so that they can be introduced in an American court. That is not the German practice, but it is not incompatible with German law and if the party seeking the evidence is willing to pay for it, a verbatim transcript can be prepared. Correspondingly, an examination in the United States may be conducted by an examiner (or even a German judge) who will prepare a summary to be signed by the witness for inclusion in the dossier of the German proceeding.[10]

All this looked quite promising, at least if the important states could be persuaded to join the Convention. Alas, it did not work out that way.

B. ARTICLE 23: EVIDENCE OR DISCOVERY

Almost on the last day of the Eleventh Session of the Hague Conference, the British Delegation put forward a new proposal, which eventually became Article 23 of the Evidence Convention:

[7] Message from the President of the United States transmitting the Convention on the Taking of Evidence, Exec. A, 92d Cong., 2d Sess., p. III (1972).

[8] Letter of Submittal from Secretary of State to President, *id.*, pp. X, XI.

[9] Plus a third, uncontroversial Hague Convention abolishing the Requirement of Legalization of Foreign Public Documents, signed Oct. 5, 1961, 527 U.N.T.S. 189.

[10] For a detailed description of the interrogation of six German witnesses in Munich for use in an American litigation, see Platto, 'Taking Evidence Abroad—A Practical Guide', 16 *Int'l Lawyer* 575, 581–5 (1982), describing the oral hearings in the *Corning Glass* case, n. 16 *infra*.

A Contracting State may at the time of signature, ratification or accession, declare that it will not execute Letters of Request issued for the purpose of obtaining pretrial discovery of documents as known in Common Law countries.

It is not clear what the British delegation had in mind. As pointed out in Chapter 7,[11] 'discovery as known in Common Law countries' is a contradiction in terms: the English view and the American view are quite different—in respect of what is discoverable, from whom discovery may be taken, and the devices available for discovery. Did the British proposal intend to authorize restrictions on American document discovery, but not on oral examinations before trial? The text would seem to indicate that, but there is no logical basis to attribute that position to the British. Did they, as Lawrence Collins has suggested, mean to record the difference in standards applicable to the procurement of *evidence*, as contrasted to *discovery*?[12] There is some logic to this interpretation, but it depends on rather strict terminology that would not be apparent to Americans. To American lawyers, all requests for assistance through the Convention would be regarded as part of the discovery process. Correspondingly everything gathered in discovery is evidence; one worries later about what fruits of discovery will be introduced or what is admissible.[13] Non-common law delegates did not even have a word for discovery, and the French text of Article 23—the only place where the word 'discovery' appears—uses the English phrase in quotation marks. At all events, it is clear that the American delegation was not at first alert to the threat to American practice posed by Article 23. In fact, the United States voted for Article 23 while Germany, France, and Switzerland voted against it, and no particular attention was drawn to Article 23 in the ratification process before the United States Senate.[14]

When ratifications to the Evidence Convention were submitted, every Contracting State except Israel and Czechoslovakia (and, of course, the United States) made the declaration permitted by Article 23, though not all in the same form.[15] And for the most part, the response to applications for evidence by American litigants was to treat all Letters of Request as falling under Article 23 and to read the declarations made under that Article literally, so that oral testimony might be permitted, but documents could not be furnished. Thus for instance a person being interrogated might be asked '*Did you attend*

[11] Ch. 7, sect. B.

[12] See Lawrence Collins, 'The Hague Convention and Discovery: A Serious Misunderstanding?', (1986) 35 *Int'l & Comp. L.Q.* 765, repr. (with new introduction) in Collins, *Essays in International Litigation and the Conflict of Laws* (1994).

[13] See for instance, Cound, Friedenthal, Miller, and Sexton, *Civil Procedure, Cases and Materials* (6th ed. 1994), the leading American case- and text-book for first year law students, at 762: 'The final major purpose of discovery is to find out what testimony and other evidence is available on each of the disputed factual issues.'

[14] See Letter of Submittal from Secretary of State, n. 8 *supra* at p. IX and the Explanatory Report on the Convention by Philip W. Amram attached thereto, 15.

[15] See 191–2 *infra* for the two most common forms of declarations under Art. 23.

a meeting with X on October 9?' Yes. *'Were Minutes kept at that meeting?'* Yes. *'Please produce those minutes.'* Objection under the declaration pursuant to Article 23.[16] That did not make a great deal of sense, and might well diminish the usefulness of the Convention in obtaining information from non-parties.[17] The real crisis in the Convention, however, turned not on third party discovery or search for evidence, but on discovery requests addressed to parties in American product liability litigation. In each case American injured parties were on one side, European manufacturers on the other. Like so many other phenomena sweeping the world, it all started in California.

C. DOES THE EVIDENCE CONVENTION PROTECT PARTIES FROM THE *LEX FORI*?

1. The California Cases

Volkswagenwerk Aktiengesellschaft v. *Superior Court, Alameda County*[18] arose out of an accident in which a Volkswagen Microbus struck a parked vehicle, severely injuring the driver. The front of the Microbus was apparently pushed back into the driver's compartment, and plaintiff, who lost a leg in the accident, alleged that the injury was due to a defective design of the vehicle, in that it did not provide sufficient 'crashworthiness'. In order to establish this contention, plaintiff sought discovery from Volkswagen, and after various motions and countermotions, the trial judge granted the request. One can get a good idea of the *Justizkonflikt* from the judge's order, as summarized by the appellate court:[19]

[16] In the best known case of this kind, Corning Glass had brought an action against ITT in a U.S. District Court alleging infringement of its optical fibre patents, and ITT counterclaimed for patent infringement and violation of the antitrust laws. ITT sought evidence from two German companies, Siemens and Siecor (a joint venture between *Sie*mens and *Cor*ning). On application of ITT, the U.S. District Judge addressed a Letter of Request to the Bavarian Ministry of Justice as Central Authority; the Ministry granted the request with respect to testimony of the officers of the two companies, but refused the request for production of documents. Both parts of the Ministry's decision were appealed to the Oberlandesgericht in Munich, and both were upheld by that Court: *Corning Glass Works* v. *International Telegraph Corp.*, OLG München, Oct. 31, 1980, Nov. 17, 1980 (1981) 36 *Juristenzeitung* 538, 540, repr. in English in (1981) 20 Int'l Legal Mats. 1049, 1025. See also Bruno Ristau, *International Judicial Assistance* (1986), 235–44; Platto, n. 10 *supra*.

[17] It is worth pointing out that the British did not interpret the Convention in this way. When the House of Lords in the *Westinghouse* case was convinced that a Request was made for use at trial, it was regarded as a request for 'evidence' and not 'discovery', and until other events overtook the Request, see Ch. 7 at 163, it was prepared to order the witnesses both to give oral testimony and to produce clearly identified documents. See *Rio Tinto Zinc* v. *Westinghouse Electric Corp.* [1978] AC 547 at 610–11, [1978] 2 WLR 81 at 88 (Lord Wilberforce); [1978] AC at 634–5, [1978] 2 WLR at 110–11 (Lord Diplock); [1978] AC at 621–5, [1978] 2 WLR at 98–101 (Viscount Dilhorne dissenting).

[18] 123 Cal.App.3d 840, 176 Cal.Rptr. 874 (Ct. App. 1st Dist. 1981).

[19] 123 Cal.App.3d at 847–9, 176 Cal.Rptr at 878.

1. *Premises*

a. *Access*: Claimants' representatives are to have access to the VWAG facilities at Wolfsburg during normal working hours on five consecutive days to inspect and photograph the premises, inspect and copy writings, and informally interview VWAG personnel. During claimant's inspection of facilities VWAG will provide a guide. Claimants may stay after normal working hours until 10 p.m. to examine and copy writings only, and during that time VWAG may designate a monitor at claimant's expense.

b. *Inspecting and photographing premises*: Claimants' representatives may inspect and photograph VWAG's facilities, subject to relevancy limitations and to existing and future protective orders.

2. *Writings*

a. *Access to technical library and plant and records*: Claimants' representative shall have access to VWAG's technical library and plant and records 'relating to the Type II vehicles and predecessor and successor vehicles within its type, including the currently produced Vanagon model,' subject to relevancy, trade secret, and personnel-record limitations.

b. *Inspecting and copying writings*: Claimant's representatives may inspect and copy writings 'which plaintiffs shall designate as bearing upon the design, testing, modification and analysis of the crashworthiness of the front end of the Type II vehicles and predecessor and successor vehicles within its type from the outset of production through the "Vanagon" model currently produced.' The order makes procedural provisions.

3. *Informal interviews*

Claimants' representatives may, during normal working hours, 'question any of defendant's employees, not under oath . . . to identify persons who possess knowledge . . . Such questioning shall not consist of detailed interrogation as to substantive knowledge, but be only that reasonably necessary for plaintiffs to select appropriate persons for depositions and to locate documents.' Claimants must minimize inconvenience; VWAG shall 'advise and request' cooperation. VWAG may have counsel present and may tape record.

4. *Depositions*

Following the Wolfsburg visit, claimants shall provide a list of deponents within 45 days. Terms and procedures for depositions of deponents so listed are spelled out with specific reference to certain diplomatic communications known as 'Notes Verbales,' discussed below.

The Court of Appeal sustained almost all of the discovery order under California law, but it ordered plaintiff to attempt to secure the necessary evidence by Letter of Request pursuant to the Hague Evidence Convention.

A strong argument can be made [the court conceded] that as a legitimate party to a California action VWAG may be required to elect between the demands of the California court and the sensitivities of the West German government, and to risk the sanctions authorized by California law should it elect not to give the required discovery. On the other hand, in cases such as this American courts traditionally and properly recognize the countervailing force of international comity:

The concept that the courts of one sovereign state should not, as a matter of sound international relations, require acts or forebearances within the territory, and inconsistent with the internal laws, of another sovereign state unless a careful weighing of competing interests and alternative means makes clear that the order is justified. Rulings based in this concept of international comity are dictated not by technical principles of jurisdiction of the parties to or subject-matter of particular lawsuits, but rather by exercise of judicial self-restraint in furtherance of policy considerations which transcend individual lawsuits. (Cf. *Rest. 2d Foreign Relations Law of the United States*, §§ 39–40.[20]

But would not the attempt by plaintiff to seek the information it wanted via the convention be futile, in view of the declaration under Article 23?

It is true [the court replied] that by the terms of its ratification West Germany has indicated that it will not execute letters of request for pretrial discovery of documents, but we suggest that this limitation should be tested, in this action, by a specific request that West Germany permit inspection of documents in light of the manifest need for full disclosure of evidence in the pending California action. In our view an order drafted to employ the discovery means least likely to antagonize the foreign government may also properly require the responding party to take all possible steps to secure the permission and cooperation of the foreign government. We have no doubt that VWAG has the attention and respect of the West German government and that a request from VWAG to suffer discovery to proceed in substantial conformity with California law would be favourably received.[21]

Plaintiff's counsel thereupon abandoned the effort at discovery and proceeded without the material he had sought from Volkswagen's factory.[22]

In *Pierburg GmbH & Co. KG* v. *Superior Court of Los Angeles County*,[23] the same pattern was repeated. Plaintiffs were injured when the engine of their Audi automobile caught fire while they were driving in the hot desert, without any kind of collision. Plaintiffs brought suit against Pierburg, among others,

[20] 123 Cal.App.3d at 857, 176 Cal.Rptr. at 884.

[21] 123 Cal.App.3d at 858–9, 176 Cal.Rptr. at 885.

[22] An earlier California decision with the same defendant but a different plaintiff and a different court, had reached the essentially same result: *Volkswagenwerk Aktiengesellschaft* v. *Superior Court, Sacramento County*, 33 Cal.App.3d 503, 109 Cal.Rptr. 219 (Ct. App.3d Dist. 1973). The court ordered plaintiff to pursue its discovery request via letters rogatory, on the ground that the embassy of the Federal Republic of Germany had informed the court that inspection of the VW plant or response to requests for deposition without proceeding through diplomatic channels would constitute an encroachment on German sovereign rights. Though the Convention was not then in effect between the United States and Germany, the court referred to documents of the Hague Conference and writings about the Convention, concluding that:

> A foreign corporation's amenability to local suit does not signal automatic subjection of its internal affairs to the courts of the forum, because the latter have no jurisdiction over persons or property outside their territory.

33 Cal.App.3d at 507, 109 Cal.Rptr at 221.

[23] 137 Cal.App.3d 238, 186 Cal.Rptr. 876 (Ct. App.2d Dist. 1982).

on the theory that the fire had been caused by a defective carburetor manufactured by Pierburg in Germany.[24] Plaintiffs served a series of interrogatories on Pierburg's Los Angeles attorney, inquiring in detail about the design, manufacture, components, known defects, testing, and operation of the Pierburg carburetor. In Germany, no doubt, this would be regarded as an attempt at an *Ausforschungsbeweis*; in the United States, there might be some effort to focus the questions, but essentially the request was a normal one. Once again, over objections of the defendant, the trial court upheld the discovery request, but the Court of Appeal (in a different district) reversed, ordering resort first to the procedures of the Convention. Against the argument that Pierburg had waived the applicability of the Convention by responding to other requests, the court raised the debate to the public law level:

> The foundation of the Convention is to avoid international friction where a domestic state court orders civil discovery to be conducted within the territory of a civil law nation that views such unilateral conduct as an intrusion upon its judicial sovereignty. The failure of one litigant in the domestic action to demand compliance with the Convention cannot divest the foreign nation of its sovereign judicial rights under the Convention. The Convention may be waived only by the nation whose judicial sovereignty would thereby be infringed upon.[25]

Once again the plaintiff's counsel abandoned the effort to procure the information requested, and eventually the case was settled for some $20 million.

If these California cases were correct, and if foreign courts and authorities functioning as requested states would use their domestic rules and attitudes, including, for instance, the broad German business privilege and rejection of broadly phrased questions, then the Hague Evidence Convention had turned out, from the United States point of view, to be less a bridge than a hindrance to fact-finding in international litigation. Certainly demands to disclose documents or submit persons for examination before trial with respect to litigants properly before a U.S. court had not previously been rejected on the basis of international law or treaty. Writing for a German journal in 1984, I urged German defendants not to take too much comfort in the line of California cases; I predicted that soon American courts would stop requiring exhaustion of the Hague Convention route in litigation with foreign parties, and would return to the procedures applicable to domestic litigation.[26] I expressed the hope that this step would be accompanied by some moderation, once the American courts had seen the vehemence with which foreign parties and their governments viewed some of the excesses of American discovery. My prediction was soon proved correct; the 'jury is still out', if I may be

[24] Pierburg did not have a permanent establishment in California, but it was served pursuant to the Hague Service Convention, n. 5 *supra*, and it apparently did not challenge the jurisdiction of the California court.

[25] 137 Cal.App.3d at 244–5; 186 Cal.Rptr. at 881.

[26] A. Lowenfeld, 'Discovery-Verfahren und internationale Rechtshilfe', [1984] *IPrax* 51.

forgiven a term from the American legal practice, on my hope. I return to this topic in the last section of this Chapter.

2. The *Aérospatiale* Case

In the mid-1980s, as the wave of product liability cases in the United States continued to mount, so did cases involving discovery from foreign manufacturers, both in state and in federal courts. Federal courts in the United States, of course, are normally required, under the *Erie* doctrine,[27] to follow state law in ordinary civil (so-called 'state-created') actions; here, however, the issue concerned interpretation of an international treaty, and federal courts were free to make their own interpretation. Indeed if there were an authoritative federal interpretation, it would be binding on state courts.[28]

Most (though not all) federal courts came out differently from the California line of cases.[29] They agreed that discovery that could be conducted only in the territory of a foreign state, for instance inspection of a plant, as requested in the 1981 *Volkswagen* case,[30] might be deemed to be an intrusion into that state's sovereignty, and therefore could be ordered only subject to that state's consent, as given in the Convention. Other types of discovery, such as inspection of documents that can be copied and mailed, or deposition of party witnesses who can get on an airplane, would not necessarily infringe on the sovereign interests of states, and accordingly could be ordered pursuant to the Federal Rules of Civil Procedure.

In the most closely watched case, *In re Anschuetz & Co*,[31] the Federal Court of Appeals for the Fifth Circuit wrote that it did not find the California cases well reasoned, and that it could find no indication that the purpose of the Evidence Convention was to restrict the exercise of *in personam* jurisdiction by United States courts over foreign nationals properly before it:[32]

> Treating the Convention procedures as exclusive would make foreign authorities the final arbiters of what evidence may be taken from their nationals, even when those nationals are parties properly within the jurisdiction of an American court.

[27] Named after the great case of *Erie R. Co* v. *Tompkins*, 304 U.S. 64 (1938), in which the U.S. Supreme Court rejected the concept of 'federal general common law' and required federal courts in 'non-federal' cases to follow the substantive law of the state where the federal court is sitting.

[28] If no treaty were applicable, for instance if the information in question were located in Switzerland, which had not joined the Hague Evidence Convention, a federal court sitting, say, in California would still be free to apply the Federal Rules of Civil Procedure, but a decision under those rules would not be binding on the state courts of California.

[29] See cases cited in *Restatement (Third) of Foreign Relations Law*, § 473, Reporters' Note 6.

[30] See text at n. 19 *supra*.

[31] 754 F.2d 602 (5th Cir. 1985), vacated in light of *Aérospatiale*, n. 35 *infra*, 483 U.S. 1002 (1987).

[32] 754 F.2d at 606.

While it is conceivable that the United States could enter into a treaty giving other signatories control over litigation instituted and pursued in American courts, a treaty intended to bring about such a curtailment of the rights given to all litigants by the federal rules would surely state its intention clearly and precisely identify crucial terms.[33]

By now the issue had absorbed a great many persons on both sides of the Atlantic. The Supreme Court practically had to grant review, but (possibly because it wanted a pure product liability case[34]) it chose not the *Anschuetz* case but a case arising out of the crash in Iowa of an airplane manufactured by the French company Société Nationale Industrielle Aérospatiale.[35] Briefs *amicus curiae* urging required first resort to the Convention were filed on behalf of the governments of France, Germany, Switzerland, the United Kingdom, and the Italy-America Chamber of Commerce, as well as by various litigants in related cases.[36]

The outcome is well known. On the issue of whether resort to the Convention was mandatory, the answer was clearly 'no'. The text of the Convention simply did not support such a reading. Article 1 of the Evidence Convention plainly says: 'a judicial authority *may* . . . request the competent authority of another Contracting State to obtain evidence, or to perform some other judicial act.' It does not say, as the Hague Service Convention does, 'The present Convention *shall apply in all cases*.[37] I always thought that the parties and *amici*

[33] *Id.* at 612.

[34] *Anschuetz* was a third party claim brought against the German manufacturer of steering gear on a ship involved in a collision on the Mississippi River.

[35] *Soc. Nationale Industrielle Aérospatiale* v. *U.S. District Court for the Southern District of Iowa*, 482 U.S. 522 (1987).

[36] The briefs of the parties and the *amici curiae* are reproduced in (1986) 25 Int'l Leg. Mats. 1475–1586.

[37] The full passage in Art. 1 of the Hague Service Convention reads:

> The present Convention shall apply in all cases, in civil or commercial matters, where there is occasion to transmit a judicial or extrajudicial document abroad.

Professor McClean, in commenting on the *Aérospatiale* case, writes that emphasis by the Supreme Court on the contrast between the two conventions was to prove a source of embarrassment, when the Court held in the following year that the Service Convention was not mandatory either: David McLean, *International Judicial Assistance* (1992) 115. The reference is to *Volkswagenwerk Aktiengesellschaft* v. *Schlunk*, 486 U.S. 694 (1988), a case arising out of a fatal automobile accident in Indiana, resulting in a product liability action against VWAG in the state court in Illinois. Plaintiff served VWAG in accordance with Illinois law by service on VWAG's subsidiary, Volkswagen of North America, and VWAG moved to set aside the service on the ground that it could only be served pursuant to the Hague Service Convention. The case went all the way to the U.S. Supreme Court, which held—correctly in my view—that the Convention provided the exclusive way for service to be effected in Germany, but did not exclude service in the forum state on a resident agent in accordance with the law of that state.

Thus I do not believe that the Supreme Court has been caught in a contradiction, as McClean suggests. The *Schlunk* case does illustrate, however, that Germany and some other states were disappointed by the Hague Service Convention, even as the United States had been disappointed by the Hague Evidence Convention.

(as well as various lobbyists) damaged their cause by overplaying it. 'Must' was clearly wrong;[38] the question was whether 'should' was appropriate.

On that question, the Supreme Court split five to four. The majority, in an opinion by Justice Stevens, wrote:

> [We] cannot accept petitioners' invitation to announce a new rule of law that would require first resort to Convention procedures whenever discovery is sought from a foreign litigant. Assuming . . . that we have the law-making power to do so, we are convinced that such a general rule would be unwise. In many situations the Letter of Request procedure authorized by the Convention would be unduly time consuming and expensive, as well as less certain to produce needed evidence than direct use of the Federal Rules. A rule of first resort in all cases would therefore be inconsistent with the overriding interest in the 'just, speedy, and inexpensive determination' of litigation in our courts. See Fed. Rule Civ. Proc. 1.[39]

To the argument that a rule of first resort is necessary to accord respect to the sovereignty of the states where the evidence is located, the majority said it was not persuaded:

> If such a duty were to be inferred from the adoption of the Convention itself, we believe that it would have been described in the text of that document. Moreover, the concept of international comity requires in this context a more particularized analysis of the respective interests of the foreign nation and the requesting nation than petitioners' proposed general rule would generate [citing what became § 442 of the *Resatement*]. We therefore decline to hold as a blanket matter that comity requires resort to Hague Evidence Convention procedures without prior scrutiny in each case of the particular facts, sovereign interests, and likelihood that resort to those procedures will prove effective.
>
> Some discovery procedures are much more 'intrusive' than others. In this case, for example, an interrogatory asking petitioners to identify the pilot who flew flight tests in the Rallye [the aircraft that crashed] before it was certified for flight by the Federal Aviation Administration, or a request to admit that petitioners authorized certain advertising in a particular magazine, is certainly less intrusive than a request to produce all of the 'design specifications, change orders and plans and all drawings concerning the leading edge slats for the Rallye type aircraft manufactured by the defendants.' Even if a court might be persuaded that a particular document request was too burdensome or too 'intrusive' to be granted in full, with or without an appropriate protective order, it might well refuse to insist upon the use of Convention procedures before requiring responses to

[38] The Court added:

> Surely, if the Convention had been intended to replace completely the broad discovery powers that the common law courts in the United States previously exercised over foreign litigants subject to their jurisdiction, it would have been most anomalous for the common law contracting parties to agree to Article 23, which enables a contracting party to revoke its consent to the treaty's procedure for pretrial discovery.

482 U.S. at 536.

[39] 482 U.S. at 542–3.

simple interrogatories or requests for admissions. The exact line between reasonableness and unreasonableness in each case must be drawn by the trial court, based on its knowledge of the case and of the claims and interests of the parties and the governments whose statutes and policies they invoke.[40]

The minority, in a long opinion by Justice Blackmun, thought the presumption—though not the obligation—should be in favor of resort to the Convention. An individualized or case-by-case analysis would be appropriate only when it appeared that it would be futile to employ the Convention or when its procedures had proved unhelpful:

The Court ignores the importance of the Convention by relegating it to an 'optional' status, without acknowledging the significant achievement in accommodating divergent interests that the Convention represents. Experience to date indicates that there is a large risk that the case by case comity analysis now to be permitted by the Court will be performed inadequately and that the somewhat unfamiliar procedures of the Convention will be invoked infrequently. I fear the Court's decision means that courts will resort unnecessarily to issuing discovery orders under the Federal Rules of Civil Procedure in a raw exercise of their jurisdictional power to the detriment of the United States' national and international interests. The Court's view of this country's international obligations is particularly unfortunate in a world in which regular commercial and legal channels loom ever more crucial.

. . . I therefore would apply a general presumption that, in most cases, courts should resort first to the Convention procedures. An individualized analysis of the circumstances of a particular case is appropriate only when it appears that it would be futile to employ the Convention or when its procedures prove to be unhelpful.[41]

In assessing the majority and minority opinions of the Supreme Court, it is useful to look at the specifics of the declaration submitted by Contracting States under Article 23. Most states, including Germany, France, and Italy, simply said:

The [Federal Republic of Germany] declares in pursuance of Article 23 of the Convention that it will not, in its territory, execute Letters of Request issued for the purpose of obtaining pre-trial discovery of documents as known in Common Law countries.

The United Kingdom, and a few other states, were not quite so harsh. The British declaration provides:

In accordance with Article 23 Her Majesty's Government declare that the United Kingdom will not execute Letters of Request issued for the purpose of obtaining pretrial discovery of documents. Her Majesty's Government further declare that Her Majesty's Government understand 'Letters of Request issued for the

[40] *Id.* 543–6. [41] 482 U.S. at 548–9.

purpose of obtaining pre-trial discovery of documents' for the purposes of the foregoing Declaration as including any Letter of Request which requires a person:

a. to state what documents relevant to the proceedings to which the Letter of Request relates are, or have been, in his possession, custody, or power; or
b. to produce any documents other than particular documents specified in the Letter of Request as being documents appearing to the requesting court to be, or to be likely to be, in his possession, custody or power.

Thus, the British were prepared to order both oral depositions and document production, provided the requests were specific.[42] In fact the requirement had been interpreted with extraordinary strictness by British courts.[43] But the French government, seeing an opening, advised the Supreme Court that it would modify its declaration, so that its refusal to execute Letters of Request would not apply 'when the requested documents are enumerated limitatively in the Letter of Request and have a direct and precise link with the object of the procedure.'

In fact the French government did so five days after the *Aérospatiale* case was argued in the Supreme Court, and five months before the decision came down. The move impressed Justice Blackmun,[44] but not, it seems, the majority.

Altogether, the *Aérospatiale* case was an interesting education in comparative procedure for the U.S. Supreme Court, and for the American legal profession as a whole. But the case did not resolve the conflict, and to some extent exacerbated it. Switzerland, for instance, which had signed the Hague Evidence Convention in 1985 but had not yet ratified it, abandoned the effort, as it had advised the Supreme Court it might do.[45] The Federal Republic of Germany, which had been the most active in asserting the primacy of the Convention in numerous cases since the *Volkswagen* litigation in California,

[42] See the discussion of the *Westinghouse* case in Ch. 7, esp. 159.

[43] For instance, letters rogatory were issued by a California state court in connection with claims by American manufacturers of asbestos against various insurance companies alleged to be liable on so-called long-tail insurance policies. (Recall the *Insurance Antitrust* case, Ch. 2 sect. D.) The Letters Rogatory sought production of:

> the written instructions from the plaintiffs or their agents to [a named broker at Lloyd's] to obtain the insurance policies set forth in exhibit (1) hereto.

Exhibit 1 was a list of policies identified by their numbers and by the numbers of brokers' slips. The House of Lords, reversing the Court of Appeal, rejected the document request, on the ground that there was no evidence that there was a document or a set of documents by which instructions were submitted to the broker; the request must thus be construed as one for 'written instructions, if any', and that was fishing: *In re Asbestos Insurance Coverage Cases* [1985] 1 WLR 331 (HL(E)).

[44] See 482 U.S. at 563–5.

[45] Brief *amicus curiae* of the Government of Switzerland (Aug. 22, 1986), 2. In Sept. 1993, the Swiss government reconsidered the question, and it became a party to the Evidence Convention, as well as the Hague Service Convention as of Jan. 1, 1995.

had also been considering regulations modifying its Article 23 declaration.[46] Following the decision in *Aérospatiale*, the German government postponed and eventually dropped the proposed regulations. Ironically in *Aérospatiale* itself on remand, the defendants agreed to supply the requested information through procedures under Chapter II of the Convention—i.e. without compulsion—and that was done, thus saving Aérospatiale the dilemma of either risking sanctions under the American Federal Rules or the French blocking statute, which as we saw[47] does not apply when international treaties provide otherwise.[48]

D. A LOOK AHEAD

1. Once More the *Restatement*

Whether judicial discovery is described as an aspect of adjudication, prescription, or enforcement, there can be no doubt that orders for discovery are exercises of jurisdiction. Though the drafters of the *Restatement of Foreign Relations Law* could not claim, as they did for the basic jurisdictional sections, §§ 402–403,[49] that they were stating (let alone *re*stating) international law, they tried in § 442 to set out some guidelines for United States law that could with time form the basis for a developing international law.

Both the majority and the dissent in *Aérospatiale* quote with approval from what became § 442, which suggests on the one hand that the *Restatement* was having some impact, even before the final version had been published,[50] but on the other hand that its prescription was not clear enough. In fact, § 442 was

[46] And had also so advised the Supreme Court. Brief *Amicus Curiae* of Federal Republic of Germany (Aug. 22, 1986), 9–10.

[47] See Ch. 7 at n. 59.

[48] For the aftermath of the *Aérospatiale* case, see Minch, 'US Obligations under the Hague Convention: more than Mere Good Will?' 22 *Int'l Lawyer* 511, 527, n. 68 (1988). The author was one of the counsel for *Aérospatiale*.

In post-*Aérospatiale* cases in the United States, most courts permitted defendants to attempt to demonstrate that discovery should be via the Convention, but then held that defendants had not met the burden of showing:

(i) that the particular facts and the interests of the foreign state justified resort to the Convention and

(ii) that such resort would not be futile.

See, generally, Born and Honig, 'Comity and the Lower Courts: Post *Aérospatiale* Application of the Hague Evidence Convention', 24 *Int'l Lawyer* 393 (1990); G. Born and D. Westin, *International Civil Litigation in the United States Courts* (2nd edn. 1992) 438–47. For an important article by a Federal Court of Appeals judge, urging that the Federal Rules of Civil Procedure be amended to adopt the dissenters' position in *Aérospatiale*, see Weis, 'The Federal Rules and the Hague Conventions: Concerns and Comity', 50 *U. Pitt. L. Rev.* 903 (1989).

[49] See Ch. 2, 17–20.

[50] See Ch. 7, n. 5 *supra*.

not addressed to the Evidence Convention,[51] but more generally to the problem of accommodating Americans' thirst for information with the rest of the world's reluctance to supply that information. It may not be out of place, therefore, to explain the thinking behind § 442 of the *Restatement*, and then to suggest how the rationale of § 442 might be combined with the experience of the Hague Evidence Convention in the search for revised, more useful international agreement.[52]

First, § 442 starts from the fundamental proposition that the law of the forum governs procedure. It follows that the court where an action is pending may order any person subject to its jurisdiction to produce documents, objects or other information, even if the information or the person in possession of

[51] The *Restatement* does have a section on the Hague Evidence Convention, § 473, which describes and explains the Convention but does not purport to set out normative standards.

[52] The 'black letter' reads as follows:

§442. Requests for Disclosure: Law of the United States

(1) (a) A court or agency in the United States, when authorized by statute or rule of court, may order a person subject to its jurisdiction to produce documents, objects, or other information relevant to an action or investigation, even if the information or the person in possession of the information is outside the United States.

(b) Failure to comply with an order to produce information may subject the person to whom the order is directed to sanctions, including finding of contempt, dismissal of a claim or defense, or default judgment, or may lead to a determination that the facts to which the order was addressed are as asserted by the opposing party.

(c) In deciding whether to issue an order directing production of information located abroad, and in framing such an order, a court or agency in the United States should take into account the importance to the investigation or litigation of the documents or other information requested; the degree of specificity of the request; whether the information originated in the United States; the availability of alternative means of securing the information; and the extent to which noncompliance with the request would undermine important interests of the United States, or compliance with the request would undermine interests of the state where the information is located.

(2) If disclosure of information located outside the United States is prohibited by a law, regulation, or order of a court or other authority of the state in which the information or prospective witness is located, or of the state of which a prospective witness is a national,

(a) a court or agency in the United States may require the person to whom the order is directed to make a good faith effort to secure permission from the foreign authorities to make the information available;

(b) a court or agency should not ordinarily impose sanctions of contempt, dismissal, or default on a party that has failed to comply with the order for production, except in cases of deliberate concealment or removal of information or of failure to make a good faith effort in accordance with paragraph (a);

(c) a court or agency may, in appropriate cases, make findings of fact adverse to a party that has failed to comply with the order for production, even if that party has made a good faith effort to secure permission from the foreign authorities to make the information available and that effort has been unsuccessful.

The text is accompanied by 17 pages of Comments and Reporters' Notes.

the information is outside of the forum state.[53] Further, failure to comply with such an order may subject the person to whom the order is addressed to sanctions, including adverse findings, dismissal of a claim or defense, or a judgment of default or dismissal, as well as contempt. So far the *Restatement* just restates American law up to the middle-1980s. But then the *Restatement* says, 'Wait'. Don't let attorneys issue sweeping demands for discovery, and then test them in a sanctions context. All requests for discovery of foreign parties or involving information located abroad should be issued by the judge, after some genuine scrutiny. In deciding whether to issue such an order, the judge is expected to introduce *reasonableness* into the process, something that foreign participants in American litigation have often regarded as in short supply. Specifically, in the *Restatement* formulation, the judge should take into account:

—the importance to the litigation of the documents or other information requested;
—the degree of specificity of the request;
—the origin of the information;
—the availability of alternative means of securing the information; and finally
—the relative interests of the forum state and of the state where the information is located.

So far the prescription makes good sense, in my view, and if it makes American lawyers do more homework than is required when simply asking for 'all documents, memoranda, correspondence, etc.', so much the better. 'Fishing' is not the entire source of the conflict, but it is a significant ingredient. But what if the state where the information is located (or of which the prospective witness is a national) has in place a blocking statute or other prohibition? Here we come back to the teaching of the *Interhandel* case.

First, the forum state may order the person to whom the request is directed to make a good faith effort to receive permission to make the disclosure. If

[53] Normally discovery requests and orders follow a determination that the court has jurisdiction over the defendants. If the defendant challenges the court's jurisdiction and that issue depends on questions of fact, such as the degree of activity the defendant has conducted in the forum state, several courts in the United States have upheld discovery requests limited to the jurisdictional question. In one case against a foreign insurance company where plaintiff made an initial showing and defendant refused to comply with a discovery order seeking to establish how many policies defendant had sold in the United States, the trial court, after several warnings, drew an adverse inference to uphold its jurisdiction pursuant to Rule 37(b)(2) of the Federal Rules of Civil Procedure, the same rule that was applied by the lower courts in *Société Internationale*, Ch.7, sect. C(1), but reversed by the Supreme Court. Here the Supreme Court approved the trial court: *Insurance Corp. of Ireland, Ltd* v. *Compagnie des Bauxites de Guinée*, 456 U.S. 694 (1982).

Whether this is acceptable or too much like Baron Münchhausen pulling himself up by his own bootstraps, it seems to me, depends on the strength of the plaintiff's initial showing.

such good faith effort is demonstrated, then ordinarily sanctions of contempt, dismissal, or default should not be imposed. Second, as in *Interhandel*, a party with the burden of proof may not be able to meet the burden without certain information; even if it does not have the burden—as for instance the defendant in a product liability case, the non-producing party may suffer from not being forthcoming in disclosing designs or manufacturing methods.[54] But it should not be punished expressly for defying the order of the court. Third, however, if a party courts an impediment, as by urging its government to issue a blocking order,[55] or even by litigating instead of attempting to comply,[56] and certainly by secretly shipping documents out of the forum state,[57] the reason for the forum to stay its hand recedes.

Is this all still too forum-oriented? Careful readers will notice that in paraphrasing § 442 of the *Restatement*, I have substituted 'forum state' for 'United States'; my purpose, I repeat, is to see if what is there set out can be a building block for some kind of broader consensus or even a formal agreement. To pursue this goal, I come back to the Hague Evidence Convention—another building block.

2. The Hague Convention: A New Look?

Like the *Aérospatiale* case, the experience with the Evidence Convention over the last two decades has been an experience in comparative procedure. The European countries (and the few other state parties) have learned what discovery is, and they have learned the significant differences on this subject between the English and the American approaches. The common law countries, and particularly the Americans, have learned some startling aspects of civil procedure in the continental manner. The effort to build a bridge between the common law and the civil law cannot be regarded as a success, but I think the experience has been instructive, and I want to offer some suggestions for benefiting from that experience.

I do not suggest that all the conflicts can be solved. As pointed out at the outset of the discussion of discovery, much of the controversy reflects deeper divisions, over jurisdiction and over substantive law including damages, and those divisions, while ameliorated in some areas, notably in connection with securities regulation, have not gone away. Still I want to view the Evidence Convention as a building block and not as a stumbling block, and to suggest how a more stable structure might be erected on its foundations.

The basic trade-off is not hard to figure out. Let the Hague Evidence Convention start out like the Hague Service Convention:

[54] Compare the experience of Beecham in the *Ampicillin* litigation, Ch. 7, sect. D(2).

[55] Recall the *Laker* case, Ch. 1 at n. 28.

[56] Recall the *Bank of Nova Scotia* litigation, Ch. 7, sect. F(2).

[57] This occurred in the *Marc Rich* case. See Ch. 7, n. 141 and the sources there cited.

This Convention shall apply in all cases—all cases in which a court of one state requires evidence located in another contracting state for use in a pending proceeding.

Note that I do not say 'for use at trial'. I think those words, which have been used in some cases to overcome Article 23,[58] could easily become an empty formula; moreover, the effort to distinguish 'discovery' from 'evidence' did not produce agreement between the leading English-speaking states, and would not be understood by the rest of the world.

Once resort to the Convention becomes mandatory as between Contracting States, the intervention of the judge of the state where the action is pending, as called for in the *Restatement*, also becomes mandatory, because it is the judicial authority that issues the Letter of Request. No more 'wide-roving' attorneys. The judge should not be required to certify that a given request concerns 'admissible' material—it is too early for such a determination and anyhow the rules of evidence of state *A*, the requesting state, should not concern state *B*, the requested state.[59] The judge should be required to certify however, that he or she has scrutinized the request, that it is specific and not open-ended, that the request is not duplicative or made for purposes of harassment, and that the information requested cannot be obtained in reliable and usable form elsewhere. (Note that these points build on § 442(1)(c) of the *Restatement*.)

The Central Authority or the court in the requested state would still be authorized to exercise some scrutiny, as it is under Articles 11 and 12 of the existing Convention, with respect to privileges and limited concerns of national security.[60] But Article 23 would be eliminated. Thus it would be understood that the request under the revised Evidence Convention could cover documents as well as oral examination concerning specified topics, and also physical evidence such as the site of an accident or manufacturing or shipping facilities. As to the breadth of the request, one might permit some 'blue pencilling' by the court (not the bureaucrats in the Central Authority), as was done

[58] e.g., in *Rio Tinto Zinc* v. *Westinghouse Electric Corp*. See Ch. 7 at n. 78.

[59] Compare the statement of Lord Keith of Kinkel in the *Westinghouse* case, quoted with approval by Lord Fraser of Tullybelton in the *Asbestos Insurance Coverage* case, n. 42 *supra*.

> In the face of a statement of letters rogatory that a certain person is a necessary witness for the applicant, I am of opinion that the court of request should not be astute to examine the issues in the action and the circumstances of the case with excessive particularity for the purpose of determining in advance whether the evidence of that person will be relevant and admissible. That is essentially a matter for the requesting court.

[1978] AC 547 at 654.

[60] Concerns of 'sovereignty', the other term used in Art. 12(b) of the existing Convention, seem to me quite unpersuasive, except possibly if the state itself is a litigant. If that is the concern to which Article 12(b) of the existing Convention is addressed, a better solution would be to write an express exemption for state parties into the convention, rather than to leave vague notions of 'judicial sovereignty' floating about in an article designed to limit the grounds for refusal to execute Letters of Request.

in *Westinghouse* v. *Rio Tinto Zinc*,[61] but an essential piece of the request (in addition to the form now annexed to the Convention) would be the determination by the requesting court that the request was limited, defined, and necessary. That determination would be entitled to respect (I do not say recognition as a judgment); it could not be disregarded, and it could be departed from only on the basis of a reasoned judgment by the court in the requested state.[62] If there is a serious initiative to amend the Convention, I would also suggest adding a definition—a broad definition—of 'civil or commercial matters', to reach at least as far as the House of Lords did in the *Norway* case,[63] and if possible to make clear that administrative proceedings or discovery in aid of execution of a judgment are not excluded.[64]

I do not suggest that I have said the last word on the trade-offs required to rebuild the Hague Evidence Convention. I do want to stress, however, that in my judgment other compromises, such as the suggestion that the United States agree to mandatory resort to the Convention in return for agreement by other Contracting States to adopt the English version of an Article 23 declaration,[65] are inadequate.[66] Article 23 is not only Delphic in its text, it is unsound in concept.[67]

In the end we are concerned here with two rules of international law. Private International Law teaches that matters of procedure and evidence are governed by the law of the forum where an action is pending. Public International Law teaches that judicial functions can be carried out in a state only by officials of that state and with the state's consent. I believe an Evidence Convention revised along the lines here suggested would preserve—and indeed strengthen—both rules.

[61] Ch. 7 at n. 79.

[62] Note that *mutatis mutandis* this proposal is similar in concept to the solution reached between the United States and Switzerland, the Cayman Islands, and others in connection with investigations by governmental authorities, as described in Ch. 7, sect. F.

[63] *In re State of Norway's Application* [1990] 1 AC 723 (HL(E)).

[64] See the Decision of the Magistrate's Court of Tel Aviv, Israel of Aug. 5, 1992 in *Securities and Exchange Commission* v. *Eddie Antar et al.*, 89 Civ. 3773 (NHP), granting a request by the United States SEC to examine and copy documents concerning the locations of assets of Eddie Antar, in implementation of the judgment of the U.S. court secured by the SEC appointing a receiver to recapture illicit gains of Antar and his associates, as described in Ch. 6, sect. C(3). Apparently the examination of the documents made available pursuant to this Decision enabled the SEC to trace and eventually recapture funds of Antar on deposit not only in Israel, but in Switzerland and Quebec as well. See Ch. 6, at nn. 50–51.

[65] See 191–2 *supra*.

[66] See e.g., Abbo Junker, *Discovery im deutsch-amerikanischen Rechtsverkehr* (1987) 284–300, 442–43. In fairness, Junker was looking to preserve the existing Convention, while I am here looking to a revised convention.

[67] I first made the suggestion that the Evidence Convention be made mandatory in return for eliminating Art. 23 some 10 years ago, but without elaboration. Lowenfeld, 'Discovering discovery, International Style', Introduction to Symposium on Transnational Discovery, 16 *N.Y.U. J. Int'l Law & Pol.* 957, 959–60 (1984). The idea found favor with Judge Weis, n. 48 *supra*, 50 *U. Pitt. L. Rev.* 903 at 927–8, but not, so far as I know, with anyone in the U.S. government.

9

Party Autonomy: The Triumph of Practical Considerations

INTRODUCTION

Throughout this volume, we have explored conflict and disagreement—about jurisdiction to prescribe, jurisdiction to adjudicate, responsibility of multinational enterprises, enforcement of judgments, and scope of disclosure or discovery in international controversies. In truth, the area of disagreement is not quite as vast as the preceding chapters would indicate. Nearly everyone agrees, today, (1) that parties to a commercial transaction (putting aside certain consumer contracts) may agree on the law applicable to their relations; (2) that they may choose the forum to resolve any disputes that may arise between them; and (3) that they can remove state organs almost completely from the process of adjudication by choosing to have their disputes resolved by arbitration. Moreover, while agreement on a judgments convention reaching beyond the European Community and its immediate neighbors has thus far been unattainable, a convention to enforce arbitral awards (as well as agreements to arbitrate) has more than a hundred adherents, including all the world's commercial states and states from all legal traditions and at all stages of legal development.[1] Thus states have committed themselves to enforce with very limited scrutiny arbitral awards rendered in countries whose judgments they might well decline to recognize or enforce, and by persons whom no state has screened—all because, it is said, the parties to the arbitration agreed to the forum of their own free will—by *autonomie de la volonté*, in the more elegant French expression.

Parties engaged in international transactions and their lawyers want to know where disputes that may arise will be adjudicated, and even if they have made no investigation of the details of the possibly applicable laws, they want to know what law will be applied by the decision-maker. Rightly or wrongly, many parties are fearful of litigating in the other party's home state, and if they can, they seek to specify 'their' forum. If the bargaining or marketing situation does not permit that, the parties look for a 'neutral' forum, which may be a court in London or Geneva but more and more turns out to be an arbitral

[1] UN Convention on the Recognition and Enforcement of Foreign Abitral Awards of June 10, 1958 (the New York Convention), 330 U.N.T.S. 3.

forum. All of this is not really free will, but rather part of the bargain, embraced within the term 'party autonomy'. Of course, when a dispute actually arises, one or both parties may well have incentives to challenge that part of the bargain.

The support of party autonomy is so widespread that it can fairly be called a rule of customary law. I want here to look first at some of the assumptions and paradoxes of party autonomy in international transactions; then to explore the limits of party autonomy, which, as one might expect, will take us back to the issues of public law with which this volume began; and finally to make some observations about the procedures of international arbitration, which in my experience has become a kind of melting pot of different approaches to civil litigation. In thinking about these topics, it is instructive to reflect on the many assertions of state interests that we have seen throughout this volume, and to ponder whether the enthusiasm for party autonomy does not cast some doubt on the persuasiveness of these assertions.

A. CHOICE OF LAW BY CONTRACTING PARTNERS: THE PARADOX REJECTED

The paradox of party autonomy in choice of law is well known. For Joseph Henry Beale, the leading American scholar on conflict of laws in the first third of this century, the issue was clear. The law gives effect to the acts of private parties, and not the other way around.[2] Judge Learned Hand, generally believed to be the greatest American jurist never to have served on the Supreme Court, and in many ways a very practical judge, wrote:

> People cannot by agreement substitute the law of another place; they may of course incorporate any provisions they wish into the their agreements—a statute like anything else—and when they do, courts will try to make sense out of the whole, so far as they can. But an agreement is not a contract, except as the law says it shall be, and to try to make it one is to pull on one's bootstraps. Some law must impose the obligation, and the parties have nothing whatever to do with that; no more than whether their acts are torts or crimes.[3]

Similar statements of the paradox were made in Germany[4] and France.[5] J.-P. Niboyet, the leading French scholar in conflict of laws of his generation, stated in his Hague Lectures of 1927 that '[t]he law is no longer entitled to its name if it is subject to being excluded without restraint by those whom it must

[2] J. H. Beale, *The Conflict of Laws* (1935), ii, § 332.2, 1079–80. Accordingly the first *Restatement of Conflict of Laws* (1934), of which Beale was Chief Reporter, made no provision for choice of law by the parties. The *Second Restatement*, with Willis Reese as Chief Reporter, made a 180 degree turn on this point, as discussed below.

[3] *E. Gerli & Co. v. Cunard S.S. Co*, 48 F.2d 115 at 117 (2d. Cir. 1931).

[4] See, e.g. Ludwig von Bar, *Theorie und Praxis des Internationalen Privatrechts* (1889), ii, ¶ 247.

[5] See, e.g., Antoine Pillet, *Traité Pratique de Droit International Privé* (1924), ii, ¶ 481.

govern.'[6] While most civil law states did not have an equally hostile view to choice of law by the parties[7]—and indeed the French Supreme Court was much more receptive to choice of law clauses than the scholars were[8]—my impression is that many scholars were troubled by what Learned Hand called pulling oneself up by one's bootstraps. Many scholars, I believe, would agree with Professor Kegel of Germany, who refers to party autonomy—not in disapproval—as a *Verlegenheitslösung*, a solution of embarrassment:

> Since in many cases a generally persuasive resolution of the interests of the parties that point to different laws is not possible, one permits the parties to make the choice.[9]

Only the English seem to have always been comfortable with applying the law chosen by the parties to a contract. In 1760, the great Lord Mansfield wrote:

> The law of the place can never be the rule, where the transaction is entered into with an express view to the law of another country.[10]

In 1796, a case that seems to have combined choice of forum with choice of law, the rule of party autonomy was expressly applied by the English court when it remitted Dutch seamen claiming their wages to courts in the Netherlands.[11] And in the *Vita Foods* case of 1939,[12] which still seems to be the

[6] J.-P. Niboyet, 'La Théorie de l'Autonomie de la Volonté', 16 *Recueil des Cours* 1, 55, 57 (Hague Acad. 1927). In his treatise published two decades later, Niboyet accepted party autonomy, but warned of its excesses: J.-P. Niboyet, *Traité de Droit International Privé* (1948), v, 51–60.

[7] See, e.g., Ernst Rabel, *The Conflict of Laws, A Comparative Study* (2nd edn., 1960), ii, 359–431; *Int'l Encyclopedia of Comparative Law* (1976), iii, ch. 24 (Lando).

[8] Notably in *American Trading Company* v. *Quebec Steamship Company Ltd.*, S.1911. 1.129, 11 Rev. Critique de Droit Int'l Privé 395 (1911) (Cour de Cassation, Dec. 5, 1910).

[9] Gerhard Kegel, *Internationales Privatrecht* (7th edn., 1995), 483. Kegel goes on to point out that party autonomy is often dispositive even when determination of the proper law would be easy without a choice of law clause, for instance in a contract of lease of real property.

Compare the following statement by Judge John Marshall Harlan (as he then was), in *Siegelman* v. *Cunard White Star Ltd.*, 221 F.2d 189 at 195 (2d Cir. 1955), in upholding a choice of law clause in a steamship ticket, against the arguments of Beale and others:

> Instead of viewing the parties as usurping the legislative function, it seems more realistic to regard them as relieving the courts of the problem of resolving a question of conflict of laws. Their course might be expected to reduce litigation, and it is to be commended as much as good draftsmanship which relieves courts of problems of resolving ambiguities. To say that there may be no reduction in litigation because courts may not honor the provision is to reason backwards.

[10] *Robinson* v. *Bland*, 2 Burr. 1077, at 1078, 1 Wm. Bl. 234, 256, 97 ER 717, 718 (1760). The passage is quoted with approval by Story (1st edn., 1834), § 280, but whether Story understood the passage as favoring party autonomy or rather as a reason to depart from the place of contracting in favor of the place of performance, is not clear.

[11] *Gienar* v. *Meyer*, 2 H. Bl. 603, 120 ER 728 (1796).

[12] *Vita Food Products, Inc.* v. *Unus Shipping Co. Ltd*, [1939] AC 277, [1939] 2 D.L.R. 1 (Privy Council).

leading case in England and countries following the English model, the highest court of the British Empire not only upheld the freedom of parties to a contract to choose the law applicable to them, but expressly rejected the argument that the choice was invalid because the transaction had no connection with the state whose law was chosen (that is with English law).[13]

Today, the debates about selection of the applicable law by the parties to a contract seem a bit old-fashioned. The Rome Convention states as its main principle, '[a] contract shall be governed by the law chosen by the parties';[14] so does the new German Law on Conflict of Laws;[15] so does the new Swiss Law on Private International Law;[16] and so on.[17] Only in the United States, among the countries surveyed in this volume, is it still said that (for issues that the parties could not have resolved by an explicit provision) the state of the law chosen must have a substantial relationship to the parties or the transaction. But § 187 of the *Restatement (Second) of Conflict of Laws*, which in this area has been very influential, adds the additional option of another 'reasonable basis' for the parties' choice, such as a neutral law or a law familiar to both parties.[18] I believe it is fair to say that in practice the law on parties' express choice of law in the United States is not significantly different from that in the countries that are parties to the Rome Convention. As the leading current American treatise on conflict of laws points out, if the 'substantial relationship' criterion of the *Restatement* were understood as an invitation to explore the interests or

[13] [1939] AC at 290.

[14] EEC Convention on the Law Applicable to Contractual Obligations, done at Rome, June 19, 1980; [1980] OJ L266, Art. 3(1).

[15] *Germany*: Law on the Revision of Private International Law of July 25, 1986, Art 27(1).

[16] *Switzerland*: Federal Statute on Private International Law of Dec. 18, 1987, Art. 116.

[17] For a convenient survey, see Ole Lando, 'The Conflict of Laws of Contracts: General Principles' (1985), 189 *Recueil des Cours* 225 at 255–84. See also the *Report on the Law Applicable to Contractual Obligations* (the Giuliano/Lagarde Report) [1980] OJ C282/1 at 15–16.

[18] The complete text of § 187 reads as follows:

Law of the State Chosen by the parties

(1) The law of the state chosen by the parties to govern their contractual rights and duties will be applied if the particular issue is one which the parties could have resolved by an explicit provision in their agreement directed to that issue.

(2) The law of the state chosen by the parties to govern their contractual rights and duties will be applied, even if the particular issue is one which the parties could not have resolved by an explicit provision in their agreement directed to that issue, unless either

(a) the chosen state has no substantial relationship to the parties or the transaction and there is no other reasonable basis for the parties' choice, or

(b) application of the law of the chosen state would be contrary to a fundamental policy of a state which has a materially greater interest than the chosen state in the determination of the particular issue and which, under the rule of § 188, would be the state of the applicable law in the absence of an effective choice of law by the parties.

(3) In the absence of a contrary indication of intention, the reference is to the local law of the state of the chosen law.

contacts of the state whose law was selected in comparison with the law of some other state, 'the simplicity and convenience of party autonomy would be lost.'[19] As in other modern states, simplicity and convenience have prevailed in this area. Whatever 'state interests'—genuine or made up—are supposed to influence decisions of choice of law cases in the United States,[20] they do not trump the express choice of law by the parties.

B. CHOICE OF FORUM BY CONTRACT PARTNERS: MORE PARADOXES OVERCOME

If parties to a contract can choose the law applicable to their relationship, why should they not be able to choose a forum to resolve any disputes that might arise growing out of that relationship?

On one level, the answer to that question is easy. Every legal system provides for consent as a basis for judicial jurisdiction, and there is no reason why consent cannot be given in advance by contract.[21] Thus the affirmative aspect of forum selection—conferring jurisdiction on a court or *prorogation*—ought to be easily accepted, unless the court selected by the parties has reasons of its own not to hear the case, for instance on the ground that the taxpayers that support it have no interest in adjudicating controversies having no connection with the forum.[22]

The negative aspect of forum selection has been more difficult, and still gives rise to a fair amount of litigation. One rarely hears, any more, of complaints about 'ousting courts of their jurisdiction'; courts nearly everywhere

[19] Eugene K. Scoles and Peter Hay, *Conflict of Laws* (2nd edn., 1992), 674.

[20] See, generally, Brainerd Currie, *Selected Essays on the Conflict of Laws* (1963), as well as a vast body of writing thereon. For a convenient, though not exhaustive, bibliography see Scoles and Hay, n. 19 *supra*, 15–19 and footnotes thereto. For a defense of interest analysis by one of Currie's disciples, see Herma Hill Kay, 'A Defense of Currie's Governmental Interest Analysis', 215 *Recueil des Cours* 9 (Hague Acad. 1989–III).

[21] I omit, for present purposes, certain contracts of adhesion such as transportation tickets, catalogue sales, and insurance contracts by individuals.

[22] See, e.g., New York Business Corporation Law, § 1314, which provides that an action against a foreign corporation may be maintained in New York courts by another foreign corporation or by a non-resident only in 5 specified circumstances, which may be summarized as defining controversies that arise in or involve parties that have permanent connections to the state.

In 1984, in connection with major negotiations concerning restructuring of debt from Latin American and other developing countries, the New York legislature adopted two provisions to encourage the choice of New York law and New York courts. Under General Obligations Law, § 5–1401 parties to a contract relating to a transaction covering in the aggregate $250,000 or more may agree that New York law will govern their rights and duties in whole or in part, 'whether or not such contract . . . bears a reasonable relation to this state'. Under § 5–1402 of the same law, parties to a contract for which a choice of New York law has been made under § 5–1401, and which covers in the aggregate $1,000,000 or more, may agree to submit to the jurisdiction of the courts of New York, notwithstanding Business Corporation Law § 1314 or a comparable provision in the New York Banking Law.

are overworked and overcrowded. But the acceptance of forum selection clauses may be seen as a counter-trend to the trend explored in Chapter 4, which has greatly expanded the available bases for suing out-of-state parties in the plaintiff's preferred forum. Thus, to take a recurring pattern, a Manufacturer in Xandia contracts with a Distributor in Patria for distribution of the Manufacturer's products. Eventually a dispute arises, the Manufacturer terminates the distribution agreement, and the Distributor wants to bring suit. Absent a forum selection clause, the suit could generally be brought in Patria—if Patria and Xandia were parties to the Brussels/Lugano Convention on the basis that the contract was to be performed in Patria or that the Manufacturer maintained a branch in Patria,[23] in common law countries such as the United States and England, on the basis also that the contract was entered into in Patria.[24] The Manufacturer, however, inserted a clause into the contract that any controversies arising out of or related to the agreement shall be submitted solely to the courts of Xandia. Should such a clause be upheld so that the courts of Patria must dismiss (or at least stay) an action brought by the Distributor?

Nearly everywhere the answer is 'yes'. The Brussels Convention states unequivocally, in Article 17 that:

> If the parties, one or more of whom is domiciled in a Contracting State, have agreed that a court or the courts of a Contracting State are to have jurisdiction to settle any disputes which have arisen or which may arise in connection with a particular legal relationship, that court or courts shall have exclusive jurisdiction.[25]

It is striking—and demonstrates the strong support for forum selection in the (now enlarged) European Community—that Article 17 reads the word 'exclusive' into a choice of forum clause even if the clause does not say so.[26] The Swiss Statute on Private International Law takes the same position.[27] I do not believe American courts, or English courts when the Brussels Convention is

[23] See Brussels Convention, Art. 5(1); 5(5).

[24] See, e.g., *England*: Rules of Supreme Court, Order 11, r. 1(1)(d)(i), (e); *New York*: C.P.L.R., § 302(a)(1).

[25] Again, I omit for present purposes references to the exceptions, such as certain insurance and consumer contracts and individual contracts of employment, which are expressly excluded from application of Art. 17.

[26] The Jenard Report on the Brussels Convention states that reading 'exclusive' into a forum selection clause 'is essential to avoid different courts from being properly seised of the matter and giving conflicting or at least differing judgments': *Report on the Convention on Jurisdiction and the Enforcement of Judgments in Civil and Commercial Matters* [1979] OJ C59/1 at 37. Compare a similar justification for rejecting the place of contracting as an acceptable basis for jurisdiction. See Ch. 4, n. 22.

For a decision upholding under Art. 17 a forum selection clause in which each party agreed to sue only in the courts of the other's domicile but permitting a defendant to file a counterclaim for set-off at its domicile, see *Meeth* v. *Glacetal Sarl*, case 23/78 [1978] ECR 2133, [1979] 1 CMLR 520 (ECJ, Nov. 9, 1978).

[27] *Switzerland*: Federal Statute on Private International Law of Dec. 18, 1987, Art. 5(1).

not applicable, would go that far.[28] But if the forum selection clause states, or can fairly be read to mean that the parties agreed to submit their disputes solely to a court other than the one selected by plaintiff, that agreement ought to be carried out under ordinary principles of contract law, and generally will be.[29]

So far so good. But what if 'ordinary contract principles' do not yield the preliminary conclusion that a contract was formed? Suppose *A* brings an action against *B* in Patria for breach of contract, basing jurisdiction of the Patrian court on a choice of forum clause in the contract naming the courts of Patria. *B* challenges the jurisdiction of the Patrian court on the ground that the contract never came into being, and therefore neither did the only basis on which the court can assert jurisdiction over him. It seems to be held everywhere that the Patrian court has jurisdiction to determine its own jurisdiction—the so-called *Kompetenz-Kompetenz*—if necessary by taking evidence on issues of capacity to contract, meeting of the minds, fraud or duress, illegality, or whatever other points *B* raises. It is possible that a contract was formed and yet the forum clause was not effectively concluded—for instance if the forum selection or arbitration clause was contained in an order confirmation sent by *A* to *B* but *B* did not sign and return the form, but the sale nevertheless went forward.[30] If, however, the Patrian court decides that no contract was

[28] For the English approach, compare *Dicey and Morris on the Conflict of Laws*, (12th edn., Collins, 1993, plus 1995 Supp.) Rule 32(2) with Rule 32(3) and comments thereto, 420–38. For the American approach, see *Restatement (Third) of Foreign Relations Law*, § 421, comment *f* (1987).

[29] A qualification is necessary concerning the U.S. practice, stemming from the federal character of the American judicial system. A few states of the United States—including Alabama, Georgia, Idaho, and Montana, but none of the major commercial states—still regard forum selection clauses as contrary to public policy. Federal courts hearing federal question or maritime clauses will almost certainly give effect to such clauses; federal courts hearing so-called diversity-of-citizenship or state-created clauses are also likely to favor upholding choice of forum clauses, but in domestic (i.e. interstate as contrasted with international) cases the rule is not clear, if they care sitting in one of the states that disfavor choice of forum clauses. See *Stewart Organization Inc.* v. *Ricoh Corporation*, 487 U.S. 22 (1988). For an up-to-date comprehensive survey of American practice, see Walter W. Heiser, 'Forum Selection Clauses in State Courts: Limitations on Enforcement after *Stewart* and *Carnival Cruise*', 45 *Fla. L. Rev.* 361 (July 1993); 'Forum Selection Clauses in Federal Courts: Limitations on Enforcement after *Stewart* and *Carnival Cruise*', 45 *Fla L. Rev.* 553 (Sept. 1993).

[30] For two cases of this kind involving arbitration clauses reaching opposite results, see, e.g., *Van Walsum NV* v. *Chevalines SA* (1968) 64 Schweizerische Juristen-Zeitung 56 (Trib. Canton Genève, June 8, 1967) declining to enforce an arbitral award; *Chemicals & Phosphates Ltd* v. *NV Algemene Oliehandel* [1971] Nederlandse Jurisprudentie 470 (Rechtbank, Rotterdam, June 26, 1970), dismissing an action in court on the basis of effectiveness of arbitration clause. Both of these cases are reproduced in English in Lowenfeld, *International Litigation and Arbitration* (1993) at 346, 347. In order to avoid the frequency of cases of this kind, Art. 17 of the Brussels Convention was amended on British initiative when the United Kingdom became a party, to add to the requirement that the agreement on a forum be in writing the alternative:

> . . . in international trade or commerce, in a form which accords with a usage of which the parties are or ought to have been aware and which in such trade or commerce is widely known to, and regularly observed by, parties to contracts of the type involved in the particular trade or commerce concerned.

formed—for instance if it finds that what *A* claims was *B*'s acceptance was actually an unaccepted counter-offer—it cannot require *B* to litigate in Patria if there is no other basis for jurisdiction over *B*. The decision of the Patrian court has to be that it has no jurisdiction over the controversy, though it had jurisdiction to determine whether or not it had jurisdiction.

Suppose, thereafter, that *A* is not satisfied with this outcome and brings suit for breach of contract against *B* in Xandia, the domicile of *B*. *B* now has no basis for challenging the jurisdiction of the Xandian court, but asserts that it has already been determined that no contract was formed between the parties. I believe that *B* will prevail. While strict principles of recognition of judgments might not fit, since it was determined that there was no jurisdiction in the first forum, a practical answer—whether based on estoppel or issue preclusion or *res judicata*—ought to, and I believe would, lead to dismissal of the second action.

Suppose, to vary the example, that *A* sues *B* in Patria for breach of contract and *B* moves for dismissal on the basis of a forum selection clause in the contract choosing the courts of Xandia. The Patrian court upholds *B*'s contention and dismisses the action, and thereafter *A* brings suit against *B* in Xandia. Is *B* now precluded from contending in Xandia that no contract was ever formed? Here the answer is no, though I could understand that someone might object that I have contradicted the assertion made in the preceding paragraph. Both examples are vulnerable to criticism based on logic. It is true that in the first case, I have suggested giving effect to a judgment rendered without jurisdiction, and in the second case I have suggested permitting one court to uphold the contract, the second one to strike it down. But what the two examples have in common is that in both instances the operative decision-maker is the forum appointed by the parties, and if a 'good arguable case' (to use the English formula) can be asserted showing that they have agreed on that appointment—for example a document that, whatever its inherent weakness, was signed by persons apparently authorized to represent the parties (i.e. not a document with forged signatures or falsified terms)—then the appointed forum should decide the controversy, and the other forum's decision should be taken as a kind of abstention, not a final determination on the merits.[31]

It is not, I think, coincidence that the principal cases on this issue involve agreements to arbitrate. Suppose *A* sues *B* in a Patrian court and *B*, as in the preceding example, moves for a stay or dismissal pursuant to a forum selection clause calling for arbitration (whether in Patria or elsewhere). It was formerly thought that if *A* challenged the existence or validity of the contract containing

[31] Not many reported cases reflect this pattern. One important such case in *Mackender* v. *Feldia, AG* [1967] 1 WLR 619 (CA), discussed in Ch. 4 at note 108 in the context of discretion properly exercised by the English court in not taking jurisdiction of an action to declare invalid a contract with a choice of forum clause selecting a Belgian court. That court should determine the issue of illegality, and unless a contrary provision appears in the contract, apply its own law.

the arbitration clause, that issue had to be determined by the Patrian court before the controversy could proceed to arbitration.[32] One by one over the past thirty years, all the major commercial states have moved away from that proposition, in favor of the practical solution that the question of the validity of a contract, as well as questions of performance, breach, damages, and counterclaims can and should be left to the arbitrators.[33] Likewise, all the major international arbitration rules and institutions make provision for determination of challenges to their jurisdiction by the arbitrators.[34] Courts, legislators, treaty drafters, and rule-makers have all been willing to delegate to arbitrators the issue of their own jurisdiction, without concern (or perhaps better overcoming their concern) that the arbitrators will pull themselves up by their own bootstraps to uphold their jurisdiction. The reverse solution, however, that is a solution reserving the validity of a contract containing an arbitration clause to the courts, would not only enable defendants in many instances to delay resolution of disputes, but would gravely distort the understanding and expectation of the parties to commercial transactions at the time they entered into the transactions. Putting the point another way, reserving questions about the validity of a contract containing an arbitration clause to the courts might be logically correct but it would be mercantilely unreasonable.

England was the last important holdout on this issue, so far as I know, and the conversion of its courts is instructive. Until recently, the prevailing English view was that if plaintiff initiated a lawsuit, defendant moved for a stay of the suit pending arbitration, and plaintiff asserted that no contract had been formed between the parties or that the contract was void *ab initio*, or conversely if plaintiff initiated an arbitration and defendant moved for stay of the arbitration on the same grounds, the validity of the contract had to be submitted for determination by the court.[35] 'For if in truth no contract was ever made', as the leading English treatise on arbitration stated, 'then the arbitration provisions of the supposed contract never bound the parties; and an arbitrator appointed under those provisions could have no authority to act.'[36] The authors realized that this reasoning had been rejected in many other countries, and that its intellectual purity had already been compromised by

[32] See, e.g., *Heyman* v. *Darwins* [1942] AC 356, discussed hereafter.

[33] e.g, *France*: *Soc. Gosset* v. *Soc. Carpelli*, 1963 Dalloz 545 (Cour de Cassation Civ. 1st ch., May 7, 1963).

United States: *Prima Paint Corp.* v. *Flood & Conklin Mfg. Co,* 388 U.S. 395 (1967).

Germany: *V. & K.* v. *H*, 53 BGHZ 315 (Bundesgerichtshof, Feb. 27, 1970.)

For similar citations from Belgium, Italy, Japan, the Netherlands, and Switzerland, see Georges R. Delaume, *Law and Practice of Transnational Contracts* (1988), § 9.07.

[34] See, e.g., International Chamber of Commerce Rules of Arbitration, Art. 8(3); London Court of International Arbitration, Art. 14.1; American Arbitration Association, International Arbitration Rules, Art. 15; UNCITRAL Arbitration Rules, Art. 21. See also UNCITRAL Model Law of International Commercial Arbitration, Art. 16.

[35] See Mustill and Boyd, *The Law and Practice of Commercial Arbitration in England* (2nd edn. 1989) 108 *et seq*; *Heyman* v. *Darwins* [1942] AC 356.

[36] Mustill and Boyd, n. 35 *supra*, at 108.

holdings that disputes concerning the continued validity of a contract or concerning damages for its wrongful termination were within the jurisdiction of arbitrators.[37] Still, not until 1993 in the *Harbour Assurance* case[38] did the English courts move away from the 'orthodox view'. Against the argument that *ex nihil, nil fit*—nothing can come of nothing, Lord Justice Gibson wrote in the Court of Appeal:

The policy consideration which is of greatest weight, in my judgment, is what the judge called the imperative of giving effect to the wishes of the parties unless there are compelling reasons of principle why it is not possible to do so.[39]

The technique by which the three speeches in the Court of Appeal coped with the doctrine of *stare decisis* and distinguished away more than a generation of precedent need not concern us here.[40] It is relevant to our overall theme of development of international law, however, that Lord Justice Leggatt sought support for the change in English law in the decision of the United States Supreme Court in the *Prima Paint* case,[41] and that Lord Justice Hoffman relied heavily on the following passage from a decision of the Supreme Court of Germany:

There is every reason to presume that reasonable parties will wish to have the relationships created by their contract and the claims arising therefrom, irrespective of whether their contract is effective or not, decided by the same tribunal and not by two different tribunals . . . Experience shows that as soon as a dispute of any kind arises from a contract, objections are very often also raised against its validity.[42]

I do not here want to open up the running debate about *lex mercatoria*.[43] I do think it is fair to say, however, that party autonomy—both for choice of law and for choice of forum, including an arbitral forum—is now part of an international

[37] Mustill and Boyd, 109.

[38] *Harbour Assurance Co. (UK) Ltd* v. *Kansa General International Insurance Co. Ltd* [1993] QB 701, [1993] 3 WLR 42, [1993] 3 All ER 897 (CA).

[39] [1993] 3 WLR at 48, [1993] 3 All ER at 903.

[40] In brief, the several commonly quoted statements in *Heyman* v. *Darwins*, n. 32 *supra*, were denominated *obiter dicta*, because in that case the holding was that the dispute fell within the arbitration clause and that accordingly the dispute should be referred to arbitration. Other intervening decisions were similarly distinguished. There was no doubt, however, that the *Harbour Assurance* case constituted a significant change in English law.

[41] [1993] QB at 717 [1993] 3 WLR at 55, [1993] 3 All ER at 909, quoting from *Prima Paint Corp.* v. *Flood & Conklin Mfg. Co*, n. 33 *supra*. Leggatt J quotes the passage, 388 U.S. at 403–4, which distinguished between a claim of fraud in the inducement of the contract—which would be for the arbitrators, and fraud in the inducement of the arbitration clause itself—which would still be for the court.

[42] *V & K* v. *H*, n. 33 *supra*, 53 BGHZ 315 at 322, translated into English in (1990) 6 Arbitration Int'l 79 at 85, quoted by Hoffman LJ [1993] QB at 724 [1993] 3 WLR at 61, [1993] 3 All ER at 915.

[43] For my views on this subject, see Lowenfeld, 'Lex Mercatoria: An Arbitrator's View', in Thomas E. Carbonneau (ed.), *Lex Mercatoria and Arbitration* (1990), also in (1990) 6 *Arbitration Int'l* 133.

customary law of dispute settlement. Moreover, this body of law, responsive to the needs of the participants in international transactions, reflects a countertrend to the assertion of national interests that we have seen throughout this volume. Some of the components of this procedural *lex mercatoria* are addressed in the last section of this Chapter. Before coming to that topic, it is necessary to give some attention to the (shrinking) limits of party autonomy.

C. LIMITS TO PARTY AUTONOMY

It is evident that, notwithstanding the modern enthusiasm for party autonomy, choice of law and choice of forum are not absolute values. Particularly when party autonomy comes up against public law, one an expect some inroads into freedom of choice. I want to discuss, by way of illustration, two English cases, one involving choice of law by the parties, the other choice of forum, both of which were defeated in the English court, and then come to three well-known American cases in which party autonomy prevailed over strong opposition and lingering doubts.

1. Two English Decisions

(a) A Choice of Law Case

Regazzoni v. *K. C. Sethia (1944) Ltd*[44] arose out of a contract by which an Indian company doing business in England agreed to sell 500,000 jute bags of specified quality to a Swiss firm, c.i.f. Genoa, Italy. The jute bags were to be exported from India and, as both parties knew, they were to be shipped onward from Genoa to South Africa. The contract, made by an exchange of telegrams between seller's agent in Germany and buyer in Switzerland, incorporated by reference the form contract of the United Kingdom Jute Trade Association, which provided that the governing law was English.[45] Seller failed to make delivery, and when buyer claimed damages for breach of contract, seller defended on the ground that the export of goods from India destined for South Africa was prohibited by Indian law. Buyer countered that the contract was subject to English, not Indian law, and that English law did not prohibit trade with South Africa. How should this case be decided?

Buyer pointed out that the House of Lords had reiterated just three years before in *Government of India* v. *Taylor*[46] that an English court would not enforce penal or revenue laws of another country. Seller argued that this case was different, that a choice of English law must carry with it a choice of

[44] [1958] AC 301 (HL(E)).

[45] These facts emerge from the report of the decision of the lower court, *Regazzoni* v. *K. C. Sethia (1994) Ltd*, [1955] 2 Lloyd's Rep. 766 at 774 (QB).

[46] [1955] AC 491, discussed in Ch. 6 sect. C(2).

English public policy, and that it would (or should) be contrary to English public policy to uphold a contract to violate the law of a friendly foreign state.

Readers who have followed these essays thus far will not be surprised that I am not impressed by the argument that a court should disregard foreign law because it is 'public'. The question remains whether, by choosing English law and an English forum, the parties could avoid the law of India. Clearly if the firm that had promised to export the goods from India later got cold feet and failed to deliver, the English court would not order it to perform the contract. But why should it not award damages to the buyer, who had invested money in the deal and had made a resale contract with a South African firm to which it might now be liable?

Lord Reid, one of the four Law Lords responding to that question, said:

> To my mind, the question whether this contact is enforceable by English courts is not, properly speaking a question of international law. The real question is one of public policy in English law; but in considering this question we must have in mind the background of international law and international relationships often referred to as the comity of nations.[47]

That led Lord Reid to the view that if both parties knew that the contract could not be performed without committing a breach of foreign law, it cannot be enforced by an English court. The question of party autonomy is not addressed at all, except by the inference that the whole of English law was chosen, including the reference to Indian law via English public policy. An alternative approach, also not stated explicitly by any of the Law Lords, is that certain kinds of rules—sometimes called mandatory rules or *lois de police*—cannot be avoided by choice of law clauses.

It is not necessary for the time being to choose between these two views; suffice it to say that choice of law by parties to an international contract has its limits, and that they tend to be found in the public law area. I would add only that I think the result in *Regazzoni* would be the same if the chosen law and the chosen forum had been American. However, if the court that heard the case followed § 187 of the *Restatement (Second) of Conflict of Laws*,[48] I believe it would have accepted only the second inference from *Regazzoni*, i.e. that 'application of the law of the chosen state [say New York] would be contrary to a fundamental policy of a state [i.e. India] which has a materially greater interest . . . in the particular issue.'[49] and that this interest cannot be avoided by choice of law by the parties.

(b) A Choice of Forum Case

Carvalho v. *Hull, Blyth (Angola) Ltd*[50] arose from a suit brought in London by a former resident of Angola against a company registered (and hence amenable

[47] [1958] AC at 323.
[48] See n. 18 *supra*.
[49] *Restatement*, § 187(2)(b).
[50] [1979] 1 WLR 1228 (CA).

to suit) in England, but with its business operations in Angola. The plaintiff, a Dr Carvalho, and his family had owned Hull, Blyth, the defendant trading and distribution company, for 100 years, but in 1970 the company had been re-organized so that plaintiff was left with a 49 per cent holding of five subsidiary companies. In December 1973, after several years of guerrilla warfare but two years before Angola gained its independence from Portugal, Dr Carvalho entered into a contract to sell all his shares in the subsidiary companies to Hull, Blyth for 76 million Portuguese escudos (about 3 million dollars or £1.5 million), to be paid in four instalments. The contract contained a clause stating:

> In case of litigation arising, the District Court of Luanda shall be considered the sole competent court to adjudicate to the exclusion of all others.

The first three instalments were paid, but the fourth instalment of about 20 million escudos was not paid. Meanwhile Carvalho had left Angola, and Angola had gained its independence. Carvalho brought suit in London to recover the remainder of the purchase price, and the company moved to dismiss or stay the action in reliance on the forum selection clause.

Plaintiff replied that he had left Angola under duress, with all his assets there being taken over and amid threats to himself and his family. If he returns to Angola, his lawyers said, Dr. Carvalho believes that he will be liquidated. Moreover, plaintiff asserted that if his action were tried in Angola, it would be adjudicated under the new constitution of the People's Republic of Angola, which guaranteed private property and activities, 'even those of foreigners, provided that they are useful to the economy of the country and the interests of the Angolan people', and stressed the 'wide front which includes all the patriotic forces engaged in the anti-Imperialist struggle'. Plaintiff contended therefore (i) that he could not obtain a fair trial in Angola, and (ii) that in any event while the court house in Luanda might still be standing, the District Court in which he had agreed to litigate—part of the Portuguese judicial system—no longer existed. Against these contentions it could be said that the independence of Angola was clearly foreseeable when Dr Carvalho signed the contract of sale, and that the overriding principle was that people should be held to their contracts. Plaintiff could not, in this reasoning, be allowed to sue on a contract yet disregard one of its terms.

How should this case be decided? Is this the case that establishes the threshold, that is that when parties can show revolutionary changes of the kind that occurred in Angola in the 1970s they may be released from their undertakings to litigate in a foreign court, but unless they can make a comparable showing—say the replacement of the Shah of Iran by the Ayatollah—choice of forum clauses will be upheld?

In the actual case, the Court of Appeal in London accepted both of Carvalho's arguments. As a matter of discretion, which it said the High Court judge possessed,[51] plaintiff had shown 'strong cause' why a stay should not be granted; as a matter of construction of the agreement, the forum selection clause failed because the District Court in Luanda was completely different from the court contemplated by the agreement. The Court of Appeal did not quite answer the question whether *Carvalho* was the threshold case, but I believe it presents a good standard by which to measure efforts to be released from forum selection clauses.

2. The American Trilogy

In contrast to the practice in England, where forum selection clauses had been honored as early as 1796,[52] such clauses had a mixed reception in the United States prior to the decisions of the Supreme Court to be discussed below. A leading decision of the highest court in the state of New York as early as 1931 had upheld an action in New York on an arbitral award rendered in England despite absence of the defendant, on the basis that he had agreed by contract to submit to arbitration in London.[53] But more often than not, courts in the United States had declined to dismiss suits in which defendant moved for a stay or dismissal on the basis of a prior agreement to submit disputes to a foreign court or arbitral tribunal. In one well known case, for instance, an American insurance company, New York Life, had issued a life insurance policy in Germany to a citizen of Germany, with a provision that any suit in respect of the policy must be brought in Karlsruhe, Germany. Plaintiff, a citizen and resident of Germany, brought suit against the insurance company in Oregon, where the company did business, and the court refused to dismiss or stay the action. The choice of forum clause, the court said, was 'contrary to public policy and void. The law prescribed the jurisdiction of courts, and it cannot be diminished or increased by the convention of the parties.'[54]

Decisions on forum selection clauses went in both directions,[55] but as late as 1971, the *Restatement (Second) of Conflict of Laws*, which had embraced party autonomy with respect to choice of the applicable law[56] and whose Reporter, Professor Reese, was a strong advocate of party autonomy,[57] had to address forum selection as follows:

[51] Citing Rule 30 in Dicey and Morris, (9th edn., 1973). The corresponding passage appears as Rule 32(2) of the current 12th edn. (Collins, 1993).

[52] See *Gienar* v. *Meyer*, n. 11 *supra*.

[53] *Gilbert* v. *Burnstine*, 255 N.Y. 348, 174 N.E. 706 (1931).

[54] *State ex rel. Kahn* v. *Tazwell*, 125 Or. 528 at 543, 266 P. 238 at 243 (1928).

[55] For a survey of cases going both ways on this issue, but with the majority declining to relinquish the courts jurisdiction, see Annotation: 'Validity of Contractual Provision Limiting Place or Court in Which Action May Be Brought', 56 A.L.R.2d 300 (1957).

[56] See n. 18 *supra*.

[57] See e.g, Willis Reese, 'The Contractual Forum: Situation in the United States', 13 Am. J. Comp. L. 179 (1964); 'The Model Choice of Forum Act', 17 Am. J. Comp. L. 292 (1969).

The parties' agreement as to the place of the action *cannot oust a state of judicial jurisdiction, but such an agreement* will be given effect unless it is unfair or unreasonable[58] (italics added).

In the following year, the U.S. Supreme Court issued its decision in the well known *Zapata* case[59] which substantially changed the outlook in the United States on forum selection, and I think on party autonomy generally, particularly in regard to international transactions.

(a) An Exculpatory Clause

The *Zapata* case involved a contract for towage by a German firm of an offshore oil drilling rig owned by an American company from Louisiana to a point in the Adriatic near Ravenna, Italy. During a storm in the Gulf of Mexico, the drilling rig's elevator legs broke off and the rig was severely damaged, in circumstances where each party blamed the other for the accident. The rig was brought to Tampa, Florida, the nearest port of refuge, and Zapata, the owner of the rig, brought suit against the German owner of the deep sea tug. The owner of the tug moved to stay or dismiss the action on the basis of a clause in the towage contract providing that 'Any dispute arising must be treated before the London Court of Justice', and on the basis of an action meanwhile begun by the tug's owner in London.[60] The District Court in Tampa declined to dismiss the action, on the ground that agreements to oust the court's jurisdiction are contrary to public policy. The Court of Appeals, sitting *en banc*, affirmed by an eight to six vote.[61] The Supreme Court, in an eight to one decision written by Chief Justice Burger, reversed, not only upholding the forum selection clause, but making a firm declaration in favor of the customs and practices of international trade:

> For at least two decades we have witnessed an expansion of overseas commercial activities by business enterprises based in the United States. The barrier of distance that once tended to confine a business concern to a modest territory no longer does so. Here we see an American company with special expertise contracting with a foreign company to tow a complex machine thousands of miles across seas and oceans. The expansion of American business and industry will hardly be encouraged if, notwithstanding solemn contracts, we insist on a parochial concept that all disputes must be resolved under our laws and in our courts . . . We cannot have trade and commerce in world markets and

[58] ALI, *Restatement (Second) of Conflict of Laws*, § 80. In the 1988 Revisions of the *Restatement*, the italicized words are omitted, reflecting the developments discussed hereafter.

[59] *The Bremen* v. *Zapata Off-Shore Co.*, 407 U.S. 1 (1972).

[60] See *Unterweser Reederei GmbH* v. *Zapata Off-Shore Company* [1968] 2 Lloyd's Rep. 158 (CA), in which the English courts sustained jurisdiction pursuant to R.S.C. Order 11, r. 1(i)(d)(iv) on the basis of the forum selection clause, though the transaction had no connection with England, and notwithstanding the action pending in Tampa.

[61] *In Re Unterweser Reederei GmbH*, 446 F.2d 907 (5th Cir. 1971).

international waters exclusively on our terms, governed by our laws, and resolved in our courts.[62]

. . .

The argument that [forum selection] clauses are improper because they tend to 'oust' a court of jurisdiction is hardly more than a vestigial legal fiction. It appears to rest at core on historical judicial resistance to any attempt to reduce the power and business of a particular court and has little place in an era when all courts are overloaded and when businesses once essentially local now operate in world markets. It reflects something of a provincial attitude regarding the fairness of other tribunals . . . No one seriously contends in this case that the forum-selection clause 'ousted' the District Court of jurisdiction over Zapata's action. The threshold question is whether that court should have exercised its jurisdiction to do more than give effect to the legitimate expectations of the parties, manifested in their freely negotiated agreement by specifically enforcing the forum clause.

There are compelling reasons why a freely negotiated private international agreement, unaffected by fraud, undue influence, or overweening bargaining power, such as that involved here, should be given full effect. In this case, for example, we are concerned with a far from routine transaction between companies of two different nations contemplating the tow of an extremely costly piece of equipment from Louisiana across the Gulf of Mexico and the Atlantic Ocean, through the Mediterranean Sea to its final destination in the Adriatic Sea . . . It cannot be doubted for a moment that the parties sought to provide for a neutral forum for the resolution of any disputes arising during the tow . . . There is strong evidence that the forum clause was a vital part of the agreement, and it would be unrealistic to think that the parties did not conduct their negotiations, including fixing the monetary terms, with the consequences of the forum clause figuring prominently in their calculations . . .

Thus, in the light of present-day commercial realities and expanding international trade we conclude that the forum clause should control absent a strong showing that it should be set aside.[63]

As is often the case in battles over judicial jurisdiction,[64] there was more to the struggle over the proper forum than the convenience of the parties, the availability of witnesses, or even finding a neutral forum in a dispute between an American and a German company. The contract of towage contained a clause stating, in pertinent part:

Urag [the towing company], their masters and crews are not responsible for defaults and/or errors in the navigation of the tow.
Damages suffered by the towed objects are in any case for account of its owners.

Under English law that clause would almost certainly be given effect, and it was assumed throughout the American litigation that the English courts would

[62] 407 U.S. at 8.
[63] *Id.* 12–13, 15.
[64] See, e.g., the discussion of the *Helicopteros* case, Ch. 4 at n. 39.

treat the choice of an English forum as a choice of English law as well.[65] The majority in the Court of Appeals, and Justice Douglas in dissent in the Supreme Court, argued that giving effect to the forum selection clause in this case should be held against United States public policy, because it undermined the American policy, recently confirmed in two decisions of the Supreme Court,[66] that exculpatory clauses such as the one in the present case were not enforceable. The majority in the Supreme Court did not reject this policy, which remains in place with respect to towage in internal waters of the United States. But—and here is the relevance of the *Zapata* case to the larger theme of this Chapter—the policy against exculpatory clauses was not strong enough to overcome the stronger value of protecting the justified expectations of parties to international commercial transactions, as expressed in their freely negotiated agreements. Only if *Zapata* could carry its 'heavy burden' of showing that a London trial would be 'so manifestly and gravely inconvenient' that it would be 'effectively deprived of a meaningful day in court', would the forum selection clause be overridden.[67]

(b) A Securities Claim

A prohibition or, as in *Zapata*, a strong public policy, against contracting out of liability for negligence could be said to be at the borderline between public and private law. Could parties to a contract choose their own forum to govern a legal relationship subject to positive regulation, such as under antitrust or securities laws? Within the United States it was clear that such claims were to be adjudicated in federal, not state courts, and it had been assumed that this also meant that they could not be arbitrated. The Supreme Court had so held in a domestic dispute between a brokerage house and a customer under the Securities Act of 1933;[68] the same issue under the antitrust laws had not reached the Supreme Court, but several courts of appeals had held that antitrust claims—including counterclaims—were not suitable for resolution by arbitration.[69] Shortly after the decision in *Zapata*, the question came before

[65] Chief Justice Burger cited *Tzortzis* v. *Monark Line A/B* [1968] 1 WLR 406, [1968] 1 Lloyd's Rep. 337 (CA) for that proposition, 407 U.S. at 14, n. 15, although by the time the U.S. Supreme Court rendered its opinion the statement by the English Court of Appeal in that case that the inference that *qui eligit iudicem eligit ius* is irresistible had been substantially cut back by the House of Lords in *Cie. Tunisienne de Navigation SA* v. *Cie d'Armement Maritime SA* [1971] AC 572, where the proposition was described as a 'weighty indication', though to be considered along with other factors.

[66] *Bisso* v. *Inland Waterways Corporation*, 349 U.S. 85 (1955); *Dixilyn Drilling Corp.* v. *Crescent Towing & Salvage Co*, 372 U.S. 697 (1963), both involving towing accidents on the Mississippi River.

[67] 407 U.S. at 18.

[68] *Wilko* v. *Swan*, 346 U.S. 427 (1953).

[69] In the leading case, *American Safety Equipment Corp.* v. *J. P. Maguire & Co*, 391 F.2d 821 (2d Cir. 1968), the Court of Appeals had held that arbitration about the validity, under the Sherman Antitrust Act, of the agreement between the parties, was not permissible:

> A claim under the antitrust laws is not merely a private matter. The Sherman Act is

the Supreme Court whether these decisions should prevail in respect to international as well as domestic controversies.

Scherk v. *Alberto-Culver Co*[70] arose out of a contract for the purchase by a United States-based cosmetics company from a citizen and resident in Germany of several European cosmetics enterprises. It was agreed between the parties that the seller would transform his enterprise into a corporation and that the buyer would then purchase the shares of the corporation. Pending completion of the sale, the shares were to be held in escrow. The agreement was to be governed by the law of Illinois, but disputes between the parties were to be settled by arbitration in Paris under the rules of the International Chamber of Commerce.

Subsequently Alberto-Culver, the buyer, accused the seller of misstating certain information concerning trademarks of the acquired firms, and sought to rescind the transaction. Seller refused and initiated arbitration proceedings before the ICC; Buyer in turn brought suit in the U.S. District Court in Chicago to enjoin the arbitration and rescind the sale, alleging that it had been defrauded in violation of section 10(b) of the Securities Exchange Act of 1934 and the famous Regulation 10(b)(5) issued thereunder.[71]

The German seller moved to dismiss the lawsuit on the basis of the forum selection clause calling for arbitration in Paris; buyer countered that it had brought a claim under the securities laws and that it was settled law that such claims could not be removed from judicial jurisdiction. Of course, as the seller pointed out, Alberto-Culver's claim was not a typical securities claim; the real controversy concerned the validity and value of trademarks on cosmetics

> designed to promote the national interest in a competitive economy . . . Antitrust violations can affect hundreds of thousands—perhaps millions—of people and inflict staggering economic damage . . . Since commercial arbitrators are frequently men drawn for their business expertise, it hardly seems proper for them to determine these issues of great public interest . . .
>
> We express no general distrust of arbitrators or arbitration . . . We conclude only that the pervasive public interest in enforcement of the antitrust laws and the nature of the claims that arise in such cases makes the outcome here clear. In some situations Congress has allowed parties to obtain the advantages of arbitration, if they 'are willing to accept less certainty of legally correct adjustments', but we do not think that this is one of them. In short we conclude that the antitrust claims raised here are inappropriate for arbitration.

391 F.2d at 827–8.

[70] 417 U.S. 506 (1974). The present writer was a member of a committee of the American Arbitration Association which submitted *amicus curiae* briefs in this case, as well as in the *Mitsubishi* case discussed hereafter, in support of upholding the agreements to arbitrate.

[71] 15 U.S.C. § 78; 17 C.F.R. § 240.10b–5. Jurisdiction over the German seller was founded on § 27 of the Securities Exchange Act, 15 U.S.C. § 78aa, which provides for jurisdiction to enforce any liability or duty created by the Act: 'in the district wherein any act or transaction constituting the violation occurred, and for service of process . . . wherever the defendant may be found'. Service of process was effected on the seller in Switzerland pursuant to Rule 4(e) and (i) of the Federal Rules of Civil Procedure and in accordance with Swiss law.

products. Nevertheless the District Court in Chicago upheld its jurisdiction and enjoined the arbitration in Paris, and the Court of Appeals, by a two to one decision, affirmed.[72] Seller appealed to the Supreme Court, arguing that the prior decisions of the Court had been overtaken by the *Zapata* case with respect to international transactions. The Supreme Court agreed, by a five to four vote. The majority emphasized that in contrast to the situation in *Wilko* v. *Swan*, the purely domestic case in which the Supreme Court had held that claims under the securities claims could not be arbitrated, the contract in this case was a 'truly international agreement' involving 'considerations and policies significantly different from those found initially in *Wilko*'. In *Wilko*, the Court said, there was no doubt that U.S. law, and particularly the federal securities laws, were applicable.

> In this case, by contrast, in the absence of the arbitration provision considerable uncertainty existed at the time of the agreement and still exists, concerning the law applicable to the resolution of disputes arising out of the contract.
>
> Such uncertainty will almost inevitably exist with respect to any contract touching two or more countries, each with its own substantive laws and conflict of laws rules. A contractual provision specifying in advance the forum in which disputes shall be litigated and the law to be applied is, therefore, an almost indispensable precondition to achievement of the orderliness and predictability essential to any international business transaction. Furthermore, such a provision obviates the danger that a dispute under the agreement might be submitted to a forum hostile to the interests of one of the parties or unfamiliar with the problem area involved.
>
> A parochial refusal by the courts of one country to enforce an international arbitration agreement would not only frustrate these purposes, but would invite unseemly and mutually destructive jockeying by the parties to secure tactical litigation advantages. In the present case, for example, it is not inconceivable that if [Seller] had anticipated that [Buyer] would be able in this country to enjoin resort to arbitration he might have sought an order in France or some other country enjoining [Buyer] from proceeding with its litigation in the United States. Whatever recognition the courts of this country might ultimately have granted to the order of the foreign court, the dicey atmosphere of such legal no-man's-land would surely damage the fabric of international commerce and trade, and imperil the willingness and ability of businessmen to enter into international commercial agreements.[73]

Referring to its holding in *Zapata*, the Court said that an agreement to arbitrate before a specified tribunal is, in effect, a specialized kind of forum selection clause that posits not only the situs but also the procedure to be used in resolving the dispute:

> The invalidation of such an agreement in the case before us would not only allow the respondent to repudiate his solemn promise but would, as well, reflect

[72] *Alberto-Culver Co* v. *Scherk*, 484 F.2d 611 (7th Cir. 1973).

[73] 417 U.S. at 515–17.

a 'parochial concept that all disputes must be resolved under our laws and in our courts . . . [quoting from *Zapata*]. We cannot have trade and commerce in world markets and international waters exclusively on our terms, governed by our laws, and resolved in our courts.

Scherk was, as noted, a five to four decision, and the dissenters worried that the protections of U.S. securities laws were being submerged to the 'invocation of the "international contract" talisman'.[74] In the event, the opposite development took place: Having approved arbitration under international rules of a securities law claim against a foreign party, the U.S. Supreme Court reconsidered the prohibition on arbitration of domestic securities claims, and in a series of decisions in the 1980s, repudiated the *Wilko* decision of the 1950s and upheld agreements to arbitrate between investment houses and their customers in wholly domestic transactions as well.[75]

(c) An Antitrust Claim

A special concern of those who feared the spread of party autonomy and in particular of arbitration has been the field of antitrust and competition law. The perception was that, while arbitrators (whether or not they were jurists) may be competent to determine the quality of merchandise and to interpret provisions in a commercial contract, they could not be trusted to be sensitive to the public interest. If, for instance, a manufacturer and a distributor made an agreement covering a given market or area, arbitrators could decide whether the manufacturer had granted an exclusive franchise to the distributor, whether the distributor had met its purchase or sales quota, and whether shipments and payments had been made on time. The arbitrators might not, however, understand or be sympathetic to defenses by the distributor based on contentions that a prohibition in the distribution agreement against resale outside the assigned territory, or a requirement that the distributor buy product *B* in order to have access to product *A* were inconsistent with the antitrust laws. Accordingly, it was understood in the United States, as it was in most European states, that disputes raising antitrust claims could not be submitted to arbitration. No provision of United States law so stated, and as noted, the Supreme Court had not passed on the question, but several courts of appeals had taken this position,[76] in some instances splitting a controversy in two, with the manufacturer's claim submitted to arbitration pursuant to an arbitration clause, but the distributor's antitrust counterclaim retained by the court.[77] In

[74] *Id.* 519.

[75] The leading cases were *Shearson/American Express, Inc.* v. *McMahon*, 482 U.S. 220 (1987) and *Rodriguez de Quijas* v. *Shearson/American Express Inc.*, 490 U.S. 477 (1989).

[76] See n. 69 *supra*.

[77] See, e.g., *Sam Reisfeld & Son Import Co v. SA Eteco,* 530 F.2d 679 (5th Cir. 1979) involving a manufacturer from Belgium and a distributor in Louisiana; see also the decision of the Court of Appeals in the *Mitsubishi* case discussed hereafter, 723 F.2d 155 (1983).

the well-known *Mitsubishi* case that came before it in 1985,[78] the Supreme court had to decide whether this approach could stand in an international transaction in the light of *Zapata* and *Scherk*.

Mitsubishi, a Japanese automobile manufacturer had entered into a joint venture with a Swiss subsidiary of the American Chrysler Corporation to distribute its automobiles through Chrysler dealers outside the United States. Among its dealers was Soler, an automobile dealer in Puerto Rico. At first, the arrangement between Mitsubishi and Soler was successful, but after some time Soler fell behind in meeting its sales quota and in meeting payments for cars delivered. Soler sought permission to transship some vehicles to Latin America or to the continental United States, but Mitsubishi declined to give permission. Eventually Mitsubishi sought an order to compel Soler to arbitrate pursuant to an article in the agreement calling for arbitration of 'all disputes, controversies, or differences which may arise between [the parties] out of or in relation to . . . the Agreements or the breach thereof'. The Agreement called for arbitration in Tokyo under auspices of the Japan Commercial Arbitration Association, with the contract subject to the law of Switzerland.

Soler denied the operative allegations of the Mitsubishi's complaint, and counterclaimed under the Sherman Antitrust Act and the Puerto Rico Dealers Contracts Act,[79] asserting (i) that the counterclaims were not covered by the agreement to arbitrate, and (ii) that in any event they raised non-arbitrable issues. The District Court ordered arbitration of all issues, the Court of Appeals reversed as to the antitrust claim,[80] and once more the Supreme Court faced the question of whether international transactions were somehow different. The answer (by a vote of five to three) was once again yes:

> *The Bremen* [*Zapata*] and *Scherk* established a strong presumption in favour of enforcement of freely negotiated contractual choice-of-forum provisions. Here, as in *Scherk*, that presumption is reinforced by the emphatic federal policy in favor of arbitral dispute resolution. And at least since this Nation's accession in 1970 to the [New York Arbitration] Convention, and the implementation of the Convention in the same year by amendment of the Federal Arbitration Act, that federal policy applies with special force in the field of international commerce. Thus, we must weigh the concerns of *American Safety*[81] against a strong belief in the efficacy of arbitral procedures for the resolution of international commercial disputes and an equal commitment to the enforcement of freely negotiated choice-of-forum clauses.[82]

The last section of this Chapter comes back to the question whether arbitrators are up to understanding complex antitrust issues, and whether they can be

[78] *Mitsubishi Motors* v. *Soler Chrysler-Plymouth, Inc.*, 473 U.S. 614 (1985).
[79] 10 Puerto Rico Laws Ann., § 278 *et seq.*
[80] N. 77 *supra.*
[81] N. 69 *supra.*
[82] 473 U.S. at 614.

trusted to do so. The Court's answer, which did not convince everyone,[83] read:

> There is no reason to assume at the outset of the dispute that international arbitration will not provide an adequate mechanism. To be sure, the international arbitral tribunal owes no prior allegiance to the legal norms of particular states; hence, it has no direct obligation to vindicate their statutory dictates. The tribunal, however, is bound to effectuate the intentions of the parties. Where the parties have agreed that the arbitral body is to decide a defined set of claims which includes, as in these cases, those arising from the application of American antitrust law, the tribunal therefore should be bound to decide that dispute in accord with the national law giving rise to the claim.[84]
>
> . . .
>
> As international trade has expanded in recent decades, so too has the use of international arbitration to resolve disputes arising in the course of that trade. The controversies that international arbitral institutions are called upon to resolve have increased in diversity as well as in complexity. Yet the potential of these tribunals for efficient disposition of legal disagreements arising from commercial relations has not yet been tested. If they are to take a central place in the international legal order, national courts will need to 'shake off the old judicial hostility to arbitration', . . . and also their customary and understandable unwillingness to cede jurisdiction of a claim arising under domestic law to a foreign or transnational tribunal. To this extent at least, it will be necessary for national courts to subordinate domestic notions of arbitrability to the international policy favoring commercial arbitration. See *Scherk*, supra.[85]

D. ARBITRATION AND THE PUBLIC LAW TABOO

In *Scherk* v. *Alberto Culver*, the assumption was that the arbitrators sitting in Paris would apply the law of Illinois—the other leg of the respect for party autonomy, and in that case probably the result of a not uncommon bargain in which one side selects the law, the other side the forum. The law of Illinois, of course, means the law applicable in Illinois, which comprises federal as well as state law, including the United States securities laws and regulations. Is the assumption that arbitrators sitting in Paris could and would apply the securities laws of the United States justified? I believe it is, but if that is correct, it is worth pausing to contemplate. It tells us that the public law taboo which is

[83] But did convince the present author. See Lowenfeld, 'The *Mitsubishi* case: Another View', 2 *Arbitration Int'l* 178 (1986), replying to Thomas E. Carbonneau, '*Mitsubishi*: The Folly of Quixotic Internationalism', 2 *Arbitration Int'l* 116 (1986).

[84] 473 U.S. at 636–7.

[85] *Id.* 638–9. Eventually, the arbitration went forward before three arbitrators at the Japan Commercial Arbitration Association, but Soler, which had in the meantime declared bankruptcy, did not participate and thus the antitrust claims were never raised before the arbitrators. The tribunal rendered its award on Apr. 14, 1987 in favor of Mitsubishi.

cherished by national courts is cast off when dispute settlement is assigned to arbitrators.

One could conclude that this shows the error of decisions such as *Scherk* and *Mitsubishi*; my conclusion is the opposite. To me, it reinforces the doubt (to put it mildly) expressed in Chapters 1 and 2 about the refusal of national courts to apply the teachings of conflict of laws when the public law of another state enters the discussion. Suppose in *Scherk*, as in *Zapata*, the forum selection clause had pointed, not to arbitration under the rules of the ICC, but, say, to the High Court of Justice in London or the Tribunal de Grande Instance in Paris. Suppose Alberto-Culver, as in the actual case, had brought suit in Chicago, Scherk had moved for stay or dismissal on the basis of the forum selection clause, citing *Zapata*, and Alberto-Culver had countered with the assertion that it could not obtain a hearing in London or Paris for its claim based on the U.S. Securities Exchange Act. Would the outcome be the same, that is dismissal of the action in Chicago in favor of adjudication in London or Paris? I now think so, but only because of the step-by-step progression from *Zapata* to *Scherk* to *Mitsubishi*. My evidence (I do not say conclusive proof) comes from a series of cases recently brought in courts in the United States involving Lloyd's of London and various participants in that market.

1. The American *Lloyd's* Cases

It is well known that a substantial number of underwriting syndicates at Lloyd's have been in distress in the past few years. Investors in some of these syndicates, known as 'Names', have lost significant portions of their investment, and in some instances have been subject to calls for additional contributions of capital and drawing against stand-by letters of credit posted by the Names at the time they made their investment.[86] Inevitably, this situation produced massive litigation, not only in England, but in the United States. In the American actions, the Names usually claimed against the Corporation or the Society of Lloyd's, against individual syndicates, and also against 'managing agents' and 'members' agents' who were alleged to have put their own interests ahead of those of the Names. A major assertion in the actions of the American Names was that the participations in the syndicates were 'securities', and that they had been sold in circumstances that violated U.S. securities laws.[87]

[86] Participations in syndicates at Lloyd's have a unique character, with some attributes of a partnership, in that the investors' liability is not limited to their initial contribution, and some attributes of a corporation, in that the liability is several and not joint, so that a 15% participant in a syndicate can never be liable for more than 15% of a given loss.

[87] In fact the U.S. Securities and Exchange Commission had never treated participation in syndicates at Lloyd's as securities. But while some correspondence between Lloyd's and SEC staff so stated, no court or formal SEC decision had so held.

All the contracts concerning the participation by the Names in syndicates at Lloyd's had been formally made in England, and all called for the application of English law. The agreements between the Names and the syndicates, members' agents, and managing agents all contained provisions calling for arbitration in London; the 'general undertaking' that all the Names signed with the Corporation of Lloyd's did not call for arbitration, but for adjudication of any disputes in English courts. Plaintiffs argued in various American courts that their statutory claims under U.S. securities laws could not be regarded as coming within a contract providing for English law, and more to the point of the present discussion, that their claims under the securities laws could not secure a hearing in English courts or arbitral proceedings. In every such case, these arguments were rejected, and the choice of law and choice of forum clauses (whether looking to adjudication or arbitration) were upheld. The Court of Appeals for the Second Circuit, for instance, wrote:

> It defies reason to suggest that a plaintiff may circumvent forum selection and arbitration clauses merely by stating claims under laws not recognized by the forum selected in the agreement. A plaintiff would simply have to allege violations of *his country*'s tort law or *his country's* statutory law or *his country*'s property law in order to render nugatory any forum selection clause that implicitly or explicitly required the application of the law of another jurisdiction. We refuse to allow a party's solemn promise to be defeated by artful pleading. . . In the absence of other considerations, the agreement to submit to arbitration or the jurisdiction of the English courts must be enforced even if that agreement tacitly includes the forfeiture of some claims that could have been brought in a different forum.
>
> Of course, the [plaintiffs] are quite right that if the substance of their claims, stripped of their labels, does not fall within the scope of the clauses, the clauses cannot apply. However, they must make this argument in the face of strong public policy in favor of forum selection and arbitration clauses [citing *Zapata*, *Mitsubishi*, and *Scherk*].[88]

Thus what we have seen in the past twenty-plus years is a steady path in the United States from acceptance of a fairly chosen foreign judicial forum in a dispute about liability for a marine accident with public policy overtones (*Zapata*), to acceptance of a foreign arbitral forum to address claims under U.S. public law (*Scherk*), to acceptance of a foreign arbitral forum in circumstances where one could not be certain that the U.S. public law claim would be addressed (*Mitsubishi*),[89] to acceptance of foreign judicial or arbitral fora

[88] *Roby* v. *Corporation of Lloyd's*, 996 F.2d 1353 at 1360–1 (2d Cir. 1993), cert. denied, 114 S.Ct. 385 (1993). To the same effect, *Riley* v. *Kingsley Underwriting Agencies Ltd*, 969 F2d 953 at 957 (10th Cir. 1992), cert. denied, 113 S.Ct. 658 (1992); *Bonny* v. *Society of Lloyd's*, 3 F.3d 156 at 161–2 (7th Cir. 1993).

[89] I argued in 1986 that the arbitrators in Tokyo instructed to apply Swiss law would also apply the laws of the relevant market (i.e., U.S. law) with respect to the antitrust claim: Lowenfeld, 'The *Mitsubishi* Case: Another View', 2 *Arbitration Int'l* 178 at 186–8 (1986). That suggestion is made somewhat easier by the adoption in 1987 of the Swiss Private International Law statute which not only accepts the parties' choice of law in

even if the claims under U.S. public law would probably not be heard (the *Lloyd's* cases).[90] To be sure, what I have been describing is an American development, or, more precisely, a development in American perception of (private) international law. But on the one hand the United States was behind the curve two decades ago in respecting party autonomy, and on the other it was and remains well ahead of the curve (if not alone) in adopting public laws with private remedies. Thus the subordination of these remedies to the value of party autonomy is, it seems to me, quite significant, both in terms of judicial philosophy and in terms of practical arrangements for persons dealing with American contract partners.

2. The Arbitrator's Dilemma and the Swiss Solution

Not long ago, an arbitral tribunal sitting in Geneva in a contract dispute between a Belgian and an Italian firm was faced with the contention by the Italian party that the contract was 'automatically void' under Article 85(2) of the Treaty of Rome because it fell within the prohibitions against anti-competitive agreements in Article 85(1) and had not been given clearances by the European Commission under Article 85(3). The arbitral tribunal, following the traditional view, held that it had no jurisdiction to decide on the validity of the agreement under the Treaty of Rome—foreign public law. Quite the contrary, said the Swiss Supreme Court in setting aside the award.[91] If the Arbitrators rendered a decision on the merits assuming the validity of the contract and awarded damages for its breach, they would be violating Article 19 of the Swiss Private International Law statute, the Swiss counterpart to Article 7(1) of the Rome Choice of Law Convention.[92] After surveying the literature

arbitration (Art. 187), but calls for application of the competition law of the country in whose market the restraint directly affects the damaged party (Art. 137), and also provides for application of a law other than the one designated by the statute if that law is meant to be applied mandatorily (Art. 19). But none of this could be predicted with certainty, either in 1985 when *Mitsubishi* was decided or today.

[90] I have been informed by an English arbitrator that claims by American Names against agents or syndicates at Lloyd's under U.S. securities laws have been heard in arbitrations conducted by English arbitrators in London. Clearly the U.S. courts in *Roby* and the other cases cited at n. 88 *supra* could not be assured of this; there is no suggestion that there has been a breach in the public law taboo in English courts.

[91] *G. SA.* v. *V. SpA* (1992) 118 BGE (ATF) II 193 (Apr. 28, 1992), also [1993] Revue de l'Arbitrage 124, excerpted in English in (1993) 18 Yearbook of Commercial Arbitration 143.

[92] Art. 19 of the Swiss PIL statute reads:

> (1) A provision of a law other than the one designated by this Statute that is meant to be applied mandatorily may be taken into account if interests of a party that are according to Swiss views legitimate and clearly overriding so require and the case is closely connected to that law.
>
> (2) Whether such a provision should be taken into account depends on its policy and its consequences for a judgment that is fair according to Swiss views.

Translation, taken from Karrer, Arnold, and Patocchi, *Switzerland's Private International Law* (2nd edn., 1994).

concerning application of Article 85, and concluding that national courts within the European Community have the authority to pronounce on the validity of a contract challenged under Article 85 with respect to which the European Commission had made no decision,[93] the Swiss Federal Court concluded:

> If contradictory decisions are to be avoided, it is essential that arbitrators examine the conformity with Community regulations of contracts that have been submitted to them. Thus the arbitral tribunal could not make its award without having first examined whether or not it could do so on the basis of a valid contract.[94]

That decision makes good sense to me. It gives substantial support, as I see it, to the widening exercise of party autonomy to choose dispute settlement by arbitration. If arbitrators can award damages for breach of a contract that may be invalid because it violates the (public) law of a state (or group of states), party autonomy loses its legitimacy; if, on the other hand, arbitrators are precluded from passing on public, mandatory competition law, as was formerly assumed,[95] then a possibly significant number of disputes between parties to contracts cannot be resolved in a single forum. The Swiss Federal Court, at least, has shown sufficient confidence in the process of arbitration to escape from this dilemma by confirming the authority, and it seems the duty, of arbitrators to pass on public law, not only under the law chosen by the parties, but under the law with which the contract has a close connection.[96]

[93] See *Delimitis* v. *Henninger Bräu, AG*, Case C–234/89, [1991] ECR I–935, [1992] 5 CMLR 210, (ECJ Feb. 28, 1991). The Court of Justice also said that in case of doubt, a court of a Member State of the Community could grant a stay pending a possible exemption decision by the Commission; that option would not be available to an arbitral tribunal, or indeed to a court of a state not a member of the European Community. See *Nordsee Deutsche Hochseefischerei GmbH* v. *Reederei Mond*, Case 102/81, [1982] ECR 1095 (ECJ, Mar. 23, 1982).

[94] 118 BGE II at 198. A slightly different translation from the French appears in 18 Yearbook of Commercial Arbitration at 149.

[95] Compare the now largely discredited holding of the U.S. Court of Appeals in the *American Safety Equipment* case, excerpted in n. 69 *supra*.

[96] The issue of divisibility of issues submitted to arbitrators can cut both ways. See, e.g., the recent decision of the Court of Appeal of Paris in *Soc. Labinal* v. *Soc. Mors et Westland Aerospace* [1993] Revue de l'Arbitrage 645, [1993] Journal du Droit International 957 (Cour d'Appel, Paris, May 19, 1993). In that case *A* and *B* had entered into a joint venture contract containing a clause calling for arbitration in Geneva of any dispute that might arise between them related to the contract. *A* subsequently accused *B* of joining with *C* in a combination in breach of joint venture contract and in violation of the competition laws of the European Community. *A* brought suit against *B* and *C* in the Tribunal de Commerce, which sustained the action against both defendants notwithstanding the agreement to arbitrate between *A* and *B*, both on the basis that the matter concerned public law (*règles d'ordre public économique*) and hence was not arbitrable, and on the basis that the claims against *B* and *C* should be heard in a single proceeding. The Court of Appeal reversed, saying:

> the arbitrability of a dispute is not excluded by the sole fact that the rules of a public policy character apply to the rights in dispute;

and

> neither the connection between the two disputes nor the proper administration of

An excellent recent article by a young Swiss lawyer approving the trend toward authorizing—and requiring—arbitrators to apply public law points out that international arbitration in the last analysis depends on the good will of states and their courts for the enforcement of arbitral awards:[97]

> The standard reached under the New York Convention, should not be put at risk by an attitude of disrespect toward national laws.[98] It is therefore advisable that arbitrators respect the rules that countries or transnational organizations like the EC have enacted in the reasonable exercise of their legislative powers.
>
> . . .
>
> The fact that international arbitrators do not owe allegiance to the law of a particular country or its *ordre public* should not result in total disregard for any national laws. Should not the fact that international arbitration is more detached from a national legal system than a national court which deals with an international dispute lead to an attitude that is less hostile and more receptive to foreign public law, as long as there is a close connection between this law and the relevant facts of the case?[99]

I agree, and I do not think the rationale is limited to competition law.[100] Thus, for instance, suppose the contract in the *Regazzoni* case,[101] involving the Swiss buyer of jute bags from India for resale to South Africa, had contained a clause calling for arbitration. I believe the arbitrators, whether sitting in London or Geneva, should have applied Indian law to invalidate the contract, regardless of the existence of any choice of law clause calling for application of English or Swiss law.[102] And in response to Hochstrasser's point that

> justice can stand in the way of competence of the arbitral tribunal in application of a freely negotiated arbitration clause.

The case is discussed with extended excerpts in English in Sigvard Jarvin, 'Arbitration of Antitrust and Competition Issues' [1994] *Swedish and International Arbitration* 55 at 75–9.

[97] Daniel Hochstrasser, 'Choice of Law and "Foreign" Mandatory Rules in International Arbitration' (1994) 11 *J. Int'l Arbitration* 57 at 85.

[98] Art. V(2) of the UN Convention on the Recognition and Enforcement of Foreign Arbitral Awards, n. 1 *supra*, reads:

> Recognition and enforcement of an arbitral award may . . . be refused if the competent authority where recognition and enforcement is sought finds that
> (a) The subject matter of the difference is not capable of settlement by arbitration under the law of that country; or
> (b) the recognition or enforcement of the award would be contrary to the public policy of that country.

[99] *Ibid.*

[100] For a contrary view by an eminent Swiss professor, see Anton Heini, 'Der Materiellrechtliche Ordre Public im Neuen Schweizerischen Recht der internationalen Schiedgerichtsbarkeit' in *Festschrift für Walther J. Habscheid zum 65. Geburtstag* (1989). See also in the same author's earlier foreign article taking the traditional view that foreign states' interests have no place in private international law: Heini, 'Ausländische Staatsinteressen und internationales Privatrecht' (1981) 100 *Zeitschrift für Schweizerisches Recht* 65.

[101] n. 44 *supra* and sect. C(1)(a).

[102] For an interesting discussion on the question of whether arbitrators should apply mandatory law when that law is not the *lex contractus*, see Pierre Mayer, 'Mandatory Rules

arbitrators should feel less hostility to foreign public law than national courts, I find it interesting and encouraging that arbitrators in London in the claims against syndicates and agents at Lloyd's have taken cognizance of claims under United States securities laws.[103] Of course this discussion assumes that there is no controversy concerning the jurisdiction to prescribe of the state that has adopted the mandatory law in question—in the words of the text quoted, that that law was enacted 'in the reasonable exercise of [the state's] legislative powers'. If there is such a controversy—for instance United States assertion of antitrust jurisdiction over aspects of the London reinsurance market[104]—one would not expect arbitrators to get in the middle.[105]

3. A Larger Lesson?

There is evidently much more to be said about party autonomy—on choice of law, on choice of forum, and on the relation between them. There is no doubt, however, that agreements to arbitrate have become by far the most widely used form of party autonomy in international transactions, and arbitration has become the most common form of international dispute settlement. This development, which in large measure has taken place since World War II and much of it even more recently, leaves me with two thoughts that may serve to tie the subject of this Chapter to the theme of the volume as a whole.

First, the experience of international arbitration shows that the incompatibilities of the several legal systems are not as great as one might have expected from the various conflicts described throughout these pages. My observation from more than two decades of participation as arbitrator in international controversies, involving parties, counsel, and fellow arbitrators from some twenty countries and all the major legal systems, is that the procedures for establishing facts, choosing and interpreting law, and deciding disputes are not very different from one case to another. The origin of the parties, the applicable law, and the background of counsel and of the arbitrators make some difference, but not as much as one might have supposed.[106] Typically the procedures of an international arbitration are an amalgam of civil and common

of Law in International Arbitration', 2 *Arbitration Int'l* 274, 280–6. Mayer eventually comes out affirmative, but not without some doubts.

[103] See n. 90 *supra*.

[104] See the discussion of the *Insurance Antitrust Case*, Ch. 2, sect. D.

[105] Also, my argument would not extend to mandatory laws that the arbitrators, or the seat of the arbitration, would regard as offensive and contrary to public policy, such as laws based on exclusion of persons from the capacity to contract on the basis of race or religion.

[106] The different rules of various arbitral institutions are important for initiation of the process, choosing the arbitrators, dealing with default, and arranging for deposits and fees. My experience, having arbitrated pursuant to nearly all the major rules, is that once an arbitration is under way, the formal rules have very little impact on the conduct of the proceedings.

law analogies. Thus there will be a concentrated hearing or trial, similar to the common law practice; the parties or principals of corporations will be permitted—and indeed expected—to testify, again following the common law model; and there is likely to be direct and cross-examination of witnesses (including party witnesses). But pleadings will be elaborate, as in the civil law tradition; discovery American-style is out, and the exchange of documents will follow what might be called a modified English approach, with each side expected to make disclosure on its own but also to respond to requests from its adversary. I have written elsewhere about the pedagogic influence of international arbitration on lawyers brought up in a single system;[107] my point here is that while the cases are typically hard fought—international arbitration is much more like litigation than like mediation or conciliation—the clash of cultures is much less sharp than in the controversies that we have seen in the preceding chapters.

Second, and contrary to earlier belief, arbitrators seem to be less affected by the public law taboo, and at the same time—also contrary to earlier belief—not wholly removed from public law and public interest. We saw in the *Scherk* case that the U.S. Supreme Court assumed that arbitrators in Paris could and would apply United States securities law, and in *Mitsubishi* that arbitrators in Tokyo would apply United States antitrust law. When arbitrators in Geneva considered themselves without authority to apply the competition law of the European Community, their decision was annulled by the Swiss Supreme Court. We have not as yet seen the next logical step. Is it asking too much to wonder whether, if arbitrators in Paris or Tokyo or Geneva can and must take foreign public law into account, courts may some day do so as well? It seems that the Swiss Private International Law Statute has paved the way for such a development, at least with respect to competition law,[108] but we have not yet seen any such cases. Apart from that specific point, I would venture the suggestion that international arbitration could serve as a mirror, leading the various protagonists of the conflicts that we have explored throughout these chapters to stand back and perhaps have second thoughts about their cherished beliefs—not only in regard to foreign public law, but in regard to the reluctance to enforce foreign judgments, in regard to different approaches to civil procedure, and in regard to viewing private controversies as if they involved deep-seated national interests.

[107] See Lowenfeld, 'The Two-Way Mirror: International Arbitration as a Comparative Procedure', 7 *Mich. Y.B. Int'l Legal Studies* 163 (1985), repr. in W. L. Craig, W. Park, and J. Paulsson, *International Chamber of Commerce Arbitration* (1986), ii, App. VII, 187.

[108] See *Switzerland*: PIL Statute, Arts. 136, 137, discussed in n. 89 *supra*.

10

The Search for a Unifying Principle

It is evident that this group of essays makes no pretence to constituting a treatise, covering all the various aspects of private international law. But the effort has been to do more than merely present a collection of short stories, linked only by the annoying fact that the United States is a participant in nearly all of them. If this volume has been long (perhaps too long) on narrative and illustration, and short (perhaps too short) on doctrine, it has not been for want of a central theme. I do think that a common principle emerges from the various cases, episodes, and short stories here set out—the principle of reasonableness.

A. THE PRINCIPLE OF REASONABLENESS

Please note that this is not, as has sometimes been supposed, the same as the 'rule of reason' as it has been developed in American antitrust law as an alternative to *per se* liability.[1] Reasonableness as the governing principle of private international law has a far wider scope. If we lived in the eighteenth century, we might call it Enlightenment. It invites questioning of mottos, maxims, axioms, and it rejects attitudes such as those of the House of Lords in *Government of India* v. *Taylor*,[2] that we do not know how a rule came about or why, but it is a rule and we are surprised that anyone would want to change it. It encourages thinking, as in *Asahi*,[3] about whether it makes sense to litigate a dispute between a Taiwanese tube maker and a Japanese valve maker in a California court, and it permits an answer to this question that would not exclude all judicial jurisdiction in an American court over the valve maker if it were the only solvent defendant available to compensate the injured plaintiff. In the debate about whether 'doing business' should be a basis for judicial jurisdiction, the principle of reasonableness prompts the question whether it is just to remit the Japanese widow to suit in Malaysia for the death of her husband, because he was killed on a domestic flight in that country and not on an international flight originating in Japan.

[1] See, e.g., P. Areeda and D. Turner, *Antitrust Law* (1986), vii, ch. 15.

[2] Ch. 6, sect. C(2).

[3] Ch. 4, sect. E(2).

Again, the principle of reasonableness invites—and informs—thinking about whether a multinational enterprise can insulate itself from liability by operating through a web of subsidiaries, and does not demand a yes or no answer to that question. Thus, Amoco/Standard Oil can reasonably be held liable for the consequences of a shipwreck caused by a granddaughter or great-granddaughter company,[4] but not for a ship's mortgage that it did not guarantee.

The principle of reasonableness does not reject all absolute values. It accepts, for example, the rule that a judgment rendered by a court in Patria without jurisdiction over the judgment debtor will not be recognized or enforced in Xandia. But it does not automatically define the jurisdiction of the Patrian court by the rules in effect in Xandia. More generally, the principle of reasonableness questions undiscriminating application of what seem like absolute values—privacy for instance. Not long ago, the *Sun*, a London tabloid newspaper, responding to Prince Charles' admission that he had not been faithful to Princess Diana after their marriage broke up, protested 'How dare he invade our privacy with this tale of adultery?'[5] Not all invocation of the right to privacy is as absurd—as unreasonable—as that one. But whether Beecham should disclose its correspondence with Bristol-Meyers,[6] or Volkswagen should explain the thinking that went into the design of the Microbus,[7] are not questions about privacy. And they are certainly not questions about that most over-used of alleged absolutes, 'sovereignty'.

I have long wondered how the concept of sovereignty crept into the subjects here discussed. I understand that sovereignty is important when one thinks of control of the Panama Canal, or the Falkland Islands or Berlin or Jerusalem. But is it really pertinent to the limits of the effects doctrine, or to procurement of evidence for purposes of discovery or trial? When we face a question about whether the surviving wife or the daughter by an earlier marriage should succeed to the New York bank account of the decedent, an Italian national domiciled in France,[8] we do not think about sovereignty. The question is simply whether the American preference for party autonomy or the French preference for protecting the inheritance of children should prevail. On some level at some time, legislatures passed on these preferences—questions of values. But neither solution is contrary to the public policy or *ordre public* of the other; neither solution offends the sovereignty of the other; and if, as happened in the *Watts* case discussed in Chapter 6,[9] the issue comes up in the context of recognition of a judgment, there is no *raison d'état* to deny recognition. Why then is the question

[4] Ch. 5, sect. C(1).

[5] Quoted by Anthony Lewis, 'Down the Tabloid Stage', *New York Times*, July 4, 1994, 19, cols. 1–6.

[6] See Ch. 7, sect. D(2).

[7] See Ch. 8, sect. C(1).

[8] See Ch. 6, sect. C(1).

[9] Ch. 6, n. 27.

different when the issue concerns 'public law'—whether state *A* prefers competition and state *B* monopoly, or state *C* prefers disclosure and state *D* secrecy?

The principle of reasonableness does not deny that different values are reflected in these decisions, and interests of varying strengths. What it calls for is balancing by states, that is by courts and governments, of the respective values and interests of their own and other states particular interests, not abstract 'sovereign interests'. Further—and this is the fundamental premise of the *Restatement* from which I have drawn throughout this volume—respect by the courts of Patria for the values and interests of Xandia will be greatly enhanced if it is established in Patria that the Xandian courts and other authorities are committed to a similar reasonable evaluation of the interests and values of Patria.

I am not speaking of reciprocity, but rather of a shared approach. The shared approach is not linked to specific expressions of substantive values—whether to prefer the daughter or the surviving spouse, or to prefer competition or monopoly, disclosure or secrecy. I refer to a shared approach to international law—private international law as here defined[10]—reasonable expectations, genuine links, the duty to evaluate and balance, the distinction between overlap in regulation and direct conflict and between potential conflict and actual clash.

I do not, of course, claim that we have reached nirvana, or that we ever will. I do contend that as a goal—a shared goal among those with broadly comparable legal traditions—the vision of reasonableness is not itself unreasonable.

B. A LOOK BACK AND A LOOK AHEAD

If reasonableness is an attractive goal, does that make it law? In particular, does reasonableness rise to a principle of international law? It is a fair question, but not, in my view, an embarrassing one.

One of my colleagues asked me not long ago whether any state could sue another state before the World Court for violation of private international law. He knew, of course, that the answer would be 'no',[11] and he was not really expecting a reply on my part. His point, which he did not need to spell out, was that it followed that the principles I was setting out were not law at all, let alone international law. My colleague reflected a common view, but not, I submit, a persuasive one, on two distinct grounds.

First, no one today would define the precepts of international law in terms of the jurisdictional rules of the International Court of Justice. In answer to a question, for instance, about the consistency with international law of a bombing attack on a civilian population—whether in Grozny or Sarajevo or Port au

[10] See Ch. 1, sect. B.

[11] The *Interhandel* case brought by Switzerland against the United States is, perhaps, an exception, but in the result not a very powerful one. See Ch. 7, n. 38.

Prince—no serious person would respond, 'It all depends on whether the World Court would have jurisdiction: if not, there is no violation.' International law is not limited to the jurisdiction of the World Court; more generally (and largely beyond the scope of these essays), the assumption that law is no more than the sum of available remedies is not only cynical, but is a grossly mistaken understanding of law.

Second (and closer to the theme of this volume), the fascination of *private* international law is that there is not one Supreme World Court of Justice, but that there is a common corpus of legal issues addressed by a large number of national courts, legislatures, regulatory agencies, and commentators. Of course, as has been evident throughout this volume, the results are not always the same—within a given country, a given court, and across the spectrum of countries whose cases we have explored. We cannot say, as one can say about physics or medicine or music, that law—even international law—knows no frontiers. But even as scientists and doctors and musicians from around the world can share their talents and experience with one another and with a wider public, so, I think, can lawyers concerned with the issues addressed here—jurisdiction to prescribe and to adjudicate, judgments to recognize and to enforce, facts to discover and to conceal, agreements to make or to set aside.

Not every reader will be convinced by the principle of reasonableness. Every reader, I trust, will be convinced, as I hope that my doubting colleague would be convinced, of the existence of the body of law that we have here explored, not only as a classification in library catalogues, but as a common intellectual pursuit with important practical consequences for individuals, companies, and states.

I would go one step further, and state my belief that if reasonableness is not yet a universally accepted principle, there has been discernible and significant progress towards that goal in the relatively short period within which the cases described in this volume took place.

Laker, at least the English phase[12] is sounder than *Westinghouse*.[13] The *Eddie Antar* cases are more constructive than the *Schemmer/Vesco* case.[14] The decisions of the Supreme Court of Germany—in 1991 in the *M* case on jurisdiction based on presence of property[15] and in 1992 in the case concerning the California judgment on sexual molestation[16]—are sounder, in my concept of international law, than many of the earlier German decisions discussed. Certainly on the part of the United States, one sees more emphasis on co-operation, and less on unilateralism, as shown, for example, in the accords on exchange of information reached with Switzerland and with the Cayman Islands following the confrontations of the early 1980s.[17] Overall, I think in a number of fields of the international economy—from banking to competition law to securities regulation to trade, the world is moving away from

[12] Ch. 1, sect. D.
[13] Ch. 7, sect. E.
[14] Ch. 6, sect. C(3).
[15] Ch. 4, sect. D(1).
[16] Ch. 6, sect. E(4).
[17] Ch. 7, sect. F.

confrontation about jurisdiction and toward seeking consensus on substance, as well as on the techniques and shared values of dispute settlement.

I do not suggest that solutions to the problems explored here are well settled. I do believe, however, that we have moved beyond the definition that I proposed some twenty-five years ago that international law is what international lawyers do.[18] Whatever the sources of the term *Private* International Law, I think it is now clear that public law is no longer out of bounds for international lawyers, that private international law embraces public law, and indeed that this is where the action is.

. . . The quest continues.

[18] Lowenfeld, 'On Teaching International Law', 1 *N.Y.U. J. Int'l Law and Politics*, 61 (1968).

BIBLIOGRAPHY

General Works

AMERICAN LAW INSTITUTE, *Restatement (Second) of the Conflict of Laws* (1971 and 1988 Revisions)

—— *Restatement (Second) of the Foreign Relations Law of the United States* (1965)

—— *Restatement (Third) of the Foreign Relations Law of the United States* (1987)

AUDIT, BERNARD, *Droit International Privé* (1991)

BATIFFOL, H., AND LAGARDE, P., *Droit International Privé* (7th edn., 1981–3)

CHESHIRE AND NORTH, *Private International Law* (12th edn. North and Fawcett (eds.), 1992)

DICEY AND MORRIS, *The Conflict of Laws* (12th edn., Collins, 1993)

FIRSCHING, KARL, AND VON HOFFMANN, BERND, *Internationales Privatrecht* (4th edn., 1995)

GEIMER, REINHOLD, *Internationales Zivilprozesrecht* (1987)

KEGEL, GERHARD, *Internationales Privatrecht* (7th edn., 1995)

MAYER, PIERRE, *Droit International Privé* (5th edn., 1994)

SCOLES, EUGENE K., AND HAY, PETER, *Conflict of Laws* (2nd edn., 1992)

WEINTRAUB, RUSSELL J., *Commentary on the Conflict of Laws* (3rd edn., 1986)

Specialized Works

BORN, GARY B., AND WESTIN, DAVID, *International Civil Litigation in United States Courts* (2nd edn., 1992)

COLLINS, LAWRENCE, *The Civil Jurisdiction and Judgments Act 1982* (1983)

—— *Essays in International Litigation and the Conflict of Laws* (1994)

GEIMER, REINHOLD, AND SCHUTZE, ROLF, *Internationale Urteilsanerkennung* (1983)

KLEIN, F.-E. (ed.), *Basle Symposium on the Rôle of Public Law in Private International Law* (1991)

LOWE, A. V. (ed.), *Extraterritorial Jurisdiction* (1983)

—— *Foreign Affairs in English Courts* (1986)

LOOKOFSKY, JOSEPH, *Transnational Litigation and Commercial Arbitration: A Comparative Analysis of American, European, and International Law* (1992)

LOWENFELD, ANDREAS F., *International Litigation and Arbitration* (1993)

—— 'Public Law in the International Arena: Conflict of Laws, International Law, and Some Suggestions for their Interaction' (1979) 163 *Rec. des Cours* 311

MANN, F. A.,'The Doctrine of International Jurisdiction Revisited after Twenty Years' (1984) 186 *Rec. des Cours* 9

MEESSEN, KARL (ed.), *International Law of Export Control: Jurisdictional Issues* (1992)

PLATTO, CHARLES, AND HORTON, W. G. (eds.), *Enforcement of Foreign Judgments Worldwide* (2nd edn., 1993)

ROSENTHAL, DOUGLAS E., AND KNIGHTON, WILLIAM, *National Laws and International Commerce: The Problem of Extraterritoriality* (1982)

Authorities Cited

Chapters 1–3

BREWSTER, KINGMAN, JR., *Antitrust and American Business Abroad* (1958)

CURRIE, BRAINERD, 'Notes on Methods and Objectives in the Conflict of Laws' [1959] *Duke L.J.* 171 (repr. in B. Currie, *Selected Essays on the Conflict of Laws* 177 (1963)

FUGATE, WILBUR, *Foreign Commerce and the Antitrust Laws* (4th edn., 1991)

GERBER, DAVID J., 'The Extraterritorial Application of the German Antitrust Laws', 77 *Am. J. Int'l L.* 756 (1983)

JENNINGS, ROBERT Y., 'Extraterritorial Jurisdiction and the United States Antitrust Laws' 22 *Brit. Yb. Int'l Law* 146 (1957)

JUENGER, FRIEDRICH K., *Choice of Law and Multistate Justice* (1993)

—— 'Constitutional Control of Extraterritoriality?: A Comment on Professor Brilmayer's Appraisal', 50 *Law & Contemp. Prob.* No. 3, 39 (1987)

LANGE, DIETER G. F., AND SANDAGE, JOHN BYRON, 'The Wood Pulp Decision and Its Implications for the Scope of EC Competition Law' 26 *CML Rev.* 139, 164 (1989)

LOWENFELD, ANDREAS F., *Aviation Law* (2nd edn., 1981)

—— Book Review of Lawrence Ebb, *International Business: Regulation and Protection* (1964) 78 *Harv. L. Rev.* 1699 (1965)

MANN, F. A., 'The *Dyestuffs* Case in the Court of Justice of the European Communities', 22 *Int'l & Comp. L.Q.* 35 (1973)

—— 'The Doctrine of International Jurisdiction Revisited after Twenty Years', 186 Rec. des Cours 9 (Hague Acad. Int'l Law 1984)

—— 'The Public International Law of Restrictive Practices in the European Court of Justice', 38 *Int'l & Comp. L.Q.* 375 (1989)

METZGER, STANLEY D., 'The Restatement of the Foreign Relations Law of the United States: Bases and Conflicts of Jurisdiction', 41 *N.Y.U. L. Rev.* 7 (1966)

JENNINGS, ROBERT Y., AND WATTS, ARTHUR (eds.), *Oppenheim's International Law* (9th edn., 1992)

Chapters 4–6

BAILEY, MARTIN, *Oilgate, The Sanctions Scandal* (1979)

BARTLETT, JAMES W. III, 'In re Oil Spill by the Amoco Cadiz—Choice of Law and a Pierced Corporate Veil Defeat the 1969—Civil Liability Convention', 10 *The Maritime Lawyer* 1 (1985)

BERLE, A. A., AND MEANS, G. C., *The Modern Corporation and Private Property* (1933)

BLANPAIN, R., *The Badger Case and the OECD Guidelines for Multinational Enterprises* (1977)

BLUMBERG, PHILLIP I., *The Law of Corporate Groups* (1983–9)

—— *The Multinational Challenge to Corporation Law* (1993)

BURBANK, STEPHEN B., 'The World in Our Courts: Review of Gary Born, *International Civil Litigation in United States Courts*', 89 *Mich. L. Rev.* 1456 (1991)

CARRINGTON, PAUL, 'The Modern Utility of *Quasi in Rem* Jurisdiction', 76 *Harv. L. Rev.* 303 (1962)

CASAD, ROBERT C., *Jurisdiction in Civil Actions* (2nd edn., 1991)

CAVERS, DAVID, *The Choice of Law Process* (1965) ch. VI, 'Principles of Preference Exemplified: Torts'

CENTER FOR SOCIAL ACTION OF THE UNITED CHURCH OF CHRIST, *The Oil Conspiracy* (1979)

COHN, E. J., AND SIMITIS, C., '"Lifting the Veil" in the Company Laws of the European Continent', 12 *Int'l & Comp. L.Q.* 189 (1963)

COLLINS, LAWRENCE, '*Harris* v. *Taylor* Revived', 92 *LQR* 268 (1976), repr. in Collins, *Essays in International Litigation and the Conflict of Laws* (1994)

—— 'The Territorial Reach of Mareva Injunctions', 105 *LQR* 262 (1989), repr. in Collins, *Essays in International Litigation and the Conflict of Laws* (1994)

CORCORAN, JAMES IRVINE WHITCOMB, 'The Trading with the Enemy Act and the Controlled Canadian Corporation', 14 *McGill L.J.* 174 (1968)

DE VRIES, HENRY, AND LOWENFELD, ANDREAS F., 'Jurisdiction in Personal Actions—A Comparison of Civil Law and Views', 44 *Iowa L. Rev.* 306 (1959)

DOBSON, JUAN M., '"Lifting the Veil" in Four Countries: The Law of Argentina, England, France and the United States', 35 *Int'l & Comp. L.Q.* 839 (1986)

DROZ, G., AND DYER, A., 'The Hague Conference and the Main Issues of Private International Law for the Eighties', 3 *Nw. J. Int'l L. & Bus.* 155 (1981)

EHRENZWEIG, ALBERT, 'Contracts in the Conflict of Laws', 59 *Colum. L. Rev.* 973 (1959)

GEIMER, REINHOLD, AND SCHÜTZE, ROLF A., *Internationale Urteilsannerkennung* (1983) i.

GORDON, MICHAEL W., 'Argentine Jurisprudence: The Parke Davis and Deltec Cases', 6 *Lawyer of the Americas* 320 (1974)

—— 'Argentine Jurisprudence: Deltec Update', 11 *Lawyer of the Americas* 43 (1979)

GOWER, L. C. B. *et al.*, *Principles of Modern Company Law* (4th edn., 1979)

HADDEN, T., 'Inside Corporate Groups', 12 *Int'l J. Sociology of Law* 271 (1984)

HAUPT, KLAUS (ed.), *Groups of Companies in European Laws* (1982), ii.

HAY, PETER, 'Transient Jurisdiction, Especially Over International Defendants: Critical Comments on *Burnham* v. *Superior Court of California*', 1990 *U. Ill. L. Rev.* 593

HAYASHIDA, KENICHIRO, 'Jurisdiction and Applicable Law in Arbitration Cases in Japan' 42 *Zeitschrift für Luft- und Weltraumrecht* 250 (1993)

HEIDENBERGER, PETER, 'Vollstreckbarerklärung von U.S. Jury-Urteilen' (1991) 37 RIW 599

IMMENGA, ULRICH, 'Abhängige Unternehmen und Konzerne im Europäischen Gemeinschaftsrecht' 48 *Rabels Zeitschrift für Ausländisches und Internationales Privatrecht* 48 (1984)

INT'L ENCYCLOPEDIA OF COMPARATIVE LAW, xiii, Ch. 3, Part IV (Buxbaum, R. M.), 'The Corporate Entity and Its Disregard'

—— xi, Torts, ch. 8 (Stoll), 'International Consequences of Liability: Remedies'

JUENGER, FRIEDRICH K., 'American Jurisdiction: A Story of Comparative Neglect', 65 *U. Col. L. Rev.* 1 (1993)

KEETON, W. PAGE, *et al.*, *Prosser and Keeton on the Law of Torts* (5th edn., 1984)

LANDO, OLE, 'The Conflict of Laws of Contracts: General Principles', 189 *Recueil des Cours* 225 (1984–VI)

LOWENFELD, ANDREAS F., 'Conflict of Laws English Style: Review Essay', 37 *Am. J. Comp. L.* 353 (1989)

—— 'Injunctions Across National Frontiers: A Tale of Two Cities', 3 *Am. Rev. Int'l Arbitration* 31 (1992)

—— 'In Search of the Intangible: A Comment on *Shaffer* v. *Heitner*', 53 *N.Y.U. L. Rev.* 102 (1978)

—— 'Thoughts about a Multinational Judgments Convention: A Reaction to the von Mehren Report', 57 *Law & Contemp. Probs.* No. 3, 289 (Summer 1994)

—— *Trade Controls for Political Ends* (2nd edn., 1983)

MANN, F. A., 'The Doctrine of International Jurisdiction Revisited after Twenty Years', 186 *Recueil des Cours* (1984)

MANN, MICHAEL D., MARI, JOSEPH G., AND LAVDAS, GEORGE, *Developments in International Securities Law Enforcement and Regulations* (1994)

MUSHLIN, MICHAEL B., 'The New *Quasi in Rem* Jurisdiction: New York's Revival of a Doctrine Whose Time has Passed', 55 *Brooklyn L. Rev.* 1059 (1990)

PLATTO, CHARLES, AND HORTON, WILLIAM (eds.), *Enforcement of Foreign Judgments Worldwide* (2nd edn., 1993)

ROSENBERG, MAURICE, 'One Procedural Genie Too Many or Putting *Seider* Back Into Its Bottle', 71 *Colum. L. Rev.* 660 (1971)

SCHACK, HAIMO, 'Vermögensbelegenheit als Zuständigkeitsgrund' 97 *Zeitschrift für Zivilprozess* 46 (1984)

SCHUMANN, EKKEHARD, 'Aktuelle Fragen und Probleme des Gerichtsstandes des Vermögens' 93 *Zeitschrift für Zivilprozess* 408 (1980)

SCOTT, AUSTIN W., *Fundamentals of Procedure in Actions at Law* (1922)

SEIDL-HOHENVELDERN, IGNAZ, 'International Economic "Soft Law"', 163 *Recueil des Cours* 165 (Hague Academy Int'l Law 1979)

SIEGEL, DAVID, 'Jurisdiction ad Infinitum: New York's "Rem" Seizure of the Insurance Policy for Jurisdiction in Accident Cases', 20 *Int'l & Comp. L.Q.* 99 (1971)

SILBERMAN, LINDA, 'Reflections on *Burnham* v. *Superior Court*: Toward Presumptive Rules of Jurisdiction and Implications for Choice of Law', 22 *Rutgers L.J.* 569 (1991)

—— '*Shaffer* v. *Heitner*: The End of an Era', 53 *N.Y.U. L. Rev.* 33 (1978)

U.K. FOREIGN AND COMMONWEALTH OFFICE, *Report on the Supply of Petroleum and Petroleum Products to Rhodesia* (1978)

U.S. TREASURY, *Treasury Investigation of Charges Made Against the Mobil Oil Corporation* (Mimeograph, 1977)

VAGTS, DETLEV F., 'The Multinational Enterprise: A New Challenge for Transnational Law', 83 *Harvard L. Rev.* 739 (1970)

VAN OMMESLAGHE, PIERRE, 'Les groupes de sociétés et l'expérience du droit belge', in Haupt, Klaus (ed.), *Groups of Companies in European Laws* (1982)

VON MEHREN, ARTHUR T., AND TRAUTMAN, DONALD T., 'Jurisdiction to Adjudicate: A Suggested Analysis', 79 *Harv. L. Rev.* 1121 (1966)

WEISSBERG, KENNETH, AND MOISSINAC, MARIE-CAROLINE, Piercing the Corporate Veil in France', 6 *Int'l Financial L. Rev.* No. 7, 33 (July 1987)

ZEKOLL, JOACHIM, 'Zur Vollstreckbarkeit eines US-amerikanischen Schadensurteils' 36 RIW 302 (1990)

—— 'Zweimal amerikanische "punitive damages" vor deutschen Gerichten' [1993] 5 IPRax 288

Chapters 7–10

APRIL, SERGE, AND FRIED, JONATHAN, 'Compelling Discovery and Disclosure in Transnational Criminal Litigation—a Canadian View', 16 *N.Y.U. J. Int'l Law & Pol.* 961 (1984)

AREEDA, PHILIP, AND TURNER, DONALD, *Antitrust Law* (1986), vii, ch. 15

BAR, LUDWIG VON, *Theorie und Praxis des Internationalen Privat rechts* (2nd edn., 1889)

BEALE, J. H., *The Conflict of Laws* (1935)

BEALE, SARA S., AND BRYSON, WILLIAM C., *Grand Jury Law and Practice* (1986 plus Supplements)

BORN, GARY B. AND HONIG, SCOTT, 'Comity and the Lower Courts: Post Aérospatiale Application of the Hague Evidence Convention', 24 *Int'l Lawyer* 393 (1990)

CARBONNEAU, THOMAS E. 'Mitsubishi: The Folly of Quixotic Internationalism', 2 *Arbitration Int'l* 116 (1986)

CHAYES, ABRAM, EHRLICH, THOMAS, AND LOWENFELD, ANDREAS F., *International Legal Process* (1968–9)

COLLINS, LAWRENCE, 'The Hague Convention and Discovery: A Serious Misunderstanding?', 35 *Int'l & Comp. L.Q.* 765 (1986), repr. (with new introduction) in Collins, *Essays in International Litigation and the Conflict of Laws* (1994)

COUND, JOHN J., FRIEDENTHAL, JACK H., MILLER, ARTHUR R., AND SEXTON, JOHN E., *Civil Procedure, Cases and Materials* (6th edn., 1994)

CURRIE, BRAINERD, *Selected Essays on the Conflict of Laws* (1963)

DELAUME, GEORGES R., *Law and Practice of Transnational Contracts* (1988)

DU BOIS, JOSIAH ELLIS, *The Devil's Chemists* (1952)

FEHRENBACH, T. R., *The Swiss Bankers* (1966)

FRANKEL, MARVIN E., AND NAFTALIS, GARY P., *The Grand Jury: An Institution on Trial* (1977)

FUGATE, WILBUR L., *Foreign Commerce and the Antitrust Laws* (4th edn., 1991)

GRUSON, MICHAEL, 'Forum Selection Clauses in International and Interstate Commercial Agreements' [1982] *Univ. Illinois L. Rev.* 133

HALPERN, SHELDON W., 'Application of the Doctrine of Commercial Impracticability: Searching for the "Wisdom of Solomon"', 135 *U. Pa. L. Rev.* 1123 (1987)

HEINI, ANTON, 'Ausländische Staatsinteressen und internationales Privatrecht' (1981) 100 *Zeitschrift für Schweizerisches Recht* 65

HEINI, ANTON, 'Der Materiellrechtliche Ordre Public im Neuen Schweizerischen Recht der internationalen Schiedsgerichtsbarkeit' in *Festschrift für Walther J. Habscheid zum 65. Geburtstag* (1989)

HEISER, WALTER W., 'Forum Selection Clauses in State Courts: Limitations on Enforcement after *Stewart* and *Carnival Cruise*', 45 *Fla. L. Rev.* 361 (July 1993)

—— 'Forum Selection Clauses in Federal Courts: Limitations on Enforcement after *Stewart* and *Carnival Cruise*', 45 *Fla. L. Rev.* 553 (Sept. 1993)

HENKIN, LOUIS, 'The Mythology of Sovereignty', Newsletter of the American Society for International Law, March–May 1993

HOCHSTRASSER, DANIEL, 'Choice of law and "Foreign" Mandatory Rules in International Arbitration', 11 *J. Int'l Arbitration* 57 (1994)

HOECHNER, KURT, 'A Swiss Perspective on Conflicts of Jurisdiction', 50 *Law & Contemp. Prob.* No. 3, 271 (1987)

HONEGGER, PETER S., *Amerikanische Offenlegungspflichten in Konflikt mit Schweizerischen Geheimhaltungspflichten* (1986)

INT'L ENCYCLOPEDIA OF COMPARATIVE LAW (1976) iii, ch. 24 (Lando)

JUNKER, ABBO, *Discovery im deutsch-amerikanischen Rechtsverkehr* (1987)

KARRER, PIERRE A., Arnold, Karl W., and Patocchi, Paolo Michele, *Switzerland's Private International Law* (2d edn., 1994)

KAY, HERMA HILL, 'A Defense of Currie's Governmental Interest Analysis', 215 *Recueil des Cours* 9 (Hague Acad. 1989–III)

KELLY, JAMES T., 'United States Foreign Policy: Efforts to Penetrate Bank Secrecy in Switzerland from 1940 to 1975', 6 *Cal. Western Int'l L.J.* 24 (1976)

LANDO, OLE, 'The Conflict of Laws of Contracts: General Principles', (1989) 189 *Recueil des Cours* 225

LANGAN, P. ST. J., AND HENDERSON, L. D. J., *Civil Procedure* (3rd edn., 1983)

LEVINE, JULIUS BYRON, *Discovery: A Comparison between English and American Discovery Law and Reform Proposals* (1982)

LEVY, LEONARD W., *The Origins of the Fifth Amendment: The Right Against Self-Incrimination* (1968)

LOWE, A. V., 'Blocking Extraterritorial Jurisdiction: the British Protection of Trading Interests Act, 1980', 75 *Am. J. Int'l. L.* 257 (1981)

LOWENFELD, ANDREAS F., 'Discovering Discovery, International Style', Introduction to *Symposium on Transnational Discovery*, 16 *N.Y.U. J. Int'l Law & Politics* 957 (1984)

—— 'Discovery-Verfahren und internationale Rechtshilfe", [1984] IPrax 51

—— '*Lex Mercatoria*: An Arbitrator's View', in Carbonneau, Thomas E. (ed.), *Lex Mercatoria and Arbitration* (1990), also in 6 *Arbitration International* 133 (1990)

—— 'On Teaching International Law', 1 *N.Y.U. J. Int'l Law and Politics* 61 (1968)

——'Sovereignty, Jurisdiction and Reasonableness: A Reply to A. V. Lowe', 75 *Am. J. Int'l Law* 629 (1981)

—— 'The *Banco della Svizzera Italiana* Case', 15 *Review of Securities Regulation* 942 (March 24, 1982)

—— 'The Mitsubishi case: Another View', 2 *Arbitration Int'l* 178 (1986)

—— 'The Two-Way Mirror: International Arbitration as Comparative Procedure', 7 *Mich. Y.B. Int'l Legal Studies* 163 (1985), repr. in Craig, Park, and Paulsson, *International Chamber of Commerce Arbitration* (1986), ii, App. VII

—— '"To Have One's Cake . . ." The Federal Maritime Commission and the Conferences', 1 *J. Maritime Law & Commerce* 21 (1969)

MANN, MICHAEL, MARI, JOSEPH G., AND LAVDAS, GEORGE, *Developments in International Securities Law Enforcement and Regulation* (1994)

MAY, TIMOTHY, 'The Status of the Federal Maritime Regulation under Principles of International Law', 54 *Georgetown L.J.* 794 (1966)

MAYER, PIERRE, 'Mandatory Rules of Law in International Arbitration', 2 *Arbitration Int'l* 274 (1986)

MCLEAN, DAVID, *International Judicial Assistance* (1992)

MERHIGE, ROBERT, 'The Westinghouse Uranium Case: Problems Encountered in Seeking Foreign Discovery and Evidence', 13 *Int'l Lawyer* 19 (1979)

MUSTILL, MICHAEL J., AND BOYD, STUART, *The Law and Practice of Commercial Arbitration in England* (2nd edn., 1989)

NIBOYET, J.-P., 'La Théorie de l'Autonomie de la Volonté', 16 *Recueil des Cours* 1 (Hague Acad. 1927)

—— *Traité de Droit Internationale Privé* (1948)

PAGET-BROWN, IAN, 'Bank Secrecy and Criminal Matters: The Cayman Islands and U.S. Cooperative Development', 20 *Case Western Res. J. Int'l L.* 369 (1988)

PILLET, ANTOINE, *Traité Pratique de Droit International Privé* (1924)

PLATTO, CHARLES, 'Taking Evidence Abroad—A Practical Guide', 16 *Int'l Lawyer* 575 (1982)

RABEL, ERNST, *The Conflict of Laws, A Comparative Study* (2nd edn., 1960)

REESE, WILLIS, 'The Contractual Forum: Situation in the United States', 13 *Am. J. Comp. L.* 179 (1964)

—— 'The Model Choice of Forum Act', 17 *Am. J. Comp. L.* 292 (1969)

RISTAU, BRUNO, *International Judicial Assistance* (1986)

SCHLOSSER, PETER, 'International Rechtshilfe und rechtsstaatlicher Schutz von Beweispersonen' (1981) 94 *Zeitschrift für Zivilprozess* 369

—— *Der Justizkonflikt zwischen den USA und Europa* (1985)

—— *Der Justizkonflikt mit den Vereinigten Staaten von Amerika* (Walter Habscheid (ed.), 1986)

SCHÜTZE, ROLF, 'Die Anerkennung und Vollstreckbarerklärung US-Amerikanischer Zivil Urteile die nach einer pre-trial-discovery ergangen sind, in der Bundesrepublik Deutschland' in *Festschrift für Ernst C. Stiefel* (1987), 697

SCOLES, EUGENE K., AND HAY, PETER, *Conflict of Laws* (2nd edn., 1992)

SIME, STUART, *A Practical Approach to Civil Procedure* (1994)

STORY, JOSEPH, *Commentaries on the Conflict of Laws* (1834)

WEIS, JOSEPH, 'The Federal Rules and the Hague Conventions: Concerns and Comity', 50 *U. Pitt. L. Rev.* 903 (1989)

ZÄCH, ROGER (ed.), *Litigation of Business Matters in the United States and Legal Assistance* (1984)

INDEX